Unleashing Web 2.0
From Concepts to Creativity

Gottfried Vossen
Stephan Hagemann

AMSTERDAM · BOSTON · HEIDELBERG · LONDON
NEW YORK · OXFORD · PARIS · SAN DIEGO
SAN FRANCISCO · SINGAPORE · SYDNEY · TOKYO
MORGAN KAUFMANN PUBLISHERS IS AN IMPRINT OF ELSEVIER

ELSEVIER

MK®
MORGAN KAUFMANN PUBLISHERS

Publisher:	Denise E. M. Penrose
Executive Editor:	Diane Cerra
Publishing Services Manager:	George Morrison
Project Manager:	Mónica González de Mendoza
Assistant Editor:	Mary E. James
Production Assistant:	Lianne Hong
Cover Design:	Joanne Blank
Cover Artist:	Laura Vossen
Composition:	Charon Tec
Interior printer:	Sheridan Books, Inc.
Cover printer:	Phoenix Color Corporation

Morgan Kaufmann Publishers is an imprint of Elsevier.
30 Corporate Drive, Suite 400, Burlington, MA 01803, USA

This book is printed on acid-free paper.

Library of Congress Cataloging-in-Publication Data

Vossen, Gottfried.
  Unleashing Web 2.0 : from concepts to creativity / Gottfried Vossen, Stephan Hagemann.
      p. cm.
  Includes bibliographical references and index.
  ISBN 978-0-12-374034-2 (pbk. : alk. paper) 1. Internet--History. 2. Internet--Social aspects. 3. Web services. 4. World Wide Web. I. Hagemann, Stephan. II. Title.
  TK5105.875.I57V685 2007
  004.67'8--dc22

                                    2007015129

ISBN: 978-0-12-374034-2

For information on all Morgan Kaufmann publications,
visit our Web site at www.mkp.com or www.books.elsevier.com

Printed in the United States of America
07 08 09 10 11 12   10 9 8 7 6 5 4 3 2 1

Dedication

To Martina, in remembrance of our Aotearoa year – Gottfried Vossen

To Julia – Stephan Hagemann

Contents

Preface

During the year 2006, everything seemed to have come out in Version 2, Release 0 (commonly abbreviated as "2.0"): The IEEE *Spectrum* journal reported on *Silicon Valley 2.0 (beta)* in its August 2006 issue, German tech news ticker heise.de stated in September that "technology keeps the *Family 2.0* together," the Australian edition of the *T3* tech magazine described *Gadgets 2.0* in its October 2006 issue, the San Jose *Mercury News* had a story on *India 2.0* in early December. There are many other such examples, including *Pub 2.0, Jobs 2.0, Health 2.0, Entertainment 2.0, Business 2.0*, or *Music 2.0*. All of this can be traced back to O'Reilly Media, where the term was coined in late 2004. As can be read at www.oreillynet. com/pub/a/oreilly/tim/news/2005/09/30/what-is-web-20.html,

> The concept of "Web 2.0" began with a conference brainstorming session between O'Reilly and MediaLive International. Dale Dougherty, Web pioneer and O'Reilly vice president, noted that far from having "crashed," the Web was more important than ever, with exciting new applications and sites popping up with surprising regularity. What's more, the companies that had survived the collapse seemed to have some things in common. Could it be that the dot-com collapse marked some kind of turning point for the Web, such that a call to action such as "Web 2.0" might make sense? We agreed that it did, and so the Web 2.0 Conference was born.

"Web 2.0" has rapidly become a label that everybody seems to be able to relate to: Hardware manufacturer Intel suddenly entered the software market and created an Internet Business Suite called "SuiteTwo," an integrated package of Web 2.0 software. U.S. marketing research giant Gartner recognized a major driver for the IT industry in Web 2.0 technologies and awarded it the "Hype Oscar" of 2006. SEOmoz, a Seattle-based search engine optimization company even rated and ranked more than 300 "Web 2.0 companies" in thirty-eight categories and gave a "Web 2.0 Award" 2006 in twenty-one of them (http://www.seomoz.org/web2.0/). Finally, *Time* magazine made "You" the *Person of the Year*

2006 in its December 2006 issue, acknowledging the fact that the Web meanwhile heavily benefits from user contributions in a variety of media forms. On the other hand, critics are already warning of a "Bubble 2.0," while the *New York Times* jumped to a "Web 3.0" in November 2006.

But what actually is "2.0" in the context of the Web? What is new and what is not? The media have tried to answer this question in the recent past. An exploding number of blogs, showcases, magazine and journal special issues, the famous O'Reilly "summit" conferences, and news messages have offered numerous "definitions" and explanations of Web 2.0, what its features are, what can be expected from it in the very near future, and how important it is to join the bandwagon. Among other effects, this has made many people and companies nervous. They now ask themselves questions such as, "Are we Web 2.0 ready?" or "Do we comply with Web 2.0?" or "What will happen to us if we do not convert to this movement?" Although various attempts have been made to provide a precise definition, we are looking at a moving target characterized by a certain amount of fuzziness that lacks a simple and concise description and impact analysis.

The aim of this book is to remedy this situation by taking a critical look at developments commonly attributed to Web 2.0, by putting them in perspective, in particular with respect to the "historic" development of the Web, and by describing the current state of things from that perspective. The approach we take does not try to bring together each and every "definition" that we could find on the subject. Instead, we take a look at the subject from a technical and from a business point of view. The former allows us to draw several lines of development whose current end point is Web 2.0, but whose roots can be clearly recognized and identified. Moreover, several services and sites have been around for a while already and turn out not to be a *result* of Web 2.0, but one of its *prerequisites*. The business perspective lets us identify various ways of monetizing the Web, and we again try to analyze what is new and what is not. One of the findings resulting from this is that the term "Web 2.0" should actually have been "Internet 2.0." However, we stick to the former term, being aware of the discussion it provokes.

We start out in Chapter 1 with a historical perspective that looks at how the Web has emerged since its inception in 1993. We look at technological advances that have paved the way for the ubiquitous spread of the Web we have experienced in recent years, and at how the perception and usage of the Web by people and their interaction with this medium have changed over the years, in particular when looking at the younger generation. In Chapter 2, we take a closer look at the advances in Web technology, with an emphasis on languages, formats, and standards that have been developed in recent years and that see a confluence today in various ways. Chapter 3 presents the core Web 2.0 technical mechanisms, which are APIs, Web procedure calls, and their mash-ups, rich Internet applications, and tagging. In Chapter 4, we complement this with sample frameworks for Web development, including AjaxTK, OpenLaszlo, and

Ruby on Rails. In Chapter 5, we study impacts of the next generation of the Web. The major ones we see are data ownership, software as a service, and the socialization and cocreation of content, which includes topics such as social networks and social software. In Chapter 6, we look at another important Web development that has been around for quite a number of years already, the Semantic Web. We contrast Web 2.0 with the Semantic Web and try to elaborate on the aspects that will make them fit together.

With a topic selection such as this, we should say a word to the intended readership for the book. The techie maintaining one of the many blogs covering the topic on an almost daily basis is certainly not our target audience. Instead, the book is intended for readers who have a basic understanding of what the Web is about and who are interested in finding the various facets of the present-day Web in one place. Depending on how deep a reader's knowledge about HTML, scripting languages, or P2P protocols actually is, he or she may skip Chapter 2 and jump right into the newer technologies dealt with in Chapter 3. By a similar token, a reader mostly technically, but less conceptually interested, may decide to skip Chapter 6. Another type of reader may take our detailed exposition of a single running example in Chapter 2 as an introduction into the various technologies underlying the Web and as a starting point for further studies. We are aware that the audience for our book will be diverse, but we hope that the brief overview of the contents given here can serve as a guideline for what to read and what to skip.

Since we are from academia, we have been thinking for some time about how to integrate Web 2.0 into Computer Science (CS) and Information Systems (IS) educational programs. We often approach new topics through seminars in which students have to prepare presentations and write papers. We have done the same with the Web 2.0 topic in the summer term of 2006, yet the material produced by our graduate IS students at the University of Muenster, Germany, was so interesting that we were motivated to develop it further. We are thus grateful to Björn Böhmer, Florian Christ, Nicolas Dillmann, Henning Eiben, Christian Heitmann, Alexander Rajko, Julian Reimann, Jens Sieberg, Björn Skall, Steffani Ungerath and Heiko Zeus for granting us access to their material. The seminar and therefore the book have also benefited from discussions with students of Professor Wojciech Cellary from the Economical University of Poznan, Poland, with whom we met in Potsdam near Berlin during May 2006 to listen to some of the presentations the students had to prepare.

When it came to finding a title for the book, one of the greatest challenges arose. We are aware that having "Web 2.0" in the title may help sell the book today, but what if tomorrow the term is replaced by "Web 3.0"? Other books have had this problem, yet we are willing to take a risk here. We are convinced that the term will stick for a while, and we will modify the title in the future if necessary.

We need to say a word about the use of URLs in this book. It is clear that Web addresses are all over the text, as they represent the numerous examples we have explored, looked at, and found worth mentioning. However, we have decided not to state URLs explicitly each time, and the rule we apply is the following. If a company by name xxx can simply be found on the Web by going to www.xxx.com, we do not mention the URL. However, we do as soon as the URL deviates in the slightest way from this generic format.

Finally, the book was designed and written during the sabbatical stay of the first author at the University of Waikato in Hamilton, New Zealand. We are grateful to Professor Jim Corner, chairman of the Department of Management Systems in the University of Waikato Management School, for his hospitality, in particular during the time when both authors stayed in New Zealand. Clearly, working in a country where November and December, known to be dark and wet months in Central Europe, fall into early summer is particularly fun, and so we were able to take the efforts of writing this book out into nature at times, for example into the famous Polynesian Spa in Rotorua (www.polynesianspa. co.nz/).

As is often the case with books, this has been an effort in which many people were involved, some in the design of the structure, and many in the development of the various chapters. In particular, we are indebted to Jim Anderton, Doug Barry, Jim Corner, Bodo Hüsemann, Catherine Legg, Andrew Otwell, Joachim Schwieren, Dennis Shasha, Andreas Simon, Todd Stephens, Gunnar Thies, and Ian Witten for all the feedback they have provided, ranging from comments on specific sections to in-depth reviews of the entire manuscript. The book has benefited considerably from these interactions, and of course it remains our responsibility what we have made of it.

We are grateful to our publisher, Diane Cerra, who believed in the project from the moment we suggested it to her, and who has once more accompanied us very professionally through an intense writing and production process. We are also grateful to Mary James (assistant editor), Monica Mendoza (production) and Misty Bergeron (marketing manager). Last, but not least, the artwork on the cover was painted by Laura, Gottfried's oldest daughter, following a suggestion from Jens Sieberg. It is based on the idea that the Web is currently getting a substantial overhaul during which old, static stuff gets replaced by fresh, dynamic new elements and colors, and the tools that are used to this end include Ajax, tags, and a few other ingredients. The image is also reminiscent of the New Zealand fern as well as Maori ornaments common all over Aotearoa, which both symbolize very well the connection between established traditions and evolving nature that we also find on the Web today.

Gottfried Vossen and Stephan Hagemann
Hamilton, New Zealand, and Münster, Germany, March 2007

We plan to make additional material available over time at
www.unleashingweb20.com

chapter 1

A Brief History of the Web

Since its inception in the early 1990s, the Web has revolutionized our lives and world more than many other technological developments in recent history. In this first chapter, we tour the history of the Web, during which we will identify three major streams of development and impact:

■ The *application stream* is simply an account of what we have experienced over the past ten to fifteen years, namely the Web as an ever-growing and omnipresent library of information that we access through search engines and portals, the Web as a commerce platform through which people and companies do major portions of their business, and the Web as a media repository that keeps lots of things around for free.

■ The *technology stream* touches upon the technological advances underneath the Web that have enabled its evolution and development (and which actually keep evolving). We keep this stream, which looks at both hardware and software, short in this chapter and elaborate more on it in Chapter 2.

■ The *user participation and contribution stream* looks at how people perceive and use the Web and how this has changed over the past fifteen years in some considerable ways. Since fifteen years is roughly half a generation, it will not come as a surprise that, especially, the younger generation today deals and interacts with the Web in an entirely different way than people did when it all started.

Taking these streams, their impacts, and their results together, we arrive at what is currently considered Web 2.0. By the end of the chapter, we try to answer questions such as: Is "Web 2.0" just a term describing what is currently considered cool on the Web? Does it only describe currently popular Web sites? Does it denote a new class of business models for the Web? Or does it stand for a collection of new concepts in information exchange over the Web? To say it right away, the point is that Web 2.0 is *not* a new invention of some clever business people, but it is the most recent consequence and result of a development that started more than ten years ago. Indeed, we identify three major dimensions along which the Web in its 2.0 version is evolving – data, functionality, and socialization – and we use these dimensions as an orientation throughout the remainder of this book. Please refer to O'Reilly (2005) for one of the main sources that has triggered the discussion to which we are contributing.

1.1 A new breed of applications: the rise of the Web

Imagine back in 1993, when the World Wide Web, the WWW, or the *Web* as we have generally come to call it, had just arrived; see Berners-Lee (2000) for an account. Especially in academia, where people had been using the Internet since the late 1970s and early 1980s in various ways and for various purposes including file transfer and e-mail, it quickly became known that there was a new service around on the Internet. Using this new service, one could request a file written in a language called HTML (the *Hypertext Markup Language*, see text following). With a program called a *browser* installed on his or her local machine, that HTML file could be rendered or displayed when it arrived. Let's start our tour through the history of the Web by taking a brief look at browsers and what they are about.

1.1.1 The arrival of the browser

NCSA Mosaic

An early browser was *Mosaic*, developed by the National Center for Supercomputing Applications (NCSA) at the University of Illinois in Urbana-Champaign in the United States. There had been earlier browser developments (e.g., Silversmith), but Mosaic was the first *graphical* browser that could display more than just plain ASCII text (which is what a text-based browser does). The first version of Mosaic had, among others, the following capabilities: It could access document and data using the Web, the File Transfer Protocol (FTP), or several other Internet services; it could display HTML files comprising text, anchors, images (in different formats), and already

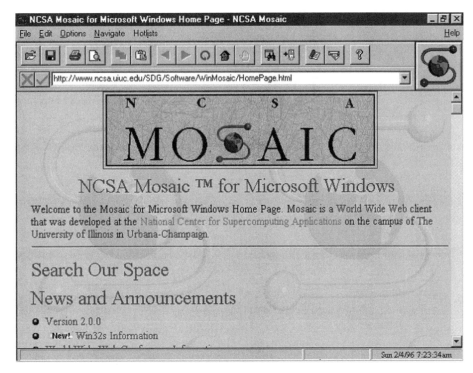

Figure 1.1 NCSA Mosaic.
Source: http://medialab.di.unipi.it/doc/SEHTML2D/figs/02fig09.gif

supported several video formats as well as Postscript; it came with a toolbar
that had shortcut buttons; it maintained a local history as well as a hotlist, and
it allowed the user to set preferences for window size, fonts, and so on. Figure
1.1 shows a screenshot of the *Mosaic for Windows* home page.

Mosaic already had basic browser functionality and features that we have
gotten used to, and it worked in a way we are still using browsers today: the
client/server principle applied to the Internet.

The client/server principle

The client/server principle is based on a pretty simple idea, illustrated in
Figure 1.2. Interactions between software systems are broken down into two
roles: *Clients* are requesting services, *servers* are providing them. When a client
wants a service such as a database access or a print function to be executed on
its behalf, it sends a corresponding *request* to the respective server. The server
will then process this request (i.e., execute the access or the printing) and will
eventually send a *reply* back to the client.

This simple scheme, described in more detail, for example, in Tanenbaum
and van Steen (2007), has become extremely successful in software applications,
and it is this scheme that interactions between a browser and a Web server are

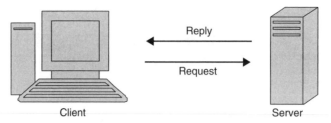

Figure 1.2 The client/server principle.

based upon. A common feature of this principle is that it often operates in a *synchronous* fashion: While a server is responding to the request of a client, the client will typically sit idle and wait for the reply. Only when the reply has arrived will the client continue whatever it was doing before sending off the request. This form of interaction is often necessary. For example, if the client is executing a part of a workflow that needs data from a remote database, this part cannot be completed before that data has arrived. It has also been common in the context of the Web until recently; we elaborate more on this in Chapter 2.

In a larger network, clients may need help in finding servers that can provide a particular service; a similar situation occurs after the initial setup of a network or when a new client gets connected. Without going into details, this problem has been solved in a variety of ways. For example, there could be a directory service in which clients can look up services, or there might be a *broker* to which a client has to talk first and who will provide the address of a server. Another option, also useful for a number of other issues arising in a computer network (e.g., routing, congestion control, consistent transaction termination), is to designate a central site as the network monitor; this site would then have all the knowledge needed in the network. An obvious drawback is that the network can hardly continue to function when the central site is down, a disadvantage avoided by peer-to-peer networks as shown in the following discussion.

HTML and HTTP

The basics that led to launching the Web as a service sitting atop the Internet were two quickly emerging standards: HTML, the Hypertext Markup Language, and HTTP, the Hypertext Transfer Protocol. The former is a language, developed by Tim Berners-Lee at CERN, the European particle physics lab in Geneva, Switzerland, for describing Web pages (i.e., documents a Web server will store and a browser will render). HTML is discussed in more detail in Chapter 2. HTTP is a protocol for getting a request for a page from a client to a Web server and for getting the requested page in a reply back to the browser. Thus, the client/server principle is also fundamental for the interactions happening on the Web between browsers and Web servers, and, as we will see, this picture has only slightly changed since the arrival of *Web services*. Over the years, HTML has become very successful as a tool to put information on the Web that can be employed even without a deep understanding of programming. The reasons for this include the fact that HTML is a vastly fault-tolerant language, where programming errors are simply ignored, and that numerous tools are available for writing HTML documents, from simple text editor to sophisticated WYSIWYG (What You See Is What You Get) environments.

Netscape

The initial version of Mosaic was launched in March 1993, and its final version in November the same year. Although far from modern browser functionality, with all their plug-ins and extensions (such as, for example, Version 2 of the Mozilla Firefox browser published in the fall of 2006 or Version 7 of the Internet Explorer), users pretty soon started to recognize that there was a new animal out there to easily reach for information that was stored in remote places. A number of other browsers followed, in particular *Netscape Navigator* (later renamed *Communicator*, then renamed back to *Netscape*) in October 1994 and *Microsoft Internet Explorer* in August 1995. These two soon got into what is now known as the *browser war*, which, between the two, was won by Microsoft but which is still continuing between Microsoft's Internet Explorer and Mozilla Firefox.

In mid-1994, Silicon Graphics founder Jim Clark started to collaborate with Marc Andreessen to found *Mosaic Communications* (later renamed *Netscape Communications*). Andreessen had just graduated from the University of Illinois, where he had been the leader of the Mosaic project. They both saw the great potential for Web browsing software, and from the beginning, Netscape was a big success (with more than 80 percent market share at times), in particular since the software was free for noncommercial use and came with attractive licensing schemes for other uses. Netscape's success was also due to the fact that it introduced a number of innovative features over the years, among them the on-the-fly displaying of Web pages while they were still being loaded; in other words, text and images started appearing on the screen already during a download. Earlier browsers did not display a page until everything that was included had been loaded, which had the effect that users might have to stare at an empty page for several minutes and which caused people to speak of the "World-Wide Wait." With Netscape, however, a user could begin reading a page even before its entire contents was available, which greatly enhanced the acceptance of this new medium.

Menu bar   Navigation Toolbar   Address Toolbar   Personal Toolbar   Netscape Icon

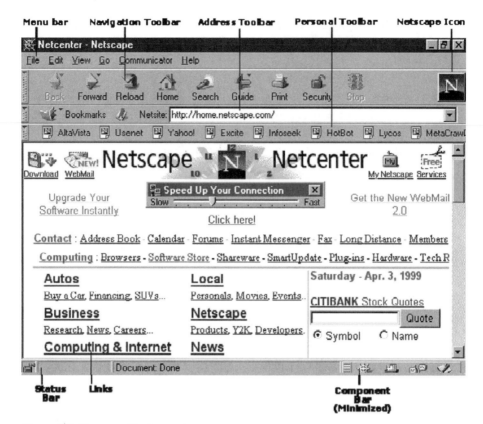

Figure 1.3 Netscape Navigator 4.
Source: http://www.3dmultimedia.com/help/internet/gifs/navigator_eng.gif

Netscape also introduced other new features (including cookies, frames, and, later, JavaScript programming), some of which eventually became open standards through bodies such as the W3C, the World Wide Web Consortium (w3.org), and ECMA, the European Computer Manufacturers Association (now called Ecma International, see www.ecma-international.org).

Figure 1.3 shows Version 4 of the Netscape browser, pointed to the Netscape home page of April 1999. It also explains the main features to be found in Netscape, such as the menu bar, the navigation, address, and personal toolbars, the status bar, or the component bar.

Although free as a product for private use, Netscape's success was big enough to encourage Clark and Andreessen to take Netscape Communications public in August 1995. As Dan Gillmor wrote in August 2005 in his blog, then at Bayosphere (bayosphere.com/blog/dangillmor/080905/netscape):

I remember the day well. Everyone was agog at the way the stock price soared. I mean, this was a company with scant revenues and no hint of profits. That became a familiar concept as the decade progressed. The Netscape IPO was, for practical purposes, the Big Bang of the Internet stock bubble – or, to use a different metaphor, the launching pad for the outrages and excesses of the late 1990s and their fallout. ... Netscape exemplified everything about the era. It launched with hardly any revenues, though it did start showing serious revenues and had genuine prospects ...

1.1.2 The flattening of the world

Let's deviate from the core topic of this section, the Web and its rise, for a moment and take a broader look at a number of events in recent history that have led to a changed world.

The initial public offering (IPO) of Netscape in 1995 is one of the events that Thomas L. Friedman, foreign affairs columnist for the *New York Times*, in Friedman (2005), calls a world "flattener."

The world as of today has become a flat one in which people from opposite ends of the planet can interact, play, do business with each other, and collaborate, and of that without knowing each other or having met, and where companies can pursue their business in any part of the world depending on what suits their goals and intentions best; they can also look at an entire world of customer base.

There are, essentially, no more serious limits to what anyone can accomplish in the world these days, since the infrastructure we can rely upon and the organizational frameworks within which we can move allow for so many unconventional and innovative ways of communicating, working together, collaborating, and information exchange. In total, Friedman (2005) accounts for ten flatteners which, in the order he discusses them, are:

1. The fall of the Berlin wall on November 9, 1989: Eastern Europe opens up as a new market, as a huge resource for a cheap, yet generally well-educated work force, and as an area with enormous demand for investments and renovation. The globalization wave swaps from the West across Eastern Europe and extends deeply into Asia. Millions of people in previously communist countries obtain a new political and economic freedom at a scale they have never known before.

2. The aforementioned Netscape IPO on August 9, 1995: For the first time in history, it was demonstrated that one can make money through the Internet, in particular with a company whose business model does not immediately imply major revenues. Netscape and the Internet become part of a digital revolution immediately picked up by the Eastern countries.

3. Software with compatible interfaces and file formats as well as work-flow software: People connect all over the world by chaining together what they are doing into a comprehensive whole. New forms of collaboration and distribution of work can now be run over the Internet, and jobs become location- and time-independent. Indeed, U.S. tax declarations done in Bangalore, India, or parts for a Boeing 777 plane manufactured in Russia are becoming a normality. A division of labor in specialized tasks has moved from a regional or domestic to an international scale.

4. Open sourcing, or the idea of self-organizing collaborative communities which in particular are capable of running large software projects: The most prominent examples in use today are the GNU/Linux operating system or the Mozilla Firefox browser project. In both cases, complex software with numerous components has been developed in a huge common effort, and is being maintained by a community of developers who respond to bugs and failures with an efficiency unknown to (and vastly impossible for) commercial software companies.

5. Outsourcing, where companies concentrate on their core business and leave the rest to others who can do it more cheaply and often more efficiently: Outsourcing occurs at a global scale (i.e., is not restricted to national boundaries or regional constraints anymore). This particularly applies to software production, parts of which are often given to Indian companies or, more recently, to programmers in Eastern Europe.

6. Offshoring, which means going way beyond outsourcing; indeed, the next step is to take entire production lines to an area of the world where labor is cheaper: This particularly refers to China since it joined the World Trade Organization in 2001, but also again to India or countries such as Russia and Brazil.

7. Supply chaining, or the idea of streamlining supply and production processes on a worldwide basis, for example through the introduction of RFID (Radio Frequency Identification) tags: Supply chains have become truly global today, with their various aspects of inbound or outbound logistics, supply chain integration, purchasing, capacity planning, inventory management, just-in-time processes often scaled to be dealt with internationally.

8. Insourcing, which is the opposite of outsourcing: It sometimes makes sense to bring specific functions into a company in order to have them executed more efficiently. An example is UPS and their handling of Toshiba laptop repairs. UPS not only picks up from the customers laptops that need to be repaired, but nowadays even repairs them in a UPS customer center in order to be able to ship them back to the customer

as soon as the repair has been completed. Apparently, this is much more efficient than shipping a laptop back to Toshiba in Japan and transporting it from there back to the customers once finished.

9. Informing, thanks to search engines such as AltaVista, Google, Yahoo!, or MSN Web Search (as well as the many others we encounter in upcoming chapters): In the flat world, knowledge and entertainment can be obtained at any time and anywhere. Information is accessed through search engines, e-mails are read on the move, and movies are downloaded on demand. A twenty-first-century person does, thus, no longer depend on printed newspapers, physical office space, or the local library.

10. Finally, the steroids (i.e., the technological developments that have made everything digital, mobile, personal, virtual). These include high-speed cabling, wireless computer access, modern personal digital assistants (PDAs), cell phones, data servers as a commodity, cheap personal and laptop computers with high computational capabilities, huge storage capacities, and excellent input/output facilities.

Interestingly, Flatteners 5 and 6 are also the subject of a recent report on the globalization and offshoring of software, prepared by Aspray et al. (2006) for the Association of Computing Machinery (ACM) in New York. The report contains the findings of a task force that looked into the rapid globalization of IT and the migration of jobs resulting from outsourcing and offshoring, and which vastly agrees with what Friedman is describing; some findings can be taken as an extension of Friedman's arguments in the specific direction of the IT industry.

Obviously, not all flatteners are related to the Internet and the Web, yet all of these developments, which go together and influence each other, heavily rely on efficient communication networks and on tools such as the Web for utilizing them. While we are not discussing all the impacts these flatteners have had since the mid-1990s or, as Friedman claims, especially in the (still pretty young) twenty-first century, some are relevant for us as well. We have already mentioned Flattener 2, the Netscape IPO, which, from today's perspective can be seen as one of the initiators of the "dot-com bubble" that erupted during the late 1990s; indeed, all of a sudden an Internet company without any highly valued product could exhibit an enormous market value. Another is Flattener 9, which refers to the entirely changed way in which people handled the Internet once the Web had arrived. All of a sudden, it became possible to access arbitrarily remote information in an easy and vastly intuitive way ("the global village"), in particular information that had not been known before to it exist. One of the slogans now was to have "information at your fingertips," and *search engines* were the tool that made this flattener possible.

1.1.3 From linking to searching

Links and navigation

The key to what has made the Web so popular early on is the fact that a Web page or an HTML document can contain *hyperlinks*, or *links* for short, which are references to other pages (or other places in a current page). The origin of this is *hypertext*, an approach to overcome the linearity of traditional text that was originally suggested by Bush (1945). Selecting a link that appears in a given HTML document causes the browser to send off a request for the page whose address is included in the link (or, if the link points to another place in the current page, to go that position); this page will then be displayed.

Figure 1.4 gives a rough idea of what that can mean at a larger scale. The Web is a large collection of hyperlinked documents and can be perceived, from a more technical point of view, as a directed *graph* in which the individual pages or HTML documents are the nodes, and in which links leading from one page to another (or back to the same page) are the (directed) edges. Figure 1.4 shows only a very small and finite subset of nodes and links, but it can easily be extended in any direction and by any number of further nodes and edges.

Links in HTML are technically *anchors* which typically are composed of a name (that will show up in the document where the links are placed) and a

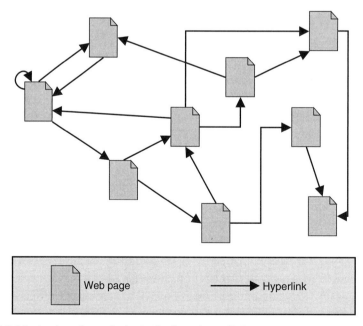

Figure 1.4 Navigation through the Web along hyperlinks.

URL, a *Universal Resource Locator* or logical address of a Web page. When a user clicks on the link, the browser will contact the Web server behind that URL through common network protocols which, among other things, will ensure name resolution (i.e., translate the URL into the physical IP address of the computer storing the requested resource) through various steps of address translation and request the respective HTML document. Links allow a form of *navigation* through the Web, the idea being that if something that a user is looking for is not contained in the current page, the page might contain a link to be followed for getting her or him to the next page, which may in turn be more relevant to the subject in question, or may contain another link to be followed, and so on. Links, however, need not necessarily point to other pages, but can also be used to jump back and forth within a single page or they can link to different types of content (e.g., images, videos). For a technical analysis of navigation, consult Levene (2006).

From a somewhat conceptual point of view, it is fair to say that the Web is a *very large* graph (with a current – spring of 2007 – estimate of more than ten billion nodes) and an even larger number of edges. Following links then means creating *paths* in that graph (i.e., sequences of nodes that have a source and a target). However, paths are not formed randomly but typically represent a *search* for a term or a combination of terms contained in a node (Web page). The size of the Web then makes it impossible to search comprehensively, since there is hardly any *a priori* indication of how long a search would have to continue, or how long a search path could become. This situation is complicated by the fact that the Web as a graph is never known completely in advance. In fact, the Web is a *dynamic* graph in which both nodes and edges come and go. Moreover, parts of the Web might be unreachable at a time due to network problems, or Web designers may add new pages with links and from time to time remove old ones. Investigations of the connectivity of the Web as a graph have revealed that it is not as interconnected as one might think. Indeed, as reported in *Nature* 405, 113 (May 2000), the Web has the form of a bow tie, shown in Figure 1.5, with several components:

A central core contains pages between which users can surf easily. Another large cluster, labeled "in," contains pages that link to the core but cannot be reached from it. These are often new pages that have not yet been linked to. A separate "out" cluster consists of pages that can be reached from the core but do not link to it, such as corporate Web sites containing only internal links. Other groups of pages, called "tendrils" and "tubes," connect to either the in or out clusters, or both, but not to the core, whereas some pages are completely unconnected.

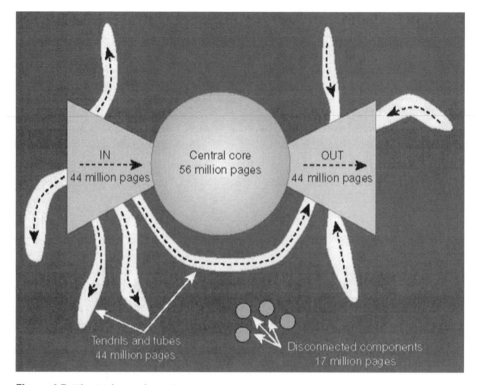

Figure 1.5 The Web as a bow tie.
Reprinted by permission from MacMillan Publishers Ltd: The Web is a Bow Tie, 2000

As a consequence, a user might not be able to find a click path between two randomly chosen Web pages for the simple reason that they are not connected!

Web exploration

As a consequence of the above, in particular the size of the Web and the fact that it is highly dynamic, traditional traversals for graphs are hardly applicable to the Web. Instead, the Web relies more on *exploration* (i.e., the progression along paths or sequences of nodes without predetermined targets).

Exploration has an extremely practical perspective, namely the question of how to find specific information in this "hyperspace," or how to make sense of this large and dynamic graph for a particular application or usage at hand. This is where the activity of *search* comes in. In the early days of the Web, exploration and search were soon identified as being relevant, if not the major form of getting to information on the Web; however, automatic tools were not yet around.

This was the time when a new type of job was created, the *information broker*. In the mid-1990s, clients could turn to an information broker to have a search done on the Internet (and, in addition, through more traditional information sources). If the client was a company, which was most often the case, the broker would typically come back with market data, data on market developments, information on the competition both domestically and internationally, typical figures of how much is spent on advertising and what common distribution channels are, and real or estimated consumer demand. Clearly, that not only required an in-depth investigation, but also analytical capabilities (i.e., ways to distinguish highly relevant information from less relevant and to aggregate the former into concise, readable and often graphical statements, and often inside knowledge of the particular area the customer was from). Indeed, there is a difference whether an information broker works for a pharmaceutical company or for a construction company that is building high-speed trains or exclusive ocean liners.

While the information broker as a job description has lost importance over the years due to the automated tools for doing this job, we discuss next an important aspect that is still around today, that of *price comparisons.* Indeed, comparing prices over the Web has become an important activity, for both companies and individual users, and is a form of information brokering still available today through companies or sites such as DealTime, mySimon, BizRate, Pricewatch, or PriceGrabber, to name just a few.

Web search

Search engines are today's most important tool for finding information on the Web, and they emerged relatively soon after the Web had been launched in 1993. "To search" the Web is nowadays often identified with "to google" the Web, with Google getting roughly 45 percent of all the search traffic today (searchenginewatch.com/2156431). Google was not the first search engine around, and will most likely not be the last. However, it has dominated the search field ever since its launch in the fall of 1998, and it has invented many tools and services now taken for granted; consult Brin and Page (1998) for the original research on Google, Vise (2005) for an account of the history of Google, and Miller (2007) for an in-depth presentation of its possibilities. Levene (2006) describes how search engines work in general; Langville and Meyer (2006) study Google's as well as other ranking algorithms. A comprehensive exposition of Web basics, Web search and issues related to search is given by Witten et al. (2007). For fairness reasons, we mention that AltaVista, Yahoo!, InfoSeek, AlltheWeb, Ask, Vivisimo, A9, Wisenut, or Windows Live Search are among the many other search engines out there; we mention a few more in later chapters. Angel (2002) describes the history of Yahoo!.

Search has indeed become ubiquitous. Today people search from the interface of a search engine, and then browse through an initial portion of the often thousands or even millions of answers the engines bring back. Search often even replaces entering a precise URL into a browser. In fact, search has become so universal that Battelle (2005) speaks of the *Database of Intentions* that nowadays exists on the Web: It is not a materialized database stored on a particular server, but "the aggregate results of every search ever entered, every result list ever tendered, and every path taken as a result." He continues to state that the Database of Intentions "represents a real-time history of post-Web culture – a massive click stream database of desires, needs, wants, and preferences that can be discovered, subpoenaed, archived, tracked, and exploited for all sorts of ends." Search not only happens explicitly, by referring to a search engine; it also happens to a large extent inside other sites, for example within a shopping or an auction site where the user is looking for a particular category or product. Also, most newspaper sites provide a search function that can be used on their archives. As a result, a major portion of the time presently spent on the Web is actually spent searching, and Battelle keeps watching the developments in this field in his search blog on the topic (see battellemedia.com/).

From a technical perspective, a search engine is typically based on techniques from information retrieval (IR) as explained, for example, in Levene (2006), Pokorny (2004) or Witten et al. (2007) and has three major components, as indicated in Figure 1.6: a crawler, an indexer, and a runtime system. The *crawler* explores the Web as indicated earlier and constantly copies pages from the Web and delivers them to the search engine provider for analysis. Analysis is done by an *indexer*, which extracts terms from the page using IR techniques and inserts them into a database (the actual *index*). Each term is associated with the document (and its URL) from which it was extracted. Finally, there is the *runtime system* that answers user queries. When a user initiates a search for a particular term, the indexer will return a number of pages that may be relevant. These are ranked by the runtime system, where the idea almost always is to show "most relevant" documents first, whatever the definition of *relevance* is. The pages are then returned to the user in that order.

As an aside, we mention that a crawler commonly revisits Web pages from time to time, in order to keep its associated index up-to-date. Thus, a search query will typically return the most recent version of a Web page. If a user is interested in previous versions or wants to see how a page has evolved over time (if at all), the place to look is the *Wayback Machine* at the *Internet Archive* (see www.archive.org/web/web.php), which has been crawling the Web on a daily basis ever since 1996.

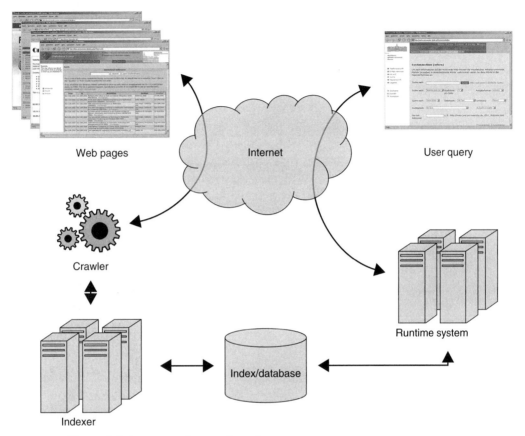

Web pages   Internet   User query

Crawler

Runtime system

Indexer   Index/database

Figure 1.6 Anatomy of a search engine.

PageRank

The popularity of Google grew out of the fact that they developed an entirely new approach to search. Before Google, it was essential to locate any site whose content was related or contained a given search term. To this end, search engine builders constructed indexes of Web pages and often simply stored the respective URLs. As an answer to a query, a user would get back a list of URLs which he or she then had to work through. Google cofounder Larry Page came up with the idea that not all search results could be equally relevant to a given query, but unlike the information broker, who can exploit his or her expertise on a particular field, an automated search engine needs additional ways to evaluate results. What Page suggested was to rank search results, and he developed a particular algorithm for doing so; the result of that algorithm applied to a given page is the *PageRank*, named after the inventor.

The PageRank of a page is calculated using a recursive formula (see infolab. stanford.edu/~backrub/google.html for details) which we are not discussing here, but the underlying idea is simple. Monika Henzinger, former Google research director, explained it in an interview with the German edition of MIT's *Technology Review* in April 2004 using the following analogy: Consider a doctor. The more people recommend the doctor, the better he or she is supposed to be. It is similar with ranking a Web page. The more pages that link to a page *p*, the higher the rank of *p* will be. However, the quality of a doctor also depends on the quality of the recommender. It makes a difference whether a colleague or a salesperson for the pharmaceutical industry recommends her or him. If the doctor is recommended by another doctor, that recommendation will count 100 percent; a recommendation from a nurse without comprehensive medical education will count only 60 percent, that from a patient, 20 percent, and that from the salesperson, having an interest completely disjoint from that of the doctor, will count 0 percent. The principle behind this (also found, for example, in classical scientific citations), is thus based on the idea of looking at the links going into a page *p* in order to calculate the rank of *p*, but to do so by recursively ranking all pages from which these incoming links emerge. The idea was first explored while Google founders Sergey Brin and Larry Page worked on a project called *BackRub* at Stanford University. Over the years, Google has added other criteria for constructing the order in which search results are presented to the user besides PageRank. Langville and Meyer (2006) give an in-depth exposition of the mathematical and algorithmic aspects behind PageRank calculations.

Beyond link analysis

An information broker can apply intuition, human expertise, and reasoning as well as experience and domain knowledge to search results in order to distinguish good and bad ones. A search engine has to do all of this based on some form of artificial intelligence. The comparison between the two points to the fact that even beyond Google there is lots of room for improvement in search. For example, a ranking algorithm may learn from the user as a search progresses, an idea behind the Mooter search engine. For another example, Yahoo! Mindset is based on the idea, shown in Figure 1.7, for the search term "bank," that a user may be somewhere in a "shopping" and a "research" mode or somewhere in between during the search, depending on whether the user is looking for commercial or noncommercial information. Mindset offers a slider (seen in the upper left portion of Figure 1.7) which the user can move left or right in order to get the search results reordered according to a changed mode. By the same token, other novel ideas have been developed around search and been realized in engines such as Ask, Wisenut, Vivisimo,

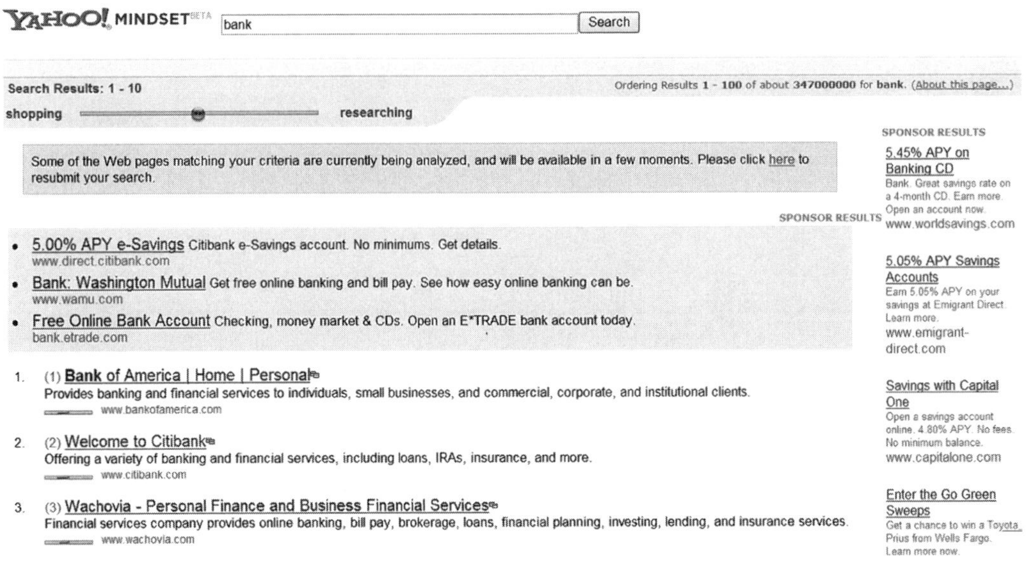

Figure 1.7 Yahoo! Mindset search result for term "bank."
Source: http://mindset.research.yahoo.com/search.php?p=bank

Snap, TransparenSee, and others. Besides keyword-based search, other ideas for search have developed around personal histories, text search, topic interpretation, word associations, or taxonomies; we mention some of them again in Chapters 5 and 6. For an up-to-date account, consult SearchEngineWatch and look under their "Search Engine Resources" section. To find out what is new in Google, refer to Google Blogoscoped at blog.outer-court.com. To take a wider view on search engine developments, optimization, and marketing, we suggest looking at WebmasterWorld.

The long tail of search

It is interesting to look at some statistics about searching. To the end, consult, for example, Google's Zeitgeist (at www.google.com/zeitgeist), which keeps recent past rankings about most popular search terms. For example, the five search queries entered at Google in 2006 with the biggest gain compared to 2005 were (see www.google.com/intl/en/press/zeitgeist2006.html):

1. bebo
2. myspace
3. world cup
4. metacafe
5. radioblog

Other statistics may be obtained from places like Nielsen//Netratings or the aforementioned SearchEngineWatch.

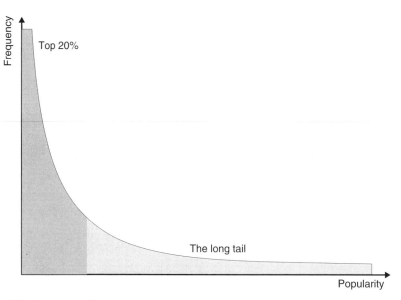

Figure 1.8 The long tail (of search queries).

What people have observed by looking at these figures is, among other things, that few queries have a very high frequency (i.e., are asked by many people and pretty often), but then a large number of queries have a considerable lower frequency. When plotted as a curve, where the x-axis represents a list of (a fixed number of) queries, while the y-axis indicates their frequency, the graph will look like the one shown in Figure 1.8. Graphs of this form follow a power-law type of distribution: They exhibit a steep decline after an initial, say, 20 percent, followed by a massive tail into which the graph flattens out. Power laws can be found in many fields: the aforementioned search term frequency, book sales, or popularity of Web pages. Traditionally, when resources are limited (e.g., space on a book shelf or time on a TV channel), the tail gets cut off at some point. The term *long tail* is used to describe a situation where such a cutting off does not occur, but the entire tail is preserved. For example, there is no need for search engine providers to disallow search queries that are only used very infrequently.

As we go along in this book, we see the long tail phenomenon in a variety of contexts related to the Internet and the Web. For example, it immediately comes back in the context of electronic commerce, where the availability of cheap and easy-to-use technology has enabled a number of companies to participate that otherwise would not have even thought about entering this arena. It also applied in the context of online advertising, as we discuss in Chapter 5. The long tail is discussed in detail in Anderson (2006) as well as on Anderson's Web site (at www.thelongtail.com/).

4,830,584 sites - 75,151 editors - over 590,000 categories

Figure 1.9 The dmoz.org example of a portal page (as of March 2007). *Source:* http://dmoz.org/

Directories and portals

We mention that Yahoo! and AOL were among the first to recognize that the Web, with its exploding number of pages already in the mid-90s, needed some form of organization, and they did so by creating *directories* containing categorizations of Web site content and pathways to other content. These were hierarchically organized catalogs of other sites, and many of them were later developed into portals. A *portal* can be seen as an entry point to the Web or a pathway to Web sources that has a number of topical sections that are owned and managed by the main site and that typically provide some personalization features (e.g., choice of language). We mention that our distinction between directories and portals is not a strict one in what follows.

As a typical directory page, Figure 1.9 shows the home page of the *Open Directory Project*, also known as *Directory Mozilla* (DMOZ), "the most comprehensive human edited directory of the Web" hosted and administered by Netscape, with its categories such as *Arts, Games, Health, News, Recreation*, and so on. Each such category will typically contain a list of subtopics, eventually together with the current number of hits in each. For example, hitting "Recreation" on the dmoz.org portal will reveal a list whose first ten entries are as follows (where the "@" sign indicates membership in another category as well):

Antiques (1,034)
Astronomy@ (1,316)
Audio (204)
Autos (8,433)
Aviation (4,713)
Birding (1,885)
Boating (2,835)
Bowling@ (656)
Camps (1,169)
Climbing (1,369)

Directories and portals are actually a bit older than search engines and originally did not accept the idea that search was a necessary feature for the Web. The reason behind this is easily identified as being commercial: If a portal has sites included in its categories and places banner ads on pages, it will be interested in many people using the portal and its listings, so that the ads can drive home some revenue. But this will only work if traffic is not distracted to other sites, which may not be listed in the portal, by a search engine. In other words, directories and portals were originally afraid that search engines would take away too much of the traffic that would otherwise reach them.

If a user is looking for very specific information, using a directory today may not be a rewarding experience, since it may not be obvious under which category to look for the term in question. Therefore, it has become common even for a directory to offer a search field that can freely be used for arbitrary searches inside the directory. The modern version of classical portals such as Yahoo! do still provide a categorization, yet this may be more difficult to find (e.g., under dir.yahoo.com), since other services have become predominant. In other words, the original portal idea of providing a single point of access to the Web still exists, yet usability has gained much more priority over the years and has modified the appearance of portals considerably. For example, a look at Yahoo! in Figure 1.10 shows that, from the home page, services such as *Mail*, *Messenger* or *Weather* are only one click away.

Directories and portals can not only be seen as an alternative (or competition, depending on the point of view) to search engines, where potential search results have been categorized in advance; they are often also highly specialized, for example towards a particular business branch or interest. Examples for the former include travel booking portals such as Travelocity,

Figure 1.10 The Yahoo! home page (as of March 2007).

Hotels, RatesToGo, or Expedia. An example of the latter is the recently launched German informatics portal io-port.net, which

> offers fast and convenient access to more than two million publications in informatics and related subject areas from all over the world. All information, which, up to then had been stored in various data sources, has been consolidated and is now available from one source. All steps required for information retrieval are available via an easy-to-use, customizable interface and supported by powerful tools.

Thus, portals have lost little of their popularity until today, and new portals are still being launched from time to time. An example of such a recent addition to the portal scene is Kosmix, which specialized in fields like health, video games, finance, travel, U.S. politics, and autos.

As we discuss later, the next evolutionary step is that a user can configure a home page entirely according to his or her preferences and services needed. Actually, even the Yahoo! starting page is partially configurable as is iGoogle (see www.google.com/ig), but sites such as Netvibes take this idea a considerable step further. Here, the user can choose from a rich menu of different search, mail, or blog services, which are then "mashed" together into a personalized page.

1.1.4 Commercialization of the Web

Roughly during the mid-90s, people started thinking about ways to monetize the Web and discovered that there is also a commercial side to the Web. We have already mentioned the Netscape IPO, but commercialization was and is not just about buying (and eventually selling) Internet companies.

A first step towards commercialization has been to attract user attention and, once obtained, to retain it. A popular approach has been to require registration in exchange for access to additional features or services. Without being historically precise about the order in which this has occurred, examples include Amazon.com, which let users create their personal wish list after logging in, as well as MySpace, Yahoo! or Google. Once you have registered for an account at any of these or many other sites, you may be allowed to use storage space, upload files, invite other participants to access your files, use their free e-mail service, and so on. Moreover, it is often possible to *personalize* your site (i.e., to customize pages according to your preferences, desires, or needs). What you may have to accept as a kind of compensation is that advertisements will be placed on your opening page (or beyond that), next to the results of searches you do on that site, or will be sent to your e-mail account from time to time. As we discuss in more depth later, advertising on the Web has become one of the most prominent Internet business models, and the idea of "free" sites just described provides a highly attractive advertising channel. Clearly, the more people register at a site (i.e., reveal some of their personal data and maybe even a user profile of preferences and hobbies), the more data the site owner will have available and the more he can do with it. Experience also shows that people do not reregister for similar service functionality from distinct providers too often. Thus, there is some form of customer retention right away, and then is it often just a small step to starting to offer these customers a little extra service for which they then, however, have to pay.

E-commerce

Commercialization of the Web has in particular materialized in the form of *electronic commerce*, commonly abbreviated as *e-commerce*, which involves moving a considerable amount of shopping and retail activity essentially from the street to the Web, or from the physical to a virtual world. More generally, e-commerce refers to selling goods or services over the Internet or over other online systems, where payments may be made online or otherwise. It was typically during the weeks before Christmas in which the success as well as the growth of e-commerce could be measured best every year; see, for example, Bertil Lindberg's collection of Web pages on global e-business and e-commerce at home.earthlink.net/~lindberg_b/GEC.htm for a number of statistics on the subject. In the beginning, customers were reluctant to do electronic shopping, since it was uncommon, it was not considered an "experience" as it may well be when strolling through physical shops, and it was often considered unreliable. Many companies entering this new form of business were not ready yet, unaware of the process modifications they would have to install in their front and back offices, and unfamiliar with the various options they had from the very beginning. Major obstacles in the beginning also were lacking security, in particular when it came to payments over the Web, and lacking trust, in particular when it came to the question of whether goods I had paid for would indeed be delivered to me. As a consequence, e-commerce took off slowly in the very beginning. However, the obstacles were soon overcome, for example by improvement in hardware and software (e.g., session handling), by encrypting payment information, by appropriate measures from credit card companies (such as Visa's *Zero Liability*, see usa.visa.com/personal/security/visa_security_ program/zero_liability.html), or by the introduction of trusted third parties for handling the physical aspects of sales transactions. Then, towards the end of the century, e-commerce started flying, with companies such as CDnow and Amazon.com, later also eBay, and sales figures soon went beyond the billion-dollar threshold. Today, "brick-and-mortar" retail chains such as Wal-Mart or Costco make considerable revenues online, in addition to the numerous stores they run in a traditional way.

However, it was also discovered that e-commerce and selling over the Web was not the only way of making money on or through the Web. Indeed, another was placing advertisements, and ultimately to introduce *paid clicks* (discussed in the following text). Besides all this is, of course, the telecommunication industry, for which technological advances such as the arrival of DSL or wireless networks brought entirely new business models for both the professional and the private customer.

CDnow

CDnow is a good example of how setting up a new type of business on the Web took off. CDnow was created in August 1994 by brothers Jason and Matthew Olim. As they describe in Olim et al. (1999), their personal account of the company, it was started in the basement of their parents' home; Jason became the president and CEO and Matthew the Principal Software Engineer. The company was incorporated in Pennsylvania in 1994 and originally specialized in selling hard-to-find CDs. It went public in February

1998, and after financial difficulties eventually merged with Bertelsmann, the big German media company, in 2000. CDnow became famous for its unique internal music rating and recommendation service, which was also often used by those who had never actually purchased a product on the site. In late 2002, Amazon.com began operating the CDnow Web site, but discontinued CDnow's music-profiling section.

What the Olim brothers detected early on was that the Web offered a unique chance to provide not only information, but highly specialized information that previously had required an enormous amount of research to come by. This is what they provided for music on CDs, and they combined their information and catalog service with the possibility to buy CDs directly from them. At some point, CDnow was probably the best online store for music, as it was able to integrate so much information on a CD, on an artist, or on a group in one place and in so many distinct categories. Their selection was enormous, and most of the time whatever they offered could be delivered within days. They also ran into problems that nobody had foreseen in the very beginning, for example that customs fees may need to be paid when a package of CDs is delivered to an addressee in a foreign country. In other words, legal issues related to commerce over a network that does not really have physical boundaries came up in this context (as it did for any other shop that now started selling internationally), and many of these issues remain unresolved today. We mention that this is different, at least in most parts of the world, for nonphysical goods, which can be distributed electronically and for which these issues do not exist. Apple's iTunes is currently by far the most popular service for distributing music electronically.

E-commerce system components

E-commerce, as said, is the process of buying, selling, transferring, or exchanging products, services, or information via computer networks and in particular the Web; see Laudon and Traver (2007) for a comprehensive introduction. It has become popular because it provides an innovative approach for conducting business for many companies, often in addition to a traditional business. It represents a reduction in the cost of transactions, it can provide unique, customized products for even small customer bases, and it allows customer access 24 hours a day, 7 days a week ("24/7"). Moreover, e-commerce *between* customers has been highly popularized through auctioning sites. Often, a fundamental characteristic of an e-commerce scenario is the absence of *intermediaries* (i.e., third parties offering intermediation services to two trading parties). For example, a publishing company can now sell directly to readers, without going through the intermediary of a book store, or individuals can sell used cars without the help of a car dealer.

A typical e-commerce system has four major components:

- **Product presentation component:** An e-commerce system must provide a way for customers, which can be individual consumers, companies, or a business, to search, select, and identify products they want to purchase. Many e-commerce Web sites have an electronic catalog which is a list or categorization of products with descriptions, pictures, and prices. Commonly, and as mentioned, some form of search function is provided that aids inspecting the catalog.

- **Order entry and shopping basket component:** After the customer has selected a desired product, he or she needs to enter an order for the product into the electronic commerce system. Order entry often allows the customer to add items to an electronic shopping basket, which is a list of the products the customer wants to purchase. Before an item is added to that basket, the e-commerce system should have the inventory control system check the product database to see if there is adequate stock on hand or if the product needs to be ordered from a manufacturer.

- **Payment component:** To allow customers to pay for the items purchased, an e-commerce system needs to have an electronic payment capability. Various approaches are used for electronic payment, including payment by credit card or by electronic funds transfer. To ensure the security of the card information sent over the Internet, special protocols such as HTTPS that provide data encryption are used.

- **Customer service and support component:** At any time before, during, or after purchasing an item, the customer may need advice or special services. For example, a customer may have a question about how a particular item of clothing fits before purchasing it. During the ordering process, the customer may have difficulty using the electronic commerce system. After receiving an item, the customer may decide to exchange or return the item. Some time later, the customer may have a warranty claim. Many of these customer service situations can be dealt with by providing detailed information and answers to questions electronically. A well-designed e-commerce system will therefore provide capabilities for customer service.

Clearly, while these components are well understood these days, it has taken more than ten years of development and experience to come up with this understanding. In the beginning, user acceptance of e-commerce was low, due to limitations in Internet access, to the limited number of companies doing e-business at all, to the mentioned lack of trust, or to the missing customer support. Indeed, a traditional retail shop will know returning customers after a short while, whereas an e-commerce site, without further measures, cannot distinguish an HTTP request by a customer today from one by the same customer tomorrow. It also took companies a while to recognize that doing their business electronically involves much more than setting up a Web site that has the components listed above. Indeed, it requires a considerable amount of process reengineering, as, for example, the Web shop and the back office must be connected in novel ways that did not exist before. This was overlooked frequently in the early days of electronic commerce and was a typical reason for failure. Apparently among the fastest to realize this and to react properly have been banks and financial institutions, since their business has moved to the Web quite considerably; electronic banking stock trade as well as fund and portfolio management are in wide use today.

Meanwhile, e-commerce has triggered the development of a whole new branch of the software industry, which not only provides software to install and run a Web shop, but also systems for click stream analysis, data mining (Han and Kamber, 2006; Witten and Frank, 2006), and customer relationship management (CRM) (Payne, 2006). Data mining has become popular for analyzing the vast amounts of data that are aggregated by a typical e-commerce installation and aims at finding information within that data previously unknown or not obvious. Prominent data mining applications include association rule determination, clustering, and classification. Click streams that have been created by users are also subject to intensive data mining, and CRM comprises a set of tools and techniques for exploiting data mining results in order to attract new customers or to retain existing ones. We mentioned that data mining is by no means restricted to the area of e-commerce, but has a number of other highly successful application areas as well.

Many software systems for e-commerce nowadays are *agent-based*, and comprise programs called *agents* for tasks such as the identification of customer needs, product search, finding best bargains, price negotiations, arrangement of payment or delivery, after-sales services, advertisement, or fraud detection. An agent in this context is a program that is autonomous, that can act based on decision-making mechanisms built into it, but that can also react to changing conditions in its environment, that can adapt to new conditions, and that can communicate with other agents. As an example of an e-commerce architecture for an enterprise, Figure 1.11 shows a typical setup of the Enfinity Suite 6 from the German software company Intershop.

As can be seen here, an e-commerce platform meanwhile serves both the buyer as well as the seller side. On the buyer side, there are typically a number of suppliers from which the company is getting its raw materials or supplies, often through some form of procurement process, and, thanks to the flattening we have mentioned, this process can be executed worldwide.

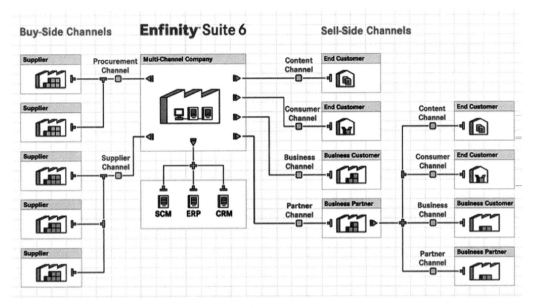

Figure 1.11 Intershop Enfinity Suite 6.
Source: http://www.intershop.de/is-bin/intershop.static/WFS/public/-/Editions/Root%20Edition/
units/webteam/Media/MiscImages/es6_scenario_de.gif

Internally, there is a supply-chain management (SCM) system at work that interacts with an enterprise resource planning (ERP) system in various ways. On the seller side, there may be several channels through which the company sells its goods or services also worldwide, including consumers, businesses, and partners. For their various customers, some form of CRM-system will be in place in order to take care of after-sales activities, customer contacts, complaints, warranty claims, help desk inquiries, and so on.

Types of e-commerce

We mention that electronic commerce has developed into various types that all have their specific properties and requirements:

- Business-to-business or B2B e-commerce, which involves a business selling its goods or services electronically to other businesses.
- Business-to-customer or B2C e-commerce, which involves a business selling its goods or services electronically to end-customers.
- Customer-to-customer or C2C e-commerce, which involves a customer selling goods or a service electronically to other customers.

B2B e-commerce, in turn, comes in three major varieties. In a *supplier-oriented marketplace*, a supplier provides e-commerce capabilities for other businesses to order its products; the other businesses place orders electronically from the supplier, much in the same way that consumers will place orders in B2C e-commerce. In a *buyer-oriented marketplace*, the business that wants to purchase a product requests quotations or bids from other companies electronically; each supplier that is interested places a bid electronically and the buyer selects the winning supplier from the submitted bids. Finally, in an *intermediary-oriented marketplace*, a third-party business acts as an intermediary between the supplier and the buyer; the intermediary provides e-commerce capabilities for both suppliers and buyers in order to identify each other and to electronically transact business.

B2C e-commerce is probably best known to the general public, although by figures alone B2B is considerably higher in value of goods traded. B2C e-commerce has become popular due to two aspects: the end of intermediaries and better price transparency. Indeed, goods are now often sold directly by a business to the end-customer, instead of going through a third-party. For example, software can now be downloaded from the producer directly (called *electronic software distribution*), instead of having it burnt on (i.e., copied to) a CD-ROM or DVD and sold through stores. As a result, prices may be lower (an expectation often not valid), or the seller will make a better profit (since nothing needs to be paid to the intermediary). Second, and as mentioned, it has become very popular on the Web to provide price comparisons, through sites such as DealTime or guenstiger.de. As a consequence, the customer will nowadays often do extensive comparisons before committing to a particular seller.

The third major type of e-commerce, C2C, is mostly manifested these days through auctions such as eBay or TradeMe.co.nz. eBay (Cohen, 2002) was founded in September 1995 by computer programmer Pierre Omidyar under the name AuctionWeb. One of the early items sold on eBay was Omidyar's broken laser pointer, which to his surprise was due to a real interest in such an item by the winning bidder. The company officially changed the name of its service from AuctionWeb to eBay in September 1997. Millions of collectibles, appliances, computers, furniture, CDs, DVDs, musical instruments, diecast models, outdoor equipment, cars, and other items are listed, bought, and sold daily on eBay. Some items are rare and valuable, while many other items would have been discarded if eBay, with its thousands of bidders worldwide, did not exist. Anything used or new can be sold as long as it is not illegal or does not violate the eBay *Prohibited and Restricted Items policy*. Interestingly, programmers can create applications that integrate with eBay through the eBay application programming interface (API) by joining the eBay Developers Program. This opens the door to "mashing up" eBay with totally different applications, an aspect we say more about in Chapter 3.

We mention that other types of e-commerce have meanwhile emerged, including G2C (government-to-customer) or B2G (business-to-government), to name just two. Each type can be combined with one or more business models in order to actually generate revenue. We discuss the details in Chapter 5.

Yet another form of commercialization of the Web is what happened in the late 1990s (roughly between 1997 and 2001) in the context of the so called *dot-com bubble*, namely the buying and selling of entire Internet companies (the "dot-coms"). With the story of Netscape, we have already mentioned a very prominent example. In 1998, Netscape was taken over by AOL. There are quite a few other examples of start-ups that had a new idea for an Internet site or service in the first place, were taken public (i.e., to the stock market) pretty soon after the incorporation, became subject to speculation, and were finally bought by another company. In the course of these happenings, many were heavily overvalued and hence overpriced which, together with rapidly increasing stock prices and the temptation to many individuals of being able to make money on the stock market fast, ultimately led to the famous crash.

Customer feedback and recommendations

For anyone interested in setting up an e-commerce site, two questions will prevail: What is an appropriate way to sell my product, and how do I attract traffic to my site? Regarding the former, an obvious difference exists between goods that can be stored on a computer, such as software or music files, and physical goods, such as cars or clothing. The former are basically easy to sell. After having made the payment, the customer is given an access code and a URL from where he or she can download what was paid for; the files just purchased will be made available at that address, and will typically be kept there for some period of time in case the download fails and has to be retried. The same is no longer true for the other type of goods. Indeed, the latter might require that the customer needs to be given advice or data for comparison (in the case of cars) or needs to be given the opportunity to return the merchandise if it does not fit or meet the expectations (an issue nowadays legally regulated in many countries).

Especially for physical goods, it has become very helpful if such *advice comes from other customers*. On places like Amazon.com, eBay, and others, this has become one of the main aspects people watch out for when shopping for a product: what others have said about that product before, how they like it, whether or not they would buy it again, and maybe how its seller has been rated or the overall experience has been. Once the importance of other customers' opinions, evaluations, and recommendations had been recognized, many Web shop providers started to install possibilities for commenting on a regular and intensive basis. Amazon.com was among the first to take this even a step further and go from pure reviews, which can be commented on by others, to a comprehensive recommendation system ("Customers who bought this item also bought . . ."), whose goal is, as an Amazon.com employee once put it, "to make people buy stuff they did not know they wanted."

While reviews often come from a professional source (such as the publisher of a book or newspaper staff) or from private customers, recommendations are generated by the data mining tools that work behind the scenes of the Amazon.com Web site. Recommendation systems look primarily at transactional data that is collected about each and every sales transaction, but also at previous user input (such as ratings) or click paths, and then try to classify a customer's preferences and to build a profile; recommendations will then be made on the basis of some form of similarity of items or categories that have been identified in consumers' profiles. Clearly, recommendations point to other items, where more customer reviews as well as further recommendations to more products can be found. More recently, Amazon.com has begun to allow registered users to place *tags* on items, which are explained as follows: "Think of a tag as a keyword or category label. Tags can both help you find items on the Amazon.com site as well as provide an easy way for you to 'remember' and classify items for later recall." The activity of placing a tag is called *tagging* and has become very popular in recent years; we say more about it in Chapter 3, as we will come across tagging in various contexts in what follows.

The possibility for customers and others to place reviews or tags on an e-commerce site marks the arrival of *user input* to the Web, an option which is included in many serious commerce sites today. Indeed, ratings and comments have been shown to have a major impact on revenues a seller may be able to obtain, and that is no surprise: If a seller is getting bad ratings repeatedly, why would anyone buy from him in the future? This input is typically exploited in various ways, including the offer of a seemingly customer-specific *Gold Box* at Amazon.com or the formation of *virtual communities*. Such communities are characterized by the fact that its members might not know each other, but they all share common interests. This phenomenon has been identified and studied by many researchers in recent years, and it represents a major aspect of the socialization of the Internet and the Web.

In the context of electronic commerce, user input to the Web typically comes in one of several forms: It may consist of collecting feedback, comments, reviews, or evaluations. Beyond e-commerce, however, it may consist of having a discussion on a specific topic or just producing a monologue of your own opinion or experience in diary form, activities that have become known as *blogging*; we say more about this topic later in this chapter.

Providing user input to the Web, or being able to write to the Web, is one of the major characteristics of the Web today.

The feature of providing feedback and ratings to an e-commerce site has only been a first step in the direction of turning a shop more and more into an application or even a collection of applications. A typical example is Amazon.com's *wish list* function, where a user can save search results for future purchases and gifts (and delete items that he or she no longer wishes to get). Another such example is the aforementioned tagging function, through which users can create their personal "subdatabase" out of the Amazon.com database. Using tags, he or she can structure or categorize items according to personal taste, needs, or demands. Apparently, functions like these go far beyond the nice book store as which Amazon.com started selling over the Web back in 1995. Today, the goal is to make a visit of this site a rich experience, similar to visiting a (book) store downtown or in the mall, so that the user will hopefully use the site for more and more of his or her shopping needs.

Advertising and its long tail

The other aspect the owner of an e-commerce business will be interested in, the attraction of traffic, as already mentioned in the context of portals, is closely related to classical disciplines from business administration: advertising and marketing. Traditionally, *advertising* is the art of drawing public attention to goods or services by promoting a business, and is performed through a variety of media. It is a mechanism of *marketing*, which is concerned with the alignment of corporations with the needs of the business market.

Advertising has become a big business on the Web. It has started out with banners that could be placed on other Web sites. It has meanwhile emerged into one of the major ways to make money on the Web, which according to Battelle (2005) is due to Bill Gross and his invention of GoTo, a service that became famous for being among the first to differentiate traffic. Indeed, what Gross, who had founded IdeaLab for helping start-up companies to establish their business, figured was that advertisement on the Web is vastly irrelevant and cannot be beneficial as long as the traffic passing by any placed ad is the "wrong" traffic (i.e., coming from people not interested in what is being advertised). If people arrive at a site due to a spammer who has led them there, due to a bad portal classification, or due to a bad search result, they are hardly interested in the products or services offered at that site. Gross hence started investigating the question of how to get qualified traffic to a site (i.e., traffic with a basic intention to respond to the goods or services found at a site), and then started calculating what businesses might be ready to pay for this. This gave birth to the idea that advertisements can be associated with the terms people search for and to pay-per-click tracking models we see today in this business. Companies like Accipiter or its new mother, aQuantive, have made this part of the software business.

Advertising has become a major business model, in particular since the arrival of Google AdSense. According to them, it is "a fast and easy way for website publishers of all sizes to display relevant Google ads on their website's content pages and earn money" and Google AdWords, which allows businesses to "create ads and choose keywords, which are words and phrases related to [their] business.... When people search on Google using one of [the] keywords, [the] ad may appear next to the search results." Again, we delay a more detailed discussion of advertising as a general business model, and AdSense as well as AdWords in particular a little bit. An important point to notice here is that through advertising on the Web, another incarnation of the long tail curve of Web applications we saw in Figure 1.8 materializes. Through Google AdWords, it has become possible not only for large companies (amounting to 20 percent of all companies) to place advertisements on the Web, but now the same can be done even for a small company. Through a cost-effective and highly scalable automated infrastructure provided by the Google search index, Google offers advertising even for very limited budgets as may only be available for a small company. In other words, small companies do not have to set up an infrastructure for advertising potentially even in niche markets themselves, but they can simply rely on what others are providing and searching for on the Web.

Trusted third parties

While we have mentioned that, from a seller's perspective, doing business over the Web may be attractive due to the absence of intermediaries who may take a little share off the profit, there are situations in which new intermediaries enter the picture. This, in particular, refers to making payments, for which *trusted third parties* have come onto the scene. The term is borrowed from cryptography, where it denotes an entity enabling interactions between two parties who both trust the third party; so that they can utilize this trust to secure their business interactions. Figure 1.12 shows a typical scenario, here using X-CART, another provider of e-commerce store software, and PayPal as an example.

PayPal allows payments and money transfers to be made over the Web, actually to anybody with an e-mail address, and it performs payment processing for online vendors, auction sites, and other corporate users, for which it charges a fee. Private users need to register and set up a profile which, for example, includes a reference to a bank account or to a credit card. PayPal will

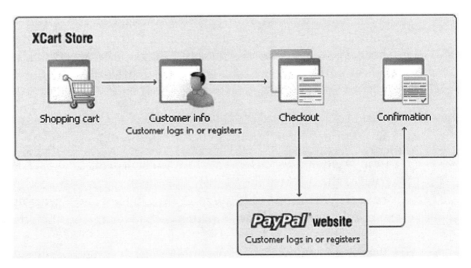

Figure 1.12 Secure payments through a third party.
Source: http://www.x-cart.com/images/paypal.gif

use that reference to collect money to be paid by the account or card owner to someone else. When a customer reaches the checkout phase during an e-commerce session, the shopping site he or she interacts with might branch to PayPal for payment processing. If the customer agrees to pay through PayPal, PayPal will verify the payment through a sequence of encrypted messages. If approved, the seller will receive a message stating that the payment has been verified, so that the goods can finally be shipped to the customer. Services such as PayPal or Escrow have invented the notion of a *micropayment* (i.e., a tiny payment of often just a few cents) which is feasible as a reimbursement only if occurring sufficiently often.

Other forms of third-party services have become common on the Web, for example companies issuing *digital certificates*. These are files containing the information such as the name to whom it is given, the location (URL) of the respective organization, the public key of that organization, a validity period, and an issuer, and they are issued by certificate authorities such as Verisign or RSA.

Summary

In conclusion, it is fair to say that, since the inception of the Web in 1993, a considerable amount of the trading and retail business has moved to electronic platforms and is now run over the Web. E-commerce continues to grow at a fast pace, as recent statistics from comScore Networks show. For example, the U.S. e-commerce retail spending excluding travel, auctions, and large corporate purchases has grown by 24 percent, from 82.3 billion dollars (U.S.) in 2005 to 102.1 billion dollars in 2006. This has created completely new industries, and it has led to a number of new business models and side effects that do not exist, at least not at this scale, in the physical world. Next, we look at another impact the evolution of the Web has had.

1.1.5 Peer-to-peer networks and free file sharing

In the beginning of this chapter, we explained the client/server principle as one of the cornerstones of early Web interactions between browsers and Web servers. This principle has, over time, undergone a generalization that has also had an impact on how users see the Web and the information it provides.

Initially, when the Web started and HTML became available as a markup language for Web pages, people composed their HTML code in a text editor, a way that still works today. A few years later, tools became available for designing Web pages and for setting up Web sites more and more easily. Some of these simply allowed for design of HTML documents and to include links, graphics, maybe even audio and video in a WYSIWYG fashion, others allowed for an easy management of entire Web sites comprised of multiple pages. The modern result of this development are *content management systems* (CMS), which are underneath most major Web sites today, in particular those maintained at an enterprise level.

What is more important to us is the fact that, over time, more and more people started setting up sites using these tools, and the obvious consequence was that the information available on the Web grew exponentially. Once a site had been created, the next important issue was to get it found, for which the emerging breed of search engines provided registration mechanisms, sometimes for free, increasingly often for a fee. This also led to the development of tricks that, for example, faked high popularity of a site just to get a good ranking with search engines. Besides text and textual documents, people soon started to place other types of documents on the Web, in particular media such as image, audio, and video files. Now every user may have experienced how easy it is to save (actually copy) an image found in an HTML document: just right-click on the image and select the "save image as" option! Similarly, audio and video files can easily be downloaded and copied to a local computer, as long as access to these files is granted. The fact that obtaining information from the Web became so easy and the sheer amount of files available on the Web paved the way for a new attitude towards information. Before we get into this, let's briefly continue the technological discussion.

Beyond the client/server model: P2P

It soon turned out that the traditional client/server model behind the Web, which we have described earlier in this chapter, was not optimal for some interactions, including the downloading of large files. Imagine a video file that contains a ninety-minute movie; with a reasonable compression rate this will easily amount to roughly 800 MB in file size. Even over an Internet connection that can guarantee a constant download rate of 80 KB/sec, this will take almost three hours! Thus, if a video server would have to serve a request for such a file from a client, the server would be kept busy with just this request for quite a while. Moreover, a *constant* rate can hardly be guaranteed these days, a fact that has so far prevented video-on-demand from becoming a big business. Clearly, this situation will change as technology advances, yet for the time being an alternative is needed.

Notice that the video download problem is not just a matter of bandwidth; it is also a matter of a single server being occupied with a large request for quite some time. The alternative people have developed for tasks like this are *peer-to-peer* (P2P) networks, which give up the idea of a central server that has to take care of all incoming requests we have outlined earlier in this chapter. Instead, a P2P network primarily relies on the computing power and bandwidth of its participants and is typically used for connecting nodes via mostly ad hoc connections; see Tanenbaum (2003) for details. A P2P network also does not know the notion of a client; any participant in the network can function as either a client or a server to the other nodes of the network, as needed by the task at hand. In fact, a P2P system comes with complete and decentralized self-management and resource usage, and it enables two or more peers to collaborate spontaneously in a network of equals (peers) by using appropriate information and communication systems.

As mentioned, one of the many uses for P2P networks is the sharing of large files, which is done on a large scale today on the Internet. The different P2P systems in use are based on distinct file-sharing architectures with different principles, advantages, disadvantages, and naming conventions. We present the most popular one next.

Gnutella

Gnutella is a file sharing network that has been set up since 2000 and is among the most popular P2P networks today. Gnutella has several million users, many of whom might be on at any given time. For using Gnutella, or for being a participant in a Gnutella network, one has to install a Gnutella client on a local machine. From there, requests for files can be issued as illustrated in Figure 1.13. Here, a participant has issued a request for a file, which is broadcasted to all other participants in the network. The one holding the

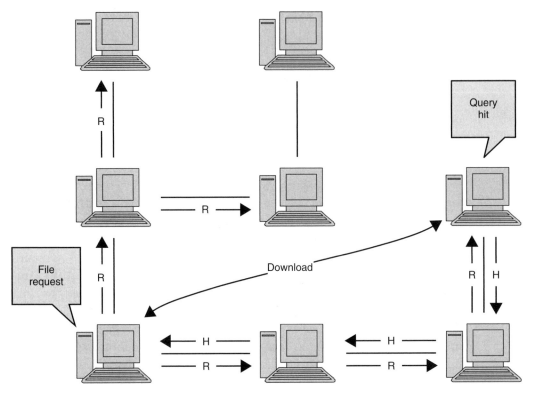

Figure 1.13 File request in a Gnutella network.

file will announce "hit" on the path through the intermediate nodes through which the hit node was found; the subsequent download will then go directly to the requester.

Notice the absence of a central server, which is typical for a P2P network. Control is entirely decentralized. A search query or request is forwarded in a Gnutella network until the TTL (time to live) of the request packet has become zero. The number of queries that are issued during a request may rise exponentially with the number of peers that receive such a query, making the network rather inefficient but resistant to failures.

There are other popular P2P networks that have different approaches to certain parts of this basic model, mostly to circumvent the exponential rise of requests that Gnutella faces. We discuss these networks in Chapter 2.

Free file sharing

One of the consequences of developments like the P2P networks, protocols, and tools just described has always been that information and files started to become available on the Web which previously had been pretty costly. We are not delving into legal issues related to services like Napster and Kazaa here or into general issues related to copyright or intellectual rights and their protection. However, the fact is that many users around the globe have started using the Internet and the Web as a free source for almost everything. For example, once the MP3 format had been invented as a digital audio encoding and lossy compression format by Fraunhofer's *Institut für Integrierte Schaltungen* in Erlangen, Germany, music got transformed into MP3 format en masse and then could be copied freely between computers and other devices. On the illegal side, people started ripping music CDs and exchanging their content over the Internet; others took videos of recently released movies with a camcorder in a cinema, compressed them into a suitable video format, and put them on a file-sharing network for general copying. More recently, videos started to get shared via specialized platforms such YouTube, Bolt, Brightcove, Podshow, or THE 9 on Yahoo (see 9.yahoo.com), to name just a few.

Open access

A net result of the developments just described is a perception of the Internet and the Web today, shared by many of their users (in particular the younger ones), that all content is, or should be, for free. As we have tried to point out, the issues here are far from being resolved today, but the fact is that sharing stuff for free, be it legal or not, has become extremely popular. Open sharing, on the other hand, also has positive effects, as can be seen from the Open Source community of software developers (see Friedman's flatteners mentioned earlier). *Open access*, at no charge and without license restrictions in particular to scientific results and literature, has become a radical demand by many people these days and has emerged into an international movement. The idea is already supported through a growing number of electronic journals that publish scientific papers exclusively in electronic form and often for free. It is also supported by numerous university sites worldwide, where scientists put their papers, talks, and other material up for free download. On the other hand, a publishing company is unable to provide all its copyrighted material, in particular books, for free. The discussion on this topic is in full swing these days, currently without a conclusion that would be acceptable to all participants in sight.

Conclusion

With these remarks we conclude the applications stream. The bottom-line we can take away from this discussion is that the Internet and in particular the Web have penetrated our lives in a number of (primarily positive) ways (even though some people have gotten addicted to it, and even shrinks worldwide have found numerous new customers due to the rise of the Web). Search is a primary activity on the Web today, e-commerce and electronic banking have become big businesses, and new models for doing business such as C2C auctions or for presenting advertisements have emerged. Refer to Pogue and Biersdorfer (2006) for further details on many of the topics we have touched upon. All of this has been made possible by a number of technological advances, both on the hardware and on the software side, as we discuss next.

1.2 Technological developments in a nutshell

We have already mentioned some of the (hardware or software) technology that has emerged in the context of the Web that has helped to make the Web popular, or that serves as a foundation in general. We now consider the second contributing stream, the technology stream, a development that has finally led to what is now being called "Web 2.0." In a little more detail, we touch upon the most relevant technological advances and communication infrastructure in this section. However, this is not intended as an in-depth treatment of hardware, networking, or software technology (which is the order in which we discuss it), so, again, please refer to the relevant literature we note in each area.

Hardware history

In hardware, there is essentially one singular development that governs it all: the fact that hardware is becoming smaller and smaller and will ultimately disappear from visibility. Consider, for example, the personal computer (PC). While already more than ten years old when the Web was launched, it has shrunk (and become cheaper) on a regular basis ever since, with laptops meanwhile being more popular (and higher in sales figures) than desktops. Moreover, with processors embedded into other systems such as cars, cell phones, watches and so on, we can now carry computing power in our pockets that was unthinkable only a few years back (and that typically outperforms the computing power that was needed to fly man to the Moon in the late 1960s). Just think of an intelligent cell phone or a modern PDA that is powered by a microprocessor, has some 64 MB or at least 32 MB of main memory, maybe even a hard drive, that can run a slightly simplified version of a common operating system, and that can have a host of applications installed (and can have many of them running simultaneously). Thus, in many applications, we do not see the computer anymore, and this trend, which has been envisioned, for example, in Norman (1999), will continue in ways we cannot fully predict today.

Another important aspect of hardware development has always been that prices keep dropping, in spite of expectations that this cannot go on forever. As has been noted recently, Moore's Law is still valid after forty years, and expected to remain valid for another ten to fifteen years. In this "law," Gordon Moore, one of the founders of Intel, predicted in 1965 in an article in the journal *Electronics* that the number of transistors on a chip would double every twelve to eighteen months. He later corrected the time span to twenty-four months, but that does not change anything significant. It turns out that microprocessor packaging has vastly been able to keep up with this law, and no reason is in sight why this should change soon. Raymond Kurzweil, one of the primary visionaries of artificial intelligence and father of famous music synthesizers, and others consider Moore's Law a special case of a more general law that applies to the technological evolution in general: If the potential of a specific technology is exhausted, it is replaced by a new one. Kurzweil does not use the "transistors-per-chip" measure, but prefers "computing power per 1,000-dollar machine." Indeed, considering the evolution of computers from mechanical devices via tubes and transistors to present-day microprocessors, it exhibits a double-exponential growth of efficiency. The computing power per 1,000-dollar (mechanical) computer has doubled between 1910 and 1950 every three years, between 1950 and 1966 roughly every two years, and presently doubles almost annually.

As a result, hardware has become a commodity, cheap and ubiquitous. To use hardware, be it processors or storage, it is not necessary anymore to purchase it, since computing power and storage capacity can nowadays be rented on-demand. With many Internet providers (as well as other companies, for example Amazon.com with its S3 service; see Chapter 5), private or commercial customers can choose the type of machine they need (with characteristics such as number of processors, clock frequency, or main memory), the desired amount of storage, and the rental period and then get charged, say, on a monthly basis. This has even become an attractive alternative to purchasing for the reason that, since hardware ages so fast, there is no more need to get rid of items no longer used.

In the academic world, the idea of *grid computing* (Grandinetti, 2006) has emerged as an alternative, where applications can request computational power in an on-demand fashion within an always available *grid* of machines (and often use them for free), just like electric power is obtained from an outlet, but is actually drawn from an electrical grid that does not need any user interaction or adaptation even at peak times. Grid computing has a number of applications, for example in particle physics, meteorology, medical data processing, or in satellite image processing. It has become widely known through the SETI@home project of the University of California, Berkeley, which uses computer idle time for a search for extraterrestrial intelligence (setiathome.berkeley.edu).

1.2.1 IP networking

Interestingly, a similar trend of evolving from an expensive and rare technicality into a cheap and ubiquitous commodity can be observed regarding computer networks, at least from an end-user perspective. This is especially true for networks that are based on the TCP/IP protocol stack and that are, hence, considered to be part of the Internet; for details of TCP (Transmission Control Protocol) and IP (Internet Protocol), refer to Tanenbaum (2003). Essentially, networks of this category break messages to be transmitted into *packets*. These packets are equipped with addressing information as well as protection against transmission errors. They travel individually, possibly all different routes between the sender and the receiver; transmission control makes this reliable by assuring that all packets will ultimately arrive at the receiver and that the latter will be able to correctly order and reassemble them into the original message. A vivid explanation of these basics can be found at www.warriorsofthe.net.

The arrival and wide spread of wireless network technology have made it possible to get connected to the Internet without cables, and many modern devices, most notably laptop computers, are able to establish a connection to the nearest hot spot just by themselves. At the same time, cable-based networks, with fiber optics having replaced copper wires to a large extent, start moving into private homes, as the technology continues to decrease in price, and convergence of technologies is beginning to materialize. For instance, some providers nowadays let users get an Internet connection over a power line, from which electricity is obtained otherwise. Increasing numbers of providers are integrating Internet and telephone communications. The latter has become known under the acronym *Voice over IP* (VoIP) and has been made popular especially by *Skype*. Skype users make telephone and video calls through their computer using Skype client software and an Internet connection. Users may also communicate with landline and mobile telephones, although this requires setting up an account in which the caller has deposited money. Skype operates on a P2P model rather than a client/server model, as is discussed in Chapter 2. The Skype user directory is entirely decentralized and distributed among the nodes in the network, so that the network can easily scale to large sizes.

As Roberts (2006) notes, the historical development of the Internet can be seen in four stages. Stage 1 refers to the period from 1980 to 1991 where the Net had a research and academic focus; Stage 2 is 1992 to 1997, which saw early public uses; Stage 3 followed from 1998 to 2005, when the Internet achieved both domestic and international critical mass. We are currently experiencing the fourth stage; the Internet has become a maturing, universal, and worldwide accessible network that continues to grow and advance technologically rapidly. Stage 3 especially was impacted considerably by the aforementioned dot-com bubble and its gigantic speculation in Internet stocks, which provided the money for establishing high-bandwidth networks. This laid the foundation for broadband Internet applications and the integration of data, voice, and video services on the single technological basis that we are used to today. As remarked also by Friedman (2005), one of the consequences of the burst of the dot-com bubble was an oversupply of fiber-optic cable capacity, especially in the United States, of which many newly created service providers were able to take advantage.

The mid-1990s also saw a growing need for administration of Internet issues, one result of which was the creation of ICANN, the *Internet Corporation for Assigned Names and Numbers*. ICANN is a private nonprofit organization based in Marina del Rey, California, whose basic task is the technical administration of the Internet, in particular the assignment of domain names and IP addresses as well as the introduction of new top-level domains. To this end, it is worth mentioning that naming on the Internet follows a hierarchical pattern as defined in the *Domain Name System* (DNS), which translates domain or computer host names into IP addresses, thereby providing a worldwide keyword-based redirection service. It also lists mail exchange servers accepting e-mail for each domain, and it makes it possible for people to assign authoritative names without needing to communicate with a central registrar each time. To give the reader an idea of how many names are around these days, in the fall of 2006 there were more than fifty-three million .com domains registered, more than ten million .de domains, or almost five million .org domains. The mid-1990s, moreover, saw the formation of organizations dealing with the development of standards related to Web technology, most notably the *World Wide Web Consortium* (W3C), founded by Web inventor Tim Berners-Lee. For Web standards in general, see w3.org and the *Organization for the Advancement of Structured Information Standards* (OASIS) for standards related to electronic business and Web services (see www.oasis-open.org).

The broadband era

With broadband and wireless technology available as a commodity (with the only major remaining exception being the developing countries), we will soon see a host of new applications and services arise and delivered over the Internet and the Web, with digital radio and television only being precursors of what is to come. Broadband communication in particular allows for an easy transfer of large files, so that, for example, it becomes possible to watch movies over the Internet on a mobile device, since at some point it will be possible to guarantee a constant transfer rate over a certain period

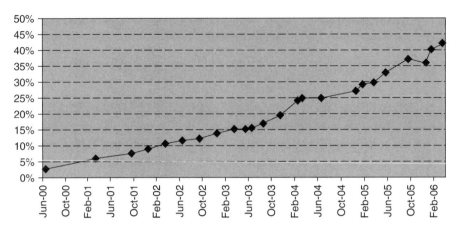

Figure 1.14 Home broadband penetration in the United States.
Courtesy of Pew Internet & American Life Project

of time. As Figure 1.14 indicates, the broadband penetration of homes in the United States has gone up considerably since the year 2000. A typical effect after getting broadband at home is that people spend more time on the Internet. Moreover, with flat rates for Internet access widely available today, many users do not explicitly switch their connection on and off, but are essentially always on.

A consequence foreseen for the near future is the delivery of television programs over the Internet and the Web ("IP television" or IPTV for short), for which many television companies are preparing. IPTV is becoming available both in the form of downloadable sections as well as streaming video; companies exploring this field include Babelgum, Joost, or Zattoo.

1.2.2 HTML and XML

On the software side of technology, we first have to mention that in parallel to hardware becoming a commodity, software development has dropped in price. What has been an expensive service some time ago is now cheap, and the "LAMP" (a common acronym for *Linux, Apache, MySQL, PHP*) manifestation of the Open-Source world has brought along a considerable number of tools through which software development is supported today.

We have already mentioned the arrival, together with the Web, of a new language, HTML, the predominant markup language for the creation of Web pages. HTML provides the means to structure text-based information in a document by denoting headings, tables, paragraphs, or lists, and to supplement that text with forms, images, links, and interaction. As mentioned, the language was originally developed by Tim Berners-Lee in the context of his creation of the Web (Berners-Lee, 2000), and it became popular through the fact that it is easy to use. An HTML document can quickly be set up using just a few structuring elements again called *tags*. Tags have to follow some simple syntactical rules and are often used to describe both content and presentation of a document (Musciano and Kennedy, 2006).

The *separation* of presentation and content became an issue when Web pages started to be rendered on more and more devices, including computer terminals, laptop screens, and cell phone displays, since each device has its own capabilities, requirements, and restrictions. It has also become important due to the fact that HTML is increasingly generated dynamically by applications, rather than being stored as static files. For example, an online database will rely on the assumption that no layout information needs to be stored for its content, but that this information will be added once its content is being accessed for display. In HTML, presentation can be specified within a document or separately within *cascading style sheet* (CSS) files.

HTML tags are all predefined, and although there are ways to include additional tags (for example, through the embedding of scripting language code), tags can generally not be defined by the individual user. This is different in XML (Harold and Means, 2004), the *Extensible Markup Language*, a W3C recommendation for a general-purpose markup language that supports a wide variety of applications and that has no predefined tags at all. Markup languages based on the XML standard are easy to design, and this has been done for such diverse fields as astronomy, biochemistry, music, and mathematics and for such distinct applications like voice or news in recent years. XML-based languages are also reasonably human-readable, since the tags used can be chosen in such a way that they relate to the meaning of the particular portion of the document that they enclose. XML is a simplified subset of the *Standard Generalized Markup Language* (SGML) and is widely used in information integration and sharing applications, in particular as they arise on the Internet. Any XML-based language should have an associated syntax specification, which can take the form of a *document type definition* (DTD, a formalism essentially based on regular context-free languages), or of an *XML Schema Definition* (XSD), which specifies a schema roughly in the style and detail of structure and type declarations found in programming languages or database schema languages.

The development of a new language based on XML typically goes through several steps (we later see that a similar sequence of steps is applicable to the other design tasks, for example ontologies or more generally vocabularies that are intended to serve a specific information integration, sharing, or orientation purpose), including the following:

1. Search for existing DTDs (or schemas)
2. Design of a namespace and a DTD (or a schema)

3. Discussion and fine tuning within the interested community
4. Publication of the language
5. Community-wide use of the language.

The concept of a *namespace* has turned out to be instrumental for XML. Namespaces provide a simple method for providing uniquely named elements and attributes in XML documents, namely by associating them with a distinct name collection that is identified by a unique URI (a *Uniform Resource Identifier* or unique Web address). An XML document may contain elements from different namespaces, as long as they are all properly referenced in the beginning of the document.

There are pros and cons regarding the question of whether to use a DTD or an XML Schema definition, but such a discussion goes beyond the scope of this chapter. XML has had an impact on HTML in that it has brought along XHTML (Musciano and Kennedy, 2006), a version of HTML that follows the same strict syntax rules as XML. More importantly, XML has become a universal enabler for a number of applications on the Web. For example, e-commerce sites use XML-based language intensively for document exchange or integration. Examples include RosettaNet (www.rosettanet.org), and ebXML (Electronic Business using eXtensible Markup Language, see www.ebxml.org), platforms that provide standardized XML documents for e-commerce items such as orders, invoices, and so on. RosettaNet is an open, nonprofit consortium of industrial companies that develops universal standards for the global supply chain. ebXML was started in 1999 as an initiative of OASIS and the United Nations/ECE agency CEFACT and is a collection of specifications that enables arbitrary enterprises to conduct business over the Internet; it provides standard methods for exchanging business messages, for conducting trade relationships, for communicating data in common terms, or for defining and registering business processes.

As we show in Chapters 2 and 6, the complexity of many XML languages that try to fully cover all information needs of a company has led to a countermovement where so called *micro-formats* define only the semantics of a very small portion of content.

Beyond plain HTML: scripting

As mentioned, an HTML document is allowed to have scripting code embedded. This arose out of the necessity to make Web pages dynamic as well as interactive. Indeed, often when users are asked for input, that input needs to be checked for correctness and completeness, or it needs to be sent off to a server for verification and most likely storage in a database. Moreover, the response a Web server creates upon the arrival of user input may have to be generated dynamically (e.g., to acknowledge or reject the input), in which case HTML needs to be created on the fly. To this end, an important distinction refers to the question of whether scripting occurs at the client side or at the server side, an issue again discussed in more detail in Chapter 2. To give the reader a warmup on it, consider the typical Web client/server scenario shown in Figure 1.15 where the client basically runs a browser, while the server has access to a number of stored documents and data sources.

Client-side scripting, very often seen in the form of *JavaScript*, makes use of the fact that a browser can not only render HTML pages, but also execute programs. These programs, which have to be written in a script language, will be interpreted just like HTML code in general. Thus, some of the tasks arising in a Web site can be off-loaded onto the client. On the other hand, certain things cannot be done at the client side, in particular when access to a database on the Web is needed. With server-side scripting using, for example, the *PHP* language, user requests are fulfilled by running a script directly on the Web server to generate dynamic HTML pages. It can be used to provide interactive Web sites that interface to databases or other data stores as well as local or external sources, with the primary advantage being the ability to customize the response based on a user's requirements, access rights, or query results returned by a database.

While PHP is primarily used on Web servers, there are other languages, originally used for other purposes, that have, over time, been extended to also support server-side scripting functionality. For example, Java, the popular programming language (java.sun.com), with its Enterprise Edition platform (java.sun.com/javaee), has constructs such as Servlets or JavaServer

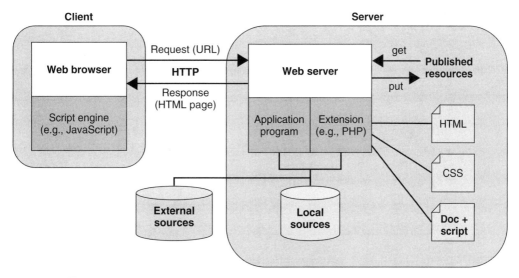

Figure 1.15 Client-side versus server-side scripting.

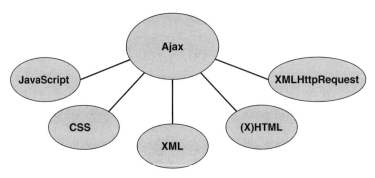

Figure 1.16 Ajax and its constituents.

Faces which allow HTML pages to be generated by Java applications running on the server (for details, see java.sun.com/javaee/5/docs/tutorial/doc/).

Both client-side and server-side scripting is based on the client/server paradigm and on the fact that any such interaction so far has been assumed to be *synchronous*. In order to enhance Web programming even further, a recent idea has been to not only allow HTML creation or modification on the fly ("dynamically"), but to be able to provide direct feedback to the user via on-the-fly HTML generation on the client. This, combined with *asynchronous* processing of data which allows sending data directly to the server for processing and receiving responses from the server *without* the need to reload an entire page, has led to a further separation of user interface logic from business logic now known under the acronym Ajax (*Asynchronous JavaScript and XML*). In a nutshell, Ajax brings together the various (software) technologies shown in Figure 1.16.

As shown in subsequent chapters, Ajax is a Web development technique that allows developers to build rich Web applications that are similar in functionality to classical desktop applications, yet they run in a Web browser. Its main functionality stems from an exploitation of XMLHttpRequest, a JavaScript class (with specific properties and methods) supported by most browsers which allows HTTP requests to be sent from inside JavaScript code.

1.2.3 Web services and RSS

Out of the numerous applications XML has seen to date, we mention just two more: Web services and RSS. Again, the discussion here will be cursory, and we delve into further details in Chapter 2.

Web services

Web services extend the client/server paradigm by the notion of an explicit registry, as indicated in Figure 1.17, thereby solving the problem of locating a service in a way that is appropriate for the Web.

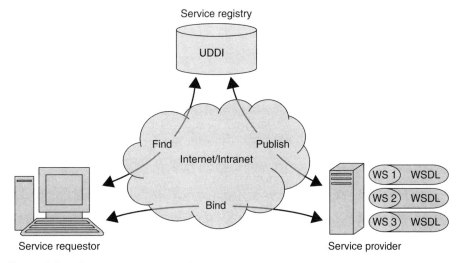

Figure 1.17 The Web service paradigm.

A service requestor (client) looking for a service sends a corresponding query to a service registry. If the desired service is found, the client can contact the service provider and use the service. The situation and proceeding is similar to looking for a service in real life by consulting the local Yellow Pages for alternative offering and contact data. The provider has previously published his service(s) in the registry. Hence, Web services hide all details concerning their implementation and the platforms they are based on; they essentially come with a unique URI that points to their provider. Since Web services are generally assumed to be interoperable, they can be combined with other services to build new applications with more comprehensive functionality than any single service involved.

To achieve these goals, Web services are commonly based on standards, in particular on the XML-based specifications SOAP (*Simple Object Access Protocol*), UDDI (*Universal Description, Discovery and Integration*), and WSDL (*Web Services Description Language*), all of which come with their distinct namespace and are described in detail, for example, in Alonso et al. (2004). These standards have typically been made a recommendation by the W3C (or are in the process of becoming a recommendation, which sometimes takes a bit of time). The benefits of a Web services architecture is well recognized in the business-to-business (B2B) area already, where companies are starting to use it for enterprise application integration, B2B integration, application construction, and a flexible approach to outsourcing. What is on the horizon today is a massive exploitation of the service paradigm to software provisioning even for customer applications. Modern Web applications tend to offer more and more services without the need of software installation, yet not every single one of them follows the paradigm shown in Figure 1.17 literally.

Web feeds and RSS

The second major XML application we mention marks a departure from the traditional way of looking for information on the Web, namely by searching and then essentially *pulling* the information found off the Web. As people have done for decades with newspapers and magazines, a more convenient way to obtain information on a regular basis is to *subscribe* to it, an idea underlying *push services* on the Web. Here the object in question is the *Web feed*, a data format used for pushing frequently updated content to interested users. Content distributors *syndicate* Web feeds, thereby allowing users to subscribe to it. Thus, in a typical usage scenario for such feeds, a content provider publishes a feed link on his site; users can subscribe to this using a feed or news reader running on their own machines. When instructed, or periodically, the reader asks all the servers in its feed list if they have new content. If so, it either makes a note of the new content or immediately starts downloading it (though, strictly speaking, this again results in a pull; we call it *push* here as the user does not have to activate this each time).

The primary format in which these feeds are specified is XML-based RSS, which may refer to *Really Simple Syndication* (RSS 2.0), *Rich Site Summary* (RSS 0.91, RSS 1.0), or *RDF Site Summary.* Using RSS or the Atom syndication format, users or clients can subscribe to a host of information from the Web, so that obtaining information (e.g., stock tickers, special offers, news, and nowadays often *podcasts*) can be automated in various ways. As we will discuss in more detail in Chapter 3, RSS and Atom have provided, in some form, what is today called a *mash-up* for several years already. A mash-up essentially brings multiple services or content sources together in order to form a new, often valued-added service.

Conclusion

This concludes our brief tour through some of the most relevant technological advances in connection with the Internet and the Web over recent years, and also the second stream of developments that have led to the arrival of Web 2.0. There has been enormous progress in networking technology and in hardware, and there have also been a number of good ideas in the software area, which together have helped to make the Web an extremely popular and widely used medium. What we look at next, when we discuss the third development stream, is how user participation in that medium as well as user contribution to it have changed drastically within a relatively short period of time.

1.3 User participation and contribution: socialization of the Web

The third preparatory stream for Web 2.0 we discuss is intended to show how dramatically different generations of people have changed their perception of and participation in the Web, and have gotten used to the Web as a communication medium, a socialization platform, a discussion forum, a business platform, a storage device for their diaries, and as a constantly growing and expanding encyclopedia. To this end, imagine an average eighteen-year-old student back in 1993. This person probably did not even notice right away that the Web came along. Clearly, there were others who did, but for the average person it took a few years to recognize that the Web had arrived and what it could do for her or him. The same person, now in his or her early thirties, will meanwhile have gotten used to electronic mail, both in business and private life, bank account and portfolio management, search for arbitrary information, photo exchange with friends, and probably a few other things that can easily be done over the Web today. What we try to summarize in this section is how a person who is eighteen years of age in early 2007 will see the Web, which typically is radically different, and how this person will now contribute to the Web.

1.3.1 Blogs and wikis

We have mentioned occasionally throughout this chapter that users have started to turn to the Web as a medium where they can easily and freely express themselves. By doing so online, they can reach a high number of other people most of whom they will not even know. We will now take a closer look at two forms of user-generated content that have become pretty popular and that are used today for vastly different purposes: *Blogs* are typically expressions of personal or professional opinion or experience on which other people can at most comment; *wikis* are pages or systems of pages describing content that other people can directly edit and hence extend, update, modify, or delete. Both communication forms have become very popular in recent years and contribute significantly to the novel read/write nature of the Web today.

Blogs and new forms of publishing

An effect the Web has seen in recent years and that we have described earlier is that people have started to write comments on products or sellers, on trips or special offers, and more generally on almost any topic; ultimately people have started to write about themselves, or have started to comment on any issue even without a particular cause (such as a prior shopping experience).

This had led to the creation of *blogs* and to a new form of activity called *blogging*. In essence, a *blog* is an online diary or a journal that a person is keeping and updating on an ad hoc or a regular basis. The word itself is a shortened version of *Web log* and is meant to resemble the logs kept by the captain of a ship as a written record of daily activities and documentation describing a journey of the ship.

A blog on the Web is typically a sequence of short texts in which entries appear in reverse order of publication so that the most recent entry is always shown first. In its most basic form, a blog consists of text only. Without any additional features and, in particular, if separated from subscriptions and from RSS, a blog is, hence, no more than a kind of diary that may be kept by anybody (e.g., private persons, people in prominent positions, politicians, movie stars, musicians, companies, or company CEOs). However, most blogs go way beyond a simple functionality today.

As a first example of a blog, let us consider Slashdot (www.slashdot.org). It was started in 1997 by Rob Malda for publishing "news for nerds, stuff that matters." He still maintains the blog today and has created one of the most lively sites for Linux kernel news, cartoons, Open-Source projects, Internet law, and many other issues, categorized into areas such as *Books, Developers, Games, Hardware, Interviews, IT, Linux, Politics,* or *Science.* Each entry is attached to a discussion forum where comments can even be placed anonymously. A second example of a blog, which also exhibits an interesting idea of how to use this medium, can be found at www.historymatters. org.uk and represents an attempt to motivate thousands of people in the United Kingdom to contribute to the largest blog in history, by writing about what they had been doing on October 17, 2006.

As a prominent example from a company, Figure 1.18 shows an excerpt from the blog kept by General Motors Vice Chairman Bob Lutz, in which he and other GM people report on new developments or events in any of the GM companies (e.g., the presentation of the new Buick Enclave at the 2006 L.A. Auto Show or the interior design of the new Chevrolet Malibu), respond to consumer enquiries, or present a link to a video that can be found on GMtv. The blog is not a simple one, since it comes with a number of features: Users can subscribe to it (i.e., be notified when new entries get posted, existing blog entries are placed in different categories; users can access an archive that goes at least two years back), and there are many links to other sites inside and outside GM. The blog is hence a good example of how an enterprise can develop new strategies for its external (but also its internal) communication.

There is a list of other blogs on Bob Lutz's blog, such as the Dilbert blog (dilbertblog.typepad.com). The latter also exhibits typical features found in

Figure 1.18 Bob Lutz's blog on auto news from Detroit.
Source: http://fastlane.gmblogs.com/

blog sites: While blogging services are often for free (i.e., users can create and maintain a blog of their own with any charges), they typically have to accept advertising around their entries. The Dilbert blog is maintained by Typepad, which hosts free blogs only for a trial period, but which explains a number of reasons why people actually do blog, namely to broadcast personal news to the world, to share a passion or a hobby, to find a new job, or to write about their current one. Moreover, companies like GM have discovered that blogs can be a medium through which they can link with customers and maybe even get new ones interested in buying their products.

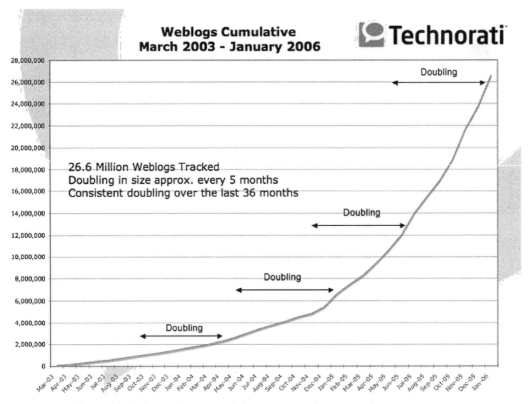

Figure 1.19 Blogosphere growth between March 2003 and January 2006.
Source: http://www.technorati.com/weblog/2006/02/81.html

Blogs are one of several modern forms of writing to the Web, and as can be seen from Figure 1.19. The source of this figure, the blogosphere (as tracked by Technorati), doubles in size almost every five-and-one-half months; it is now sixty times bigger than it was three years ago, and new blogs are added daily at a high pace. Indeed, according to Dave Sifry, "on average, a new weblog is created every second of every day – and 13.7 million bloggers are still posting 3 months after their blogs are created."

Providers where a blog can be set up (typically within a few minutes) include Blogger, Blogging, Yahoo! 360º (360.yahoo.com), or LiveJournal. UserLand was among the first to produce professional blogging software called Radio (radio.userland.com). If a blog is set up with a provider, it will be often the case that the blog is immediately created in a structured format such as RSS so that readers of the blog will be informed about new entries.

The activity of blogging, which is often enhanced, for example, with images, audio or video podcasts, can be seen as the successor to bulletin boards and forums, which have existed on the Internet roughly since the mid-90s. As seen in Figure 1.19, their numbers have increased enormously in recent years, which is why the advertising industry is taking a close look at them. And in a similar way as commenting on products on commerce sites or evaluating sellers on auction sites have done, blogging is starting to contribute to consumer behavior, since an individual user can now express his or her opinion without someone else executing control over it.

The party hosting a blog has an ethical responsibility and can block a blog or take it off-line, yet people can basically post their opinions freely. Many blogs take this issue seriously and follow some rules or code of ethics, such as the one established by Charlene Li at forrester.typepad.com/charleneli/2004/11/blogging_policy.html, which requires bloggers to adhere to the following:

> We will tell the truth. We will acknowledge and correct any mistakes promptly. We will not delete comments unless they are spam, off-topic, or defamatory. We will reply to comments when appropriate as promptly as possible. We will link to online references and original source materials directly. We will disagree with other opinions respectfully.

On a related topic, ethical implications of new technologies have recently been investigated by Rundle and Conley (2007).

Studies are showing that trust in private opinion is generally high. Blogs may also be moderated which applies, for example, to the aforementioned Slashdot. This site is also a good example for the influence a blog may have on the public or politics or both, demonstrated, for example, by the story of the Russian programmer Dmitri Sklyarov, who was arrested after giving a talk at the DefCon 9 Conference in Las Vegas in 2001 for an alleged violation of U.S. copyright law (see slashdot.org/yro/01/07/20/1332227.shtml).

Blogs have also been discovered by search engines and are meanwhile visited by crawlers on a regular basis. Since blogs can contain links to other blogs and other sites on the Web and links can be seen as a way for bloggers to refer to and collaborate with each other, and since link analysis mechanisms such as Google's PageRank give higher preference to sites with more incoming links, bloggers can influence the ranking of sites at search engines. Besides search engines like the ones we have mentioned, more specialized ones have meanwhile been developed for searching through or for blogs, including Daypop and Technorati.

Obviously, blogging has also opened the door for new forms of misuse. For example, blogs or blog entries can be requested in the sense that people are asked to write nice things about a product or an employer into a blog, and they might even get paid for this. Conversely, a blog could be used for mobbing a person or a product. An easy way to avoid some of these misuses is to require that blog writers identify themselves. Nevertheless, blogs have become a highly popular medium for people to express themselves. To learn more about the topic, see Yang (2006).

Wikis and Wikipedia

A second prominent form of user participation on and contribution to the Web today is represented by wikis. A *wiki* is a Web page or a collection of pages that allows its users to add, remove, and generally edit some of the available content, sometimes without the need for prior registration if the wiki is a public one. Thus, a wiki is an editable page or page collection that does not even require its users to know how to write a document in HTML. The term "wiki" is derived from the Hawaiian word "wikiwiki" which means "fast." Thus, the name suggests having a fast medium for collaborative publication of content on the Web. A distinction is commonly made between a single "wiki page" and "the wiki" as an entire site of pages that are connected through many links and which is, in effect, a simple, easy-to-use, and user-maintained database for creating content.

The history of wikis started in March 1995 when Ward Cunningham, a software designer from Portland, Oregon, was working on software design patterns and wanted to create a database of patterns to which other designers could contribute by refining existing patterns or by adding new ones. He extended his already existing "Portland Pattern Repository" by a database for patterns that he called *WikiWikiWeb*. The goal was to fill the database with content quickly, and in order to achieve this, he implemented a simple idea which can be seen in Figure 1.20: Each page has at its bottom a link titled "EditText" which can be used to edit the text in the core of the page directly in the browser. For example, pressing the edit link in the page shown in Figure 1.20 will lead to the page shown in Figure 1.21.

As can be seen, users can now write within the bordered area shown, and they can save their edits after entering the code number seen above this area. The important point is that no HTML is needed to edit the page; instead, the new or modified content will be converted to HTML by appropriate wiki software. Some rules apply in case a user wants to input headlines, emphasized words, and such.

Often, there is no review before the modifications that a user has made to a wiki page are accepted. Commonly, edits can be made in real time, and appear online immediately. There are systems that allow or require a login which allows signed edits, through which the author of a modification can be identified. In particular, login is often required for private wiki servers only after which a user is able to edit or read the contents. Most wiki systems have the ability to record changes so that an edit can be undone and the

Software Design Patterns

Most of the discussion of <u>DesignPatterns</u> on this Wiki are specific to <u>SoftwareEngineering</u> and are therefore <u>SoftwareDesignPatterns</u>, as contrasted with Alexander's original <u>ArchitecturalDesignPatterns</u>, which inspired the ones in software.

<u>SoftwareDesignPatterns</u> include famous examples such as **<u>SingletonPattern</u>**, **<u>AbstractFactoryPattern</u>** (see **<u>BuilderPattern</u>**), **<u>PrototypePattern</u>**

<u>SoftwareDesignPatternsIndex</u> with cross references to different names for the same pattern.

See <u>CategoryPattern</u> for a moderately exhaustive list.

Somewhat related topics:

- **<u>ExtremeProgramming</u>**
- **<u>UnitTest</u>s**

<u>EditText</u> of this page (last edited <u>June 2, 2005</u>)
<u>FindPage</u> by searching (or browse <u>LikePages</u> or take a <u>VisualTour</u>)

Figure 1.20 Software Design Patterns' Wiki in presentation mode.
Source: http://c2.com/cgi/wiki?SoftwareDesignPatterns

SoftwareDesignPatterns

Advice to visitors: Spam is not allowed on this site. Unwanted links are removed before indexing is allowed. If you are new here, please consider reading <u>GoodStyle</u> before contributing. If you just want to try out how Wiki works, please edit <u>WikiWikiSandbox</u> instead of existing pages or adding new ones. Thank you.

Type the code word, 567, here [   ] then press [Save] to finish editing. Read <u>MoreAboutCodes</u>.

```
Most of the discussion of DesignPatterns on this Wiki are specific to SoftwareEngineering and are
therefore SoftwareDesignPatterns, as contrasted with Alexander's original ArchitecturalDesignPatterns,
which inspired the ones in software.

SoftwareDesignPatterns include famous examples such
as '''SingletonPattern''', '''AbstractFactoryPattern''' (see '''BuilderPattern'''), '''PrototypePattern'''

SoftwareDesignPatternsIndex with cross references to different names for the same pattern.

See CategoryPattern for a moderately exhaustive list.
----

Somewhat related topics:
*'''ExtremeProgramming'''
*'''UnitTest'''''s'''
```

☐ I can not type tabs. Please <u>ConvertSpacesToTabs</u> for me when I save.

<u>GoodStyle</u> tips for editing.
<u>EditPage</u> using a smaller text area.
<u>EditCopy</u> from previous author.

Figure 1.21 Software Design Patterns' Wiki in editing mode.
Source: http://c2.com/cgi/wiki?edit=SoftwareDesignPatterns

respective page be brought back into any of its previous states. They can also show the most recent changes and support a history, and often there is a "diff" function that helps readers locate differences to a previous edit or between two revisions of the same page. As with blogs, there is an obvious possibility to abuse a wiki system and input garbage.

There are currently more than 100 systems for creating and maintaining wikis, most of which are Open Source (see c2.com/cgi/wiki?WikiEngines for a pretty up-to-date listing). A prominent example is *Wikia*. Wikia was founded by Angela Beesley and Jimmy Wales, the latter of whom also created Wikipedia, under the name "Wikicities," in October 2004 and relaunched as "Wikia" in March 2006. It also thus does not surprise that there are meanwhile wikis for almost each and every topic, a prominent example being *The Hitchhiker's Guide to the Galaxy* (www.bbc.co.uk/dna/h2g2). This wiki was created by *The Digital Village*, a company owned by author Douglas Adams who also wrote the famous book by the same title. It is nowadays run by the BBC which took it over after Adams' untimely demise. Adams created it in an attempt to realize his vision of an open encyclopedia authored solely by its users.

The largest wiki today is definitely the multilingual Wikipedia project that contains several million articles in about 100 languages and a large number of pictures. Wikipedia started out as an experiment in 2001 to create the largest online encyclopedia ever, but was soon growing faster than most other wikis. It soon got mentioned in blogs and various print media including the *New York Times*. Wikipedia has gone through several cycles of software development, and has always strictly separated content from comments and from pages about Wikipedia itself. Wikipedia has many distinct features that make its use transparent, among them instructions on citations, which anybody who wants to refer to a Wikipedia article elsewhere can easily download. For example, the bibliographic details for entry "Wiki" look as shown in Figure 1.22.

Bibliographic details for "Wiki"

- Page name: Wiki
- Author: Wikipedia contributors
- Publisher: *Wikipedia, The Free Encyclopedia.*
- Date of last revision: 15 March 2007 04:31 UTC
- Date retrieved: 15 March 2007 04:59 UTC
- Permanent link: http://en.wikipedia.org/w/index.php?title= Wiki&oldid=115248053
- Page Version ID: 115248053

Please remember to check your manual of style, standards guide or instructor's guidelines for the exact syntax to suit your needs. For more detailed advice, see **Citing Wikipedia**.

Figure 1.22 Bibliographic details for Wikipedia entry "Wiki."
Source: http://en.wikipedia.org/w/index.php?title=Special:Cite&page=Wiki&id=

The Wikipedia administration has established pretty strict rules regarding content or users and, in a similar spirit as blogs, establish ethical rules. For example, a page to be deleted must be entered into a "votes for deletion" page, where users can object to its deletion; this reflects the Wikipedia idea of making decisions vastly uniform. By a similar token, a user may only be excluded from Wikipedia right away in a case of vandalism, which has turned out to be rare. In general, discussions that take place about the content of articles are highly civilized most of the time, and Wikipedia has become prototypical for proving that the ease of interaction and operation make wikis an effective tool for collaborative authoring.

How especially effective Wikipedia is indeed came out in a study the famous British science journal *Nature* reported upon in December 2005. In an article titled "Internet encyclopaedias go head to head," *Nature* wrote that "Jimmy Wales' Wikipedia comes close to Britannica in terms of the accuracy of its science entries, a Nature investigation finds" (see www.nature. com/news/2005/051212/full/438900a.html). For this study, Nature had chosen articles from both Wikipedia and the Encyclopaedia Britannica in a wide range of topics and had sent them to experts for peer review (i.e., without indicating the source of an article). The experts compared the articles one by one from each site on a given topic. Forty-two of the returned reviews turned out to be usable, and *Nature* found just eight serious errors in the articles, of which four came from either site. However, the reviewers discovered a series of factual errors, omissions, or misleading statements; in total Wikipedia had 162 of them, while the Encyclopaedia Britannica had 123. This averages to 2.92 mistakes per article for the latter and 3.86 for Wikipedia.

The accuracy of Wikipedia may in part be due to the fact that its community has developed several methods for evaluating the quality of an article, including stylistic recommendations, tips for writing good articles, a "cleanup" listing articles that need improvement, or an arbitration committee for complex user conflicts, where these methods can vary from one country to another; some articles show in their header that they "need improvement." The bottom line is that Wikipedia is presently one of the best examples for an online community that, in spite of permanent warnings such as Denning et al. (2005), works extremely well, that has many beneficiaries all over the world, that is in wide use both online and off-line (through DVD distributions that are made available from time to time), and that enjoys a high degree of trust. Wikipedia also is an excellent example of a platform that is *social* in the sense that it gets better the more people use it, since more people can contribute more knowledge, or can correct details in existing knowledge for which they are experts.

Social software like wikis enable the creation of communication and relationships among individuals as well as among groups, and it supports the establishment, maintenance, and extension of social networks. We see next that this concept of social software can be found elsewhere as well.

1.3.2 Social networks

According to Levene (2006), *social networks* bring another dimension to the Web by going way beyond simple links between Web pages; they add links between *people* and *communities*. In such a network, direct links will typically point to our closest friends and colleagues, indirect links lead to friends of a friend, and so on. In this section, we take a brief look at social networks and the impact they are having on the Web today; we return to this topic in Chapter 5.

The networked generation in 2006

Let us return to a picture we started drawing earlier in this section, and imagine an eighteen-year-old today. This youngster not only grew up with the Web, but he or she has never considered it to be a utopia, and probably started using it a few years back already! Moreover, the younger generation is well underway with respect to abandoning traditional media. Recent investigations, such as the Office of Communications (2006) report, show that the "networked generation" (young adults like our eighteen-year-old) is driving a radical shift in media consumption. British broadband users spend on average 12.7 hours per week online. Seventy percent have used some kind of online social networking site such as MySpace. Moreover, the report says

> ... there is also evidence of a significant difference in communications usage patterns between young adults and the general population: for example, 16–24 year olds [in 2006] spend on average 21 minutes more time online per week [than 2005], send 42 more SMS text messages, but spend over seven hours less time watching television.

In other words, the sixteen- to twenty-four-year-olds are spurning television, radio, and newspapers in favor of online services. Increasingly, households are turning to broadband and digital TV. As the Office of Communications (2006) report states, "this generation has grown up with new technologies – and it is this generation for whom the uptake is instinctive." Yet the report also found technology adoption is not limited to the young. "The sector is being transformed by greater competition, falling prices, and the erosion of traditional revenues and audiences."

Thus, while it initially took a while until average users and consumers started to accept the Web as a medium or platform, or actually trusted it, this young generation is now growing up with it and is hence integrating it into everyday life much more comprehensively. This observation is, by the way, perfectly in line with Friedman's Flattener 10, the steroids, and the way in which they have made their way into everyday life and usage.

Online social networking

The information available on the Internet and the Web, as well as the tools by which this information has meanwhile become accessible, have led to the establishment of a number of distinct Internet *communities* (i.e., groups of people with common interests who interact through the Internet and the Web). Today, we can identify at least the following types of communities:

- Communities of *transactions*, characterized by the fact that they facilitate buying and selling as well as auctioning
- Communities of *interest*, commonly centered around a specific topic (e.g., movies, diecast cars, health food, dietary supplements)
- Communities of *relations*, organized around life experiences (e.g., traveling New Zealand on a budget, coping with breast cancer, or coming from the same high school)
- Communities of *fantasy*, based on imaginary environments and game playing (e.g., SecondLife or Entropia).

A prominent example and at the same time one of the oldest communities of interests on the Internet is the *Internet Movie Database* (IMDb), which emerged in 1990 from a newsgroup maintained by movie fans into the biggest database on movies in cinemas and on DVD and that is now owned by Amazon.com. A currently very vibrant example is the news community *digg*. Its users can add links to news items, comment on them, and vote on which items are considered important. The digg home page displays a list of items with the highest number of diggs, thus providing a snapshot of what the digg community is currently interested in.

This considerable change in perception and usage has opened the door for the present-day willingness of people to share all kinds of information, private or otherwise, on the Web for a new open culture, as observable in blogs, wikis, and, for example, at MySpace. MySpace was founded in July 2003 by Tom Anderson, Chris DeWolfe, and a team of programmers. Since it is considered a *social networking* site, we say a few words about this term before we take a closer look at this service.

The Internet offers various ways to make contact with other people, including e-mail, chat rooms, blogs, and discussion boards (which, unfortunately, are also heavily exploited by spammers, hackers, and other users with unethical intentions). However, while these services just support ad hoc interaction or focused discussions on a particular topic (or less focused conversations on the world at large), a *social network* on the Web (i.e., an online social network) goes a step further and is typically the result of employing some software that is intended to focus on building an online community for a specific purpose. Many social networking services are also blog hosting services where people can deliver longer statements than they would otherwise, and the distinction between blogs and social networks is often blurred. Social networks connect people with different interests, and these interests could relate to a specific hobby, a medical problem, or an interest in some specific art or culture. Often, members initially connect to their friends whom they know, for example, from school or college and later add new contacts (e.g., from their professional life) found through the Web.

While there are, as mentioned, obvious possibilities for misusing such a service, there are also professional business applications of it today. Indeed, consider a large, multinational company comprising numerous departments, employees, and products. Such a company typically has a *knowledge management* problem, since there is a large body of knowledge available among its employees, yet making effective as well as efficient usage of that knowledge is not always easy. For example, a particular project might need expertise from a variety of distinct areas, and it may not be straightforward to spot the appropriate people throughout an enterprise who can actually contribute that expertise. Or a product might have a design flaw or a technical or production problem, and the best help would be to identify those people in the company who can find the cause of the flaw and eliminate it. Numerous techniques and systems have been developed to support knowledge management, to establish profiles of employees' expertise, and to bring the right people together for a particular job or project, yet many companies are still struggling with this issue and have no good policy of handling it properly.

A social network can act as a means of connecting employees of distinct expertise across departments and company branches and help them build profiles in an often much easier way, and it can do so in a much cheaper and more flexible way than traditional knowledge management systems. Once a profile has been set up and published within the network, others can search for people with particular knowledge and connect to them. A typical example of a social network often used professionally and for business purposes is LinkedIn, a network that connects businesses by industry, functions, geography, and areas of interest. Other such examples include XING and the *Open Business Club* (openBC) as well as Ryze Business Networking. Upcoming.org is a social events calendar owned by Yahoo! in which registered users can post event entries and share them with other users. Since social networks can usually be set up free of charge (or for a low fee), they are an attractive opportunity for a company to create and expand their internal contact base. However, a social network needs not be restricted to a company's internal operation; it may as well include the customers to which the company sells goods or services (and hence be used for *customer relationship management*).

MySpace

The social networking site that is probably most popular among members of the networked generation is MySpace, a Web site offering an interactive, user-supplied network of friends, personal profiles, blogs, groups, photos, music, and videos. MySpace also features an internal search engine and an internal e-mail system. According to Alexa Internet, a company monitoring Internet traffic, it is currently the world's fourth most popular English-language Web site. The service has become an increasingly influential part of contemporary popular culture, especially in English-speaking countries. Figure 1.23 shows a recent screenshot of the MySpace home page that shows the *login* area, the *cool new videos* area, the *cool new people* area, as well as other areas related to music, videos, specials, and the functionality of mail, blog, forum, groups, events, classifieds, and so on.

A user profile at MySpace has two standard sections, "About Me" and "Who I'd Like to Meet," as well as several others, such as "Interests" and "Details." Fields in the latter sections will not be displayed if not filled in. Profiles also contain a blog with fields for content, emotion, and media. MySpace supports an uploading of images, one of which can be chosen to be seen on the main page of the profile and as the image that will appear next to the user's name on comments, messages, and such. Like other sites, MySpace now supports an uploading of videos as well. A core MySpace functionality that also makes it a social site is the *User's Friends Space*, which contains a count of a user's friends, a "Top Friends" area, and a link to view all of the user's friends. Each user can choose a limited number of friends to be displayed on his or her profile in the "Top Friends" area. In the "Comments" section a user's friends may leave comments for everybody to read, where each comment could require approval or even be deleted by the user. MySpace also allows users to modify their pages through an application of HTML and CSS and hence to create a *personalization* of their page. Users can put music and movies into their profiles, a feature intensively used, for example, by bands in order to promote their music.

More details on how to use MySpace can be found in Magid and Collier (2007). To complete the picture, we also mention a few other sites where social networks can be created or set up: *Facebook* is "a social utility that connects people with friends and others who work, study and live around them." *Friendster* is seen today as the site that gave a big push to social networking since 2003, although the development itself, just like blogs and wikis, goes back to the 1990s. Friendster founder Jonathan Abrams, noticing

Figure 1.23 MySpace Global home page (as of March 2007).

that its popularity has been on the decline recently, has meanwhile founded *Socializr*, where published information is supposed to be more important than the community member who publishes it. Another site is *Ning*, which distinguishes groups from photo and video networks. *Tribe* is a service that looks at the IP address of a user's machine and redirects her or him to a domestic site to find friends more locally (www.tribe.net). *Pendosoft* is a Swedish company offering social networking software, where a sophisticated client (and hence not the ad hoc user) can retain some control over the code included in the network's site. More on the entertainment side are places like the Japanese community entertainment network *Mixi* or the *Singshot* network for online singers and Karaoke artists. *MoveOn* is a community of people (actually a roof for several organizations), "from carpenters to stay-at-home moms to business leaders," who are interested in political issues in the United States (www.moveon.org). For the sake of completeness, we mention that online communities actually go back to 1985, the founding year of *The Well* (www.well.com), which still exists today. Another early community, almost as old as the Web itself, is *Bianca's Smut Shack* (www.bianca.com/shack).

We finally mention YouTube in this context, which can be seen as a mixture of a video blogging site and a social networking site, but which exhibits an interesting phenomenon. Due to the size of networks that now exist on the Web, and due to the enormous functionality which these sites offer, IT and media companies have discovered an interest in social networks. To be on the safe side, they have started acquiring such sites (e.g., Google has bought YouTube, while Rupert Murdoch of News Corporation bought MySpace; see the cover story in *Wired* magazine, July 2006).

Social networks on the Web have also triggered a renewed interest in sociological questions regarding how the Internet and the Web are changing our social behavior (including the question of why people send out spam mails and try to hack into other people's accounts). Social networks can be extracted from the Web, for example, by looking at people's home pages or pages they have set up with one of the services mentioned above. Home pages typically tell about people's interests, hobbies, idols, maybe family and friends, and they link to corresponding other pages. An analysis of such a page in the style it is done by the indexer of a search engine can then reveal fragments of texts or individual phrases that are also used by other people on their home pages, and in this way commonalities, common interests, relationships, and even entire communities can be discovered.

As an example, *The Stanford Daily* reported the following on June 1, 2001, under the header "New Web site weaves social web":

A new Web site sketches the "Stanford Social Web" by deducing the connections between people from the information contained on their Web sites. The Web site was developed by Lada Adamic, an applied physics graduate student at Stanford, and Eytan Adar, who works at the Hewlett-Packard Sand Hill Labs. Their research was supported by the Internet Ecologies Area of the Xerox Palo Alto Research Center. According to Adamic and Adar's research proposal, "the links and text on a user's home page and the mailing lists the user subscribes to are reflections of social interactions a user has in the real world." Thus, by searching the Web sites of Stanford students for matching text and analyzing the links between Stanford students' pages, it is possible to recognize pairs of friends or acquaintances. . . . Provided that people's friends have Web sites hosted by a Stanford server, the Stanford Social Web can provide an intriguing sketch of their social lives. After entering a Stanford system user name onto the main Web site, one is led to a page showing a diagram of one's friends mapped out in the form of a constellation. The links between friends are inferred from the pattern of in-links and out-links that connect their Web sites. The Stanford Social Web not only indicates existing ties between students, but suggests pairs of students who share common experiences or interests, regardless of whether they are already acquainted with each other. The text on students' Web sites is compared within categories such as "cities," "persons" and "organizations," in order to generate a "likeness score."

On a broader scale, *social network analysis* investigates metrics that measure the characteristics of the relationships between the participants of a network. In particular, such an analysis looks for *ties* (between pairs of participants) and their *strength* as well as their specialization into *bridges*, for *triangles* (involving three people), and for issues such as the *clustering coefficient* of a participant or the *density* of the network. For a brief introduction, refer to Levene (2006), and for a more detailed one, to Brandes and Erlebach (2005).

Conclusion

In conclusion, the current expectation for several years to come is that user participation in and contribution to the Web, which has increased considerably in recent years, will continue to grow, and that the social life of individuals, families, and larger communities of people will increasingly be enriched by online applications from social Web networks. It remains to be seen whether this will indeed have anything more than local effects in the sense that people may now take their network of friends online, but do not necessarily include people they have never met or that they most likely will never meet. On the other hand and as a result of this development, the social Web will become increasingly relevant to companies as a vehicle for marketing, advertising, and communication internally as well as with their customers. For an in-depth look at this last aspect refer to Tapscott and Williams (2007), who study the effects and opportunities of mass collaboration over the Web.

1.4 Merging the streams: the arrival of "Web 2.0"

In this chapter we have tried to draw a picture that is determined by three parallel streams of development. The *applications stream* has brought along a number of services anybody can nowadays use on the Internet and the Web. The *technology stream* has provided the underlying infrastructure groundwork for all of this with fast moving and comprehensive advances in networking and hardware technology and quite a bit of progress regarding software. And, finally, the *user participation and contribution stream* (which we might also call the *socialization stream*), has changed the way in which users, both private and professional ones, perceive the Web, interact with it, contribute to it, and in particular publish their own or their private information on it. These three streams have brought along a number of techniques, technologies, and usage patterns that at present converge, and the result is what has received the preliminary and – especially during 2006 – fancy term "Web 2.0." We next try to provide a brief characterization of what is behind the term, as well as a summary of what has led to it.

In summarizing the discussion from this chapter, we have seen the emergence of

- The arrival of HTML, of the browser, and of search as a dominant activity in many Internet applications these days
- Electronic commerce as an addition to (and often a replacement of) traditional retail through stores, now being a major, if not the only, source of income for many businesses, and also a major driver of new algorithmic applications of software (think, for example, of data mining through transaction data or automatic recommendation systems as made popular by Amazon.com and others)
- Advertising as a major business model and way of making money on the Internet, in particular as a vehicle that can provide the financial basis for services that are offered for free to end users
- The long tail as an illustration of a number of phenomena that the modern Web allows to respect, in particular advertising in niche markets once the necessary technology is available as a commodity (and, as a consequence, doing commerce in these niches)
- Customer feedback, blogging, and wikis as novel ways of obtaining user input
- A disappearance of the general consensus that goods and services that are taken up basically have to be paid for, and a replacement of this consensus by the questionable understanding that computer-storable goods, which are transported mostly by being copied from one place to another, should more or less be for free; this is technologically supported by the advancement of file-sharing networks and psychologically by the open-access movement
- HTML scripting, XML, and Ajax as fundamental language and development paradigms upon which present-day Web applications can be built

- Service orientation and content syndication as new ways of providing software and content and of composing applications
- Online communities, online encyclopedias, and online social networks as (often anonymous) places where people can create collective knowledge and intelligence, and can meet and share experiences, made popular, for example, by the "MySpace generation."

When we compare these core aspects of the history of the Web that we have seen so far (where it may be a bit far-fetched to use the term "history" a little over years after its inception already), we can recognize that the Web has emerged from a medium where a few people centrally determined what all others had to use to one where very many people participate and jointly create and publish content. In other words, while initially content was mostly *read from* the Web, content is meanwhile more and more *written to* the Web. This is why some people speak of Web 2.0 as the "read/write Web."

An immediate consequence of the fact that more and more people publish on the Web through blogs, wikis, communities, tagging, and otherwise is that increasing amounts of *data* have to be stored. More data arises from commercial sites, where each and every user or customer transaction leaves a trace in a database. As mentioned, search engines have already discovered this and started incorporating blogs into their crawling activities, and companies commonly employ data warehouse technology for online analytical processing or the application of data mining tools to large data collections in order to generate new knowledge. As a common saying in data mining goes, "there's gold in your data, but you can't see it." Making the most of large data collections will be even more crucial in the future than it has been in the past. This is especially true for data collections that are in some way unique or specialized; control over such a collection will be an invaluable asset in the future. However, it should be noted that this is not a *new* fact; indeed, holding control over a specific data pool has always been very valuable, the major difference today being that so many data collections are available online.

The technology stream that we have only sketched in this chapter and that we will explore further in Chapter 2 has contributed a major paradigm shift in software development, namely a departure from large and monolithic software applications to lightweight services which ultimately can be composed and orchestrated into more powerful services that finally carry entire application scenarios. While the original Web service paradigm shown above in Figure 1.17 is not in full swing as far as the Web is concerned, a much simpler version is, which boils down to what we will soon call *Web procedure calls.* Service-orientation, especially in the form of service calls, to an open application programming interface (API) that can be contacted over the Web as long as the correct input parameters are delivered have not only become very popular, but are also exploited these days in numerous ways, particularly giving users an increased level of functionality from a single source. A benefit of the service approach to software development has so far been the fact that platform development especially on the Web has received high momentum in recent years. Yet it has also contributed to the fact that services which a provider delivers behind the scenes to some well defined interface can be enhanced and modified and even permanently corrected and updated without the user even noticing, a phenomenon that has been called "perpetual beta" by O'Reilly (2005) and others.

Taking the developments we have described together, considering them in conjunction, and putting them into a perspective of time and evolution, it becomes clear that the aspects we have described in our three streams represent the core of the developments and the evolution of the Web, the Internet, its underlying technology, and the user perception of all this. It is justified to say that the essence of Web 2.0 boils down to the following three core aspects:

■ Ways to utilize and combine *data* and *data streams* from various sources into a representation that allows for the derivation of new information or added value; the appropriate and intelligent (and legal) utilization of data that is kept current by its owner has become a driver of many new applications that nowadays come under the name "mash-ups"

■ *Functionality-* as well as service-oriented approaches to build new applications as a composition of other, already existing ones and in order to enrich user experiences on the Web, or to create "Rich Internet Applications" (RIAs), and the services provided let the Web exhibit features previously known from stationary computers only

■ Tagging, blogging, and "wiki-ing" as important steps into a *socialization* of the Web, where all of a sudden a user no longer considers his personal entries private anymore, but makes them available to friends, a certain community, and ultimately the general public, and where this often leads to an improvement of the underlying platform.

These core aspects can be seen as three dimensions spanning a "Web 2.0 space" as illustrated in Figure 1.24. We keep these three dimensions as a yardstick in the remainder of this book.

To give a first indication that our "Web 2.0 space" captures the essence of the topic, let's briefly return to Wikipedia and blogs that we discussed earlier. Both can be seen as typical examples for a Web 2.0 development and can hence be positioned within the Web 2.0 space, as shown in Figure 1.24. A blogging site puts most emphasis on data (the data that the user puts into his or her blog) and on socialization (by letting other users read the blog entries

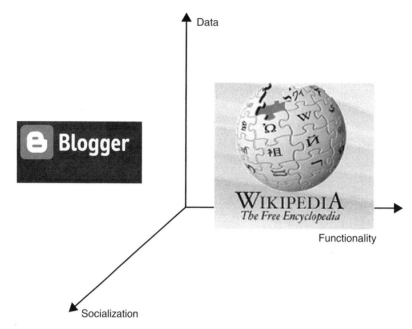

Figure 1.24 The three core dimensions of Web 2.0.

and comment on them). Wikipedia, on the other hand, is a good example of a system with advanced functionality, yet also lots of data and an important social component based on expertise, social behavior, and trust. In the following chapters, we provide more examples for placements into this space.

We finally mention that the term "Web 2.0" is already under interrogation regarding its lifespan. For example, an article in MIT's *Technology Review* in December 2006 asked the question "What comes after Web 2.0?" and reminded its readers of several other developments that might be overlooked within the current Web 2.0 hype. The most prominent of them is the *Semantic Web*, a vision that was laid out by Web inventor Tim Berners-Lee several years ago and whose goal is to add more semantics or meaning to the Web and its applications, so that it becomes easier for them to talk to each other. We say more about this in Chapter 6. Many Web sites also discuss the term "Web 3.0" already and see a fusion coming of semantic technologies and architectures of participation as we currently experience. On the funnier side, Jonathan Abrams, the aforementioned founder of Socializr, states on www.socializr.com/about that "Socializr is a 'Web 3.1' company. 'Web 3.1' is an arbitrary and silly label like 'Web 2.0', but even sillier, and 55% cooler! And everyone knows nothing works right until the 3.1 version." This should let us handle the term with care, and should prevent us from overestimating the novelty behind it.

chapter 2

A Review of the Technological Stream

In this chapter, we elaborate on the overview of technological advances we have only sketched in the previous chapter. More precisely, we focus on the languages and Web technology that have glued together the Web from the very beginning but have evolved over time as well. We also discuss the disruptive technology of P2P networks, their structures, and applications. Our aim in this chapter is twofold: First, we show what the relevant Web technology is about and how it can be used, in particular when it comes to languages such as HTML and XML or to programming in JavaScript or an Ajax environment. Second, we prepare for subsequent chapters where we look in more detail into the foundations of the software side of Web 2.0 and what it comprises.

2.1 Developments in Web technology

For more than a decade, the way in which users navigate the Web has not changed much. Only recently have a number of Web pages started to behave differently. Indeed, while most Web sites are still what we are used to, namely a set of pages that contain information (of which we see an example in Figure 2.1), some Web pages nowadays behave more like programs. As we saw in the previous chapter, this process is a clear evolution, not a revolution of the Web that is mirrored in the development and use of the underlying Web standards and technologies. In fact, what we are

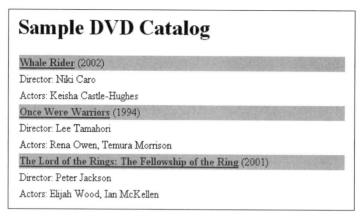

Figure 2.1 Sample DVD catalog written in HTML.

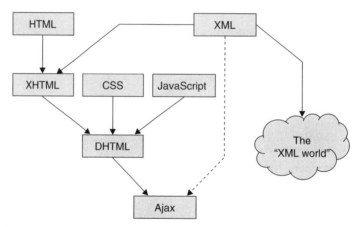

Figure 2.2 Evolution of Web (language) standards..

experiencing here is the shift from a "page-based" Web to an "application-based" Web, in which many pages host application programs, often more than just one.

In order to emphasize this observation, we will retrace the evolution steps of Web standards, from the simple beginnings to the complicated reality of today's Web standards landscape, as illustrated in Figure 2.2. As can be seen, HTML as well as XML are cornerstones of Web languages from which several other standards have emerged. Their immediate confluence has been XHTML, yet XML by itself has spawned an entire "world" of new languages. By adding style sheets and programming language elements such as JavaScript, HTML becomes DHTML (with "D" for "dynamic"), and we finally arrive at one of the core Web 2.0 technologies: Ajax. Figure 2.2 covers languages that are visible to clients (i.e., they are transported over the Web); languages that are used to create the former remain on the server-side (i.e., server-side scripting languages, see Section 2.1.4) and are invisible to clients, which is why they are not shown here.

For illustration purposes, we use the sample DVD catalog from Figure 2.1 and rephrase and extend it in each subsequent section to highlight and emphasize the characteristics of the language or concept in question. We start with a version of the catalog that one would have been able to find on the Web already in the mid-1990s. At the other end of the spectrum, in Chapter 3, we end up with an implementation that employs scripting to add dynamic behavior to the page, and that incorporates other services by "mashing them up" through the use of what we will call *Web procedure calls*. The chapter concludes with a closer look at languages that are based on XML, namely RSS and the Web Services–related specifications of WSDL, UDDI, and SOAP.

2.1.1 HTML

Web pages are commonly described using *Hypertext Markup Language* (HTML); see Musciano and Kennedy (2007). This is a language that uses *markups*, also called *tags*, in plain text files to transport information about the structure and presentation of a page. It is pretty easy to get started writing HTML documents, which has certainly contributed to its huge success. It is, however, also pretty easy to write documents in a "bad style," which has consequences, for example, when a user wants to reuse these files in different settings (e.g., for different types of displays such as a computer screen or a cell phone). The intention of this section is to point out the main characteristics of HTML, and to highlight the aforementioned deficiencies to explain why the development of Web languages did not stop with HTML.

As the name indicates, HTML uses markups to define hypertext (i.e., text and other material organized in a way that tries to overcome the inherent limitations of traditional "linear" text). Tags are used to indicate that parts of the text have a special meaning or semantics. The set of tags that can be used and the meaning of these tags are both defined in the HTML standard.

A running example

Let us look at the code in Listing 2.1, which is the source code of the Web page shown earlier in Figure 2.1; we use this code to discuss the main characteristics of an HTML file, and we look at the different parts of this code in some detail to understand how an HTML document is structured.

Listing 2.1: Sample DVD catalog source code.

```html
<!DOCTYPE HTML PUBLIC "-//W3C//DTD HTML 4.01 Transitional//EN"
      "http://www.w3.org/TR/html4/loose.dtd">
<html>
 <head>
  <title>Sample DVD Catalog</title>
  <meta name="author" content="Vossen, Hagemann">
 </head>
 <body>
  <h1>Sample DVD Catalog</h1>
  <table width="500">
   <tr>
    <td bgcolor="silver">
     <b><a href="http://www.imdb.com/title/tt0298228/">
      Whale Rider</a></b>
     (2002)
    </td>
   </tr>
   <tr><td>Director: Niki Caro</td></tr>
   <tr><td>Actors: Keisha Castle-Hughes</td></tr>
   <tr>
    <td bgcolor="silver">
     <b><a href="http://www.imdb.com/title/tt0110729/">
      Once Were Warriors</a></b>
     (1994)
    </td>
   </tr>
   <tr><td>Director: Lee Tamahori</td></tr>
   <tr><td>Actors: Rena Owen, Temura Morrison</td></tr>
   <tr>
    <td bgcolor="silver">
     <b><a href="http://www.imdb.com/title/tt0120737/">
      The Lord of the Rings: The Fellowship of the Ring</a></b>
     (2001)
    </td>
   </tr>
   <tr><td>Director: Peter Jackson</td></tr>
   <tr><td>Actors: Elijah Wood, Ian McKellen</td></tr>
  </table>
 </body>
</html>
```

Document Type Definitions

The first tag in this document defines its type. We have chosen to make our Web page "HTML 4.01 Transitional." This is a version of HTML that was introduced by the W3C in 1999 and that provides backward compatibility to older versions of HTML. Our critique of HTML is based on this version. There are two other variations of HTML Version 4, namely "Frameset" and

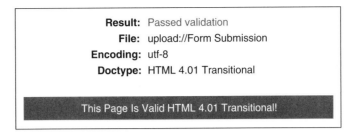

Figure 2.3 Result of validation.

"Strict." The former allows the use of framesets that enable a browser to display separate files in a single browser window. The "Strict" variation is the version that the W3C endorses as the desired type for Web documents, since it avoids the problems we describe here. However, most Web pages today still give "Transitional" as their document type. To test whether a page conforms to its DTD (that is, correctly implements the DTD it claims to implement), *validators* can be used. Such validators analyze the structure of the document at hand and check every item in it, whether it is allowed according to the DTD. Several validators can be found on the Web, such as the validator of the W3C: validator.w3.org/. If we upload the example from Listing 2.1, we obtain the result shown in Figure 2.3 telling us that the page is indeed HTML 4.01 Transitional.

It should be noted that most pages do not conform to the DTD they mention, or they do not mention one at all. For example, as of December 2006, the Amazon.com home page does not provide a reference to a DTD. Indeed, studies show that the proper use of DTDs is very rare. The ValiWatch study of 2005 (www.validome.org/lang/ge/html/valiwatch-web-2005), conducted by the authors of the Validome validator, shows that only 3.9 percent of the studied pages were valid HTML. Of these, more than 60 percent were of type "Transitional." Moreover, it shows that only 41.5 percent of pages give a valid DTD reference.

Tags used in the example

The main part of the document starts with the opening `<html>` tag, indicating that the following document is written in HTML. The chevrons that enclose the keyword are common to all tags. At the end of the code we see a closing tag: `</html>`. It indicates that the part of the document, which in this case is the entire document, ends here. All lines between the opening and closing `<html>` tags are indented. This is just for clarity; it is not required by the browser, but it indicates that all these elements are nested within the tags that surround them.

An HTML document conceptually consists of a *head* and a *body*. Although these tags are optional in the standard they are found in almost all Web pages. We see that the first tag nested within the `<html>` tag is `<head>`, which tells the browser that header information describing the current document will now be following. The head section in our example tells the browser that this page has the title "Sample DVD Catalog," which the browser will usually display in its own title bar or in the tab that the page is opened in. The `<meta>` tag gives more information about the page, in this case it tells the browser who the authors of the page are: here "Vossen, Hagemann." A `<meta>` tag does not have a closing tag. The latter is not necessary since the tag does not contain any text. It does, however, include the attributes `name` and `content`. Attributes give additional information about tags and are stated as pairs of attribute name and value. In the example we are looking at, the first attribute name is `name`, its value is `author`. The `</head>` tag concludes the head section of the document.

The `<body>` tag starts the part of the HTML document that the browser is going to render in the main part of its window. Nested into the body part of the document here is a level-one heading (indicated by the tag `<h1>`) the content of which can be seen in Figure 2.1 as large, bold text. Following the heading is a table (`<table>`) with several table rows (`<tr>`) and table data cells (`<td>`) nested into it. The width of the table is set to 500 pixels in the `<table>` tag. The cells contain parts of the description of movies. The title is always in a cell that has a silver background specified by the `bgcolor` attribute of the `<td>` tag. Moreover, titles are displayed in a bold font through the use of `<b>` and contain an anchor that links to the entry of this movie in the *Internet Movie Database* (IMDb). This information is contained in the `href` attribute of the `<a>` tag surrounding the title. In HTML, there are many ways to express this content that would look similar to the one we have chosen here. The table, for example, limits the text width to 500 pixels, which could have been achieved differently. Indeed, the use of a table for this purpose is a misuse, nevertheless one that is working in this case.

The HTML standard comprises a number of additional tags and features (e.g., to format text, to include structures such as lists, tables, and objects, or to include scripting information) which, as we see later in this chapter, allows for dynamic Web pages. A detailed discussion of the possibilities of the HTML language is beyond the scope of this book. For further details on this language, refer, for example, to Musciano and Kennedy (2007) or to one of the many other introductory texts on HTML.

Structure versus presentation

Most tags used in our small example define the structure of the document: They denote a certain part to be a heading, a table cell, or a link.

The `<b>` tag, however, demands that the title is to be rendered in a bold font, thus defining a way in which the content is to be presented. Indeed, a browser cannot identify DVD titles as what they are; it just recognizes that text has to be displayed. This is different with the first page heading since that was marked as `<h1>`. The use of the table construct is also unintuitive: looking at the table structure alone, one cannot distinguish where an entry starts and where it ends, since all rows are treated equal. Some tags used in this example, namely `width` and `bgcolor`, also define how the page is to be rendered and have nothing to do with the structure of the document.

The HTML standards prior to Version 4 as well as its "Transitional" variant allow the usage of tags and attributes that explicitly state what the output should look like; they are therefore also called *presentational* tags and attributes.

Why do we care whether presentation and content are separated or not? The answer to this question is *reuse*, more precisely reuse of content and reuse of style. Content is limited in its reuse if it is specifically and *unnecessarily* designed to be accessed in only one way. One does not only want to view Web pages on a computer screen; one may also want to print it or view it on a mobile device such as a PDA or a cell phone with a small screen. Accessibility is also an issue here (Paciello, 2000). Indeed, people with disabilities might not be able to read the content of a page if it is badly presented. Different contexts may require different presentation styles, so it is best not to tie appearance to content. As an example, take the fixed width of the table in our earlier example: on a mobile device with a display that is less than 500 pixels wide, the table would have to be scrolled sideways in order for the entire content to be viewable, which can quickly become very inconvenient when the page gets longer and wider.

Reusing style is a particular issue if one cares for consistent Web design to be applied over a large collection of pages or even across multiple sites. Here, it makes sense to format similar concepts in a similar way. The pages of a Web site should look similar so that a user can immediately notice that they belong together. If every page defines its presentation anew, controlling that the presentation is consistent is difficult. We already saw this in our small example: The silver background for the title of a DVD had to be explicitly specified every time such a title occurred.

Further issues

It should be mentioned that the HTML standards are just one part of the reality of HTML today. The competing browsers of Mozilla, Opera,

Microsoft, and others have, over time, come to define their own tags to resolve design issues or just in the hope of gaining competitive advantage through the support of a richer set of features. The `<marquee>` tag, for example, lets text scroll over the screen; it was and still is supported by Internet Explorer but not by Firefox. The opposite is true for the `<blink>` tag, which causes an element to blink (i.e., alternate between visible and invisible). Both tags have never been part of the HTML standard.

Popular browsers are relatively fault tolerant. They will display pages as expected or at least reasonably well even if the HTML code does not explicitly comply with the respective W3C standard. This is easily done since browsers *interpret* the code they are presented with and simply ignore parts they cannot interpret properly. This has led to a multitude of different attitudes towards the usage of HTML tags. Many sites are written browser-aware so that the different issues the designers have with the presentation of their site can be treated for each browser individually.

Before we turn to the solution that the W3C offers concerning the separation of presentation and content we look at XML, a markup language that is quite similar in spirit to HTML, but much more rigidly defined.

2.1.2 XML

As we mentioned in Chapter 1, the *Extensible Markup Language* (XML) is a W3C recommendation for a general-purpose markup language that supports a large variety of applications. See www.w3.org/MarkUp/#recommendations for an explanation of what that means, or Harold (2004) for a comprehensive introduction to the language. This is in significant contrast to HTML, which has always been specifically intended for the design of Web pages. XML can also be seen as a "meta language," or a language framework, as it can be (and is) used to define markup languages for specific applications such as mathematics, astronomy, chemistry, biology, business processes, news, as well as many others.

Since its introduction in 1995, there has been a flood of languages defined on the basis of XML, which can generally be classified as *application-oriented* (in areas such as the ones just mentioned) or as *technology-oriented*. The XML-based languages we deal with in this chapter fall into the latter category and include standards such as XHTML, SOAP, WSDL, RSS, and ATOM. In Chapter 6, we return to RDF and OWL.

In order to validate, process, and transform XML documents, a huge set of tools has been developed: specification languages such as DTDs and XML Schema, query languages such as XPath and XQuery, and transformation languages such as XSL and XSLT. Together with XML these form the *base*

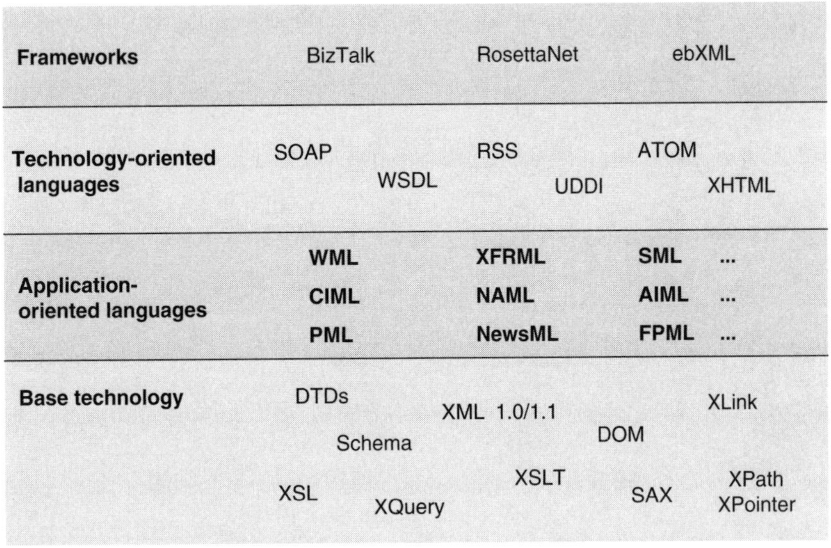

Frameworks	BizTalk	RosettaNet	ebXML	
Technology-oriented languages	SOAP WSDL	RSS UDDI	ATOM XHTML	
Application-oriented languages	WML CIML PML	XFRML NAML NewsML	SML ... AIML ... FPML ...	
Base technology	DTDs Schema XSL XQuery	XML 1.0/1.1 XSLT	DOM SAX	XLink XPath XPointer

Figure 2.4 Parts of the XML world.

technology for the languages mentioned before. *Frameworks*, such as ebXML and RosettaNet, employ tools and languages to specify business processes and documents. Figure 2.4 gives an (admittedly incomplete) overview of what we tend to call the "XML world."

XML shares with HTML that it uses plain text as the basis and that tags are enclosed in chevrons. A major difference is that tag names can be freely chosen and that there is no meaning, no semantics, attached to tags. Semantics is only added to XML documents via their interpretation in the context of a specific application.

XML documents have to be *well formed* (i.e., every tag that has been opened needs to be closed again at the same level of nesting). Due to this property, XML documents are structured as *trees*, and a number of features related to XML documents result from this fact. For example, searching for the occurrence of specific tags within an XML document amounts to descending on a path from the root of the document to some node within the underlying tree structure. As a consequence, a language such as XPath (Melton and Buxton, 2006), as the name suggests, provides ways of specifying such paths.

Tags are said to define XML *elements*. There always has to be a single root element. As an abbreviation, an empty element can be written as `<element-name/>`. Listing 2.2 shows an example of an XML document that describes our catalog of DVDs.

Listing 2.2: XML Document for a sample DVD catalog.

```
<?xml version="1.0" encoding="UTF-8"?>
<DVDCatalog>
 <Title>Sample DVD Catalog</Title>
 <DVD category="Drama/Family" language="en">
  <Title>Whale Rider</Title>
  <IMDBLink>http://www.imdb.com/title/tt0298228/</IMDBLink>
  <ASIN>B0000CABBW</ASIN>
  <Director>
   <Person>
    <Firstname>Niki</Firstname>
    <Lastname>Caro</Lastname>
   </Person>
  </Director>
  <Actors>
   <Person>
    <Firstname>Keisha</Firstname>
    <Lastname>Castle-Hughes</Lastname>
   </Person>
  </Actors>
  <Year>2002</Year>
  </DVD>
 <DVD category="Drama" language="en">
  <Title>Once Were Warriors</Title>
  <IMDBLink>http://www.imdb.com/title/tt0110729/</IMDBLink>
  <ASIN>B0000A02Y4</ASIN>
  <Director>
   <Person>
    <Firstname>Lee</Firstname>
    <Lastname>Tamahori</Lastname>
   </Person>
  </Director>
  <Actors>
   <Person>
    <Firstname>Rena</Firstname>
    <Lastname>Owen</Lastname>
   </Person>
   <Person>
    <Firstname>Temura</Firstname>
    <Lastname>Morrison</Lastname>
   </Person>
  </Actors>
  <Year>1994</Year>
  </DVD>
 <DVD category="Fantasy" language="en">
  <Title>The Lord of the Rings: The Fellowship of the Ring</Title>
  <IMDBLink>http://www.imdb.com/title/tt0120737/</IMDBLink>
  <ASIN>B00005U515</ASIN>
  <Director>
```

```
      <Person>
        <Firstname>Peter</Firstname>
        <Lastname>Jackson</Lastname>
      </Person>
    </Director>
    <Actors>
      <Person>
        <Firstname>Elijah</Firstname>
        <Lastname>Wood</Lastname>
      </Person>
      <Person>
        <Firstname>Ian</Firstname>
        <Lastname>McKellen</Lastname>
      </Person>
    </Actors>
    <Year>2001</Year>
    </DVD>
  </DVDCatalog>
```

It is easy to check that the document shown in Listing 2.2 is well formed. Although we have said that there are no semantics attached to the elements, the document is self-explanatory for a human reader, which is generally seen as one of the core advantages of XML. For example, the document describes a DVD catalog containing three DVDs, the second of which has the title *Once Were Warriors* and actors *Rena Owen* and *Temura Morrison*.

XML documents can be restricted by the use of schema formats. These define which elements can be used in a document, what attributes they have, and how the elements can be nested within each other. If an XML document conforms to such a schema it is said to be *valid*; notice that a document can be well formed without being valid, but not vice versa. In our case, we would like to make sure that only DVD elements are entered into the catalog. One way to specify a schema is through a *Document Type Definition* (DTD). As an example, the DTD in Listing 2.3 defines the structure of our sample DVD catalog.

Listing 2.3: DTD for the sample DVD catalog.

```
<!ELEMENT DVDCatalog (Title, DVD+)>
<!ELEMENT DVD (Title, IMDBLink, ASIN, Directors, Actors, Year)>
<!ATTLIST DVD category CDATA #REQUIRED language CDATA #REQUIRED>
<!ELEMENT Director (PERSON)>
<!ELEMENT Actors (PERSON+)>
<!ELEMENT Person ((Lastname, Firstname) | (Firstname, Lastname))>
<!ELEMENT IMDBLink (#PCDATA)>
<!ELEMENT ASIN (#PCDATA)>
<!ELEMENT Title (#PCDATA)>
<!ELEMENT Year (#PCDATA)>
```

```
<!ELEMENT Lastname (#PCDATA)>
<!ELEMENT Firstname (#PCDATA)>
```

The DTD shown in Listing 2.3 states that as a subelement of DVDCatalog, a valid document needs to contain a Title, at least one DVD indicated by the "+" in Line 1. Next, a DVD entry has elements Title, IMDBLink (i.e., a link to the Internet Movie Database at www.imdb.org), ASIN: the *Amazon Standard Identification Number* (we later make use of this information in programs operating on respective documents), Directors, Actors, and Year, each of which is detailed further in subsequent lines. DVDs may also have attributes, they may or may not have a director, they have at least one actor, and ultimately each value is of type "PCDATA" (parsed character data), the only data type available for DTDs. Notice that a Person element consists of a Firstname and a Lastname subelement in either order. It can easily be verified that the XML document from Listing 2.2 complies with the DTD from Listing 2.3 (i.e., is valid with respect to that DTD).

As we have stated already, there are many languages that are based on XML and are specified using a DTD. For example, the *Extensible Hypertext Markup Language* (XHTML) (Musciano and Kennedy, 2007) is a reformulation of HTML 4 in XML format (the corresponding DTD can be found at www.w3.org/TR/xhtml1/#dtds). It is called "Extensible" because it uses the XML construct of namespaces to allow other XML-based languages to be included in the code. Examples for other languages include MathML (www.w3.org/Math/) for mathematics or SVG (www.w3.org/Graphics/SVG/) for vector graphics. We say more about namespaces when we talk about Web services later in this chapter.

Remember that we have chosen the names of elements and attributes in our example to make them fit with the data we wanted to store in the document. However, we did not give instructions on how this information should be represented or displayed. A browser would therefore have no idea how to render this document into a proper Web page. If we open the XML file in a Web browser, it will simply show us the text content with all the tags, as it does not know what to make of them. Figure 2.5 shows the beginning of how the Firefox browser would display our XML file.

Next, we discuss how presentation instructions can be added to XML documents and then see how the same technique can be used to format the content of HTML documents with a so-called *style file*.

2.1.3 CSS

Cascading Style Sheets (CSS) (Briggs et al., 2004 or Meyer, 2006) allow the definition of styles for the elements of structured documents. The term

```
 − <DVDCatalog>
     <Title>Sample DVD Catalog</Title>
   − <DVD category="Drama/Family" language="en">
       <Title>Whale Rider</Title>
       <IMDBLink>http://www.imdb.com/title/tt0298228/</IMDBLink>
       <ASIN>B0000CABBW</ASIN>
     − <Director>
       − <Person>
           <Firstname>Niki</Firstname>
           <Lastname>Caro</Lastname>
         </Person>
       </Director>
     − <Actors>
       − <Person>
           <Firstname>Keisha</Firstname>
           <Lastname>Castle-Hughes</Lastname>
         </Person>
       </Actors>
       <Year>2002</Year>
     </DVD>
```

Figure 2.5 XML DVD catalog opened in Firefox.

structured document implies that it is possible to apply CSS to XML as well as to HTML, both of which we briefly look into.

CSS with XML

As we have seen, XML documents do not come with a predefined semantics and a browser does *a priori* not know how to render them. However, using CSS we can define for the various elements how they are to be presented. Let's directly look at the example in Listing 2.4, where we have defined styles for the elements in our DVD catalog example.

Listing 2.4: CSS for the sample DVD catalog.

```
DVDCatalog {
  display: block;
  margin: 5px;
  width: 500px;
}
Title {
  display: block;
  padding: 0.1em;
  margin-top: 0.1em;
}
DVDCatalog > Title {
  font: bold large sans-serif;
  text-align:center;
}
```

```
DVD > Title {
  font: large sans-serif;
  background-color: silver;
}
DVD {
  display: block;
  font: normal medium sans-serif;
}
Person {
  display: inline;
}
Director > Person:before {
  content:"Director: ";
}
Actors:before {
  content:"Actors: ";
}
Actors {
  display: block;
}
Year:before {
  content:"Year: ";
}
Year {
  display: block;
}
IMDBLink, ASIN{
  display: none;
}
```

The file consists of *sections* of the form selector { property: value; }. There can be multiple property-value pairs inside the curly braces. The meaning of a selector section is the following: All elements that match the selector are formatted using the properties and values from the respective block. If more than one selector matches all formatting rules are applied.

In the example shown in Listing 2.4, the first section defines the formatting rules for the DVDCatalog element. Whenever such an element is encountered it will be rendered as a block with a width of 500 pixels and a margin of five pixels in all directions. The second section defines the rules for Title in a similar way; note that this selector selects all titles, that is, the title of the catalog and the title of each DVD. To differentiate between the catalog title and DVD titles, sections three and four use more advanced selectors. DVDCatalog > Title selects only the title directly below the DVDCatalog element, while DVD > Title selects the title belonging to DVDs. As one can see, the catalog title is shown in bold letters, whereas the DVD titles are shown on a silver background. We can see this form of selector again with Director > Person:before, which additionally uses the *pseudo-element* before. This indicates that before such an element is output, additional formatting is to be applied. However, the property content allows additional text to be displayed before the actual element. We use this selector to display "Director:" before the name of the director. A similar text is displayed before Actors, so that once before the list of names, "Actors:" is displayed. In general, a pseudo-element is implicitly addressable whenever there is an ordinary element. Other pseudo-elements select the first letter or the first line of an element containing text. The last section specifies that *IMDBLink* and *ASIN* are not displayed at all. All other blocks have selectors of one of the forms discussed above and define styles for all other elements contained in this XML document.

Now that we have defined a CSS file, we still have to tell the browser that it ought to use it to format the output of the XML file in the desired way. We therefore create a link from our XML file to the CSS file by inserting the following line after the first line of the XML document:

```
<?xml-stylesheet media="screen" type="text/css" href="sample_
    04.css"?>
```

The media attribute in this special style sheet element states that the CSS file linked to by the href attribute of the file specifies the display properties of a document when it is rendered for a high-resolution, colored computer screen. There are several other media types available that are all tailored for special use cases. Among these are

- aural, for speech synthesizers
- handheld, for small screen devices with limited bandwidth
- print, for paged material, such as printing or previewing of a print.

If we now open the XML file again, the browser does have the necessary information on how to render the document and will hence display it quite differently from before. The result is shown in Figure 2.6.

We have seen how a CSS file can bring rendering information to an XML file, but it is not common to put XML files on the Web directly. An important reason is that XML documents tend to become large (think of an entire catalog of DVDs for an electronic store) and are, thus, often kept in a database. Usually it is not intended to publish all the data of such a database unprocessed on the Web. More typically is to rearrange the output, to select only certain parts, or to integrate several data sources into a single Web page. To achieve this, the XML data stored is accessed with a query or transformation language such as XSLT or XQuery (Melton and Buxton, 2006). These languages are then used to construct an XHTML or HTML page. Thus, it is far more common to attach style information to an HTML document. We see next how this can be done.

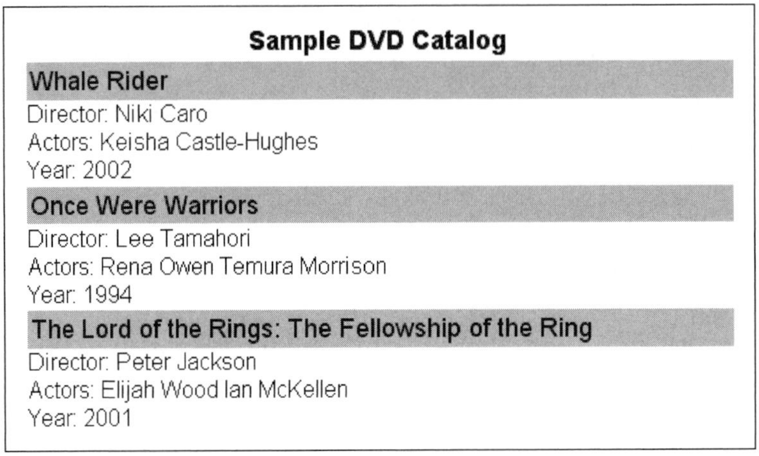

Sample DVD Catalog

Whale Rider
Director: Niki Caro
Actors: Keisha Castle-Hughes
Year: 2002

Once Were Warriors
Director: Lee Tamahori
Actors: Rena Owen Temura Morrison
Year: 1994

The Lord of the Rings: The Fellowship of the Ring
Director: Peter Jackson
Actors: Elijah Wood Ian McKellen
Year: 2001

Figure 2.6 Properly rendered sample DVD catalog.

CSS with HTML

We first go back to our original HTML example, where we had the presentational tags included with the structural tags. In order to make full use of CSS, we erase these presentational parts from the code and replace the table by nested `<div>` elements. These elements generate a block of text without giving more information about the semantics of this block. Therefore, `<div>` elements should only be used when there is no semantically meaningful tag available. As can be seen in Listing 2.5, we have erased the specification of the background colors, and the `<b>` tag highlighting for the DVD title has been replaced by the use of `<h2>`. The table has disappeared; instead several `<div>` elements have been introduced that all carry a `class` attribute with the values DVDCatalog, DVD, and DVDHead, respectively.

Just as we have done with the XML file, a link to the style sheet has to be included in the file. In the case of HTML, this link can be found in the `<head>` section of the respective document.

Listing 2.5: New code for the DVD list.

```
<!DOCTYPE HTML PUBLIC "-//W3C//DTD HTML 4.01 Transitional//EN"
    "http://www.w3.org/TR/html4/loose.dtd">
<html>
  <head>
   <title>Sample DVD Catalog</title>
   <meta name="author" content="Vossen, Hagemann">
   <link rel="stylesheet" type="text/css" href="sample_05.css">
  </head>
  <body>
   <div class="DVDCatalog">
```

```
<h1>Sample DVD Catalog</h1>
<div class="DVD">
 <div class="DVDHead">
   <h2><a href="http://www.imdb.com/title/tt0298228/">
    Whale Rider</a></h2>
   (2002)
 </div>
 Director: Niki Caro<br>
 Actors: Keisha Castle-Hughes
</div>
<div class="DVD">
 <div class="DVDHead">
   <h2><a href="http://www.imdb.com/title/tt0110729/">
    Once Were Warriors</a></h2>
   (1994)
 </div>
 Director: Lee Tamahori<br>
 Actors: Rena Owen, Temura Morrison
</div>
<div class="DVD">
 <div class="DVDHead">
   <h2><a href="http://www.imdb.com/title/tt0120737/">
    The Lord of the Rings: The Fellowship of the Ring</a></h2>
   (2001)
 </div>
 Director: Peter Jackson<br>
 Actors: Elijah Wood, Ian McKellen
</div>
</div>
</body>
</html>
```

Looking at the CSS file "sample_05.css," the content of which is shown in Listing 2.6 and which is the one referenced from the HTML document in Listing 2.5, it becomes clear how the display is now entirely separated from the content. The first selector defines that every text in the document is to be displayed without serifs unless this is overridden by a more specific selector. The second selector uses the dot notation which signifies that all `<div>` elements that belong to class DVDCatalog (i.e., those that have an attribute class whose value is DVDCatalog) are to be 500 pixels wide with a five pixel margin. We used the same construct to style the div.DVDHead selector.

Listing 2.6: CSS for HTML DVD catalog.

```
* {
 font-family: sans-serif;
}
div.DVDCatalog {
```

```
  margin: 5px;
  width: 500px;
}
h1 {
  text-align: center;
}
h2 {
  font: bold large sans-serif;
  display: inline;
  background-color: transparent;
}
div.DVDHead {
  padding: 0.2em;
  margin-top: 0.3em;
  background-color: silver;
}
```

It can be seen from Figure 2.7 that the new code results in a Web page that looks very much like the first one did (Figure 2.1). The only visible difference is that the first example uses a serif font, whereas the second uses a sans serif font. However, from the source code we have seen, the second example has a clearer internal structure and can therefore be adapted more easily to different uses. Moreover, since we have used the <h2> tag it is now clear that the respective text is some sort of heading, which was not the case before.

Although the previous examples are small, they nevertheless show the differences between proper and improper usage of HTML. The addition of CSS and its consequent use leads to cleaner and semantically more meaningful code. In larger projects, the advantages of using style sheets over not using them are considerable, so that nowadays no large Web site can do without them.

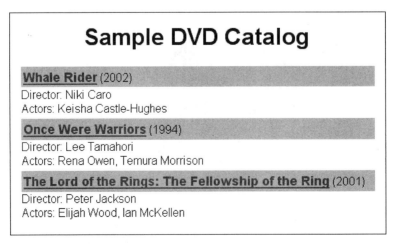

Figure 2.7 DVD catalog styled with CSS.

2.1.4 Scripting technologies

We next consider how to make Web pages more interactive. To this end, we first need to discuss a little more of the underlying technology in order to then be able to position various HTML extensions properly. These extensions will ultimately lead to the some of the core technology on which feature-rich Web applications can be based.

As we have said in Chapter 1 already, Web communication particularly between a browser and a Web server is based on the client/server paradigm. The important observation is that although all *information* including *programs* is stored on the server, the latter can be executed on either side. A browser will typically execute code that is embedded in an HTML page, while a Web server can execute independent programs that may, for example, generate HTML code to be returned to a browser. In both cases, it has become common in the context of the Web to employ *scripting languages,* also called *scripting programming languages* or simply *script languages* (i.e., programming languages that are typically interpreted and whose programs can in principle be typed directly from a computer keyboard). Programs written in a scripting language, or *scripts*, are often distinguished from programs that need to be compiled before they can be executed, since they always remain in source form and are interpreted on a command-by-command basis each time they are executed.

Client- versus server-side scripting

We speak of *client-side scripting* if we employ a scripting language to enhance HTML code that is rendered by a browser (i.e., if the script code is to be executed directly by the browser). The main application of this feature is to make Web pages dynamic, as shown shortly. We restrict our attention here to JavaScript (Keith, 2005), an object-oriented scripting language developed by Netscape Communications that is unrelated to Java, contrary to what the name may suggest. The principle of client-side scripting is shown in Figure 2.8: A browser running on the client is requesting an HTML document as before, but this document is now assumed to contain JavaScript code. The browser will recognize this while rendering the HTML document, and will then execute that code right away. Note how this form of scripting automatically leads to publishing the source code of the application. One can say that client-side scripting is intrinsically Open Source.

Alternatively, we speak of *server-side scripting* if the scripting happens entirely on the server side. In server-side scripting, user requests are fulfilled by running a script directly on the Web server to generate dynamic HTML pages. It is often used to provide interactive Web sites that interface to

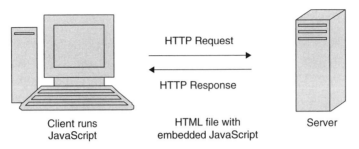

Figure 2.8 Client-side scripting using JavaScript.

databases, which can customize the response based on a user's requirements, access rights, or queries. There are numerous server-side scripting technologies available today, among them ColdFusion, Java Server Pages, Server-Side JavaScript, and PHP. We concentrate in this chapter on the latter two; in Chapter 4, we discuss more recent technologies such as Ruby on Rails.

Server-side scripting is commonly based on the *Common Gateway Interface* (CGI), a standard protocol for running programs on a Web server. CGI (Bates, 2006) requires a two-way form of communication, roughly along the following lines:

1. First, the client triggers the execution of a CGI script from within the browser, often with parameters taken from a form.
2. The Web server then recognizes and starts the CGI program. This program can perform arbitrary actions (e.g., accessing databases for storing the data sent by the browser), but it finally generates XHTML code which is sent back to the browser.
3. The client's browser finally renders the new page returned by the server.

CGI calls require a copy of the program needed, which in the case of scripts is the interpreter for the scripting language, to run for each page request. Since this can cause serious execution overhead, Web servers typically have modules that include a wide variety of scripting languages directly into the Web server.

Client-side scripting: JavaScript and DHTML

Every user of the Web has come across this form of scripting at some point. There are pages that show menus that can be unfolded dynamically, and many pages check forms even before a page is submitted to the server. Probably not all encounters with scripting in Web pages are pleasant, however. There are pages that do not seem to work: the links seem to be broken or the download just does not want to start. Other pages annoy by moving images, or windows popping up or resizing. The reasons for this are browser incompatibilities and bad uses of scripting. The first reason is merely technical, and there is more on it in this section. The second reason has discredited scripting and has led to many users turning off scripting in their browsers. Whether good or bad, it is all part of the reality of the use of client-side scripting, which is the topic of this section.

JavaScript is a scripting language originally written for the Netscape Navigator in 1995 (see developer.mozilla.org/en/docs/About_JavaScript). For an interesting article about its inventor, Brendan Eich, see wp.netscape.com/comprod/columns/techvision/innovators_be.html and Keith (2005) for a reference. As Eich states there, the reason for the success of JavaScript is as follows:

> JavaScript attracted a lot of developer attention, because what people wanted back then (and still want) is the ability to go one step beyond HTML and add a little bit of code that makes a Web page dynamic – that makes things move, respond to user input, or change color [. . .].

This statement was written in 1998 and is still valid today. As shown in Chapter 3, one idea to allow for today's feature-rich Websites is to extend the functionality of JavaScript.

JavaScript has gained so much popularity so quickly that it was implemented as JScript into the Internet Explorer in 1996 and has subsequently been standardized under the name of ECMAScript in 1997 (the latest version of ECMAScript can be found at www.ecma-international.org/publications/files/ecma-st/ECMA-262.pdf). Its development is ongoing and, as we have seen with the development of the HTML standard, it is not only the standards body that pushes the development of the language. Various browsers implement distinct dialects or extensions of ECMAScript.

As with HTML we do not want to go into any detail, but discuss only what our example does. This is hardly enough to introduce the characteristics of the language. For an introduction to the concepts of JavaScript, refer to Bates (2006) or Keith (2005).

We have seen earlier in this chapter that a browser is able to distinguish HTML as well as CSS portions of the document it is supposed to render. This is achieved through specific tags, in particular the `<html>` and `<style>` tags. In a similar way, JavaScript code is included in `<script>` tags so that a browser can easily recognize a script that it should execute. Everything inside a `<script>` tag is treated as code, and these tags can basically appear anywhere in a given HTML document. Alternatively, the script code could be placed in a separate .js file, which requires an `src` attribute within the `<script>` tag with the respective file name and its location as value.

We are not going into too many details of JavaScript here, but instead demonstrate its use by way of our running example. We set out from the version of the DVD catalog which we saw in Listing 2.5, respectively, Figure 2.7, where we had already introduced the <div> elements to structure the entries of the catalog. We will make the page responsive in that every entry can expand or collapse the details (i.e., director and actors of a movie) with a click on the head of the entry. This may come in handy when the catalog becomes longer and we want to hide some entries to make it shorter. Listing 2.7 contains the source code with those parts highlighted that are new compared to Listing 2.5.

Listing 2.7: Sample DVD catalog with JavaScript.

```
<!DOCTYPE HTML PUBLIC "-//W3C//DTD HTML 4.01 Transitional//EN"
    "http://www.w3.org/TR/html4/loose.dtd">
<html>
 <head>
  <title>Sample DVD Catalog</title>
  <meta name="author" content="Vossen, Hagemann">
  <link rel="stylesheet" type="text/css" href="sample_05.css">
  <script type="text/javascript">
   function toggleDVDDisplay(id) {
    var contentElement = document.getElementById(id);
    if (contentElement.getAttribute('expanded')=='false') {
     contentElement.style.display = 'block';
     contentElement.setAttribute('expanded', 'true');
    } else {
     contentElement.style.display = 'none';
     contentElement.setAttribute('expanded', 'false');
    }
   }
  </script>
 </head>
<body>
 <div class="DVDCatalog">
  <h1>Sample DVD Catalog</h1>
  <div class="DVD">
   <div class="DVDHead"
       onClick="toggleDVDDisplay('B0000CABBW')">
    <h2><a href="http://www.imdb.com/title/tt0298228/">
    Whale Rider</a></h2>
    (2002)
   </div>
   <div class="DVDContent" id="B0000CABBW">
    Director: Niki Caro<br>
    Actors: Keisha Castle-Hughes
   </div>
  </div>
```

```
<div class="DVD">
 <div class="DVDHead"
    onClick="toggleDVDDisplay('B0000A02Y4')">
  <h2><a href="http://www.imdb.com/title/tt0110729/">
  Once Were Warriors</a></h2>
  (1994)
 </div>
 <div class="DVDContent" id="B0000A02Y4">
  Director: Lee Tamahori<br>
  Actors: Rena Owen, Temura Morrison
 </div>
</div>
<div class="DVD">
 <div class="DVDHead"
    onClick="toggleDVDDisplay('B00005U515')">
  <h2><a href="http://www.imdb.com/title/tt0120737/">
  The Lord of the Rings: The Fellowship of the Ring</a></h2>
  (2001)
 </div>
 <div class="DVDContent" id="B00005U515">
  Director: Peter Jackson<br>
  Actors: Elijah Wood, Ian McKellen
 </div>
</div>
  </div>
 </body>
</html>
```

Structurally, there are three changes: the `<script>` tag in the head section, the change of the `<div>` element of class DVDHead, and the introduction of a new `<div>` element around the content of a DVD. Let's first turn to the script tag and the code therein, before we look at how the example works.

JavaScript example

Listing 2.7 contains the JavaScript code in the head section, or more specifically the `<script>` tag of the header. The following discussion refers to the lines of JavaScript code between these tags.

The first line of code defines a function `toggleDVDDisplay` that takes a parameter of the name `id` as input. Note that no data type is given. This is because JavaScript is a dynamically typed language. This means it allows one variable to be of different types in different steps of the execution of a script. Just as in C and so many other languages, blocks of code are specified by curly brackets. The second line defines a variable `contentElement` to which the result of the function call `document.getElementById(id)` is assigned. Its meaning is that the function `getElementById(id)` is called for the object `document`, which is the entire page being displayed, signified by the dot that connects the two names. Both the object and its function are always present in JavaScript when executed in a browser. We look at this and similar functions in the DHTML section. So, the function selects an element from the HTML document by the identifier it carries and which has to equal `id`, the variable that `toggleDVDDisplay` has as parameter).

The third line of code opens an if-then-else block, which switches depending on the value of the `expanded` attribute of `contentElement`. Statement `contentElement.getAttribute('expanded')=='false'` tests whether `expanded` is true or false. If it is already expanded and the test thus yields true, lines 4 and 5 will be executed, which will hide the element; otherwise lines 7 and 8 will be executed and the element will be expanded. Lines 4, 5 and 7, 8 complement each other to produce the behavior described here.

Let's look at the first of these two blocks in more detail. Line 4 assigns the value `block` to the display attribute of the style connected with `contentElement`. In effect, this leads to `contentElement` being visible. Line 5 sets the value for the attribute `expanded` of `contentElement`, which we use as a storage for the current expanded status of the element and thus ensure that subsequent calls of `toggleDVDDisplay` will result in the desired behavior of the page.

It should be clear from the code that the display property alternates between "none" and "block" just as the value of the expanded attribute alternates between "true" and "false" whenever the function is called more than once with the same identifier as parameter. Exactly *how* the function is called is what we see next. We have seen how the `<script>` tag defines the `ToggleDVDDisplay` function for our example. However, without further action, this function would never be called. We must turn to the other changes made in this version of the example to see how the function call is embedded into the HTML code.

We first note that every DVD header now contains an attribute `onClick="toggleDVDDisplay('XYZ')"` where XYZ is the ASIN number of the DVD at hand. The `onClick` attribute is a so-called *intrinsic event attribute*. Such attributes allow scripts to be executed on events that occur. Different events are specified for the body of a document, for forms, and for page elements. The `onClick` event occurs for an element when the user clicks on it. Subsequently, the script code that is included in the value of the attribute is executed. In our case, the `ToggleDVDDisplay` function is called with the given ASIN number. If we now turn to the `<div>` elements of the class `DVDContent`, we see that they have an attribute `id` attached to them, which is again the ASIN number of the movie. `id` can give an identifier to any element; an identifier has to be unique in one document and is a means of easily accessing the element. So, if a click is done on the header of a DVD, `ToggleDVDDisplay` will switch the corresponding content block to visible or invisible depending on the current status of the element.

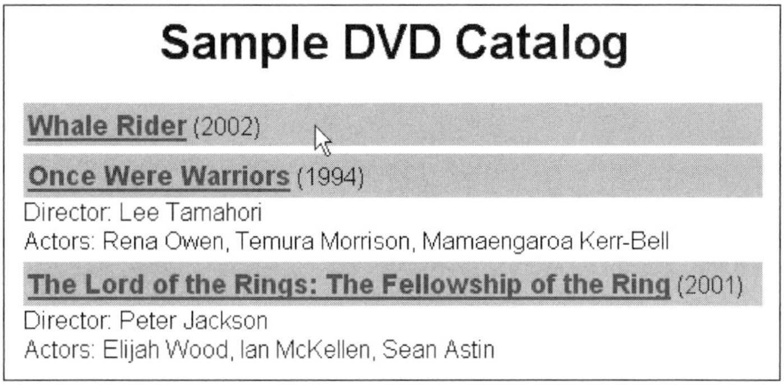

Figure 2.9 Collapsed DVD entry in the sample DVD catalog.

In Figure 2.9, we see that the content of the DVD "Whale Rider" has just been toggled invisible.

The Document Object Model and dynamic HTML

The short script we have introduced in the previous section accesses parts of the HTML document to retrieve the status of variables, which represent HTML attributes, and to set styles of elements. It does not do this directly (i.e., by manipulating HTML tags and their contents), but through objects that are present in the context of the executed script. We have already mentioned the `document` object which contains the current page with all its contents. We want to look at the relationship between the HTML document and the object representation we have used in our script.

The *Document Object Model* (DOM, see Bates, 2006 or Keith, 2005) is the description that tells the browser how to represent HTML elements as a tree structure of objects. This means that the HTML tree is represented as a set of objects, with nesting relationships among them and methods to access these objects through various structures. It is the DOM that gives a script the ability to work with content from the page; it is its perception of the page. Unfortunately, the DOM is in one aspect similar to all the other languages we have mentioned so far: It is not something that is the same for every browser that is out there. The W3C started in 1998 to define a standard which has regularly been updated since then (www.w3.org/DOM/). Different browsers still offer different object models and thus different access paths to the content of a page. Luckily, the W3C standard is so widely used that if programmers stick to it the popular browsers are able to work correctly.

A part of the DOM of the DVD catalog is shown in Figure 2.10 on the right-hand side. This in particular shows the window of the *DOM Inspector*, a tool of the Firefox browser that allows for analyzing the DOM (see www.mozilla.org/projects/inspector). One of the `div` elements in the DOM has

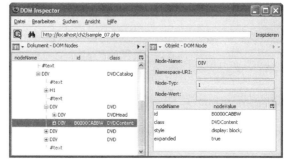

Figure 2.10 DOM of the DVD catalog.

been selected, as can be seen in the left-hand pane of the DOM Inspector window. The corresponding node data, such as its class or its style properties, is shown in the right-hand pane of that window. The Web page that we are analyzing can be seen on the left-hand side of Figure 2.10 with the element selected being highlighted. As seen here, we have selected the detail data for the movie *Whale Rider*.

This example has made use of the DOM. Object `document` is, as mentioned, the object containing the entire Web page. We have used its `getElementById(id)` method to select elements through their identifiers. Since identifiers are unique, this is a convenient way to select an element – one can be sure that the function will return at most one element. Of course the identifier has to be defined by the author of the page. There are other functions that can be used to retrieve elements, such as `getElementByClassName` or `getElementsByName`, both of which can return, as their names indicate, more than one element since the selection is not based on a unique identification.

All three functions do not yet make use of the tree structure of the DOM. The functions that allow this are all named according to a family tree metaphor. For example, `firstChild` navigates to the first subelement, and `nextSibling` moves to the next element that has the same parent node. With these and similar functions it becomes possible for a script to fully traverse arbitrary HTML documents and work on the elements found therein.

We want to mention that the combination of HTML, CSS, scripting (most often JavaScript), and the DOM widely comes under the collective name of *Dynamic HTML* or *DHTML*. This is to accentuate that this combination is considerably more than plain HTML, which is static in that once fully loaded, the presentation of that page will not change anymore. With HTML for content, CSS for style, scripting for program logic, and the DOM to glue the three together, pages that change their appearance on events but without loading additional data or other pages are enabled. This combination goes quite a long way: Bates (2006) presents an example where

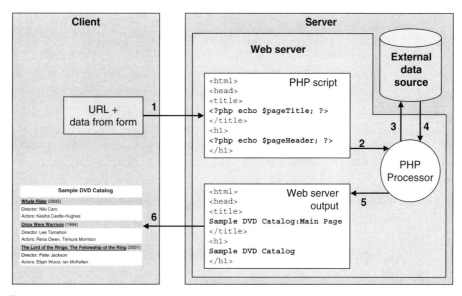

Figure 2.11 Server-side scripting with PHP.

DHTML is used to construct a menu system for a Web page that expands and shrinks in reaction to the user navigating in it.

The term *Dynamic* in DHTML does not include a change of the underlying HTML. Once it is loaded, its appearance is manipulated but its content remains the same. If we let go of this restriction, we need a mechanism to load additional content, which is exactly what *Ajax* offers, and what we cover in Chapter 3. *Dynamic* also does not refer to pages that are different every time they are visited, that are different for each user, or that present a constantly changing product catalog. Such pages do not need to be dynamic in the way used here. They are, however, dynamic in that they very probably make use of external data sources (e.g., a database) and apply *server-side scripting* for generating content based on these data sources the moment the user requests a page. This is what we look at next.

Server-side scripting

The basic principle behind server-side scripting is illustrated in Figure 2.11. The client requests a Web page by sending a URL, potentially plus data that the user has entered into a form (1). The Web server will execute a PHP script by calling its PHP processor (2); this in turn may interact with a database or another external data source, such as an XML file, in which the form data is stored or where additional data is present (3 and 4). The PHP processor will then generate HTML code as Web server output (5), which is finally shipped back to the client (6).

PHP is a "recursive" acronym standing for *PHP: Hypertext Preprocessor* (Powers, 2007). In the form known today, the project developing the PHP language started in 1997. Its predecessor was initiated in 1995 by Rasmus Lerdorf, who soon began cooperating with Andi Gutmans and Zeev Suraski for work on PHP 3. PHP can run on most Web servers and most systems and is considered free software. A popular and easy way to run PHP is through precompiled packages that not only include PHP, but also a Web browser, and a database. XAMPP is such a package that is available for GNU/Linux, Windows, Mac, and Solaris (www.apachefriends.org/en/xampp.html).

Basics of PHP: the DVD catalog with a data source

Figure 2.11 has already shown a tiny fraction of PHP code in the "PHP Script" part of the figure. If it weren't for the lines in bold, the code would behave like ordinary HTML. And indeed, the parts not in bold will subsequently not be changed, they will be output to the client and rendered there as ordinary HTML. This can be seen in the part "Web server Output" of the figure: all non-bold lines are just repeated in the output. What is happening there? We discuss the basics of PHP with this and the DVD catalog example to show the different capabilities that server-side scripting has compared to client-side scripting.

Although it may sound silly, an HTML file stored as a PHP file is a valid PHP program. Should there be a request for the file, the server will identify it as a PHP script and use the processor to run it. The processor will look for PHP code in the file. When used with a Web server, PHP code is always surrounded by `<?php` (sometimes `<?` is used instead) and `?>`. Each line the processor finds outside such a PHP script block will simply be passed on to the output, which means it will eventually be shipped to the client. This is why the code in Figure 2.11 resembles HTML so much: PHP is only embedded into it.

Let us turn to the PHP code segments from Figure 2.11. The first PHP line is `echo $pageTitle;` when written without delimiters. `echo` is a function that simply outputs the parameters that follow. In this case, what follows is just one variable. It can be identified as such, since all PHP variables start with the dollar symbol. The name of the variable is "pageTitle." It is easy to see that the second PHP code line is identical only the variable name is "page-Header" this time. The code from the figure does not show how the variables receive their values; to this end we assume that they were fetched from an external data source. However, the output shows their values: the content of `pageTitle` is "Sample DVD Catalog." Even if the variable had not been set before it was used, this would have been okay for the PHP processor. Variables not or not yet declared default to an empty string, so the title would have been empty instead. Note how the HTML code that was just passed through by the processor, since it is not denoted as PHP code, and the result of the function call of `echo` intertwine in the resulting output. A user receiving this result is not able to tell if a part of the HTML code has been generated or not. Thus, here the code remains private. This is in contrast to the case of client-side scripting where the code is always public when executed.

Listing 2.8 contains the source code for yet another version of the DVD catalog. This time it is a PHP file that will generate the code we saw in Listing 2.7 on the basis of the XML file from Listing 2.2.

Listing 2.8: PHP code generating DVD catalog.

```php
<?
  $dom = new DomDocument();
  $dom->load("sample_07.xml");
  $xp = new domxpath($dom);

  $title = $xp->query("/DVDCatalog/Title");
  printDocumentHead($title->item(0)->nodeValue);

  $dvds = $xp->query("/DVDCatalog/DVD");
  foreach ($dvds as $node) {
   $asin = getSubNodeContent($node, 'ASIN');
   $imdbLink = getSubNodeContent($node, 'IMDBLink');
   $title = getSubNodeContent($node, 'Title');
   $year = getSubNodeContent($node, 'Year');
   $director = getFullNamesOfPersons(
      $node->getElementsByTagName('Director')->item(0));
   $actors = getFullNamesOfPersons(
      $node->getElementsByTagName('Actors')->item(0));
   printDVD($asin, $imdbLink, $title, $year, $director, $actors);
  }
  printDocumentFoot();
  function printDocumentHead($titleText) {
?>
  <!DOCTYPE HTML PUBLIC "-//W3C//DTD HTML 4.01 Transitional//EN"
       "http://www.w3.org/TR/html4/loose.dtd">
  <html>
   <head>
    <title><?echo $titleText?></title>
    <meta name="author" content="Vossen, Hagemann">
    <link rel="stylesheet" type="text/css" href="sample_05.css">
    <script type="text/javascript">
    function toggleDVDDisplay(id) {
     var contentElement = document.getElementById(id);
     if (contentElement.getAttribute('expanded')=='false') {
       contentElement.style.display = 'block';
       contentElement.setAttribute('expanded', 'true');
```

```php
      } else {
        contentElement.style.display = 'none';
        contentElement.setAttribute('expanded', 'false');
      }
    }
    </script>
  </head>
  <body>
   <div class="DVDCatalog">
     <h1><?echo $titleText?></h1>
<?
 }

 function printDocumentFoot() {
 ?>
  </body>
 </html>
<?
 }

 function printDVD($asin, $imdbLink, $title, $year, $director,
   $actors){
  echo '<div class="DVD">';
  echo '<div class="DVDHead" onClick="toggleDVDDisplay(\''.
    $asin.'\')">';
  echo '<h2><a href="'.$imdbLink.'">'.$title.'</a></h2> ';
  echo '('.$year.')';
  echo '</div>';
  echo '<div class="DVDContent" id="'.$asin.'">';
  echo 'Director: '.$director.'<br>';
  echo 'Actors: '.$actors;
  echo '</div>';
  echo '</div>';
 }

 function getFullNamesOfPersons($personList) {
  $persons = $personList->getElementsByTagName('Person');
  $i = 0;
  foreach ($persons as $person) {
   $fullNames[$i] .= getSubNodeContent($person, 'Firstname').' '.
        getSubNodeContent($person, 'Lastname');
   $i++;
  }
  return implode(", ", $fullNames);
 }

 function getSubNodeContent($node, $subNodeName) {
  return $node->getElementsByTagName($subNodeName)->item(0)-
   >nodeValue;
 }
?>
```

The example is longer and more complex than those that we have seen before, which is why we take a closer look at its different parts. We start, however, not with the beginning, but with the end of the file. There we find the definitions of five functions that we look at in the following. Note that these functions are not run as the code from Figure 2.11; instead they are only executed if another portion of the code makes an explicit call to them.

The last block in this example defines a function, in fact, the function definition is done in exactly the same way as for JavaScript as we have seen earlier. Function `getSubNodeContent` takes two parameters `$node` and `$subNodeName`. Just as with JavaScript, there are no variable types accompanying the variables, they are optional as PHP is also a dynamically typed programming language. The two parameters will take a node from the XML document and the name of a nested node, respectively. It contains only one line of code which begins with the `return` command, indicating that the result, whatever code follows, is the return value of the function. So, when this function is called, the return value will be calculated according to the given parameters, and will be returned to wherever the function was called from. The rest of the line contains the access to an object that the function expects to be in `$node`. The `->` symbol that follows signifies on the one hand that `$node` is an object and that on the other hand its function `getElementsByTagName` has to be called, getting as a parameter the name of a nested node. The function will return this node, which is again an object. This is again accessed with the `->` symbol to extract the first item of an array of items (`item[0]`). And this, in turn, is *again* yet another object, of which the `nodeValue` is accessed. Just as in the JavaScript example where we accessed the DOM of an HTML page, we are now using PHP and its DOM model to access the contents of an XML file. The DOM model PHP 5 uses is compliant to the W3C DOM standard that was mentioned already. Usually, a function should and would be written with some form of error handling, which kicks in when the result of code statements cannot be correctly calculated. Our code would simply fail and produce unknown results. We accept that for the sake of simplicity.

`getFullNamesOfPersons($personList)` is the second to last function in this file. It takes an XML node that contains persons and returns their names as a string with the names separated by commas. The DTD of Listing 2.3 has defined `Person` nodes to contain `Firstname` and `Lastname` in any order. Also persons occur as nodes nested within `Director` nodes where exactly one person has to occur and `Actors` nodes. The tree traversal that this function needs to do is therefore somewhat more complex than that of `getSubNodeContent`. First, `getElementsByTagName('Person')` stores all persons in $persons. Since possibly more than one element will be returned, $persons is an array of values. The following lines of code loop through this array of persons to construct a second array, which contains the names of persons already in the order first name then last name. You see that none of the variables was defined before it was used. Whenever PHP finds a variable it does not yet know, it will simply create it in the type needed on the fly. The last line of the function returns the array of names only after applying the implode function. This function reduces an array to one string, where the elements of the former array are separated by "," as specified by the first parameter.

The two functions discussed so far did not output anything yet, instead they used return to give back values to another part of the script. The remaining three functions all output part of the page as a result of being called. There are two easy ones: printDocumentHead($titleText) and printDocumentFoot(). These two functions have the ?> tag after their declaration and the <? just before their end. As stated before, whenever the PHP processor comes across text that is not PHP code it simply outputs it, so these functions do exactly what we want them to: They can output the mainly unchanging top and bottom part of our page. The head of the document is parameterized with $titleText, which is included twice as <?echo $titleText?>, which prints out the title of the DVD catalog.

What remains is to have a look at function printDVD. It takes five parameters that contain the information about a DVD. All lines start with the echo function to output the rest of the line. One can see that the parameters are included in some of the lines. If their occurrence is compared to the places where the textual content is in Listing 2.7, one sees that these places coincide. That is not surprising since we want to generate exactly the same file.

To make everything work, there needs to be some sort of main program that uses the functions to generate the output. This is what we find in the first lines of the source code. The first four lines create and initialize three variables that are needed to process the XML file that is going to be used as the data source for this script. The variable $dom is initialized as a DOM document with $dom = new DomDocument() and the file sample is loaded into the document: $dom->load("sample_07.xml"). The next line creates a DOMXPath object $xp that can be used to query the DOM with an expression of the XPath query language as the next two blocks do. The first one selects /DVDCatalog/Title, that is, the title of the catalog, which is used to fill the parameter for the printDocumentHead function. The next block starts with the XPath expression /DVDCatalog/DVD that selects all those DVD elements that are nested within the DVDCatalog element. In effect, an array of DVD nodes is stored in the array $dvds.

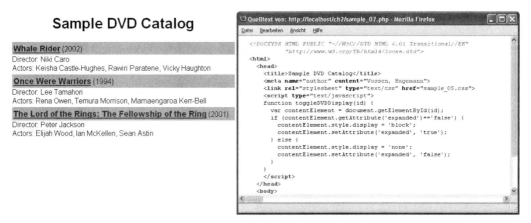

Figure 2.12 Code and Web page resulting from a call to the PHP code.

The rest of the main program of the source code takes care of the HTML output. After the header is printed using `printDocumentHead`, which contains all header information, including the JavaScript code from the previous section, a `foreach` loop runs over the array of DVDs and runs the code in the loop for every DVD contained in `$dvds`. Now functions `getSubNodeContent` and `getFullNamesOfPersons` come into play as they are used to prepare the variables for the output of the code for a DVD. For example, variable `$asin` is filled with the content of the element with the Name ASIN. As the last line in the loop, `printDVD` is called to output the DVD. After all DVDs have been processed, the page footer is printed.

When the above script is run, or rather, its URL entered into a browser, the PHP commands will execute as explained above and the result will be returned to the client. Figure 2.12 shows the returned Web page on the left-hand side, which looks exactly the same as the one from Figure 2.9. It does not only look the same, to the client it *is* the same. Looking at the source code on the right, there is no way for him to distinguish the former from the latter since all PHP code has been replaced by the calculated values.

We have seen how CSS gives a mechanism to style and format HTML and XML so that the former can be formulated without presentational aspects and the latter can be properly presented in the first place. Scripting technologies have added two forms of dynamic behavior: client-side scripting leading to Dynamic HTML, allowing for changing presentations of unchanging HTML, and server-side scripting allowing for the dynamic creation of HTML and its connection to data sources. We see in Chapter 3 that Ajax, in some ways, combines these two ideas to allow for a more dynamic presentation of dynamically requested data.

2.2 Web applications of XML

In this section, we study two important applications of XML in more detail. First, we discuss Web services, which are commonly based on standards that make heavy use of XML for description, publication, execution, and other purposes pertaining to services. Second, we take a look at RSS and ATOM, two XML-based formats for content syndication and content subscription. Both examples make use of a variety of XML features and represent applications that are in wide use today. Therefore, they serve as good illustrations of what is currently possible and how XML can fruitfully be exploited.

2.2.1 Web services

As we briefly mentioned in Chapter 1, Web services promise to enable partners to exploit arbitrary applications via the Internet. In a nutshell, a *Web service* is a stand-alone software component that has a unique URI (Uniform Resource Identifier), and that operates over the Internet and especially the Web. Web services come with a specification that is published by a service provider, and that can ideally be found by potential users or subscribers through querying a service repository. The latter can compose Web services in order to build comprehensive applications with specific and customized functionality.

From an industrial perspective, Web services can be seen as the latest answer to the quest for functioning and failure-free software, for designing and implementing systems that work, and for devising manageable application landscapes. This is a quest and challenge that has been around for more than thirty years, ever since the arrival of the so-called "software crisis" in the late 1960s and early 1970s, which refers to the difficulty of producing computer programs on budget that do not contain errors, are testable, are easily maintainable, and fulfill all requirements. As every experienced programmer will know, previous answers have included remote procedure call (RPC) as a programming technique, object orientation as a paradigm, the *Common Request Broker Architecture* (CORBA) as a middleware concept, and remote method invocation (RMI) as another programming technique. Many of these techniques have led to programming environments, yet most major failures in computing are still due to software, not hardware errors.

Features commonly attributed to Web services include distribution, loose coupling, or a directory service. The basic scenario including a service requester, a service provider, and a repository that can be queried by a client and in which a provider can publish service descriptions, already mentioned in Chapter 1, is repeated in Figure 2.13 for the sake of completeness.

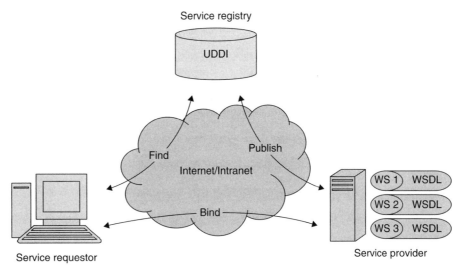

Figure 2.13 The Web service paradigm.

Publishing, finding, and binding services are all activities performed by service requestors and providers that utilize specific standards. These standards have evolved in a bottom-up fashion, in which the basic aspects of transportation have been dealt with first; this has brought along SOAP (see w3.org/TR/soap/). At a more abstract level, a Web service needs a description which may be composed using WSDL (*Web Services Description Language*, see w3.org/TR/wsdl).

Web services typically follow the standards stack shown in Figure 2.14. At the lowest layer is ordinary network transportation, in the case of the Web via the HTTP protocol. On top of this is SOAP-based messaging. As mentioned, at a more abstract perspective, WSDL is employed for services description, and UDDI (*Universal Description, Discovery and Integration*, see www.uddi.org/) for their publication and discovery. It should be noted that although UDDI is a specification it is itself the specification of a Web service in that it is described using WSDL. A detailed introduction to these standards beyond W3C documents can be found in Alonso et al. (2004).

In the past, the stack shown in Figure 2.14 has received a new layer of abstraction whenever it was detected that the existing ones were not sufficient anymore, or did not capture an aspect that turned out to be useful or necessary. So atop UDDI, the stack continues: Since often several services need to be composed in order to obtain a desired functionality, languages such as WSFL, BPEL are needed. These languages specify processes where steps in the process are comprised of Web services. Finally, several services in action need some form of coordination or transactional guarantees,

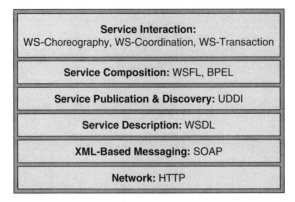

Figure 2.14 The Web services standards stack.

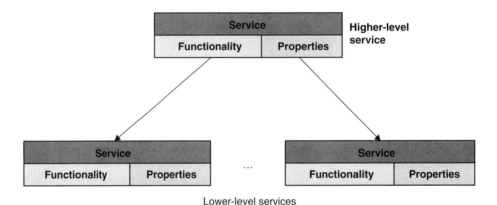

Figure 2.15 Service-orientation fundamental view.

which are achievable through standards such as WS-Coordination and WS-Transaction.

We mention that service orientation is indeed a fundamental paradigm of computer science based on the idea that complex functionality can typically be decomposed into a collection of more elementary services, as indicated in Figure 2.15. Service orientation has been seeing an increasing interest through the rise of Service-Oriented Architectures (SOAs) where large-scale systems are built around the idea of services. One possibility for the implementation of an SOA is using Web services. Implementations can also be based on the aforementioned CORBA or on DCOM, the *Distributed Component Object Model*. Important differences between the latter and Web services are the loose coupling Web services offer and their use of XML as the common vocabulary.

Under this perception of a layered approach, a single service can always be seen as some functionality with specific properties. In a top-down view, the *decomposition* is important (i.e., the idea that a service as seen from above is typically composed of more fundamental functionality and can hence be broken down into some number of components). In a bottom-up view, on the other hand, lower-level services are considered to join forces in order to provide more comprehensive functionality to the next higher level. It is always up to the application at hand how many service layers are needed or appropriate.

Web services are perfectly in line with the service layer view just described, which can also be found in a number of typical computer science scenarios (e.g., computer hardware, application architectures, computer networks, to name just a few areas where it has been successful). The important addition that Web services have brought along is the fact that they are now linked to a central (and ultimately public) repository (i.e., a "lookup" facility). Moreover, service providers and service consumers are no longer tightly, but now loosely coupled, since each Web service, which essentially is an individual software component, has a URI through which it can be placed and located anywhere in the Web. In addition, WSDL enables the automatic creation of stubs, respectively, skeletons (i.e., the structure of a client, respectively server conforming to the interface). This situation is depicted in Figure 2.16.

Clearly, a Web service application scenario that follows the general outline we have just given will require a design process that reflects the underlying business processes as well as the already available computational infrastructure. Formal design processes intuitively make sense to us. They require a structured approach, a precise requirements specification, and, ultimately, project documentation that can form the basis of future evolutions. However, they are too often considered an "overhead" in practice, in particular when it comes to Web development. As a consequence, we currently see a fundamental difference between what we have just described as being a "Web service" and what is often referred to as a "service" in modern literature (and product announcements). In particular, Web services are clearly based on standards and utilize the aforementioned repository facility. Many other types of services found on the Web do not have these properties, but represent modern forms of remote procedure calls, which differ from their predecessor essentially by the fact that they can be called over the Web. This is why we call them *Web procedure calls* (WPCs) from now on. Among those one can further distinguish whether or not they use a standardized and formal way to describe their interface (e.g., WSDL). Furthermore, they may or may not use SOAP as their message format. This differentiation can be seen in Figure 2.17. If the interfaces are formally

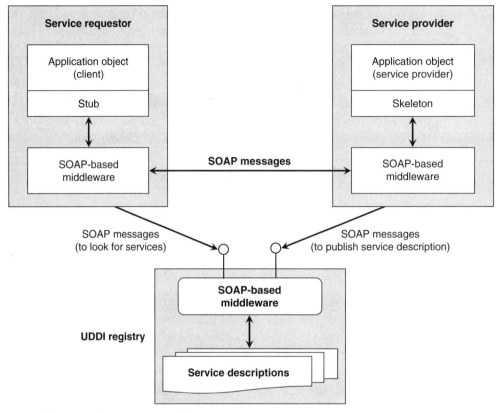

Figure 2.16 Web service infrastructure.

described, stubs and skeletons can be automatically created; this is indicated by the dotted lines.

Take as an example the Simple Storage Service (S3) Amazon.com offers (see aws.amazon.com/s3). As the name indicates, this service offers hard-drive storage space to customers. The costs are currently (end of 2006) at fifteen cents per GB stored per month plus twenty cents per GB transferred. The specification, a WSDL document, of their service can be found at s3.amazonaws.com/doc/2006-03-01/AmazonS3.wsdl. The service can process data sent to it via several protocols including SOAP. There is, however, no standards-based way to discover S3, which is why we classify it as an API supporting *Web procedure calls*. Often WPCs are even further from the idea of Web services: Google offered the API to its search engine via WSDL and SOAP, but has discontinued this as of December 2006 (see code.google. com/apis/soapsearch/). Instead they now offer an Ajax Search API (see code.google.com/apis/ajaxsearch). So, although we refrain from calling this a Web service, it is still an API for *Web procedure calls* in our view.

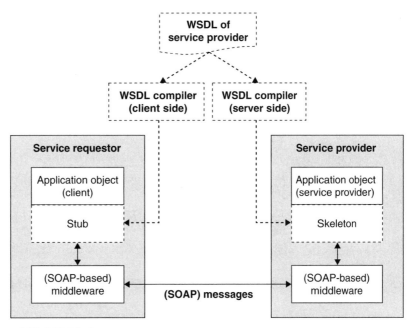

Figure 2.17 WPC infrastructures.

A closer look at SOAP and WSDL

To exhibit the intrinsic relationship between Web services and XML, we take a closer look at SOAP and WSDL next. Both these languages are formally defined by the W3C and more information is available at w3.org/TR/soap and w3.org/TR/wsdl, respectively. As we have done previously, we do not present the details of the specifications but show and explain examples that give a feel for what documents of these languages look like and what characteristics they have.

We continue our sample setting of the DVD catalog. This time, however, we do not extend the example but prepare possible future steps by taking a look at an existing service, namely the service that accesses the Amazon E-Commerce (ECS) information. This information can in our example be used to augment the data from our local data source and include it in the presented catalog data.

The ECS API can be called free of charge and is a rather popular one. Indeed, ProgrammableWeb, a place where a lot of Web 2.0 APIs can be found, lists more than 100 of their 1,400 mash-ups to involve this service. Following our exposition on these topics, we consider the Amazon.com API as supporting *Web procedure calls* only and not the full vision of Web services; yet it employs SOAP and WSDL, the two Web Services standards we want to cover here. We should mention that another way of accessing ECS is through its REST interface, which we do not cover at this point. We say more about the REST paradigm in Chapter 3, however.

WSDL

Amazon.com's description of ECS using WSDL can be found at webservices. amazon.com/AWSECommerceService/AWSECommerceService.wsdl.   The current version (as of November 2006) is more than 3,000 lines long and will therefore not be shown here in full. However, the document does not need to be repeated in full, since there are eighteen *operations* specified in the WSDL file and we look only at one of these. Operations resemble methods of a class in object-oriented programming. Similarly, a WSDL specification is comparable to interface descriptions languages (IDL) from object-oriented programming. However, due to the loosely coupled nature of Web services, its support for different protocols, and the lack of an authority that keeps track the locations of services, there is typically more information that needs to be specified in a WSDL file than in an IDL file.

The operations offered by Amazon.com span functions such as finding items (through IDs, search phrases, or similarity), sellers, customer content, or managing a shopping cart. In this section, we use the operation that retrieves items based on an ID value, the *ItemLookup* operation.

The WSDL document shown in Listing 2.9 has been reduced to only include elements that are relevant to ItemLookup. What is more, element <types> has been stripped of its content, since the type definitions contained take up most of the document's space.

Listing 2.9: Partial Amazon E-Commerce WSDL document.

```xml
<?xml version="1.0" encoding="UTF-8"?>
<definitions
  xmlns="http://schemas.xmlsoap.org/wsdl/"
  xmlns:soap="http://schemas.xmlsoap.org/wsdl/soap/"
  xmlns:xs="http://www.w3.org/2001/XMLSchema"
  xmlns:tns="http://webservices.amazon.com/AWSECommerceService/2006-
    11-14"
  targetNamespace=
    "http://webservices.amazon.com/AWSECommerceService/2006-11-14">
  <types>
  <xs:schema
    targetNamespace=
      "http://webservices.amazon.com/AWSECommerceService/2006-11-14"
    xmlns:xs="http://www.w3.org/2001/XMLSchema"
    xmlns:tns="http://webservices.amazon.com/
  AWSECommerceService/2006-11-14"
    elementFormDefault="qualified"/>
      <!-- TYPE DEFINITIONS OMITTED -->
```

```
  </types>
  <message name="ItemLookupRequestMsg">
   <part name="body" element="tns:ItemLookup"/>
  </message>
  <message name="ItemLookupResponseMsg">
   <part name="body" element="tns:ItemLookupResponse"/>
  </message>
  <portType name="AWSECommerceServicePortType">
   <operation name="ItemLookup">
     <input message="tns:ItemLookupRequestMsg"/>
     <output message="tns:ItemLookupResponseMsg"/>
   </operation>
  </portType>
  <binding
     name="AWSECommerceServiceBinding"
     type="tns:AWSECommerceServicePortType">
   <soap:binding style="document"
     transport="http://schemas.xmlsoap.org/soap/http"/>
   <operation name="ItemLookup">
     <soap:operation soapAction="http://soap.amazon.com"/>
     <input>
      <soap:body use="literal"/>
     </input>
     <output>
      <soap:body use="literal"/>
     </output>
   </operation>
  </binding>
  <service name="AWSECommerceService">
   <port
     name="AWSECommerceServicePort"
     binding="tns:AWSECommerceServiceBinding">
     <soap:address
      location="http://soap.amazon.com/onca/soap?Service=AWSECommerce
   Service"
       />
   </port>
  </service>
</definitions>
```

First, the reader should notice that the WSDL document is a rather "flat" XML document where a lot of elements are nested in the first level under definitions. Nesting can occur within type definitions, which are omitted. Before we look at the nested elements, we look at the attributes of the definitions element.

Namespaces

The attributes starting with xmlns define *XML namespaces*. These represent the XML mechanism to ensure that no conflicts among the interpretation or meaning of identically named items occur. A namespace describes the vocabulary that an element belongs to. The value of a namespace attribute is a URI, which can, but does not have to, link to a valid Web address. In our case, all URIs resolve to valid addresses. Namespaces have to be unique for their use to make sense, and URIs are used to reduce the chance of duplicate namespace identifiers. The vocabulary of a namespace can be defined using an XML Schema or DTD file, but this is not required.

The namespace defined by the attribute `xmlns` is used whenever an element in the document does not explicitly define its namespace. All elements nested directly under `definitions` do not state their namespace, so they belong to namespace `http://schemas.xmlsoap.org/wsdl/`. Other namespaces can be used if they are explicitly referenced. For example, to denote that an element belongs to the namespace `xs`, the prefix `xs:` is added to an element name, as is the case for the `schema` element under `types`. Note that the namespace of `schema` is not `xs`, but `http://www.w3.org/2001/XMLSchema`. `xs` could be replaced by any other identifier if all its occurrences in the document were replaced and the document would still have the same namespace.

The attribute `targetNamespace` denotes which namespace this document defines. The value of this identifier tells us that this is indeed the ECS from Amazon.com. As we see in the following, SOAP messages sent to the service this WSDL document defines have to refer to this namespace.

Structure of WSDL

Nested into `definitions` are `types`, `message`, `portType`, `binding`, and `service` elements. These elements reference each other through attributes contained in subelements as shown in Figure 2.18.

A `service` groups `bindings` and, through those, `operations`; it is thus essentially a set of operations. `Service` and `binding` are often called the concrete part of a WSDL document because they define the location and the protocol binding of the service. Here, `service` tells us that its SOAP interface can be reached at `http://soap.amazon.com/onca/soap?Service=AW SECommerceService`, while `binding` tells us that the service uses HTTP for transport by referencing the namespace of HTTP (i.e., `http://schemas. xmlsoap.org/soap/http`). Theoretically, there could be more than one transport protocol or more than just SOAP for data serialization, but this is rarely done in practice. `Binding` references `portType`, which can be considered as a method interface. Here, we see that operation `ItemLookup` has `ItemLookupRequestMsg` as its input message and `ItemLookupResponseMsg` as its output. There is a third type of message, `fault`, which specifies the message in case of an error. The message elements which are, of course, referenced from the `portType` part specify which type the `message` uses. For input

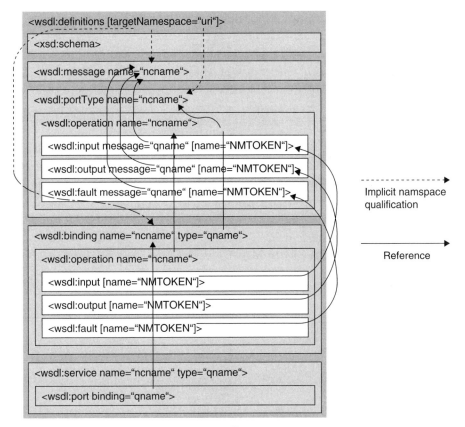

Figure 2.18 Relationships within a WSDL file.

and output we see types `tns:ItemLookup` and `tns:ItemLookupResponse`, which are both from the vocabulary defined by `targetnamespace`, thus they are both types that can be found in the `types` element, the first subelement of `definitions`.

The `types` element defines types using XML Schema. This can be seen from the namespace of the `xs:schema`, the only element in `types` we have retained from the original document. This means that nested into this WSDL file is a valid XML Schema file, which specifies the special types needed, for the `ItemLookup` operation, but also for all the other operations mentioned. Note that the XML Schema could also just be referenced from within the `types` element. We get a glimpse below of what the schema specifies for the `ItemLookup` operation when we look at the SOAP messages that can be sent to it.

The discussion of WSDL should have shown that it is a complex language which has the potential of describing services interfaces and their invocation.

It should be noted that WSDL most often does not have to be written by hand. As Web services often provide access to preexisting functionality, it is usually possible to automatically generate most of a WSDL file which may then only need a little bit of additional configuration or editing to work. Conversely, the user of a WSDL can use it to generate a stub for the service consumer he is writing.

SOAP

We have seen above how the Amazon.com WSDL file specifies that communication is done over HTTP with SOAP as the message format. So, let's look a SOAP message that can be sent to ECS. Listing 2.10 shows a SOAP message directed towards the ItemLookup operation of ECS. As specified in the WSDL file in Figure 2.18, this message would have to be sent over HTTP to the SOAP port mentioned there.

Listing 2.10: SOAP request message to Amazon.com's E-Commerce service.

```
<?xml version="1.0" encoding="UTF-8" standalone="no"?>
<SOAP-ENV:Envelope
   xmlns:SOAP-ENV="http://schemas.xmlsoap.org/soap/envelope/"
   xmlns:soap="http://schemas.xmlsoap.org/wsdl/soap/"
   xmlns:xs="http://www.w3.org/2001/XMLSchema"
   xmlns:tns="http://webservices.amazon.com/AWSECommerceService/2006-
     11-14"
   xmlns:xsi="http://www.w3.org/2001/XMLSchema-instance"
   xmlns:xsd="http://www.w3.org/2001/XMLSchema">
 <SOAP-ENV:Body>
  <tns:ItemLookup
     xmlns:tns="http://webservices.amazon.com/
  AWSECommerceService/2006-11-14">
   <tns:MarketplaceDomain/>
   <tns:AWSAccessKeyId>MY_ACCESSKEY</tns:AWSAccessKeyId>
   <tns:Request>
    <tns:IdType>ASIN</tns:IdType>
    <tns:ItemId>B0000CABBW</tns:ItemId>
    <tns:ResponseGroup>Small</tns:ResponseGroup>
   </tns:Request>
  </tns:ItemLookup>
 </SOAP-ENV:Body>
</SOAP-ENV:Envelope>
```

The listing again shows a heavy use of namespaces, referring to SOAP specific namespaces for the message itself, XML Schema namespaces, which is unused in this case, and the Amazon ECS namespace defined in this WSDL document.

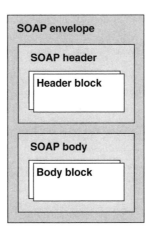

Figure 2.19 Structure of a SOAP message.

The SOAP namespaces define the structure of SOAP messages. As Figure 2.19 depicts, a SOAP message is an envelope containing a header, which is optional, and a body. Both of these elements can contain multiple blocks, called *header* or *body blocks,* respectively. The body contains the payload of a message, the header is information that can be processed by intermediaries. These may have to look at the header to perform actions of their own, such as tracking a conversation. As we are sending the message directly to the Amazon.com service no header is necessary in our case.

The body in Listing 2.10 contains only one element, ItemLookup, which has been typed by the WSDL document of ECS. The elements contained therein make it a valid ItemLookup element, which can be proven by validating the message with the schemas for the vocabularies used. The information we send to Amazon.com contains the empty element MarketplaceDomain and the author's AWSAccessKeyId, without which our request would not be processed. Furthermore, it contains our actual request, namely that we are looking for the content stored for the ASIN (IdType) identifier B0000CABBW (ItemId). ResponseGroup requests only the small and no larger versions of the result.

To complete the example, Listing 2.11 contains the response from ECS. We again see that it is a SOAP message without a header, the body this time containing the ItemLookupResponse element. After some operational information such as the time it took to process our request, the message contains the answer to our query. The item element, for example, contains the URL of the page containing the requested product, actors (of which we have omitted many), the director, the manufacturer, the product group, and finally the title of what we requested, which tells us that we have looked up *Whale Rider*.

Listing 2.11: Response SOAP message from Amazon.com's E-Commerce service.

```xml
<?xml version="1.0" encoding="UTF-8"?>
<SOAP-ENV:Envelope
  xmlns:SOAP-ENV="http://schemas.xmlsoap.org/soap/envelope/"
  xmlns:SOAP-ENC="http://schemas.xmlsoap.org/soap/encoding/"
  xmlns:xsi="http://www.w3.org/2001/XMLSchema-instance"
  xmlns:xsd="http://www.w3.org/2001/XMLSchema">
 <SOAP-ENV:Body>
  <ItemLookupResponse
    xmlns="http://webservices.amazon.com/AWSECommerceService/2006-
       11-14">
   <OperationRequest>
    <HTTPHeaders>
     <Header Name="UserAgent" Value="SQLData Client/3.02"/>
    </HTTPHeaders>
    <RequestId>MY_ACCESSKEY</RequestId>
    <Arguments>
     <Argument Name="Service" Value="AWSECommerceService"/>
    </Arguments>
    <RequestProcessingTime>0.0265100002288818</
RequestProcessingTime>
   </OperationRequest>
   <Items>
    <Request>
     <IsValid>True</IsValid>
     <ItemLookupRequest>
      <IdType>ASIN</IdType>
      <ItemId>B0000CABBW</ItemId>
      <ResponseGroup>Small</ResponseGroup>
     </ItemLookupRequest>
    </Request>
    <Item>
     <ASIN>B0000CABBW</ASIN>
     <DetailPageURL>
       http://www.amazon.com/gp/redirect.html%3FASIN=B0000CABBW%26t
       ag=ws%2 6lcode=sp1%26cID=2025%26ccmID=165953%26location=/o/
       ASIN/B0000CABBW%2 53FSubscriptionId=1RPF28QJYKDDFEDRT902</
       DetailPageURL>
     <ItemAttributes>
      <Actor>Keisha Castle-Hughes</Actor>
      <Actor>Rawiri Paratene</Actor>
      <Actor>Vicky Haughton</Actor>
      <!-- SOME ACTORS OMITTED-->
      <Director>Niki Caro/Director>
      <Manufacturer>Sony Pictures</Manufacturer>
      <ProductGroup>DVD</ProductGroup>
      <Title>Whale Rider</Title>
     </ItemAttributes>
    </Item>
```

```
        </Items>
      </ItemLookupResponse>
    </SOAP-ENV:Body>
  </SOAP-ENV:Envelope>
```

For a simple look at using WSDL and SOAP, check out the services offered at soapclient.com. They allow building forms for SOAP messages based on WSDL documents that are available on the Web.

2.2.2 Web feed formats

In Chapter 1, we mentioned the great popularity blogging has today. Blogs are used by professionals, by researchers, or by enthusiastic private writers commenting on almost every topic. Commenting on current developments or, more generally, actively *writing* about anything is not what makes Web logs new and interesting to look at. It is that this commenting and writing is heavily relying on specifications of formal languages for the simple creation and distribution of content, namely Web feed formats. This, the diffusion of these formats, is the technical counterpart to the *usage phenomenon* that so many people are using the Web to write and comment.

The value of Web feed formats lies both on the creator/provider side and on the reader/subscriber side. From the subscriber's perspective, Web feeds ease the process of receiving updates on a changing content source, which can be a single source or multiple sources. From the point of view of an information provider, Web feeds enhance their own presentation on the Web, since they allow consumers to more easily use the content through different channels. A more widespread use of the provided material can be hoped for and often happens. As we see in the remainder of this section, Web feed formats represent another prominent application of XML, and it is this aspect that we concentrate upon here; for a more detailed introduction to Web feeds see Johnson (2006).

Web feed specification and history overview

Web feed formats demonstrate that XML development and programming does not necessarily result in bloated specifications as we have seen with them in the case of Web services. Nevertheless, the bias of covering all relevant topics and at the same time keeping it simple can even be seen when looking at the development of Web feed standards.

In the current state of Web feed formats, two names have to be mentioned: RSS and Atom. While the latter really is just one format specification – and a *standard* – the RSS story is a bit more complicated. There are various competing RSS versions. All of these are based on a release published by

Netscape in 1999 in state 0.9. Based on this release, two main development strategies have emerged. These strategies are divided into an RDF-based and a non-RDF-based philosophy. RDF, the *Resource Description Framework* that we cover in Chapter 6, is an XML-based format that is specially designed for the representation of metadata and as such is used in approaches directed towards the Semantic Web.

The latter of the philosophies just mentioned, the non-RDF-based approach, can be traced back to the early stages of the Weblogging Community. UserLand Software (www.userland.com) has specially influenced the development of an RDF-free feeding technology. As a consequence, RSS 0.91 was released in the summer of 1999 and included a number of features demanded by UserLand. Discussing enhancements and extensions of the 0.91 release, the RSS developing community was finally split into two groups, each pursuing a contrary philosophy. In December 2000, RSS 1.0 (web.resource.org/rss/1.0/spec) was released by the RSS-DEV community as an RDF-based version featuring modules for extensibility of the standard.

UserLand synchronously improved the 0.91 version to 0.92 and finally to 0.94, still RDF-free and following the philosophy of having a simple, entry-level specification, in contrast to RSS 1.0 as a more complex specification. After a lot of work on joining 0.9x and 1.0, UserLand released RSS 2.0 (blogs.law.harvard.edu/tech/rss), integrating the use of modules but still leaving RDF support aside (interestingly, RSS 2.0 is now maintained at the Web site of the Harvard Law School).

As a third approach, Sam Ruby, an IBM programmer, initially started a community process to redefine the philosophy of syndication feeds. As a result, the Atom format was created in an incremental, wiki-based community developing process. Atom tries to wipe out common criticism of both RSS 2.0 and 1.0, as it is vendor-neutral and based on a very detailed specification. Up to now Atom also makes no use of RDF and is in current state 1.0. It was published as RFC 4287 and became an official Internet standard in 2005 (www.ietf.org/rfc/rfc4287.txt).

Elements of syndication feeds

Despite competing versions and different names, the different formats have more or less the same structure. The XML elements they comprise can be divided into two categories. In the first category are channel (or feed) elements that include general information about a feed. Containers are composed of a number of items, known as entries, each with an extensible set of metadata attached, and which with their subelements form the second category of elements. Table 2.1 provides an overview of all those XML elements that are required in the current version of at least one

Table 2.1 Overview of container elements of syndication formats.

	Element names in feed formats		
Description	RSS 2.0	RSS 1.0	ATOM
Feed Container	channel	channel	Feed
Feed title	title	title	Title
Feed URL	link	link	Link
Feed description	description	description	(subtitle)
Author	webMaster/ managingEditor	dc:creator	Author
Time of last update	lastBuildDate	dc:date	Updated
Unique identifier	–	–	Id
Feed entries	item	item	Entry
List of content	–	items	–

Table 2.2 Overview of entry elements of syndication formats.

	Element names in feed formats		
Description	RSS 2.0	RSS 1.0	ATOM
Entry title	title	title	title
Entry URL	(link)	link	link
Unique Identifier	guid	–	id
Entry description	description	(description)	(summary)
Date of the publication	pubDate	dc:date	updated

standard for the channel. Table 2.2 provides the same overview for the entries of a feed.

In Table 2.1 and Table 2.2, element names in parentheses indicate that the element is optional. Note that there are many more elements in all the standards, which are optional in all of them. Row 1 ("Feed Container") of Table 2.1, for example, gives the name of the element that contains the content of the feed. All other elements in this table are subelements to this element.

Note especially how elements missing from the specification are treated in RSS 1.0: "author" and "time of last update" are not contained in the standard. This is why these fields are usually substituted with elements from the Dublin Core Element Set (an ISO standard for metadata on the Internet; see dublincore.org/documents/dces/ or Chapter 6), denoted by the prefix dc:.

Note also the row with "list of content." As you can see, it is only used in RSS 1.0 where XML referencing is used to reference the item elements. This is because, as opposed to the other formats, the `item` element is not a subelement of the channel element in RSS 1.0.

In their terseness, Table 2.1 and Table 2.2 are somewhat misleading. We have used them here to show that all the formats are principally built the same way. However, the interpretation of what exactly is to be contained in one element is a different story. Take, for example, the `description` element from RSS 2.0 entries: It is not clear whether it contains a short summary of the content or an entire article. So, from a technical point of view, having to deal with these different and incompatible versions is a pain.

A closer look at the formats

Statistics from Syndic8 (see www.syndic8.com/stats.php), a directory of Web feeds, indicate that roughly 18 percent of all feeds are using Atom, while 82 percent are using RSS. Among the RSS feeds, version 2.0 has the greatest share with 75 percent, followed by versions 0.91 and 1.0 with both more than 10 percent share. Due to these numbers and the fact that we return to RDF in Chapter 6, we look here at examples for Atom and RSS 2.0 only.

As an example, we have created the blog "DVD Reviews" using the Blogger service. This blog could subsequently be integrated into the DVD catalog, adding another form of information presentation. Blogger, just as the other services we have mentioned in Chapter 1, allows a user to easily create blogs with only a minimum setup hassle. After setting up an account, the user has to specify basic information about the blog, namely its name and an address. There are many options that user can set later (e.g., to control the blog's organization, its appearance on the Web, or access rights). For the blog we have created, we only chose a template, leaving all other options unchanged.

Creating a blog essentially creates the information that is necessary to fill the channel-level elements that were introduced above. Creating an entry is just as easy: Figure 2.20 shows the form when using the Blogger site to create a post on the left-hand side; on the right-hand side is the resulting Web page, where the entry just created is the only entry, but where such information as blog title, archive overview, and information about the author are already available.

Apart from this Web page, Blogger now has also automatically created Web feeds and linked to these from the page of our blog. Blogger automatically creates an Atom and an RSS 2.0 feed. We look at these next.

ATOM

Listing 2.12 is the source code that Blogger has created for the Atom feed of the DVD Review blog. The information that we entered into the system

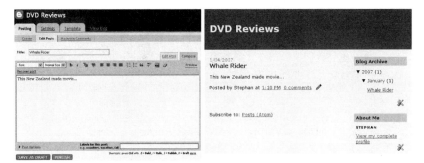

Figure 2.20 Creation of an entry and resulting page.

is highlighted, the rest is automatically filled in by the system. As one can see, there is a lot more to the actual content of this feed than the discussion of the elements so far has suggested. This is, on the one hand, because of attributes that come with the elements, and because of additions that the Blogger makes to the feed. Let's look at the elements we have not seen in Table 2.1 or Table 2.2.

Listing 2.12: Example DVD review feed in Atom format.

```xml
<?xml version="1.0" encoding="UTF-8"?>
<?xml-stylesheet href="http://www.blogger.com/styles/atom.css"
  type="text/css"?>
<feed
  xmlns="http://www.w3.org/2005/Atom"
  xmlns:openSearch="http://a9.com/-/spec/opensearchrss/1.0/">
<id>tag:blogger.com,1999:blog-58191699260754638</id>
<updated>2007-01-04T13:20:32.155Z</updated>
<title type="text">DVD Reviews</title>
<link rel="alternate" type="text/html"
  href="http://exampledvdreviews.blogspot.com/index.html"/>
<link rel="http://schemas.google.com/g/2005#feed" type="application/
  atom+xml"
  href="http://exampledvdreviews.blogspot.com/feeds/posts/default"/>
<link rel="self" type="application/atom+xml"
  href="http://exampledvdreviews.blogspot.com/feeds/posts/default"/>
<author>
  <name>SH</name>
</author>
<generator version="7.00" uri="http://www2.blogger.com">Blogger</
  generator>
<openSearch:totalResults>1</openSearch:totalResults>
<openSearch:startIndex>1</openSearch:startIndex>
<openSearch:itemsPerPage>1</openSearch:itemsPerPage>

<entry>
 <id>tag:blogger.com,1999:blog-58191699260754638.post-
  2159959054193247559</id>
```

```
<published>2007-01-04T13:10:00.000Z</published>
<updated>2007-01-04T13:20:31.855Z</updated>
<title type="text">Whale Rider</title>
<content type="html">This New Zealand made movie...</content>
<link rel="alternate" type="text/html"
   href="http://exampledvdreviews.blogspot.com/2007/01/whale-rider.
html"/>
<link rel="self" type="application/atom+xml"
   href="http://exampledvdreviews.blogspot.com/feeds/
     posts/default/2159959054193247559"/>
<link rel="edit" type="application/atom+xml"
   href="http://www.blogger.com/feeds/
     58191699260754638/posts/default/2159959054193247559"/>
<author>
  <name>SH</name>
</author>
</entry>

</feed>
```

First we note that line 2 of the feed code contains a reference to a style sheet just as we saw for the XML example in Section 2.1.2. If this page were opened in a browser directly, it could style the feed with this CSS information. However, the current versions of popular browsers recognize Web feeds, present them in a way they specify, and automatically offer the user to subscribe to the feed using feed aggregators incorporated into the browsers.

We note three `link` elements among the channel-level elements, all with different `rel` attributes describing the meaning of the respective link. Whereas the link with relation `http://schemas.google.com/g/2005#feed` is Blogger specific, the links with relations `alternate` and `self` are specified in the Atom standard. The former points to the HTML version of this feed while the latter is a pointer to the original address of the feed. With the latter information, the source of a feed can be found, even if the first access was through a copy of the feed. We find these same relations for our only feed entry. In that case, the links do not point to the entire feed, but to that particular post of the feed. The `generator` element shows that this feed was created with the Blogger service.

There are three elements (`totalResults`, `startIndex`, `itemsPerPage`) from the `openSearch` namespace. OpenSearch (see opensearch.org) is a specification to add metadata to search and search results with the intended use, described by the specification (see opensearch.org/Specifications/OpenSearch/1.1) as:

Search clients can use OpenSearch description documents to learn about the public interface of a search engine. These description documents contain parameterized URL templates that indicate how the search client should make search requests. Search engines can use the OpenSearch response elements to add search metadata to results in a variety of content formats.

The three elements contained in our feed belong to the Response part of the specification, i.e., elements that are contained in the results of a search.

As the content element in an entry is optional, we have not seen it in the two tables but it is this element that contains the content of a feed entry, in the case that the content is text and not a reference to a file, such as video or audio, available somewhere else. Here, it contains our rather incomplete review of the *Whale Rider* movie.

RSS 2.0

The code of the RSS feed from Listing 2.13 looks quite similar to that of the Atom feed, as was to be expected. It is interesting to note that the RSS feed contains the id and the updated elements from the Atom standard. This is okay, because the Atom's namespace has been included into the rss element (see line 3). These elements are used as a workaround as these or equivalent elements are missing in the RSS specification.

Listing 2.13: Example DVD review feed in RSS format.

```
<?xml version="1.0" encoding="UTF-8"?>
<rss
  xmlns:atom="http://www.w3.org/2005/Atom"
  xmlns:openSearch="http://a9.com/-/spec/opensearchrss/1.0/"
  version="2.0">
 <channel>
  <atom:id>tag:blogger.com,1999:blog-58191699260754638</atom:id>
  <lastBuildDate>Thu, 04 Jan 2007 13:20:32 +0000</lastBuildDate>
  <title>DVD Reviews</title>
  <description/>
  <link>http://exampledvdreviews.blogspot.com/index.html</link>
  <managingEditor>SH</managingEditor>
  <generator>Blogger</generator>
  <openSearch:totalResults>1</openSearch:totalResults>
  <openSearch:startIndex>1</openSearch:startIndex>
  <openSearch:itemsPerPage>25</openSearch:itemsPerPage>

  <item>
   <guid isPermaLink="false">
    tag:blogger.com,1999:blog-58191699260754638.post-
2159959054193247559
   </guid>
   <pubDate>Thu, 04 Jan 2007 13:10:00 +0000</pubDate>
   <atom:updated>2007-01-04T13:20:31.855Z</atom:updated>
   <title>Whale Rider</title>
   <description>This New Zealand made movie...</description>
```

```
    <link>http://exampledvdreviews.blogspot.com/2007/01/whale-rider.
      html</link>
    <author>SH</author>
  </item>
  </channel>
</rss>
```

As we already know, XML documents can be validated against specifications restricting the occurrence of tags in the document. Checked against a validator (such as Feed Validator at www.feedvalidator.org), the Atom feed of our example turns out to be valid, but the RSS feed is invalid. This is because an e-mail address is expected in the elements `managingEditor` and `author`. Only when this has been changed will the RSS feed also be valid. Invalid feeds are a problem as invalidity may prevent less forgiving clients from parsing the feed correctly, which may, for example, lead to incorrectly displayed feeds.

Promoting feeds

So far we have seen for just one example how easy it can be to produce a blog that also offers Web feeds. And from a publisher's perspective, it is just about as easy to integrate Web feeds into programs in a lot of contexts to benefit from their popularity. In order to do so, it is necessary that Web feeds are found, which can be done in various ways.

Promoting feeds is achieved by publishing a link to the RSS file that the aggregator application is able to refer to. Publishing is provided either by placing a link directly on the main Web page whose contents are syndicated, by enabling auto-discovery, or by registering it with a feed directory. The first option requires manual copying of the link into the aggregator program by the user. Mostly standard orange buttons labeled "XML," "RSS," or the common Web feed icon (see Figure 2.21) are placed onto the Web sites hosting the link to the feed.

This practice is getting more and more out of fashion, as auto-discovery allows for a much easier way for users to get to their desired feeds. With this, applications determine the location of the Web feed automatically when

Figure 2.21 Web feed icon.
Source: http://feedicons.com/

given the URL of the respective Web page. To enable auto-discovery, a link tag is placed inside the HTML codes' head section as follows:

```
<link    rel="alternate"
         type="application/rss+xml"
         title="RSS 2.0"
         href="url/feed.xml" />
```

In this case, the tag conforms to XHTML. It has at least the three attributes `rel`, `type`, and `href`, which we have already seen in the `link` element of the Web feeds above. And indeed, the function of the element here is exactly the inverse of the `link` element with the `alternate` relation in the feed: The one form of content delivery points to the other. Programs consuming feeds and supporting auto-discovery notify the user when accessing a Web page that a feed is available for the source.

In addition to linking the feed or enabling auto-discovery, a publisher may register his feeds at a feed directory service for publication. The information a directory requires for registration is usually just a link to the feeds' location.

Taking Syndic8 as an example for a directory service, the link to the feed is used to fetch the feed file from the publishers' location. Syndic8 then parses the feed and stores the parsed components in a repository. This database provides a basis for multiple services offered, including a search engine, operating on the metadata provided by the feeds. Syndic8 serves as a centralized Web aggregator application. In addition, it offers several interfaces for third-party aggregators to access the collected feeds links.

For example, one can create a feed of feeds that is created dynamically from the database:

```
http://www.syndic8.com/genfeed.php?Format=rss&Where=language:en&
    Scheme=DMOZ&BaseCategory=Top%2FSports&WithChildren=1
```

The call here returns an RSS list containing links as feed entries to all English feeds belonging to the DMOZ category Top/Sports. Notice that the front slash must be encoded in the URL using %2F. Syndic8 also offers Web service functionality for programmatic access to the feed collection.

Future Developments

Due to the fact that Web feeds offer benefits to all parties involved, the usage of feeds will certainly increase in the future. Because of its simplicity, the programs and services in common use will feature or integrate feed creation modules. It is also due to this simplicity that the quantity of applications comprising RSS parsing functionality will continuously increase. As can be seen from the new versions of the major browser, such as Internet Explorer 7 and Firefox 2, Web feeds are a commodity already.

However, the inconsistent and unfinished specification process of RSS may adversely affect the further development and acceptance. Up to now, none of the existing specifications is qualified to serve as an overall accepted standard. Therefore we believe that Atom will gain more and more popularity.

A further issue that needs to be addressed is that asynchronous feed updates result in unnecessary increases of network traffic. As the reader application determines the download interval for updates detached from the server feed-update interval, the downloaded file is often in the same state as the local copy. There are attempts to solve this problem in both the RSS and the Atom communities (consult, for example, the RSS specification at blogs. law.harvard.edu/tech/rss for the `cloud` element), but no implementation is widely used yet.

2.3 P2P

We have mentioned in Chapter 1 that Web activity has spawned a new interaction model beyond the classical client/server concept: Peer-to-peer (P2P) communication, particularly attractive for file and document exchanges in large volumes and without centralized control. The P2P concept gained its first big popularity when it was used to form huge file-sharing networks. Although the discussion always seems to become emotional when it comes to this topic, P2P is, at another level, just an architectural concept that, in a sense, competes with the client/server paradigm. There are more reasonable uses for P2P than just file sharing. However, since this is possibly still the largest field of application, we are first going to take a look at several different networks from this field. After that we turn to two pieces of software that also utilize P2P, and provide an insight into the wide variety of applications that this form of application organization has: Skype and AllPeers. For more on P2P nets and related issues, refer to Oram (2001).

2.3.1 P2P file-sharing networks

We now continue and complete our discussion from Chapter 1, where we already introduced the Gnutella network, with three other network structures from the same domain, namely Napster, FastTrack, and BitTorrent. These networks differ in the way they coordinate communication. While in Gnutella there are truly no central authorities; this changes for the models we present next. Clearly, this instantly changes the way in which a network can be controlled; it can, for example, prevent a network from splitting into two separate networks that do not know anything of each other.

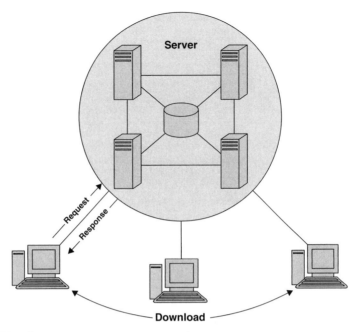

Figure 2.22 File request in a Napster network.

Napster

Napster is an online music service that was created by Shawn Fanning while he was still a student in Boston. It became famous for being the first, widely used P2P music sharing system. In particular, it allowed music files in MP3 format to be shared among users, which has led to accusations by the music industry of copyright violations at a large scale. Although the original service was shut down by court order, it paved the way for other P2P systems including Kazaa and Limewire, which are used for similar purposes.

The centralized P2P model implemented in the Napster network has several central servers that store information on every peer and respond to requests made to the network. New peers sign in with the servers and send a list of resources or files they have to offer. This is illustrated in Figure 2.22. The servers may also hold additional information about the peers such as their connection bandwidth and the time since their log-in. This data is made available to other peers so that they can choose a peer to download a certain file from. Downloading follows the same rules as mentioned earlier for Gnutella; a direct connection between two peers is made without any further server assistance and the file is then transferred from the peers.

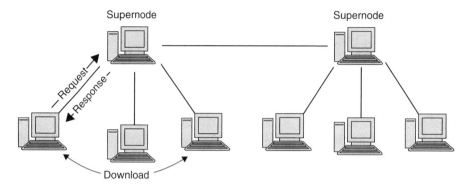

Figure 2.23 File request in a FastTrack network.

FastTrack

The FastTrack model used by Napster successor Kazaa can be seen as a fusion of the centralized and decentralized models, because the peers themselves can become a so-called *supernode*, providing similar features as a central server would offer. Supernodes were introduced to reduce search time as opposed to the decentralized model by reducing the number of search packets sent to adjacent peers. In addition, they can hold information about neighboring peers just like a server.

A search query or request is made to the supernode a peer is connected to. If one of the peers that is connected to the same supernode has the desired file, information for a direct download is submitted, as indicated in Figure 2.23. If the supernode does not list the file, it sends search queries to its neighboring supernodes, and they will look up the requested file. In the end, there is less traffic and less broadcasting than in the other networks discussed so far, and the search process is simplified.

BitTorrent

The BitTorrent P2P model is different from the previous three models (including Gnutella) because it implements a strategy where downloading automatically leads to uploading. Like the other models, BitTorrent allows choosing whether a completed file should be shared with the network, but makes it technologically impossible not to share already during downloading, a feature that is common in P2P protocols. However, as in the other models, BitTorrent downloads a file not only from one peer at a time, but from several simultaneously.

To prepare a file for a download a torrent file needs to be downloaded from a Web server, as shown in Figure 2.24. This file contains information about the length of the desired file, its name, its hash-value(s) for verification purposes,

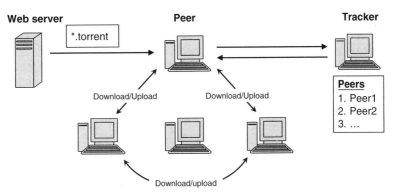

Figure 2.24 The BitTorrent network.

and a URL to a tracker. Trackers help peers to find other peers sharing the same file. A tracker responds with a list of peers that are either downloading ("leech") or uploading ("seed") the file and information about what parts of the file they already have. This is indicated in Figure 2.24 by the list on the right.

To start a download, one peer, the initial "seed," has to offer the entire file and must have uploaded it completely at least once to other peers. Files are split into pieces that are broken down in subpieces, and every peer usually has a pipeline of five subpiece requests pending to other peers. Once a subpiece has been transferred, a new subpiece of the same piece is requested. This ensures that complete pieces spread fast. To decide which pieces to download BitTorrent uses the "rarest first" algorithm except for the first piece that is downloaded as it follows the "random first piece" rule. Downloading the rarest pieces first increases the amount of available pieces that are shared by only a few peers so that the entire file is distributed evenly.

In the BitTorrent network, each peer has to maximize its download rate by itself. A peer that offers fast download rates will also receive a high upload rate. When a peer decides to "choke" another peer it cuts off uploading to it. Each peer "unchokes" a fixed number of peers according to their download rate. Uploading to only currently connected peers according to their download rate is not very efficient, because a peer with an even better rate would not be discovered. BitTorrent solves this by assigning an "optimistic unchoke" which rotates every thirty seconds. This means that even if the selected peer offers the highest download rate, it will get choked and another peer is selected for downloading.

To speed up the download's last pieces in "endgame mode," the peer sends out requests for all missing pieces to all other peers. If a piece comes

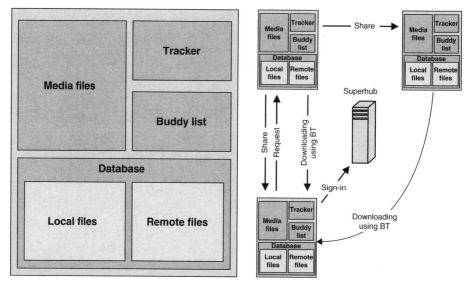

Figure 2.25 Architecture of a peer (left) in an AllPeers network (right).

in, other requests for the same piece are cancelled in order to minimize the waste of bandwidth. Once the download is completed, the peer can choose to continue uploading to other peers. During the download process, the peers contact the tracker from time to time to receive and submit information about the downloading status of the file.

2.3.2 Other P2P applications

AllPeers

After having seen several approaches of organizing a P2P network, we now look into a tool that makes this technology usable in a convenient way. Since most browsers allow for multiple extensions and add-ons, it is no surprise that P2P has also arrived at the browser.

AllPeers is a Firefox extension that adds to the browser file sharing, buddy lists, chat, and tagging, via a BitTorrent network with all the functions appearing in the "AllPeers MediaCenter." This media center allows file sharing with a closed group of people and will alert them when any of their buddies have new files. Figure 2.25 shows the architecture of a peer and the basic idea of how the AllPeers network works.

Media files such as pictures, music, or movie files are imported by just dragging them into the AllPeers window, where they can be organized into groups. When a file is imported, an RDF resource is being created (as mentioned, we discuss RDF in the context of the Semantic Web in Chapter 6). Resources are the basic units of the AllPeers data model and are written into a database that is kept in the user's local Firefox folder. Each resource has a unique, network-wide I.D. to distinguish it from other files. Additional information, such as date, size, location on disc, tags, and comments are also stored in the local database.

Although there is no centralized server in the AllPeers architecture that would coordinate file transfers, there is a central connection point called the *super hub*. This hub manages certain alerts that are exchanged between peers and stores information on the IP addresses of peers. When signing in, peers will contact the hub to deliver their IP address and to receive alerts that could not have been delivered to them because they have been off-line. The presence mechanism is decentralized, because each peer individually informs its buddies about a change in its presence. If a peer requests presence information from another peer, this is sent only if the requesting peer is on the buddy list of that particular peer and therefore has the appropriate authorization.

A functionality that is used in other contexts on the Web as well (e.g., in Flickr, as we discuss in Chapter 3), is that AllPeers allows to decide individually who will be able to see and download a resource. When a file is shared, data relevant for the transfer is sent to the corresponding peer. If that peer is online, it receives the information and writes it into its local database. The user will also receive an alert informing him or her that one of the buddies has new data to offer. However, there is no central database that keeps track of which file is located at what user. If the peer is not signed in with the AllPeers network, the sharing information is sent to the super hub where it will be stored until the peer signs in again and receives messages that are waiting for him.

To start downloading a file, a peer will choose a file of interest from his local database. The peer will then contact the peer that is hosting the file and request a data transfer as shown in Figure 2.25. Depending on the size and the level of distribution of the desired resource, AllPeers will decide which protocol to use, which can be either HTTP for smaller files or BitTorrent for larger ones. In the latter case, the peer offering the resource will run his tracker indicated by a little "T" in one of the peers in Figure 2.25, and the original BitTorrent protocol will coordinate the download process.

BitTorrent is said to implement an *architecture of participation*. AllPeers makes use of this file-sharing protocol and is our first example of a "social" service that is characterized by the fact that it gets better the more people use it and that value can be added to the service without actively contributing to it.

Skype

So far, we have seen how P2P is used to take the load off individual computers when it comes to file sharing. Skype takes the idea one step further and offers an online telephony client, which uses a P2P infrastructure in many ways instead of a central server structure. The software was introduced in August 2003. It has since then grown rapidly, with eight million concurrent online users, reported for the first time in November 2006. What started out as a VoIP solution has meanwhile evolved into a platform for voice and video telephony, instant messaging, and file sharing from which it is possible to call or receive calls even from ordinary mobile or landline phones. The details of how Skype's P2P structure works are not available publicly, so we only sketch the network structure from what is known. The information we present here is largely based on an administrator guide (Skype Limited, 2006).

The Skype client that a user needs to download contains more than most users will be expecting, since it has the potential of not only working as a client, but also as a node in the P2P network that supports the operation of a part of the network. Every client logs in with the Skype login server, where the Skype account is checked. Upon successful authentication the client receives a credential from the login server that it uses to prove its identity for a limited amount of time. The credentials are based on a public-key infrastructure, and public keys for buddies are stored locally. It is thus possible for a client to check the proper authentication of a client without contacting the login server again.

After the login process is completed, the login server, as a central server, is no longer needed. The network of Skype clients is maintained as a P2P network instead (see Figure 2.26). For that, certain clients can take the role of a *supernode*. As explained in Skype Limited (2006), "each supernode's capabilities are based on the computer's available memory, bandwidth, and uptime characteristics." Supernodes use a portion of their bandwidth to support network functions. Each client selects one supernode out of a list it keeps updated as its "upstream" link to which it keeps a persistent connection. It sends search requests to this supernode which communicates with other nodes to answer the query. A client's buddy list is maintained locally on the computer as well as in the network of supernodes.

Communication between two clients is initiated by a client who looks up the partner's IP address through the net of supernodes. First, the client tries to establish a direct connection. P2P networks usually run into trouble when peers are behind a firewall that partially blocks network traffic or a network that uses network address translation (NAT). In such a case a direct connection is not possible. Skype circumvents this problem by a cascade of

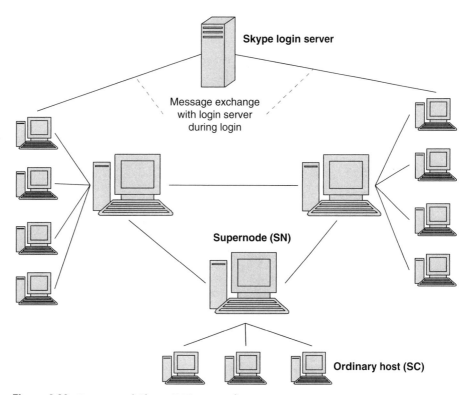

Figure 2.26 Conceptual Skype P2P network structure.

other options that two peers have to set up a call. As a second option, the calling client will notify its partner, so that he in turn may try to connect to the caller. In both cases, if the connection attempt works, the clients can communicate directly thereafter. But even if the direct connection fails, the peers still have a chance to talk to each other. As a last resort, the supernode calls a *relay host* for help, which is again an ordinary Skype peer taking on an additional responsibility. The relay host will contact both peers and set up and route all traffic between the two to support the call. In reality, more than one relay host is often used, so that the communication is immune to the loss of relay hosts.

Supernodes and relay hosts, which are selected from all those peers that have not opted out of this functionality – which has become possible in the newest version of Skype – ensure that calls can be made. As mentioned, supernodes store client information, while relay hosts route traffic. In order to prevent sniffing on other users' communication, every interaction over the Skype network is encrypted.

The addition of calling and receiving calls to and from landline or mobile phones changes the situation a bit. It may be assumed that there are special Skype clients at endpoints of phone companies that transform calls from such devices into packets of the Skype protocol.

So far, the Skype network has been pretty effective at delivering high-quality calls. The scalability of the architecture depends on the question whether the number of clients that can reliably function as supernodes grows such that it can support the growing numbers of clients connected to the system.

2.4 Summary

This chapter discusses several central aspects of the technological advances of the Web in more detail. It has first touched upon the development of the technologies directly linked to Web pages and their creation. The languages that surround HTML or are related to it all address issues that HTML suffers from. CSS allows the creation of Web pages that are free of a conflict and mixture between content and presentation. XML has made XHTML possible that has and will continue to increase the possibilities for including semantics into Web pages; we have to say more about this in Chapter 6. We have seen two complementary forms of scripting: The first is client-side scripting, which allows for parts of the program logic to reside on the client-side and thus to execute commands that give direct user feedback. The second form is server-side scripting, which is used to generate large and complex Web pages. Here, the focus is on generating HTML from databases or otherwise and based on complex program logic. The technologies show that the Web has become more dynamic, through a consequent and consistent evolution of these software technologies (and a multitude of others that we did not mention).

Web services and Web feeds were introduced in the section on XML-related technologies. Web services, the powerful but complex set of standards and languages, theoretically allows for applications to talk to each other via the Web and to do so in a dynamic, technology-independent, and automatic fashion. They have, however, not yet completely lived up to their promise. As we have seen with Web procedure calls, it is only this lean version of the entire picture of Web services that plays a significant role in the Web. This is because the Web favors less sophisticated, yet simple solutions over very powerful but complex ones. The only scenario in which Web services are fully implemented is in corporations and some B2B scenarios.

On the other hand, Web feeds are as simple as it can get: Add markups to the page, generate one file in addition to the usual ones, and other users can start subscribing to the feed and potentially syndicate it with other feeds to create their own custom-made information source. Even the version chaos of RSS does not seem to be able to stop the success of Web feeds. Of course, the requirements for Web services and Web feeds could not be more different: If a Web feed does not work, it is annoying to the reader, but he or she will usually be able to still find the entire information on the provider's Web page. Web services, on the other hand, strive to provide rigidly defined, reliable services, with a much broader range of applications than Web feeds. But to say it again, in the battle between "lean but single-purpose" and "multi-purpose but mean," the lean approach is currently in the lead.

Lastly, P2P was presented as an architectural paradigm that competes with the client/server principle. There are numerous applications in which the fact that P2P works as a distributed network leads to benefits. As applications, we have discussed file sharing, instant messaging with AllPeers, and VoIP telephony with Skype. All of these work by pushing computation or bandwidth usage from the center to the edges of the network and thus providing better scalability. It can be expected that future uses of the P2P idea will include new scenarios as well.

Enabling Techniques and Technologies

In this chapter, we take a closer look at some of the most prominent technical mechanisms that are commonly attributed to Web 2.0 developments and in particular to Web 2.0 services. We start with *Rich Internet Applications* which, today, exist for a broad variety of functions (e.g., for personal information management or for office applications including the writing of documents or the execution of spreadsheet calculations). These online applications allow for a kind of functionality and interactivity that have so far been exclusively reserved for desktop applications; they can hence be considered as a materialization of the *network computer* (i.e., the "NC" as opposed to the PC, the personal computer) that had first been predicted in the mid-1990s.

In the second section, we turn to *mash-ups*, which roughly implement the idea of bringing multiple services or sources of content together in one place in order to form a new, often valued-added service. Our primary example in this section will be Google Maps, a service from which map information can be obtained in order to mash it up, say, with textual address information in order to make it more lively and visual. We will also take a closer look at content syndication in this context and present some recent tools for making this even more convenient than doing it by hand as described in Chapter 2.

The third main topic of this chapter is *tagging* (i.e., user-generated keywords or metadata attachable to Web resources), which will be primarily exemplified through a discussion of Flickr and del.icio.us. We see in Chapter 6 how tagging actually carries the potential of bringing Web 2.0 and what has been termed the *Semantic Web* together.

3.1 Rich Internet Applications

The look and feel of page-based *Web applications* strongly differs from that of desktop applications. As HTML is a page-oriented language, most requests require the regeneration of an entire page. Moreover, HTML comes with only little support for building graphical user interfaces (GUIs), except for filling out and submitting forms. By contrast, a *rich client* provides advanced GUI features such as drag and drop, menus, or toolbars. However, as we have seen in Chapter 2, scripting on the client side is an approach to changing this situation.

The novel use of existing technologies such as Ajax and the widespread availability of broadband access to the Internet nowadays allow for the creation of Web sites that can do much more than present pages and connect them via hyperlinks. Indeed, it is now possible to execute entire programs within a Web browser, as is done with e-mail clients, chat programs, or even office suites. Clearly, advantages and disadvantages stem from the applications being available over the Net. While the applications and their data can be accessed from anywhere on the Web, currently, this holds true most often only as long as that connection exists. Users do not have to worry about program installation or updates, but the security of the Web browser becomes an ever more important issue.

To avoid page reloading and thus coming closer to the feel one is used to from desktop applications, the view of a page has to be generated and manipulated within a client's browser, while the client-server connection is only used for data exchange. The aim is to make the interfaces more responsive and to rely on the Internet connection, which is potentially slow, only when really needed. There are several technical approaches for the client-side implementation, such as Java Applets, Macromedia Flash, or Ajax. In such Web applications, the server is usually responsible for the data handling and the generation of the visualization of the application, while the browser displays the visualization and forwards user actions.

Feature-rich applications have been around for many years. Indeed, every desktop program supports functionality implemented with a manifold of interaction patterns, comprised by all that we have become used to with desktop applications: menus, movable windows, dialog boxes, drag and drop, or immediate responses. Take, for example, an office program such as Microsoft Outlook, which nowadays comprises a variety of features including e-mail, a calendar, to-do lists, contact management, or group functions, such as group calendars or folders. They are all supported by a variety of ways to interact with them. In other words, rich applications have been available *off-line* for a long time already; the novelty we are currently recognizing is that many such applications have recently moved *online*. We mention that "recently" has to be seen with some care here, since, for example, Outlook's online counterpart, Outlook Web Access, which has such rich features, has been around since 1997. While some applications move from off-line to online, far more new rich applications are being launched directly on the Web.

The yardstick for a Web application in determining whether the term "rich" is appropriate is the level to which it behaves and feels more like a classic desktop application than like a classic Web page. One can say that richness is related to functionality, and Rich Web Applications or (the more common name) *Rich Internet Applications* (RIAs for short) can be classified as function oriented, as opposed to mash-ups, which as we see later, are more data oriented.

The term *Rich Internet Application* (combining the terms *Rich Client* and *Internet Application*) was coined by Allaire (2002) to describe the benefits of a new version of the Flash Player. The idea, however, is older, and has had other names such as *Remote Scripting*, *X-Internet*, or *Webtops*. As we have seen with the technological advances in Chapter 2, Internet development is evolutionary, not revolutionary. RIAs are yet another example for this. RIAs come in a variety of forms and range from being more playful interfaces to Web pages to being a full incarnation of the *software as a service* (SaaS) idea that provides entire application systems over the Web.

In this section, we introduce several Rich Internet Applications to show their characteristics, especially their capabilities and the challenges they have to face. As mentioned, RIAs can be built using several Web development frameworks. We also exemplify the basis for building RIAs on Ajax: the mechanism for asynchronous data exchange.

3.1.1 Sample RIAs: e-mail applications

In this section, we take a look at e-mail applications. They provide a good basis for exemplifying the characteristics of Rich Internet Applications for several reasons. First, virtually everyone using the Internet uses e-mail as a way to communicate with other Internet users. Second, an e-mail program may only require a text console (see, for example, Pine from Washington University at washington.edu/pine), but might as well be a full-fledged graphical client (like Thunderbird from Mozilla, see mozilla.com/thunderbird). Both types have their pros and cons, and both types have their followers and fans. At the core, a client has to support the reading and writing of e-mails, with some management functions to search, sort, or delete e-mails. These frugal minimum requirements have led to e-mail clients being available as Web applications since the early days of the Web (note the word "client" here; e-mail as an Internet service is, of course, much older than the Web). Noncommercial users have always been able to open free mail accounts at the major portals we have mentioned in Chapter 1. These portals offer Web interfaces to e-mail accounts, which differ significantly in the feature-richness of the user interaction. Third, since sending and receiving e-mail requires Internet connectivity anyway, it is not a strong additional prerequisite to demand that the connection must be established to write e-mail in the first place; as opposed to writing them off-line and then uploading them to an e-mail server. This is becoming ever more true in our time of broadband access and flat-rate payment systems.

In this section, we look at the development of the e-mail clients designed for the use with the Microsoft Exchange Server (see microsoft.com/exchange), as they are in widespread use today, especially among business users. As we demonstrate, the arrival of a Rich Internet Application can be recognized here already.

Outlook and Outlook Web Access

Microsoft *Outlook* basically is a desktop e-mail application, yet also supports a wide variety of personal information management tasks, such as the management of contacts, a calendar, to-do lists, and notes. Combined with the Exchange server it supports special group communication features such as group scheduling, task assignment, or shared folders of mail, contacts, or calendars.

As Outlook is a desktop application running on top of the operating system of a user's computer, it needs to be installed before it can be used. A computer accessing the resources of an Exchange Server through Outlook is furthermore often required to be in the same Intranet as the Exchange Server itself. In this case, a remote user establishing a connection over the Internet is obviously not in the Intranet. He or she may still be able to access the server after connecting to a virtual private network (VPN). Such networks tunnel the traffic of connected computers through secure channels, the accessing computer then *virtually* belongs to the Intranet.

For the use with Outlook, the computer has to be able to run it and properly set up, but when this is fulfilled, one has the full flexibility of desktop applications: all the GUI features already mentioned are available. In the screenshot from Outlook shown in Figure 3.1 one can see blog entries that were downloaded with an Outlook RSS plug-in. There is a multitude

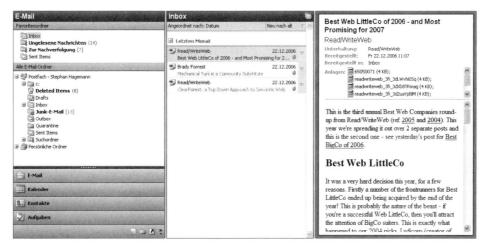

Figure 3.1 Microsoft Outlook 2003.

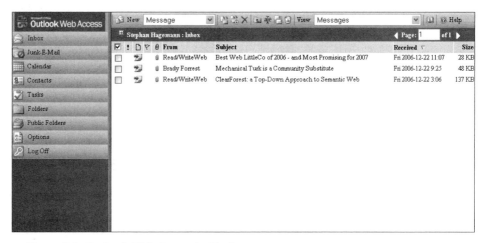

Figure 3.2 Outlook Web Access in Firefox.

of plug-ins from as simple as an integrated PDF creator to CRM solutions based on Outlook.

A popular alternative to accessing Exchange via Outlook or another desktop e-mail client is the use of the Web front end called *Outlook Web Access* (OWA). OWA comes with the Exchange server, and all its functions are tightly integrated with Exchange. For example, as opposed to Outlook, where it is possible to manage multiple accounts as well as ordinary e-mail accounts from other providers, OWA only accesses the information on the Exchange Server. Moreover, there is no way for users to add plug-ins to OWA.

Figure 3.2 shows the interface of OWA when opened with Firefox. It is important to note what browser was used, as OWA comes in two versions: one

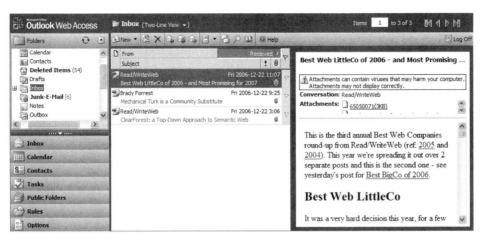

Figure 3.3 Outlook Web Access in Internet Explorer.

for the Internet Explorer and one for all other browsers. The difference between these two versions is notable, since for the latter it offers a truly page-based experience. There are two visible HTML frames: the menu on the left-hand side and the content area on the right-hand side. Almost every action triggers a reload of the content frame. Moving e-mails into subfolders is, for example, a quite inconvenient process. For every navigational step in the folder hierarchy, a new page has to be loaded. This is because a folder tree as well as drag-and-drop functionality are missing from the interface. It also lacks popup menus and independent windows: viewing or writing an e-mail hides the list of folders and e-mails.

For the non-Internet Explorer version of OWA, major drawbacks come from the low support for the efficient handling of e-mails one has in Outlook. Everything from writing, or searching, to sorting mails is rather unhandy. It nevertheless has its purpose, namely for those who cannot run Outlook on their computers, such as GNU/Linux users, or for users accessing Exchange from a remote location. It can be doubted that this version of OWA is used as a full replacement of Outlook, for compared to Outlook it is too inefficient.

The OWA version for the Internet Explorer looks and behaves quite differently from OWA for other browsers and in particular much more like its desktop brother Outlook. The similarity between Figure 3.1 and Figure 3.3, which shows OWA in Internet Explorer, should be notable at first glance. Furthermore, the interaction that OWA allows in this version is much more sophisticated. The menu on the left-hand side is what one is used to from navigating hierarchies in desktop applications. In fact, the list is the same as that in Outlook. Popup menus are present allowing fast access to actions on e-mails, for example, drag and drop allows moving e-mails using the menu on the left-hand side. There are differences to Outlook here as well: The e-mail list is paginated, which makes scanning through large folders of mail more tedious than in Outlook.

Nevertheless, comparing OWA for Internet Explorer with the former version of OWA, there is a huge difference in the interactions supported. What was true for that version is not true for this version: It is possible to replace the use of Outlook as OWA can be almost as productive.

The two versions of OWA already point to the great challenge for software development for the Web. The capabilities of browsers and their various versions differ considerably and are, in part, incompatible with each other. Likewise, if a solution for Rich Internet Applications is in some way dependent on a browser extension, this becomes an additional prerequisite. This is somewhat similar with desktop applications that have to be written for specific operating systems, because these differ in their capabilities even more. This situation would of course change if there was a standard computing model for browsers accepted by all competing browsers. From what we have learned of the history of Web development in the previous chapters, we know that this is very unlikely. For it would again become very interesting for a browser with a dominant market position to push a nonstandard yet nice feature into development and thus locking in developers and users alike.

The history of OWA provides another anecdote for this behavior. In this case however, the move to include nonstandard features actually provided the technology that has sparked the Ajax boom in 2005.

The birth of XMLHttpRequest

Jim Van Eaton, member of the OWA development team, tells a bit about the history of OWA in the Exchange blog (at msexchangeteam.com/archive/2005/06/21/406646.aspx). When Exchange 2000 was being developed, an ActiveX control was created that allowed the Internet Explorer to make requests to servers controlling distributed authoring and versioning (so-called DAV servers). ActiveX is a technology that allows the linking and embedding of objects from one document to another and can be used to embed multimedia data into Web pages. Bill Gates apparently liked the prototype of the new version of OWA, which led to the necessary component being included into Internet Explorer Version 5 and it was called XMLHTTP.

The object essentially allows a Web page to make *asynchronous* requests for data. As we know from Chapter 2, DHTML allows the appearances of pages to be altered using client-side scripting and style sheets. It has the limitation that only content that is already loaded with the page can be used when restyling the appearance of a document. Now, however, it becomes possible to load content *after* the page has been displayed, and the DHTML techniques can be used to incorporate the newly loaded data into the page. This is a disruptive change to what a Web page can do!

In 2002, an object compatible to XMLHTTP called XMLHttpRequest (XHR) was implemented for the Mozilla browser. Other browsers started to follow soon thereafter. In 2006, the W3C started working on a standard definition of this object. This is a crucial step, as the importance of the object is likely to keep growing and interoperability between browsers is crucial for keeping development as simple as possible. In 2005, the term *Ajax* was coined as an acronym for "Asynchronous JavaScript and XML." The first part refers to JavaScript employing the XMLHttpRequest object to allow for data transfers "in the background," the second refers to XML providing the vocabulary. The term is actually a misnomer, since any scripting language supporting this object can be used, and since the use of XML is not required. It nevertheless does capture the disruptiveness of the combination of techniques by giving it a concise name.

The only addition that was needed to make DHTML this much more powerful was the XMLHTTP object. It has to be noted, of course, that once we leave the world of HTML and look at other formats used on the Web (e.g., the Flash format), there are other mechanisms that allow the same kind of asynchronous data loading. But, as we have pointed out, HTML is the most important language on the Web and, as opposed to other languages, is natively supported by browsers.

Other Web-based e-mail applications

We briefly present some other Web-based e-mail clients next, in order to highlight some of the features that have been implemented and to thus discuss the extent of possibilities and design choices for RIAs. Complementing Outlook and Exchange with their strong distribution in businesses, the clients presented in the following are popular among private users. OWA was developed to complement an off-line version of the same product, and this is no longer the case for the products mentioned next.

The mail clients from Yahoo! (see mail.yahoo.com) and Google (see mail.google.com) both use Ajax to enhance the user interfaces. Their clients can be seen in Figure 3.4 and Figure 3.5, respectively. The extent to which Ajax is used and how it is used differs from one example to the other. Yahoo!'s interface offers tabs for opening different folders or mails at the same time, which Google does not. In general, Yahoo! makes intensive use of icons,

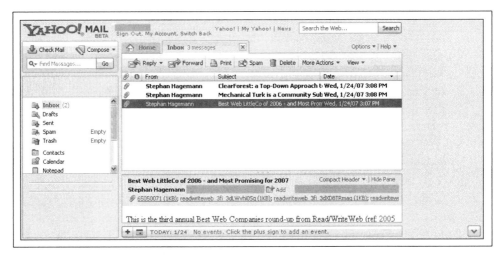

Figure 3.4 Yahoo's Web-based e-mail client.
Source: http://mail.yahoo.com

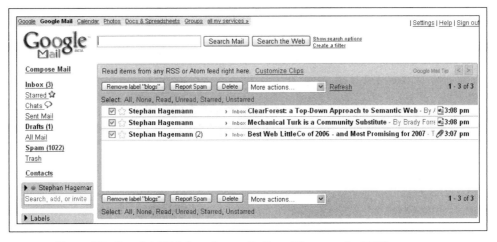

Figure 3.5 Google's Web-based e-mail client (Hammersly, 2006).
Source: http://mail.google.com

which symbolize the action connected to a button. The Yahoo! interface has special-purpose pop-up menus for most of the elements in the application and allows resizing the individual parts of the work area, two features that Google does not offer. Both mail clients can display advertisements: the white space on the right side of Figure 3.4 is the space where Yahoo! and roughly also Google will display it. Google, however, only displays ads when e-mails are opened. To bring order to e-mails, the two clients employ slightly different approaches: whereas Yahoo! uses nonhierarchical folders in which an e-mail can be sorted, where one e-mail is always in exactly one folder; Google Mail uses labels, which we have called and continue to call *tags*, where an e-mail can have one or more tags attached to it.

It is interesting to note that the discussion from this is not specific to Rich Internet Applications. Indeed, the same discussion could be held for desktop applications. The important differences refer to different design principles and different user interface philosophies, and are unrelated to the fact that the applications are transported via a Web browser. This is only possible because the capabilities have risen to a level where these distinctions become clearly visible.

As a further example for the feasibility of provisioning online mail application these days, we mention that several universities have moved their mail management to the services hosted by Google within the *Google Apps for Education* program (see www.google.com/a/edu). Check also, for example, www.itbusiness.ca/it/client/en/home/News.asp?id=41761 or www.thehoya.com/news/102406/news6.cfm.

Beyond plain e-mail

As an alternative client that tries to extend the use of e-mails to voice and video mails, we mention Springdoo. This application does not try to compete with the clients just mentioned by providing a better interface. Instead, it focuses on support for multimedia mails, namely voice and video mails. Using a Flash interface, users can record audio or video next to or instead of writing. The support for multimedia is one of the very strong features of Flash programs. The interface for writing such a "SpringMail" is depicted in Figure 3.6. As can be seen, the main part of the window contains the "Recorder" tab, which is the Flash element. In Figure 3.6, an audio snippet has already been recorded and the mail is ready to be sent. When mail is sent, the audio file is not transferred to the recipient; instead he or she will get an e-mail with a link to the audio file where the latter can be listened to.

There are plenty of other competitors in the area of online e-mail clients. As a last field of play, we mention online solutions for groupware applications. These provide functionalities similar to the Exchange Server we have already discussed, but which are accessed through a browser. For example, Joyent offers its *Connector* as one such solution, which can be bought either as a hosted solution with monthly or yearly plans, with the software and data residing on Joyent's servers, or as a dedicated server installed on the site of the client's business. Another player is Zimbra with its *Zimbra Collaboration Suite*. The software has also been released under an Open Source license. Most notably, Zimbra provides interfaces for developers to create so-called *Zimlets*. These are small pieces of code that mash-up data from Zimbra and outside sources.

Figure 3.6 Springdoo's video e-mail client.

Comparison and roundup

There are two different groups of services we have discussed so far. On the one hand, OWA and the entire Exchange world still follow the classic pattern of software distribution. A consumer buys a software product, in this example the Exchange server, and installs and manages it. As part of this product, there is also a client distributed through the browser.

On the other hand, the other clients we have briefly looked at follow the *software as a service* approach. Users do not run the software on their own hardware, but buy or receive for free the product to be used (in this case the e-mail client and with some packages also the server), and all administrative tasks related to running the product are done by the service provider. Clearly, this has become a very convenient solution for many users. It has to be noted that contracts for free services typically contain the possibility for the provider to end the service at any time. Check, for example, the terms of use of Google Mail at google.com/mail/help/terms_of_use.html. One might think that this is only because Google is a free service, but a similar clause can be found in the Joyent terms of services joyent.com/tos, which also states that users are responsible for backing up their data. It is therefore crucial for prospective clients to evaluate both alternatives, but the bottom line is that the responsibility cannot be outsourced.

We have seen how e-mail clients available on the Web today have become as feature-rich as was once reserved for desktop applications. The first steps were eased by e-mail being a communication task, depending on the Web anyway. But major steps in Web development have amplified the reasons for their adoption. Next, we look in more detail at the technical base for Ajax applications, before we then turn to more applications, which are not about communication, and how even these can be efficiently distributed over a Web browser.

3.1.2 XMLHttpRequest, the link needed for Ajax

DHTML makes Web pages more dynamic. Snippets of scripting languages allow for the manipulation of page elements that can be used to change the appearance of the page. As long as there is no way for a page to access data from other sources, the possibilities are limited. As we have seen earlier in this section, this has changed with the arrival of the XMLHttpRequest.

The reason for the unresponsiveness of traditional client/server Web applications is that Web pages are displayed in a synchronous way. As explained already in Chapter 1, in the classical Web application model, user activity on the client side results in page requests, which are transmitted to the server, processed, and finally sent back as HTML pages. In the meantime, the client has to wait for the response. Information is handled inefficiently because the results are always transmitted as a whole, often containing large amounts of redundant data. This alternating sequence of user activity and server processing is illustrated in Figure 3.7.

The primary purpose of Ajax is to speed up these interactions between a user and a Web application by making them asynchronous and by omitting redundant data from the transmissions. The new sequence of interactions is shown in Figure 3.8.

In the new Ajax model, user input is handled by the Ajax engine at the client side as shown in Figure 3.9. This engine is loaded into the browser upon the first call of the respective page. From then on, many tasks can be processed and displayed at once. Only when needed, a request for further information is sent to the server. This request is transmitted and processed asynchronously, so that user activity is not interrupted. On the other side, the server response can be constructed so that it contains only new information, reducing the amount of data transmitted. Although the details vary, every Ajax scenario consists of similar steps. When the user triggers

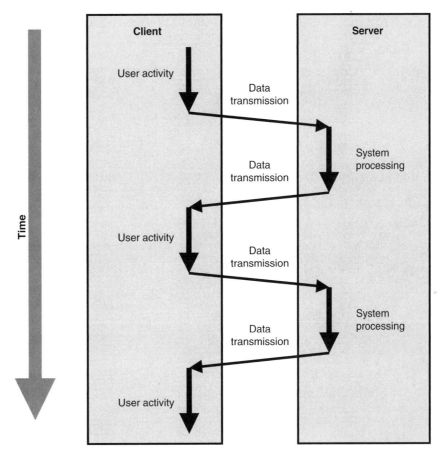

Figure 3.7 Synchronous page requests and refreshes.

an event, the Ajax engine, or more precisely the responsible JavaScript function, has to handle it in a meaningful way. If additional information from the server side is needed to accomplish the task, an asynchronous Ajax request is issued.

The Ajax engine that is depicted in Figure 3.8 as well as Figure 3.9 is not an independent entity, but represents an interaction of the Web technologies described in Chapter 2 and the XMLHttpRequest object mentioned earlier, with the aim to provide asynchronous and desktop-like interface behavior.

The general procedure of an Ajax request can be summarized by the following steps:

1. First, the `XMLHttpRequest` object is created. The corresponding statement is something like `resObject = new XMLHttpRequest()`.

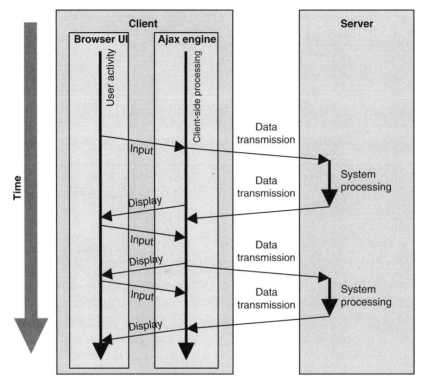

Figure 3.8 Asynchronous page refreshes.

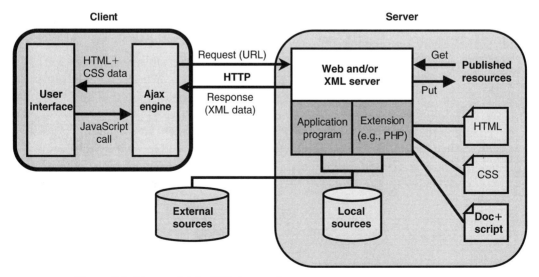

Figure 3.9 Ajax model for Web interaction.

2. For a handling of the response, a callback function must be defined. The statement would be similar to `resObject.onreadystatechange = handleResonse`, where `handleResponse` is the name of the callback handler. This function gets called whenever the status of `resObject` changes. The `resObject.readyState` field indicates the status, the `XMLHttpRequest` object is in. When it is set to `Loaded`, the transmission is finished. It is up to the callback handler to appropriately react to the status.

3. Calling `open` on the `XMLHttpRequest` object opens the HTTP connection to the server. `open` expects three arguments: the type of the HTTP request, the target URL of the server-sided application, and a flag indicating whether the transmission should be asynchronous or not. For example, for an asynchronous request with the GET-method, which is the HTTP method to retrieve a specific resource, the statement would be `resObject.open('get', targetURL, true)`.

4. To start the request, the `send` method of the `XMLHttpRequest` object is called with one argument, which contains the message in case of a POST request, which is the HTTP method to post data for processing. If GET is chosen as the method, the message parameters are encoded in the target address, so `null` is passed as argument.

5. Once the callback handler gets called and the status is COMPLETED the requested data can be accessed via the fields `responseText` and `responseXML` of the `XMLHttpRequest` object. The former returns the message as plain text, the latter in XML format.

The Ajax engine can now use the information to complete its tasks and to present the results, for example by replacing certain parts of the Web page via DHTML. The following example is to explain the function of `XMLHttpRequest`; it is by no means a Rich Internet Application. There are numerous books, such as Asleson and Schutta (2006), Crane et al. (2006), or Gehtland (2006) devoted to Ajax and how RIAs can be built with it. Nakhimovsky and Myers (2004) go into detail about how to create and consume Web procedures.

WPC server for the DVD catalog

In order to show how we can extend the DVD catalog from Chapter 2 with an XMLHttpRequest function, we now need a provider of data, a Web procedure call server (WPC server), or a Web service provider who will process the requests that are generated on the DVD catalog page. We will therefore change the PHP script we have presented in Chapter 2 and which could generate the complete catalog page. Now, instead of generating the entire page, the script will, upon request, return the detailed data that is attached

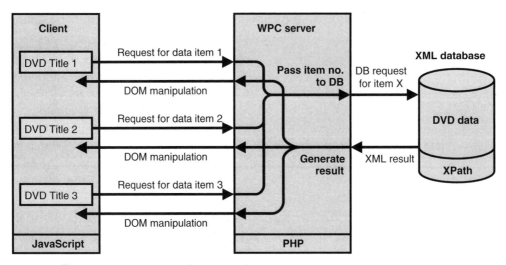

Figure 3.10 Ajax setup of DVD catalog.

to the movie. We will use the director and actors names as our detailed data. We will also use the same database that we already used in Chapter 2 (see Listing 2.2).

Figure 3.10 shows which components are now part of the example. The client executes JavaScript code to make Ajax requests to the WPC server. The server running PHP in turn generates the database requests, which in our case means accessing the XML file with XPath. It then takes the result to produce the output for the client and returns it. The client again uses JavaScript to manipulate its DOM. Listing 3.1 shows the code for the WPC server.

Listing 3.1: WPC server for the DVD catalog.

```
<?
 $asin = $_GET['ASIN'];

 $dom = new DomDocument();
 $dom->load('sample_01_database.xml');
 $xp = new domxpath($dom);
 $dvds = $xp->query('/DVDCatalog/DVD[ASIN="'.$asin.'"]');

 foreach ($dvds as $node) {
  $director =
   getFullNamesOfPersons($node->getElementsByTagName('Director')->
    item(0));
  $actors =
   getFullNamesOfPersons($node->getElementsByTagName('Actors')->
    item(0));
```

```
        returnDVDCode($director, $actors);
    }

    function returnDVDCode($director, $actors){
      echo 'Director: '.$director.'<br>'."\n".'Actors: '.$actors;
    }

    function getFullNamesOfPersons($personList) {
      $persons = $personList->getElementsByTagName('Person');
      $i = 0;
      foreach ($persons as $person) {
        $fullNames[$i] .= getSubNodeContent($person, 'Firstname').' '.
              getSubNodeContent($person, 'Lastname');
       $i++;
      }
      return implode(", ", $fullNames);
    }

    function getSubNodeContent($node, $subNodeName) {
      return $node->getElementsByTagName($subNodeName)->item(0)->
      nodeValue;
    }
  ?>
```

The WPC server in Listing 3.1 has exactly the same functions getSub-NodeContent and getFullNamesOfPersons as the page creation script from Listing 2.8 of Chapter 2 had. The functions printDocumentFoot and printDocument-Head have been deleted from the document. They are not needed any more since the script will now only function as a way for a client script to access the database of DVD catalog information. We therefore do not need to create an entire page – that would be redundant. Instead, the script uses the function returnDVDCode to deliver only the content that is not yet available at the client side. It can be seen that that function resembles the role that the printDVD function had before which, however, was complex as it generated an entire DVD entry. Here, all that is returned are the names of director and actors.

The script from Chapter 2 returned all DVDs contained in the catalog, which we do not want anymore. How can that be prevented? The line defining the $dvds object has changed slightly; it now has the following form:

```
$xp->query('/DVDCatalog/DVD[ASIN="'.$asin.'"]').
```

The code in squared brackets is a special XPath selector, which checks that the ASIN element, which is a subelement of DVD, has the same value as the $asin variable. Only those DVD nodes that satisfy this condition are selected and stored in $dvds. As one can see in line 2 of the script, the $asin variable has the value of `$_GET['ASIN']`. This array contains a value `ASIN` if a value with such a name has been handed to the script via the HTTP GET method.

With GET requests parameters are appended to the URL of the invoked script after an introductory question mark:

```
http://localhost/ch3/sample_01_server.php?ASIN=B0000CABBW
```

The request above invokes the WPC server with an ASIN parameter of B0000CABBW, which was the movie *Whale Rider*. The script will then return the following result:

```
Director: Niki Caro<br>
Actors: Keisha Castle-Hughes, Rawiri Paratene, Vicky Haughton
```

Since we have added no functions that catch and handle bad or missing ASIN numbers, in that case the script will just return an empty string.

WPC consumer

Let's turn to the client (i.e., the left-hand side of Figure 3.10). We will again start out with what we already had in Chapter 2. In Listing 2.7, we had the DVD catalog where the details could be hidden through a click on the title of the DVD. We will use that script as a starting point. As we will see, the changes needed are minimal. Listing 3.2 contains the source code for the client of our current scenario with the parts that changed in comparison to Listing 2.7 highlighted. First, one should notice that the page does not contain the information on director and actors any more. It does, however, contain empty `div` elements with the `ASIN` number of the DVD; these are used as placeholders for the content we will get from the server. The rest of the body of the document is unchanged.

Listing 3.2: WPC consumer for the DVD catalog.

```
<!DOCTYPE HTML PUBLIC "-//W3C//DTD HTML 4.01 Transitional//EN"
       "http://www.w3.org/TR/html4/loose.dtd">
<html>
  <head>
    <title>Sample DVD Catalog</title>
    <meta name="author" content="Vossen, Hagemann">
    <link rel="stylesheet" type="text/css" href="sample_05.css">
    <script type="text/javascript">
      function toggleDVDDisplay(id){
        var http = new XMLHttpRequest();
        http.onreadystatechange = function() {
          if(http.readyState == 4 && http.status == 200) {
            var contentElement = document.getElementById(id);
            contentElement.innerHTML = http.responseText;
```

```
        contentElement.style.display = 'block';
        contentElement.setAttribute('expanded', 'true');
    }
  }
      http.open("GET","http://localhost/ch3/sample_01_server.
      php?ASIN="+id, true);
  http.send(null);
  }
  </script>
</head>
<body>
  <div class="DVDCatalog">
   <h1>Sample DVD Catalog</h1>
   <div class="DVD">
    <div class="DVDHead"
        onClick="toggleDVDDisplay('B0000CABBW')">
     <h2><a href="http://www.imdb.com/title/tt0298228/">
     Whale Rider</a></h2>
     (2002)
    </div>
    <div class="DVDContent" id="B0000CABBW">
    </div>
   </div>
   <div class="DVD">
    <div class="DVDHead"
       onClick="toggleDVDDisplay('B0000A02Y4')">
     <h2><a href="http://www.imdb.com/title/tt0110729/">
     Once Were Warriors</a></h2>
     (1994)
    </div>
    <div class="DVDContent" id="B0000A02Y4">
    </div>
   </div>
   <div class="DVD">
    <div class="DVDHead"
       onClick="toggleDVDDisplay('B00005U515')">
     <h2><a href="http://www.imdb.com/title/tt0120737/">
     The Lord of the Rings: The Fellowship of the Ring</a></h2>
     (2001)
    </div>
    <div class="DVDContent" id="B00005U515">
    </div>
   </div>
  </div>
 </body>
</html>
```

The most important change is the new version of the `toggleDVDDisplay` function. It now follows exactly the general process for Ajax calls that was sketched above. First, a new `XMLHttpRequest` object is instantiated. Second, the `XMLHttpRequest` function `onreadystatechange` is defined to handle the result of the WPC call. Third, the open function sets the parameters of the WPC call and send opens the connection. When the result is returned from the server and its status is okay (meaning `http.readyState` is `4` and `http.status` is `200`), the code handling the data insertion is executed. The function `responseText` returns the result as plain text, which is inserted into the empty `div` that was held as placeholder in the body of the page, with its selection working exactly as it has done in Chapter 2. This insertion is done via overwriting the content of the `div` element's `innerHTML` property.

Note that the `toggleDVDDisplay` function we have created is so simple that it will make repeated requests to the WPC server when repeatedly clicked. This is, of course, not a desired behavior, as the Ajax is intended to reduce the amount of data that travels between server and client, and this is totally redundant data! Nevertheless, this simple example has shown what this seemingly simple construct of XMLHttpRequest can achieve.

To give a hint of what else is possible, we look a bit more at the possibilities one has with this object. So far, we have only used the XMLHttpRequest state 4 (loaded), which is used to inform the script that a data transfer is completed. Overall the following states are distinguished:

0: uninitialized
1: open
2: sent
3: receiving
4: loaded

State 1 indicates that the open function has successfully been called; state 2 means that the request is acknowledged; state 3 says that all HTTP headers have been received and that the message body is about to be received. Together these functions can be used to inform the client of the state of a request. In our example, we did not do this since the amount of data is always tiny, but should one want to load larger amounts of data, such functions are a good way of enhancing the communication with the user.

Should the data a server returns not only contain content in the form of new data, but also in the form of new script code, one can imagine a page that successively increases the amount of actions it is able to perform. The possibilities are for developers to dream up and this is hardly in any way related to the development of static Web projects! Doing all this by hand is obviously rather tedious and too low level for big project development. Therefore, in Chapter 4 we look at some of the tools that take away some of the trouble when programming Ajax.

3.1.3 More RIAs: Office and map applications

This section gives an overview of several other types of applications that have meanwhile been moved to the Web, and shows how they work.

Office applications

First, we look at more typical office programs. Thinkfree is a company that offers an application suite for word processing, spreadsheet calculation, and presentation (see also Table 5.1 in Chapter 5). It is compatible to the Microsoft Office Suite, but as it is programmed in Java, which is available on various operating systems. So the software runs not only on Windows, but on GNU/Linux, and Mac OS X. As one can see from Figure 3.11, the look and feel of the user interface is very much like that one known from Microsoft Office. There are several variants of the program available. Users can store their files online and all versions of a file are automatically saved. Folders are used to structure the data. The files can also be downloaded to be used elsewhere. Files and folders in the online storage can be shared, so that users can collaboratively work on files.

The online version runs using the Java Web Start Technology (see java.sun.com/products/javawebstart/). This allows Java programs to be started in any browser, and it takes care of administrative tasks such as checking whether any dependencies such as additional libraries need to be

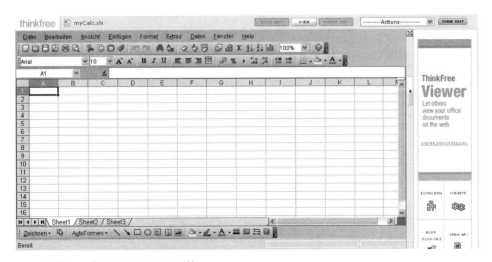

Figure 3.11 ThinkFree Office.

loaded as well. It also allows applications to cache code so that starting up the application is accelerated on successive runs. As Java is used, there is full support for menus, right-click pop-up menus, or drag and drop.

The server version and the desktop version are applications that need to be paid for, downloaded, and installed before they can be used. The former allows multiple users to work on one dedicated server; the latter allows a user to run ThinkFree locally on his or her personal machine. These last two versions are sold as products, not as services.

Gliffy complements ThinkFree as it allows for drawing diagrams. It is similar to, but not quite as sophisticated as Microsoft Visio. There are palettes of symbols supporting the creation of flow charts, UML diagrams, network diagrams, which is the one used in the sample document seen in Figure 3.12, and several others. There is a free, online version of Gliffy which comes with file storage that tracks revisions and allows several users to cocreate diagrams. Files can only be downloaded from the online storage when they are exported to svg, jpg, or png files.

The user interface of Gliffy is based on the Macromedia Flash plug-in for browsers. This gives the application a very reactive feel, and great graphical and multimedia capabilities. It is interesting to note, however, that many applications based on Macromedia Flash do not support right-click menus. Or rather, the standard right-click menu which contains the settings of Flash and a link to the Flash homepage is not altered to be made use of in the context of the program. This is also the case for Gliffy.

As mentioned, the online version of Gliffy is free of charge. There is, however, also a variant that has to be paid for, which is integrated into the

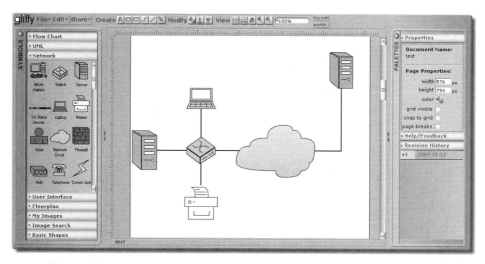

Figure 3.12 A Gliffy diagram.

wiki system *Confluence* (see atlassian.com/software/confluence). There it allows users to create diagrams for wiki pages. Creating diagrams can be imitated from any wiki page, the completed diagrams are stored within the page, and are directly visible on it.

Again there are many other services falling into this category, our following list includes word processing and spreadsheet applications: Google Docs & Spreadsheets (docs.google.com), NumSum, Peepel, Writeboard, and the various applications from Zoho (again, see Table 5.1 for further examples).

Map applications

As a final example for RIAs we turn to map applications. There are several providers of online maps today, which are typically free to use and are advertisement supported, and which usually provide additional information supplementing the content of a map. Providers include Ask Maps (see maps.ask.com), Google Maps (see maps.google.com), Map 24, Mapquest (see mapquest.com/maps), Windows Live Local (see local.live.com), or Yahoo! Maps (see maps.yahoo.com); this is not an exhaustive list. The maps interface from Yahoo! is shown in Figure 3.13. The elements that can be seen in this screenshot are typical for most map applications available. There is a search bar for location or directions searching in the top left, and a search bar to search for content on the map such as local businesses. There is often a little overview map, as in the top right corner.

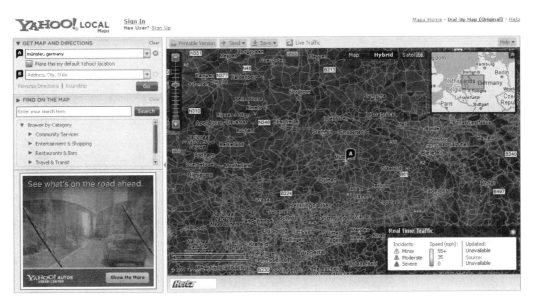

Figure 3.13 Yahoo! Maps.
Source: http://maps.yahoo.com

The map can be moved by dragging it with the mouse and can be further controlled by a zoom slider. For this, the procedure of Google Maps is as follows: the map server stores a grid of square images of every place covered. Each of these tiles has a fixed position within the coordinate system and a unique URL through which it can be retrieved. There are different tiles for the different zoom levels of the map. When a specific map is requested, the server sends back all the tiles that lie within the area covered by the map. Figure 3.14 shows an example of this for the New York-Newark area. Tiles B2 and B3 are shown completely on the screen. All other named squares are shown in part, but the images have been fully transmitted to the client, so that if the user drags the map down, the map will be shown without a need to transmit further data from the server to the client. To enable dragging further without the user having to wait for the transmission to complete, additional squares lying around the map are transmitted in the background. If a map is dragged to a part that has not been transmitted yet, the user will see a grey square until the data is completely loaded on the client side. All these transmissions are done in the background, so one can go on dragging the map even if there are parts that have not been transferred yet.

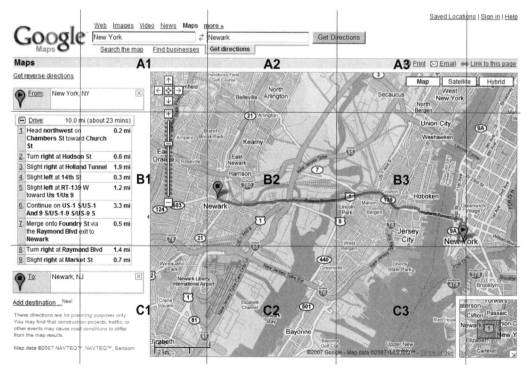

Figure 3.14 Square images ("tiles") used in Google Maps.
Source: http://maps.google.com

Map type selector buttons select between map, satellite, hybrid, or bird's eye views (Figure 3.14 shows a map, Figure 3.13 a satellite image). Not all features are available on all mapping services. For example, the bird's eye view is only available in Live Local; Map 24 does not have satellite imagery, but instead allows very detailed calculations of directions. Some services offer real-time traffic information, but as one can see from Figure 3.13, this information is not available everywhere. If present, it is typically only major U.S. cities that are covered (although we expect that similar, if not more advanced services are available in Japan or South Korea).

In terms of technology, there are several approaches. Most services use an Ajax-based interface; only Yahoo!'s service is based on Macromedia Flash. This is, however, mostly invisible to the client, as the services' performances do not differ very much. It is nevertheless interesting to note that the Google Maps implementation does not use an XMLHttpRequest object to retrieve new data as one could have expected from our introduction earlier. Instead, it uses two different mechanisms for map movement and search requests. When the map is moved, the images displaying the tiles are moved, and should a new tile be needed, the source of an image is redirected to the new URL. To update map tiles a query is submitted and the results are processed in a hidden inline frame of the HTML page as shown in Figure 3.15. The server responds with an HTML file that contains the search results in XML format. The inline frame contains a JavaScript function that is executed

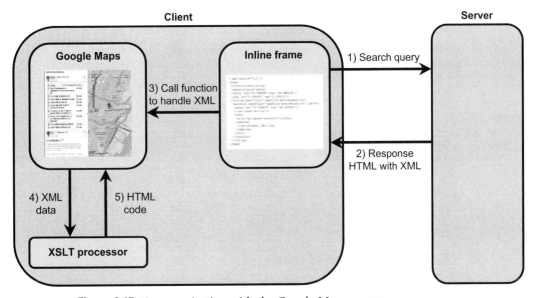

Figure 3.15 Communication with the Google Maps server.

via the `onload` attribute of HTML as soon as the page has been transmitted completely. This function calls a load function of the outer frame which handles the XML data. This way of asynchronous communication replaces the `onreadychange` function of the `XMLHttpRequest`, as the browser does not have to determine when the transmission has finished, and it has the advantage that the back and forward buttons of the browser will still work, as a history entry is made for each query.

For processing the XML data received, Google uses the XSLT Processor of the browser. This converts the XML data and ensures that the search results are shown in the HTML page and as markers within the map.

The rationale for bringing map applications online is easily understood once one sees the variety of additional information that is added to the map information. It starts with local search features, where users can search and the search is narrowed down, or localized, to the area covered by or near the visible map. The idea is that local information is more relevant than geographically unrestricted information, and this is of course the case if one searches (e.g., for stores, gyms, or manufacturers). Traffic information is another example: As real-time data is essential, any map application has to have access to the Internet to download such information anyway; with online applications the information can be integrated without users having to configure anything. Another important issue is the timeliness of the map information itself. If mapping software is distributed via CDs or DVDs, updates have to be performed to get new information on roads or new satellite images. Such upgrades can now be performed silently by the map provider, without the costly redistribution of the data to many distributed sites.

From a developer's perspective, it is interesting to note that map providers have started to offer publicly available application programming interfaces (APIs) to their map and image data. As we see in the next section, this allows for even more information sources to be integrated, through what is called *mash-ups*. Map data then is one source that can be combined with any type of geographical or other data, such as weather, house prices, classified ads, or location, pollution, and travel information.

Providing map information online is not without challenges, however. The connection speed is still a major issue, as slow connections practically prevent a fluid interaction with the mapping service, since the client is unable to load images fast enough. Clearly, this problem is a technicality which will disappear over time.

RIAs versus desktop applications

In this section, we have looked at a number of different RIAs. We have highlighted their characteristics and pointed out advantages and shortcomings when they are compared to desktop applications. In conclusion, it is safe to say that there are elementary prerequisites that have to be met for running applications online, such as fast connections and a virtually full-time connectivity. As we have pointed out in Chapter 1, the age of broadband and always-on started in the years after 2000. So it is reasonable for software and service providers to develop alternative ways to distribute software than to pack and physically ship them to their customers. And as these technical prerequisites are more and more fulfilled, the decision between RIAs and desktop applications will no longer be a question of faith, but a measuring of alternatives: Integration into the operating system and large availability across systems via the availability within browsers. We can already see the convergence of desktop and Internet applications. For example, Java Web Start is a technology that makes applications programmed in (the desktop programming language) Java available in the browser. So, based on common source code, we see two versions of the same software being deployed quite easily. This trend will continue in the future and the boundary between RIAs and desktop applications will continue to blur.

3.2 APIs, WPCs, and their mash-ups

As we have seen above, the development of Ajax applications requires the programmer, among other things, to build application programming interfaces (APIs) to the program logic via Web procedure calls. While it would be possible to only allow one's own application to invoke these procedures by restricting the addresses of accepted clients or by using authentication and encryption, there are numerous sites that have opened up these interfaces for use by others. Some of the more prominent examples here are Flickr, Google, and Amazon.com. The availability of these procedures allows for the integration of formerly disconnected sites of information, an approach for which the term *mash-up* has been coined.

Mash-ups represent a radical departure from the possibilities that existed before this trend started. The Web site of a provider often was the only way to access his data. And the only way of automatically integrating information from distinct Web sites was through page scraping, that is trying to automatically extract meaningful parts of a page. However, this allows only limited access patterns and is error-prone. Most importantly, while scraping may work well for certain scenarios, it is the shift to actively endorsing the usage of services in different contexts, it is the "design for remixability" according to Musser and O'Reilly (2007), which makes mash-ups qualitatively different.

We have stated in Chapter 2 that there is a considerable difference between Web procedure calls and Web services. That said, we also have to state that most services currently reachable publicly are in fact Web procedure calls. Although from an academic perspective, this may be seen as an inferior solution to an implementation with Web services, it nevertheless remains the marking point of a major shift in the way data is organized and accessed on the Web.

In this section we look at how mash-ups are implemented, what different kinds of mash-ups exist, and what has to be taken into account when building them. We do so by using Google Maps as one of the more prominent examples. However, we start with an application from a time when Web site owners were not so eager to publish their content with annotations to make automatic processing easier. We then look at the situation when pages are organized to allow integration, which is often the case with Web feeds, and finally we look at the mash-up of public APIs.

3.2.1 The situation in Web 1.0

As we laid out in Chapter 1, there is a lot that can be done and that actually is done on the Web. One of the many uses is the retrieval of information. This comes in forms as diverse as the users of the Web. It may happen that someone searches for an old friend, tries to find the solution to a computer problem, is interested in a new recipe for dinner, or wants to get information on the company she has stock in. Companies have similar tasks: Find information on the prices of goods, applicants, the current weather, news on competitors, or flight schedule changes. Directories, portals, and in particular search engines are all different attempts to address the need for finding information effectively and efficiently. They all do, however, require surfing to them and sometimes navigating within them to get to the exact location of where the desired information is found.

Depending on the nature of the search task both efficiency and effectiveness can be improved. Efficiency could be improved for a search task that needs to be performed repeatedly, which requires several navigational steps by a user before he gets to the desired information. Monitoring a specific auction on an auction platform requires searching for the auction, possibly sifting through pages of search results, before the desired information is obtained. The effectiveness of a search task is limited by the amount of sources on the Web. It is infeasible go to all news Web sites to monitor all the opinions on the unfolding of a current event, since there are just too many.

Searches can be characterized by their grades of repetitiveness and specificity. The higher the repetitiveness, the higher is the incentive to increase the efficiency of a search because efficient search saves the more time the more it is repeated. The higher the specificity, the more interesting it is to retrieve only the desired result. An example for a search with a high specificity is the search for a current stock market price: having to surf through a trade portal does not improve the result. On the other hand, surfing through a cooking portal when one is looking for a new dish may be crucial in providing ideas on the type of dish one could do.

Clearly, there are tools to enhance surfing the Web for information retrieval. Bookmarks, also called *favorites*, are the most basic means to do this. They allow for storing Web addresses, which get names, usually the title of a page, and can often be stored in folders. While surfing the Web, bookmarks can be collected, stored in the browser (or via services on the Web, as is becoming more and more popular; take del.icio.us or Foxmarks as examples), and can later be reused to have a direct entry point into the respective resource. Bookmarks can store where a piece of information was found. However, sometimes they do not point to items of information directly, but to their providers instead. They do not, however, contain information on which information was actually intended to be stored: indeed, it could happen that the bookmarked page contains the information directly or that a page linked from that page contains it. This ambiguity makes bookmarks flexible, but limits the increase in efficiency they can provide. There are now services that can reduce the ambiguity of bookmarks. For example, Clipmarks allows users to select parts of a Web page for them to store. We see that this is not a singular idea, but can be found behind several approaches towards making better use of the Web.

Figure 3.16 summarizes this situation. The axes are formed by repetitiveness and specificity. When the repetitive character of a retrieval task is low, a

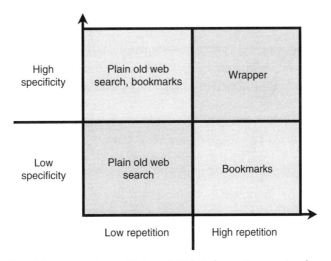

Figure 3.16 Repetitiveness and specificity of Web information retrieval.

Web search or browsing directories are reasonable means to find the needed information. However, when some very specific information is needed, it still makes sense to somehow store it, for example, through bookmarks in order not to forget it. The higher the repetitive character is the more sense it makes to use techniques that make the gathering of information more efficient and effective; this is precisely what *wrappers* do, which we cover now.

Page scraping with wrappers

A precursor to mash-ups as we see them today can be seen in *wrappers* that have been developed roughly since the mid-1990s. Wrappers grew out of the need to integrate information from multiple Web sources and of the missing query capabilities of the HTML language. As a motivation, consider the following example from Baumgartner et al. (2003): A client wants to monitor a certain Web site for financial news about car manufacturers BMW and DaimlerChrysler and wants to receive this news in e-mails. However, this site does not offer the possibility to select news items based on content and have them sent out in an e-mail, while it may allow showing news items covering a specific company. As a consequence, the client will have to visit all this news manually to get to the desired information. If he or she wants to collect information on these companies from several news sites, the situation is even worse, since there is commonly no convenient way to directly collect information from different sites into a single structured file. A solution to this problem is to use *wrapper* technology to extract the relevant information from HTML documents and translate it into XML, which can then be easily queried or further processed. The idea of wrappers falls into the broader subject of *business intelligence* on the Web, or *Web intelligence*, which is covered, for example, in Zhong et al. (2003). For a book covering wrappers in the context of data mining on the Web, refer to Liu (2007).

We present the solution proposed by Baumgartner et al. (2003), which has resulted in the *Lixto* company. Its main program, the *Lixto Suite*, can automate regularly occurring surf tasks and enhance information retrieval by extracting semantics as well. After an initial setup process, it tracks exactly that information which the user has indicated to be interested in, leaving out unnecessary information from the page or pages visited. So, as compared to bookmarks, it is not only about storing information on *where*, but also *how* the information can be found and extracted from a Web resource. With the Lixto Suite, a crawler-type of application can be configured that will periodically visit the selected page or pages, extract the relevant information, and wrap the content into a new page, which then can be accessed and which only contains the content that has been selected. Instead of having to access several sources, these can now be integrated at one place.

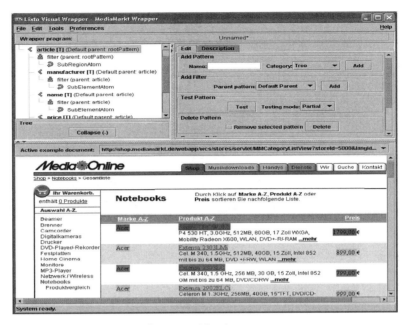

Figure 3.17 Visual pattern specification with Lixto.
Source: Baumgartner et al. (2005)

Lixto essentially does *page scraping*. This means that pages that were made for humans to read are analyzed such that specific content can automatically be extracted. This is defined by *patterns*, which give the information to be extracted a name and allow for hierarchical ordering. In the Lixto component called the *Visual Wrapper*, a user highlights those parts of a page that he or she is interested in and wants to add to a given pattern. The system then identifies which HTML (or XHTML) tags this is equivalent to, and saves information on how it has selected this within the page. This is called a *filter*. It then shows which other pieces it would select with the same filter. If a user had, for example, selected a row in a table, the wrapper would select the filter to look for the <tr> (table row) elements of that table, and mark every row of that table in the same way. The user has the option of reducing the number of selected elements by adding restrictions to a filter. Possible restrictions are *(not) before/after* conditions, expressing that an element must (not) have a specific predecessor or successor. Other restrictions check the internal structure of elements in a filter, or range values of filter elements. Interactively building patterns from pages using filters is the first step that has to be performed within the information extraction process with Lixto (depicted on the left in Figure 3.18).

The *Transformation Server* of the Lixto Suite, depicted in the center of Figure 3.18, covers all steps in the process of extracting information, called

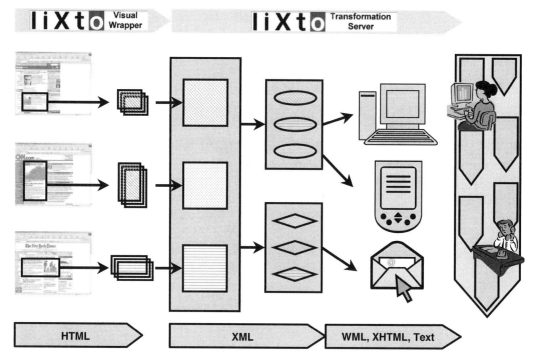

Figure 3.18 Lixto information extraction process.

the processing pipeline: acquiring, integrating, transforming, and delivering. As a first step, it performs the actual extraction of content from pages as specified. Using XML transformations several sources can be integrated. Different output methods can be specified and any application that can process XML can be used as a target of the information flow.

Details of Lixto, its components, and its algorithms and methods can be found in sources such as Baumgartner et al. (2001, 2001a, and 2005), and Gottlob et al. (2004). It can be seen as a precursor to mash-ups, to be used when Web pages contain physical annotations, but no direct data access is endorsed.

Obviously, the wrapper approach only makes sense if it is used for repetitive tasks, since surfing the Web in a random way does not lend itself to be preprogrammed. But all those applications that are characterized by a high degree of repetitiveness can significantly increase their efficiency through the use of wrappers. The strength of visual wrappers is at the same time their weakness: they use a visual extraction mechanism. Users select what they see. Whenever the code of a Web page is changed and the change is such that the system cannot find the original content anymore, the system has to be reconfigured.

The latter is a problem because Web pages are not designed to be scraped by programs in the first place, and they therefore do not necessarily support the needs of a scraper well; even worse, site providers may even want to prevent automatic page scraping. In contrast to this approach, the Semantic Web tries to embed semantic highlights into pages so that computers as well as humans are able to not just read, but even understand the semantics of elements. A page could then change in structure, but a computer would still be able to find it as long as the concepts used stay the same. We say more on the Semantic Web in Chapter 6. And probably the most important difference between the two approaches is that one endorses automatic processing, while the other one does not.

As an alternative to making Web pages readable *also* by applications, which requires complex algorithms and is a task a user has to perform, there is the option for the provider to offer the content in such a way that is *mainly* meant for automatic processing. We have earlier mentioned APIs, which are used because Ajax requires WPC servers to be able to add content to pages without reloading. APIs complement Web pages, as the former are for computer use while the latter are for human use. With APIs, servers are aware and endorse that software applications are accessing their content. Changes to the structure are therefore typically much less frequent or accompanied by versioning mechanisms, which ensures that applications based on these WPCs continue to work after changes have been made to the server. As we show in the remainder of this section, content syndication and mash-ups achieve the same effect – a (partly) automated use of the Web – in a different way: not through *consumer effort*, but through *provider provision*.

3.2.2 Content syndication with Web feeds

We have mentioned the move from pull- to push-oriented access to information on the Web in the preceding chapters already, of which wrappers are yet another example, and we have briefly mentioned content syndication as well as the RSS and ATOM standards. Content syndication, in the context of the Web, is a *(re-) combination of document-oriented content*. The next section on WPC mash-ups covers similar topics for data-oriented content.

Content syndication

In the corporate field, press reviews, which contain news from newspapers, magazines, and other written sources, have a long tradition. They contain aggregated information that is relevant to a business at large. Clearly, "relevant" here means that every article is found relevant by *someone*, not that every article is relevant for everyone. The strong points of press reviews are that they concentrate the efforts of selecting what is relevant and of pushing this to decision makers who get valuable information without putting effort into it. The steps carried out by the analysts are the same as the steps in the processing pipeline as we have seen it above for wrappers: acquiring, integrating, transforming, and delivering. *Acquiring* here means getting and reading the newspapers and magazines which are to be integrated. *Integrating* may mean photocopying or scanning of the relevant articles. A *transformation* may not be necessary, but could involve the reformatting of articles that are to big for a page. The last step of *delivering* then may be putting the compilations in the corporate mail, or sending out e-mails with the scanned articles attached. One could, of course, also provide scanned articles as Web feeds.

Indeed, with many news sources on the Web providing their document-oriented content like news and comments through the Web in feed formats already, the press review application becomes a natural target for these technologies. The four steps then again have a slightly different realization, which is shown in Figure 3.19.

Acquiring requires subscribing to the pool of news sources that are to be scanned. Integrating takes place within a news aggregator, an application that can read Web feeds. At first the entire combined content from all sources is present. Figure 3.20 shows the integrated view of several feeds in

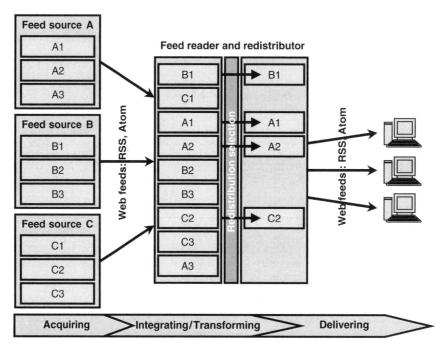

Figure 3.19 Web feed-based press review.

an online feed reader, in this case the Google Reader (see www.google.com/reader). The source, which is here a mixture of blogs as well as international news sites, of an entry is shown in the left column. The title of each entry and, if present, the first words of the content are shown next. The entries are sorted by date, which is shown in the rightmost column.

A transformation may need to be performed if the feeds are present in different feed formats, but only requires an XML transformation from one feed language to another. As such, this task is a lot easier than the routines that need to be applied in the page scraping example above, where completely arbitrary sources need to be transformed to XML in order to be integrated. The delivery step is a matter of selecting the elements that are to be redistributed, which may need to be performed manually. However, it may happen that in the future, this selection can in part be automated, when the content of entries is described, for example, through the use of tags. For redistribution the news aggregator has to act as a Web feed provider. There, the selected entries are compiled into a feed, which subsequently can be accessed by the feed readers the recipients of the press reviews use.

Google Reader offers a function to redistribute content through the selection of *shared items* (see Figure 3.21), these being the entries from the various feeds one has subscribed to. These are then automatically entered into

☆ gmane.comp.db.dbworld	**[Dbworld] 2nd CFP for 2nd International Workshop on XML DataManagement Tools and Techniques (XANTEC 2007)** - CALL FOR	5:07 AM
☆ Daniel Lemire's blog	**Why building software is hard** - Why is building software difficult? Why do so many projects fail? I recently had an argument with a	3:38 AM
☆ Elektrischer Reporter	**18: Marissa Mayer über Google** - Über Google zu sprechen, ohne Superlative fallen zu lassen, ist wahrscheinlich nahezu unmöglich, also	3:07 AM
☆ gmane.comp.db.dbworld	**[Dbworld] 2nd CFP: Track on Healthcare Knowledge Management atCBMS2007** - Special Track on Healthcare Knowledge	2:07 AM
☆ gmane.comp.db.dbworld	**[Dbworld] Conference on Spatial Information Theory (final CfP)** - FINAL CALL FOR PAPERS	1:07 AM
☆ Green Car Congress	**V100 Golf Aces EPA Emissions Tests** - Results of the emissions testing. Click to enlarge. Source: AAE. A 2002 Volkswagen Golf TDi	12:46 AM
☆ gmane.comp.db.dbworld	**[Dbworld] 2nd CFP: Query Log Analysis workshop < at > WWW2007** - Call for Papers - WWW2007 Workshop Query Log Analysis:	12:07 AM
☆ TechCrunch	**Google PowerPoint Clone Coming** - Somebody took what appears to be a header file from an existing Google application and posted it	Feb 4, 2007
☆ Green Car Congress	**DOE Awards $5.7 Million to Universities for Nuclear Energy Research, Including Nuclear Hydrogen Initiative** - The US Department	Feb 4, 2007
☆ heise online news	**Telepolis-Special "Kosmologie" jetzt am Kiosk** -	Feb 4, 2007
☆ O'Reilly Radar	**Is Tim O'Reilly Out of His Mind?** - By Tim O'Reilly A number of you have forwarded to me spam email messages with the subject line " Is	Feb 4, 2007
☆ Green Car Congress	**Komatsu to Introduce Hybrid Excavator** - A rendering of a hybrid excavator. Source: Kobe Steel. Nikkei. Komatsu Ltd. plans to introduce	Feb 4, 2007
☆ O'Reilly Radar	**Superbowl Sunday Reading Link List** - By Tim O'Reilly Since most of you are not likely to be gearing up for the superbowl, you've got	Feb 4, 2007
☆ heise online news	**Zeitung: Neuer Interessent für Benq Mobile** -	Feb 4, 2007
☆ Daniel Lemire's blog	**The paperless office finally coming?** - In the seventies, some made the prediction that we soon would have paperless offices. What	Feb 4, 2007
☆ TechCrunch	**SuperBowl Ads (Not Really) From Startups** - Today's the day - SuperBowl XLI. Hundreds of millions of people around the world will eat	Feb 4, 2007
☆ heise online news	**Ex-US-Vizepräsident Al Gore drängt IT-Unternehmen zum Klimaschutz** -	Feb 4, 2007
☆ Green Car Congress	**Report: US and Brazil to Launch Biofuels Initiative** - McClatchy reports that the US and Brazil will soon launch a partnership to expand	Feb 4, 2007
☆ Dilbert	**Comic for 04 Feb 2007** -	Feb 4, 2007
☆ Ogle Earth	**Censorship in India coming?** - A strange report by AFX this morning, referencing a Times of India article that I can't quite find online:	Feb 4, 2007
☆ Google Operating System	**Google Prepares a Presentation Tool** - I'm sure many people wondered if Google will release a presentation tool, after building Google	Feb 4, 2007
☆ heise online news	**Google Earth verschleiert Verteidigungsanlagen in Indien** -	Feb 4, 2007
☆ heise online news	**Webseite der Miami Dolphins verbreitet Trojaner** -	Feb 4, 2007
☆ heise online news	**Michael Dell will sparen und Bürokratie abbauen** -	Feb 4, 2007
☆ heise online news	**Microsoft äußert sich zu fehlerhaft beschrifteten Vista-DVDs** -	Feb 4, 2007
☆ heise online news	**Multimedia-Unternehmen Magix erwartet von Vista kräftigen Zuwachs** -	Feb 4, 2007
☆ heise online news	**EU-Kommissionsvize: Lobbyisten sollen Geldquellen offenlegen** -	Feb 4, 2007

Figure 3.20 Aggregated Web feeds in a feed reader.
Source: www.google.com/reader/

STEPHAN'S SHARED ITEMS

SmugMug: The (Anti) Web 2.0 Company

via <u>TechCrunch</u> by Michael Arrington on Jan 22, 2007

<u>SmugMug</u> CEO Don MacAskill, who has said "<u>maybe I just don't get this 'Web 2.0' term</u>" in the past, is proceeding to teach those of us who claim to know exactly what it means a thing or two. The company launched a suite of stunning new features tonight.

SmugMug, which took its first customers in late 2002, is the go-to service for serious photography nuts. 100,000 paying customers have uploaded over 100 million photos. The company has 19 employees, is profitable, and has never taken outside funding. Revenues are in the $10 million per year range, MacAskill tells me.

There is no free version of the service. People pay a minimum of $40 per year to upload photos to the site. Pro accounts, which are

These items were shared using **Google Reader**

Google Reader allows you to easily keep track of your favorite websites and see all the updates in one convenient location.

<u>Get started with Google Reader</u>

Figure 3.21 Redistribution of aggregated content.
Source: http://www.google.com/reader/shared/15702995824561894167

a Web feed and offered as a public part of the Reader program. In effect, the only two things a redistributor has to do are (1) select the news sources that are to be aggregated, and (2) select the entries for redistribution. All other steps in the process are taken care of by the feed aggregator application. To stress it again, because of the use of the feed standards RSS and Atom, the computational effort that a feed aggregator has to perform is much simpler than what a wrapper has to do. This makes it possible for virtually everyone to become a content aggregator and redistributor.

There are now even service providers that can bridge the gap to pages that are not offering feeds: For example, Feed43 offers a service to make Web feeds from any HTML page. However, it does not have the same strength in specifying patterns as a full-fledged wrapper and does not support a visual specification. However, it is available as a service and outputs RSS 2.0.

Advanced content syndication with Pipes

With *Pipes* (see pipes.yahoo.com), Yahoo! now offers a visual design tool for custom-made content syndication. The service offered goes far beyond taking the content of several Web feeds and selecting parts for redistribution manually. Here, complex rules can be used to control entry selection.

Basically, Pipes can take Web feeds from any location, although there is special support for some services such as Yahoo! Search and Yahoo! Local. For other sources, the Web feed address can be composed using a URL builder. Generally, the pipe can take user inputs as parameters, which can be of several supported types, like date, location, or URL. Operators can be applied to feed entries or entire feeds. Operators supported at the feed level

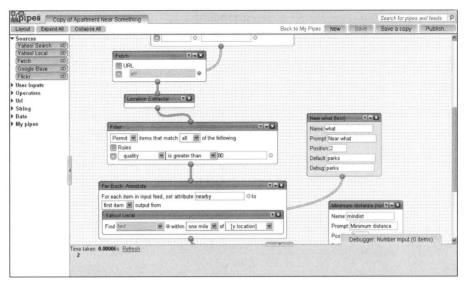

Figure 3.22 Yahoo! Pipes editor.
Source: http://pipes.yahoo.com

include counting the number of entries, filtering entries, or sorting entries. Among the operators supported at the entry level are annotation, replacement, translation, content analysis, and location extraction. Content analysis identifies important keywords from the text of an entry and appends these to the entry. Location extraction tries to find references to locations in the text, and should it find any, it appends these to the entry. As can be seen especially from these latter operators, the possibilities stemming from these operators are quite powerful.

A pipe is constructed by connecting the individual steps of source integration and operator application in the pipe editor. Figure 3.22 shows the visual editor of Pipes. Sources and operators are shown as a menu on the left. The pipe constructed so far is shown in the central pane. One can see the connectors depicting the flow of data.

At the time of writing, Pipes is very new. It remains to be seen how well it is accepted and if Pipes can be created that significantly increase the usability of Web feeds. What can already be said is that the technology provided by Pipes sets the ground for new ways to relatively easy connect resources based on Web feeds. The functionality of Pipes is comparable to that of wrappers, which also allow for complex rules and processes for wrapper processes generation and execution. We can see a trade-off between functionality and complexity here, as wrappers are able to deal with arbitrary Web resources for which rules can become very intricate. On the other hand, Pipes deals manly with Web feeds, which are easier to access.

Attribution of content and permalinks

The content (re-) distribution process based on Web feeds has shown a clear potential for the consumer of content. Let's look at the rationale for content providers. First, the provision of Web feeds eases the integration efforts on the client side so vastly that the content provider can hope for a broader readership of his work. For this to lead to a higher reputation the correct attribution is essential. How is this ensured? In fact, the Web feed formats *default* to a correct attribution of the content creator. We have seen in Chapter 2 that a field containing the author is required on the *channel level* of the XML document, and that it is available but optional on the *entry level*. As the redistribution of entries essentially copies them from the source feed to a target feed, all entry-level attributes are usually preserved. As one can see from Figure 3.21, the original Web feed, the author, and the original publishing date are present under the title of the news entry, automatically giving correct attribution to the creator of the content.

In addition to correct attribution, the content creator is probably interested in increasing the traffic on the page on which she offers the feed. One part of this is the link to the Web page of the Web feed. This is interesting as there may be additional material that is available there, potential advertising revenues when visitors of the site click on ads, possibly there are even products for sale. A very common reason for feed consumers to go to the original source of an article is the possibility to read comments on it there. While these are sometimes offered in a separate feed, more often one has to actively look them up – which makes sense when the comments are not the essential part of the content provided, but are rather discussions or pointers to further readings. A link to the homepage of the *feed* does not suffice here, since the entry will usually soon vanish from the page, especially when new articles are published. The title of an entry as seen in Figure 3.21 therefore points to the original address of the *entry*. For this link to work it should ideally be valid indefinitely, which is why the term *permalink* has been coined for these kinds of links. Permanent validity is something one would wish for many links, but as it seems the true value of this has only recently been widely recognized, although it has long been promoted by insightful people like Tim Berners-Lee (see w3.org/Provider/Style/URI). Most modern blogging and content-syndication systems including Wordpress, Movable Type, LiveJournal, RapidWeaver, and Blogger support permalinks.

3.2.3 Mash-ups based on WPCs

While Web feeds work well for document-oriented content, they only provide a very basic approach when it comes to the combination of data-oriented content. Take as an example the reporting on stock markets. There are quite a few feeds on the topic: At finance.yahoo.com, one can get feeds with news on individual quotes; at nyse.com, there are feeds on various topics such as "Financial News," "Products and Services," or "Unusual Trading." There are, however, few sites that offer just stock quotes via Web feeds (such as QuoteRSS.com). Stock quotes are not document-oriented; they are about *Symbol, Quantity, Bid, Ask*, or *Volume*. Similarly, there are no Web feeds providing aerial or map images with coordinates, one map tile a day.

In the case of stock quotes, it does make sense, however, to provide a stream of information, and when such a stream comes without time lag it even captures the movement of a stock. However, it is essential to differentiate between the different types of information that come with the quote.

In the case of mapping, entirely different access patterns are needed. Indeed, access to data needs to be organized around geographic coordinates and address information. Thus, it is fair to say that in both scenarios Web feeds are not a good option.

We see in this section that WPCs and APIs are a solution for the *(re-) combination of data-oriented content*. The essence is easy to explain: As the name suggests, Web procedure calls can be used to implement any kind of *procedure call over the web*. What can be called, with which parameters can freely be chosen, and access methods tailored to the application at hand can be created. In this section, we specifically take as an example mash-ups with Google Maps and mash-ups of multiple sources for the creation of flexible start pages.

WPC styles

We want to briefly turn to the question of how WPCs are parameterized. This may seem like a technicality, but there are alternatives that define how a Web procedure interacts with a client and how extensible it is.

In Section 3.1.2, we have already seen how WPCs mimic remote procedures calls by defining a location, a procedure, and parameters. We have used HTTP GET to call a PHP-coded function that returns additional information on a DVD. We have used the following statement:

```
http://localhost/ch3/sample_01_server.php?ASIN=B0000CABBW
```

While the GET method could also be used to send requests to the server, that would change its state and is hence considered misuse. The GET method is defined as *safe*, meaning that it should only be used for *retrieval* of information. The preferred way of sending update information to a server is the POST method. With this method, the parameters of the request are embedded into the body of the request. The visible consequence of this is that the parameters are not appended to the URI anymore; moreover, the size the parameters can have is much larger with GET.

In Chapter 2, we discussed SOAP, which is a natural way to enhance the formalization of the data sent: XML, in particular SOAP envelopes are used, for formatting the message. The interface definition of services is specified using XML Schemas (e.g., WSDL), which defines interactions supported between server and client. Finally, SOAP is the natural basis for other Web service standards as it forms the basis of the Web service stack. As a consequence, SOAP increases the formalization, but does not change the general picture of WPCs.

Due to the way we have used procedures so far, the semantics of GET and POST are unclear: They depend on the usage of the parameters in the script that is accessed. When the semantics of GET and POST and that of other HTTP methods are rigidly defined and rigidly used, the result is the *Representational State Transfer (REST)* architectural style. The name was coined in Fielding (2000), which describes how Web applications ought to be designed. Namely, as "a network of Web pages (a virtual state-machine), where the user progresses through an application by selecting links (state transitions), resulting in the next page (representing the next state of the application) being transferred to the user and rendered for their use." All functionality and the application state are considered *resources*. These are uniquely addressed, typically in the form of URIs. Taking again the DVD catalog example, the following URIs point to resources:

```
http://localhost/DVD/
http://localhost/DVD/FindDVD
http://localhost/DVD/B0000CABBW
http://localhost/DVD/B0000A02Y4
http://localhost/DVD/B00005U515
```

The first line may point to a resource containing all DVDs, the second line to a form offering the possibility to search for DVDs, and the last three lines are resources for each DVD in our catalog. The methods that can be used on the resources are GET, POST, PUT, and DELETE only. These correspond to the HTTP methods of the same name. We have already explained GET and POST. PUT adds a resource, the parameters are given in the body of the request, while DELETE removes a given address. When GET is used on a resource, a *representation* of the resource is downloaded to the client. What this representation looks like is up to client and server to decide, as there is no formal mechanism to express the interface of a server. As an example, just take a Web page loaded into a browser: The representation of the page is returned to the client because the GET method has been called. With Web browsing the representation could take, for example, the form of HTML pages, of images, or of PDF documents. When representations with links such as HTML pages are returned, users can move through the application by selecting links and thus moving through the state of the application.

We have seen two different implementations of WPCs: procedure-oriented and resource-oriented. Both styles are common on the Web and which one fits an application best needs to be determined individually. The answer is easy only when an application is to be integrated into a Web service architecture, which heavily relies on Web service standards. In that case, the advantage of using SOAP, the basis of the stack, is clear. For simpler projects, REST may be an option, as simplicity is its main offer: just four methods applied to resources identified by URIs.

Google Maps API

Google has been offering an API to their map service since June 2005. It allows for an integration of maps into other Web pages and for customizations such as markers and overlays with data from other sources. The first major update so far to Version 2 of the Maps API occurred in April 2006.

The usage of the Google Maps API (which can be found at www.google.com/apis/maps) requires signing up for a key and includes a JavaScript file from Google. Strictly speaking, this is not necessary as one could build the necessary calls into any scripting language, yet the API is documented only via the provided JavaScript class. Requests to the API are only processed when a correct key is used and when the requesting site is the one that the key was registered for. The Google Maps API library consists of a set of JavaScript objects and event listeners. Objects, for example, represent a map, a marker, or a control. Listeners allow reacting to special events that are initiated by an object or by the user. Each map is represented by an instance of the GMap2 class. The constructor of a map receives the location within the HTML document, which is defined by a <div> element as an argument. Control buttons to set the location and zoom levels can be added to the map, yet GMap2 offers interfaces and classes that can override the default behavior.

The API offers a rich set of functionality to control visual aspects of a map. To mark special locations, GMarkers can be stuck on a map. Locations are represented by a GLatLng object that contains the respective latitude and longitude. An instance of GMarker is shown as an icon (GIcon) on the map, and it is possible to define various icons to represent different objects. GMarkers can contain a GInfoWindow that will appear by clicking on the marker or other events. In addition to markers, lines and polygons which can, for example, be used to represent driving directions can be added to a map.

Listing 3.3 shows how to create a map (the source code only shows the JavaScript part of the page) and how to add controls as well as a marker to

Large Map Control   **Map Type Control**

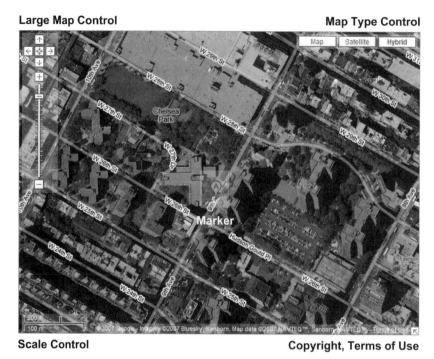

Scale Control   **Copyright, Terms of Use**

Figure 3.23 Hybrid view of a part of New York City.

the map. In particular, a map is centered on the coordinates of 40.75 latitude and −74 longitude, and has a marker in the center of the map. Figure 3.23 shows the result where the parts laid onto the map image are highlighted. In addition to the explicitly specified objects, there is scale info, the Google logo, and references to the licensers of the map content that is present on the map.

Listing 3.3: Producing a map with controls.

```
//test if the browser can display the map
if (GBrowserIsCompatible()) {
    //create the map and bind it to the div with the id "map"
    map = new GMap2(document.getElementById("map"));

    //define a point and center the map to it
    var point = new GLatLng(40.75, -74);
    map.setCenter(point, 16, G_HYBRID_MAP);

    //add controls to the map
    map.addControl(new GLargeMapControl());
    map.addControl(new GMapTypeControl());
    map.addControl(new GScaleControl());
```

```
//define a marker
var marker = new GMarker(point);

// Create text and display it in
// the info window when the marker is clicked.
var html = "Text within the InfoWindow";
GEvent.addListener(marker, 'click', function() {
        marker.openInfoWindowHtml(html, 100);
});
map.addOverlay(marker);
}
```

A standard map consists of three map types: map, satellite, and hybrid (showing a combination of the former two). The current type can be changed by using the map type control or by the setMapType method of the GMap2 object. It is possible to create a user's own map type and add it to the map. A type consists of an array of GTileLayers which are all shown in the map type at the same time. An example of a type with more than one layer is the standard "Hybrid" layer. Each tile layer may display its own copyright text at the bottom of the map and has to implement the getTileUrl method. This method expects a GPoint and the current zoom level as arguments and returns the Web address of a tile image which can be on one's own map server. A GPoint consists of two integer coordinates to locate a point within a coordinate system used by Google. So the server can either store all needed tiles according to the GPoint system or has to convert the GPoint data to GLatLng objects that contains geographical coordinates and then generate the image with this data. With this construct, it is possible to add new layers that contain more detailed images or images with a different content than the standard images of Google Maps.

A prerequisite to this approach is that it is necessary to build an entire map type of tiles that exactly fit in point of size and location, and it is not possible just to include an overlay on the map, for example to add a street map of a city where the data offered is of low quality. This can, however, be done with the unofficial extension TPhoto (gmaps.tommangan.us/tphoto.html), which allows adding pictures to a map by specifying their upper left and bottom right position. For doing this, images do not have to have the same size as the tiles; however, zooming does not work for these images.

The Google Maps API also offers some possibilities to ease asynchronous communication with one's own server and the handling of XML data. For example, function GDownloadUrl encapsulates the various different implementations of the XmlHttpRequest object and thus reduces coding effort. The methods of GXml and GXslt enable parsing of XML files into their DOM representation and subsequently working with the resulting DOM via XSLT.

In order to create new applications based on Google Maps, it is often necessary to have geo-coded data available, that is, data which maps address information to geographical coordinates and vice versa. In fact, when searching for a place via the Google Maps search bar, geo-coding is what takes place in the background. This functionality is available in the Google API via the `GClientGeocoder` object. Its function `getLatLng` can be used to retrieve the geographical location for an address asynchronously from the Google Maps servers. A second function `getLocations` returns the address information hierarchically structured with accuracy information, and the geographical coordinates.

When developing novel applications with an API from a service provider, it is important to understand the provider's terms and conditions, as they define the options a programmer has using the provided data and functionality. The Google Maps API Terms of Use (see www.google.com/apis/maps/terms.html) allows displaying Google map images on Web sites "that are generally accessible to consumers without charge." The images may only be used in the way they appear on the map, but may not be altered or distributed, nor may the Google Logo be altered or hidden. It must remain obvious that the site is not affiliated with Google. Google also reserves the rights to include advertising into map images in the future and to release new versions of the API. There is a corporate license available that takes away some of these conditions. As can be seen, these terms can have quite intricate consequences and therefore need to be kept in mind when creating mash-ups.

Developing mash-ups with Google Maps

On the technical side, developing new mash-ups requires enabling a server to be able to work together with the map data provided by Google Maps. In order to do this the server has to provide access to additional local or remote data sources. For this, WPCs can be used such as the ones we have seen in the Ajax example. What such data can be is up to the imagination of the developers, and we see some examples of existing mash-ups next.

The Google Maps API does not only enable putting a client's own data onto maps, but also mixing it or mashing it up with data from other sources. Google Maps can be used to create mash-ups with sites that have location-based data. A typical example is HousingMaps, which takes the classified real-estate ads from craigslist (see craigslist.org) and displays them on a map. To do so, it reads the RSS Feed of craigslist that provides a machine-readable version of the listings for each real-estate category (e.g., apartments, rooms, sublets, and so on.). Within the description of a particular real estate, it contains a link to the Web site of the announcement. This site contains tags with the street and city name of the real estate. HousingMaps then converts this address to its geographical coordinates and displays it on the map.

Other Web sites show news items, as can be seen in the screenshot shown in Figure 3.24. Markers are used to identify the place covered by the news item. A click on the marker reveals the headline and a link to the news page. Other projects mash-up weather forecasts with maps, and thus make them accessible much more intuitively (e.g., Weather Bonk). Google Maps might also be integrated into social networking Web sites such as MySpace. As we have explained, MySpace offers the possibility to invite friends and thus to build a "network of friends." As most members insert their personal data into MySpace, it would be quite easy to create a map showing where all friends are located. An idea quite similar has been implemented

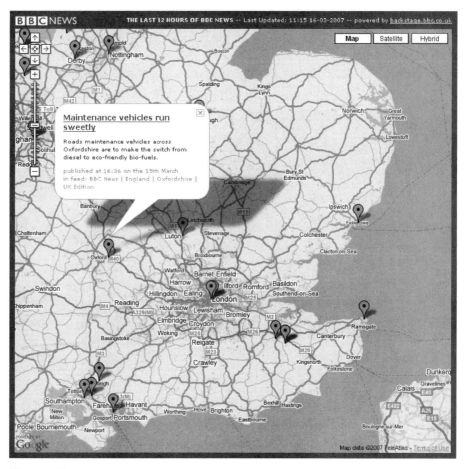

Figure 3.24 BBC news map.
Source: http://www.benedictoneill.com/content/newsmap/

at myspacemaps.info, which shows the locations of visitors to a MySpace account. Other usage scenarios for Google Maps include mobile applications: If shown on cell phones that can be located, a group of peers might meet just by localizing each other on a map. This idea has been implemented on plazes.com: Create a profile that can be linked to the big social networks and that is constantly updated with a user's location. These mash-ups mainly use the possibility to add markers to maps, in which they display additional information.

OnNYTurf offers a map that uses the option of adding an extra tile layer to a map in order to show all subway lines and stations in New York City. As seen in Figure 3.25, an additional button is present in the top right corner, which selects the subway mode of the map. The subway layer has its limitations: outside of the area covered by the subway it is empty with the map warning of "crazy ocean monsters" if one goes too far to the east, for example. Also, zooming out is only possible to some degree.

All these examples show the possibilities a programmer has for creating new services just by mashing-up data from existing Web sites. And next to maps, there are lots of other fields for mash-ups such as photo, video, shopping, mobile communication, and sports sites. Further details on Google Maps can be found in Gibson and Erle (2006) as well as in Purvis et al. (2006). There are many more mash-ups based on Google Maps: as of March 2007, ProgrammableWeb lists more than 900.

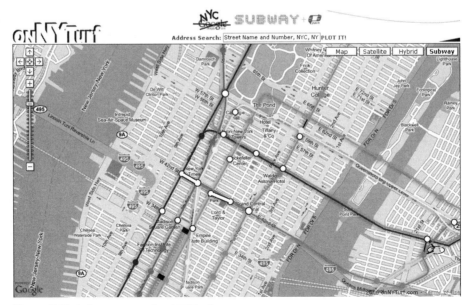

Figure 3.25 Subway map of onNYTurf.
Source: http://www.onNYTurf.com/subway/

Other examples of mash-ups: start page personalization

In Chapter 1, we mentioned portals and how they position themselves in the process of efficiently accessing information on the Web. Traditionally, the content on portals has been defined by its developers. It should not come as a surprise that with the arrival of mash-ups due to Web feeds, WPCs, and open APIs, the options for laying out a portal have dramatically increased. Instead of preselecting content that can go on a page once and for every user, it is now possible to let users decide what they want to see on their start page themselves. There has been a flood of new startups concerned with exactly this, including eskobo, Netvibes, Pageflakes, or Protopage. The major players such as Google, Microsoft, and Yahoo! have also redesigned their portals or extended their search pages and now allow users to select their content. While the big players produce content themselves and can use the portals as a way of distributing this content, the smaller pages heavily rely on mashing-up content from different sources.

Figure 3.26 shows a typical start page from Pageflakes. Most other start-page providers have similar looking pages. The main part of the page contains several so-called *widgets* (which are called "flakes" in Pageflakes). These widgets contain content from various sources. In our case, we have financial information, photos, blogs, news, a cartoon, and an event list. There are a

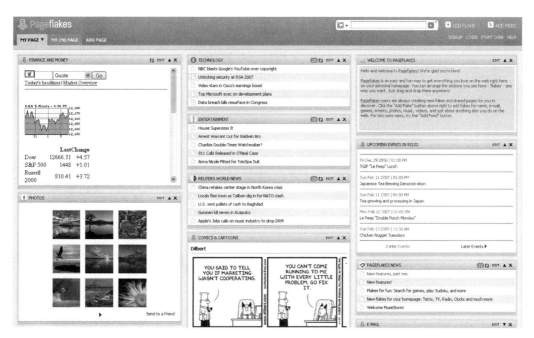

Figure 3.26 Pageflakes personalized start page.

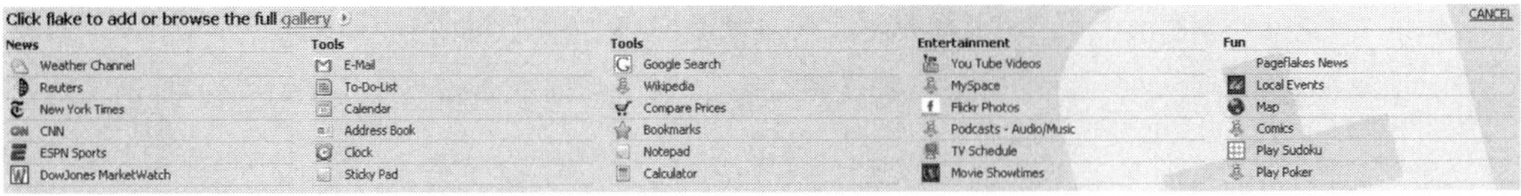

Figure 3.27 Some of the widgets available in Pageflakes.

lot more options like mailbox alerts, access to online disc space, or monitoring auctions. It is possible to reorder and resize widgets for which Ajax (as in the case of Pageflakes) or Flash is typically used. It is common to have tabs with which several start pages can be organized and search be made available. In Figure 3.26, these can be found at the top of the page.

The variety of possibilities for widgets of Pageflakes is shown in Figure 3.27. Again, other pages have similar offerings (e.g., iGoogle). One can see that many different sources are already available without further configuration. However, any Web feed can be included and only the address is needed to create a widget. Adding content from another source, for example, one which provides an open API is a matter of writing a new widget. Moreover, small single-purpose tools that do not integrate other sources such as to-do lists or notepads usually round up the available widgets.

It is important to note that the mash-ups that personalized portals provide are different in quality from the mash-ups we have seen with Google Maps, for example. The value of a start page is that it shows customized content on a single page. It does not, however, link to and thus integrate content from the different sources. Personalized start pages are faced with an increasing competition from *desktop widgets* (also referred to as *desktop gadgets*). These are offered for all popular operating systems, for example through *Dashboard* for OS X (see apple.com/macosx/features/dashboard), or as gadgets in Microsoft Vista (see microsoftgadgets.com). Environments to easily build new widgets, sometimes even without programming skills, such as Proto (see protosw.com) are also becoming available.

A lot of mash-ups are nowadays created by private people without commercial interest. The numbers of companies, such as the start-page projects mentioned earlier, that are building mash-ups is on the rise, nevertheless. These companies face the problem that by basing their services on the services of others, they become dependent on these other parties. Clearly, provider dependency is nothing new and not *per se* undesirable, but the dependence of these companies is very direct: Should the APIs change without notice, the mash-up probably breaks; should the base service become unreachable, the mash-up will not work anymore.

Problems can also be more subtle. The terms of service under which APIs are provided typically gives the provider the right to discontinue the service in the future or to disallow requests from sites where malicious use could be the reason for high traffic. Moreover, when mash-ups become popular, they face the problem that the provider of an API might find it interesting to provide the service the mash-up provided himself. These issues are in the same tone as what in Musser and O'Reilly (2007) is described as "for competitive advantage, establish a data strategy not just a product strategy." Mash-ups face the problem that they initially most likely do not have any data. Therefore they are so vulnerable to changes on the provider side. One strategy could be for mash-ups to create data through operation. Whereas the sources that they integrate only have the individual data, the mash-up provider may learn, through data mining, new facts during operations that could provide the base for "leveling the playing field."

As a final note on mash-ups at this point, we mention that the situation for mash-ups in companies is somewhat different from what we have just described. In a company, one can expect that there is general interest in increased and more efficient usage of data and of services. Mash-ups could be used as a way to leverage existing sources. Opportunistic behavior is less likely when mash-ups stay within a company. A lightweight integration of business IT-based on mash-ups (called by some the *Web-Oriented Architecture* or WOA, see blogs.zdnet.com/Hinchcliffe/?p=27) is seen as a likely candidate to replace the heavyweight approach of the Service-Oriented Architecture based on the Web services stack we saw in Chapter 2.

3.3 Tagging

Search engines before Google have often relied on meta-tags that the author of an HTML page would define to catalog or categorize that page. On-purpose manipulation of these tags has been used a lot to obtain higher ranks in search results. The use of meta-tags was therefore dropped by most search engines. Google was among those that presented radically new attempts to gather meta-information. As mentioned, they started interpreting the link structure of pages as meta-information, which resulted in a much better search engine. Manually created meta-tags are recently seeing a revival in the form of *tagging*: Users may attach any number of keywords to an object or a Web resource, which could be an entire Web site, a photo, or a link. This is meant to ease their storing of and searching through these objects. A major difference to the use of meta-tags within Web pages is that tags, although created by individuals, are frequently used within communities. Indeed, tags can be made available and hence visible to other users, so that when searching through the tags they may adopt them for their own use. This process is the basic creation mechanism for so-called *folksonomies*: collaboratively created open-ended labeling systems. They are called *folksonomies* in contrast to tax-onomies, which are generally based on rigid directories. The publication of tags or their sharing with others, which has been unknown for meta-tags, is also seen as an important form of *socialization* of user-generated content on the Web. Although the definition of tagging is as simple as we have just stated, the consequences of its use are manifold and powerful.

Flavors of tagging

Broad acknowledgment of tagging as a concept started only in 2004, and at the time of this writing, research on tagging is still in its infancy. It is never-theless worthwhile to look at various tagging flavors that can already be dis-tinguished in order to systematize our presentation. Marlow et al., (2006) report on key dimensions that define the way tags are created and used, not all of which are independent of each other. The dimensions span user-fac-ing as well as system-level characteristics, which all together determine the way a tagging system behaves. We present them here, as they allow us to characterize the examples we later look at:

- Object type: Any object that can be represented can be tagged. However, it is expected that the usage of tags differs significantly depending on the nature of an object.
- Source of material: When objects are available in a system, these objects can either be provided by users or by the system itself. An alternative is that resources outside the system (e.g., on the Web) are tagged.
- Tagging rights: The decision on who is able (or even encouraged) to add, edit, or delete tags is certain to affect the tags that occur and the patterns in which they occur. If there are restrictions, this is usually connected to the contributor: Either only he can tag, or he may be able to set permissions for others.
- Tagging support: Users may receive support when tagging objects. If the tagging rights allow several users to tag an object, already existing tags could be shown to them. Moreover, the system might make suggestions on which tags should be used for an object. Depending on which method is chosen, one can expect different developments in tag occurrences.
- Aggregation model: Under this dimension, one can essentially distin-guish between set-based and bag-based approaches. The former only allow a tag to be added to an object once, whereas in the latter case tags can be added more than once, which allows their frequency to be evaluated and used, say, for analysis purposes.
- Resource connectivity: Resources may be connected through other means than tags. Indeed, objects could be grouped together, or they

could link each other. It can be expected that such connected objects have more similar tags than unconnected ones.

- Social connectivity: This dimension refers to connections between the users of a system. The aspects worth looking into here are similar to those on resources connectivity.

Marlow et al. (2006) also mention different drivers of the motivation of users for creating tags. They identify two high-level reasons: There are *organizational* and *social* tags. The former can be subdivided into a personal and an intrapersonal form of organization. Users want to sort and find their own items, to be able to retrieve them in the future, and maybe share and want others to be able to use their scheme of organization as well. Social drivers for tagging include the attraction of attention, self presentation, opinion expression, and the creation of tags as a byproduct to play and competition.

In this section, we repeatedly see instances of the dimensions and drivers we just listed. First, we look at one of the most prominent services that supports tagging, the photo site Flickr. We then turn to ideas of socializing bookmarks, and will finally look into folksonomies.

We conclude our introduction to tagging by mentioning that it has received wide attention and many applications. For example, news sites such as that of German news magazine *Der Spiegel* (www.spiegel.de) have started to put it on their home page, in order to "socialize" the top news hits.

3.3.1 Flickr and tagging

In a nutshell, Flickr is a Web-based community for organizing and sharing photos. It was launched in February 2004 and has been and still is being developed by Ludicorp. Both Flickr and Ludicorp were acquired by Yahoo! in March 2005. Since its initial release, Flickr has become more and more popular among a growing community of Web users and has reached the 100-million photo mark in early 2006. It is described also in Bausch and Bumgardner (2006) or in Wilkinson (2007).

A comprehensive set of functions supports the organization and sharing of photos. Pictures can be uploaded though a Web interface or by sending them to a Flickr account via e-mail. There are also third-party desktop applications that make uploading more comfortable. Once uploaded, photos can be grouped into photo sets. Flickr allows a user to define privacy settings and to release photos under certain licenses. Photos always remain the property of a user. To provide more information about photos, one can add a description as well as identifying tags.

Together with del.icio.us, which we say more about in the following text, Flickr has introduced a new concept of categorizing content with user-defined keywords or *tags*. The creation activity is called *tagging*, and in contrast to defining a language based, for example, on XML or on XHTML, which is usually a *structured process*, tagging does not have a specific goal in the first place nor does it impose any restrictions on the choice of keywords. Rather than grouping photos into rigid categories, users can freely add chosen tags that allow for very flexible and natural associations. Tagging is a simple, yet powerful concept that is believed to have great potential as a foundation for future search algorithms and a Semantic Web; we elaborate on this aspect of tagging in Chapter 6 and outline its (potential) relationship to ontologies.

Because tags are publicly viewable, they are an important part of the social network represented by Flickr. Besides tagging, Flickr fosters community activities by offering numerous additional ways to get into contact with other participants, for example by writing comments on photos, by messaging, or by contributing to ongoing discussions. Users can distinguish and are encouraged to manage friends, contacts, and family members. People can share their interests in photo groups with specific topics.

Flickr offers several ways to access, publish, or manipulate data. While most users will use the Web interface to browse and view photos, pictures can also be published to blogs or Web feeds automatically. More elaborate applications can use the open API to provide additional functionality (see www.flickr.com/services/api).

Using tags with Flickr

Figure 3.28 shows a typical Flickr photo page. The photo itself is surrounded by (clockwise from top) its title, the upload date, and the uploader's name, more recent images from the uploader (called the *photostream*), groups the image has been added to, tags, additional information (such as license or date on which the photo was shot), and finally below the photo are a description and comments. All in all, there are three places where text information about an image can be placed by the author: title, description, and tags (or four if the comments are counted as well). Note that in Flickr, only the owner of a photo can add tags to it.

There are many aspects that make tags special. First, tags are treated separately in search. When search terms are entered into the Flickr search box, these terms are usually searched for in all text fields. However, it can be specified that only tags are to be used for search. To understand why this is helpful, we have to rethink why people use tags and what they use them for. One of the drivers for the use of tags is the organizational interest in finding content or sharing it with others. Let's take a look at the tags used in Figure 3.28, where three categories can be distinguished: information

Figure 3.28 Typical photo page on Flickr.
Source: http://www.flickr.com/photos/55368254@N00/379385491/
Reproduced with permission of Yahoo! Inc. © 2007 by Yahoo! Inc. YAHOO! and the YAHOO! logo are trademarks of Yahoo! Inc.
Photo used by permission from FXR - www.routhier.net

on *where* (Paris, 75001, France), *what* (Notre-Dame, Cathédrale), and *how* (Noir et Blanc, Black & White). Although these categories are not in any way encoded in the tags, they are obvious to a human user. Except for 75001, which is a zip code in Paris, all the other tags can be understood by any person understanding English (plus a bit of French). After having read these, without seeing the image, the content that can be expected is quite clear.

This is totally different for the title "Our Lady. . .". This title could also be a reasonable title for a photo of a woman, for example. The description in this case contains "Cathédrale Notre-Dame," which is equivalent to the tags on what can be seen on the picture. Often however, the description tells more than this. There are photos where the story behind the picture is explained, sometimes there are even poems attached to the image. The comments usually contain praises for the photographer on how good the photo is, or in the case of sad stories sympathy may be expressed in connection to an image.

There are techniques from artificial intelligence, such as natural language processing, that try to understand human language. One could argue that these could be used to extract meaning from the contents of title, description, and comments entries, in order to then provide the same benefits one has from tagging. This would, however, involve a number of complex steps that have to deal with the ambiguity of natural languages, which is present in its syntax, in word meanings, and in the intention of sentences or phrases. We present an alternative to natural language processing in Chapter 6 that is based on the notion of an *ontology*, yet that still requires quite a bit of effort in proper usage.

Tags, on the other hand, are much simpler to use and to understand. Two tags match only if they have the same string representation (this is not entirely true, since white spaces as well as special characters are removed from tags when searching). This makes the search for tags trivial, but it also makes the reason for an image being shown in the search on a specific tag absolutely clear. The most dramatic impact, however, is on the users: They are intuitively aware of the way that tags are used and use them accordingly. This does have its limitations: Among the tags above the author has used the two tags "noir et blanc" and "black & white" to *mean* the same. And someone searching for "cathedral" will not find this image, as this does not match the French equivalent "Cathédrale." We later look at the shortcoming of tag systems in more detail. It should be noted that there are also problems with tag spamming; just as we have already reported from search engines that used meta-tags to guide their indexers, people are (mis-) using tags to attract (undeserved) attention.

A final aspect we want to mention where tags are treated specially in Flickr is the structure of the Web site's URIs. It follows the REST principle and allows navigating the site very easily. For a start, let us look at some of the main addresses in the Flickr URI structure:

```
http://flickr.com/explore/
http://flickr.com/groups/
http://flickr.com/photos/
```

Explore contains photos that have been selected by a Flickr algorithm to be interesting, explained on www.flickr.com/explore/interesting/ as

There are lots of things that make a photo "interesting" (or not) in the Flickr. Where the clickthroughs are coming from; who comments on it and when; who marks it as a favorite; its tags and many more things which are constantly changing. Interestingness changes over time, as more and more fantastic photos and stories are added to Flickr.

With this, Flickr is using its rich data on the use of its site to add value to the stored photos. Remember that the photos are not the property of Flickr, the usage of data is, however!

Groups are a major way for supporting the social interaction on the site. Groups are controlled by administrators, who can make them private, by invitation, or public. Users can submit photos to groups. The members of a group can use a discussion board as an additional way of communicating.

The *photos* URI is the way to all photo resources on Flickr, and the *tags* subfolder is one way in which the photos are structurally accessible. Figure 3.29 shows the page www.flickr.com/explore/interesting/. The page shows so-called *tag clouds*: popular tags of all time, the last twenty-four hours, or the last week are shown, with the size of each tag indicating the frequency of its use. This offers a way for users to explore the available tags and the photos that these are attached to. *Exploration* is needed since there are so

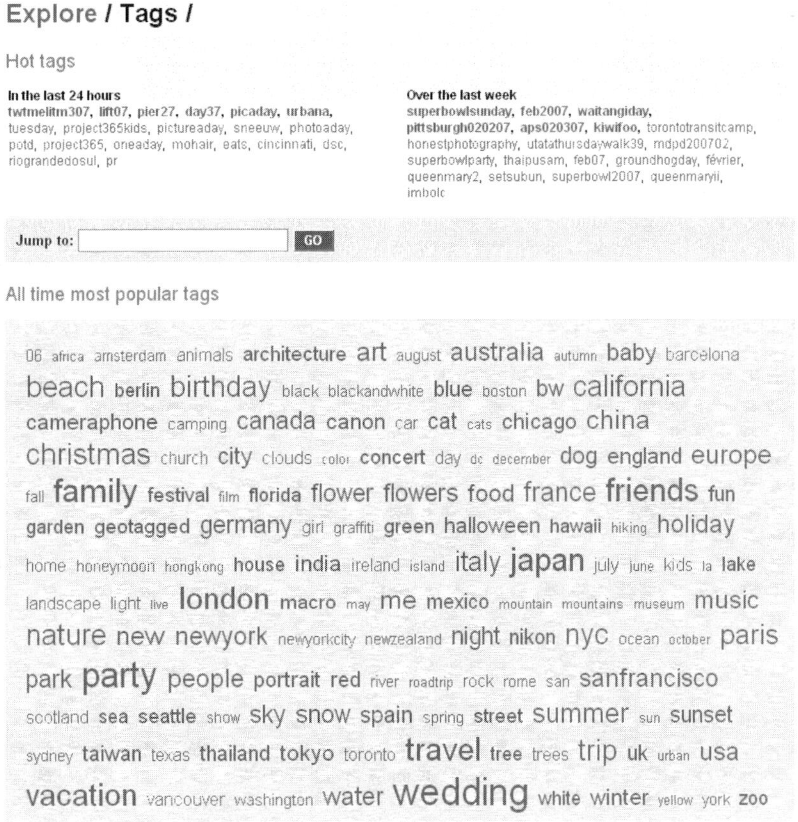

Explore / Tags /

Hot tags

In the last 24 hours
twtmelitm307, lift07, pier27, day37, picaday, urbana, tuesday, project365kids, pictureaday, sneeuw, photoaday, potd, project365, oneaday, mohair, eats, cincinnati, dsc, riograndedosul, pr

Over the last week
superbowlsunday, feb2007, waitangiday, pittsburgh020207, aps020307, kiwifoo, torontotransitcamp, honestphotography, utatathursdaywalk39, mdpd200702, superbowlparty, thaipusam, feb07, groundhogday, février, queenmary2, setsubun, superbowl2007, queenmaryii, imbolc

Jump to: [   ] GO

All time most popular tags

06 africa amsterdam animals **architecture** art august australia autumn baby barcelona beach berlin **birthday** black blackandwhite blue boston bw california cameraphone camping canada canon car cat cats chicago china christmas church city clouds color concert day dc december dog england europe fall **family** festival film florida flower flowers food france **friends** fun garden geotagged germany girl graffiti green halloween hawaii hiking holiday home honeymoon hongkong house india ireland island italy japan july june kids la lake landscape light live london macro may me mexico mountain mountains museum music nature new newyork newyorkcity newzealand night nikon nyc ocean october paris park party people portrait red river roadtrip rock rome san sanfrancisco scotland sea seattle show sky snow spain spring street summer sun sunset sydney taiwan texas thailand tokyo toronto travel tree trees trip uk urban usa vacation vancouver washington water wedding white winter yellow york zoo

Figure 3.29 Flickr tag cloud.
Source: http://www.flickr.com/photos/tags/

many tags in use that one cannot simply present a full list. Furthermore it allows a user to grub through the available resources and find something unexpected. Thus, intuitive ways to explore the tag space enable serendipity.

By clicking on any of the links in one of the tag clouds from Figure 3.29, a user can navigate to an address of the form:

```
http://flickr.com/photos/tags/<tag name>
```

This address contains the collection of all images that are tagged with the particular tag.

Tag clouds are just one of the possibilities to navigate through the multitude of tags that are used in Flickr. Other mechanisms use the simultaneous presence of tags to allow users to navigate through the tag space. Figure 3.30 shows the Flickr cluster exploration. Given a popular tag (e.g., one that is used on a lot of photos), clusters within these photos are created. The clusters are based on several tags that tend to be used together. The Flickr cluster mechanism creates four clusters, which, as can be seen, are not in any way exact, but which can sometimes differentiate quite well: For example, one can see from the sample photos that the clusters based on "birthday, cake, dinner" and "people, portrait, boy, man" contain very different kinds of photos.

There are also external applications created independently from Flickr that offer solutions to the question of how to explore that tag space. The

Figure 3.30 Flickr tag clusters.
Source: http://www.flickr.com/photos/tags/friends/clusters/

Flickr Related Tag Browser (see airtightinteractive.com/projects/related_tag_browser) shown in Figure 3.31 starts with a text field to enter a tag. It then presents some photos tagged with that keyword, which can be enlarged. Additional photos with the same tag can be reached by browsing through the paged results. To support exploration of the tag space, it displays a ring of tags which are selected on the basis that these are used in conjunction with the original tag. By clicking on one of them, new pictures are presented in the center, and a new ring of tags is created. *Tagnautica* (see quasimondo.com/tagnautica.php), shown in Figure 3.32, follows a similar approach, but it focuses even more on the tags. It also starts with one tag to which a ring of related tags is constructed. For each related tag the number of photos on Flickr is shown.

Mash-ups based on tags

Tags are meant for human use. Since there is no way to explicitly communicate *what* the person adding a tag had in mind or why the tag has been added, it is difficult to provide tags for machine use. An example for this

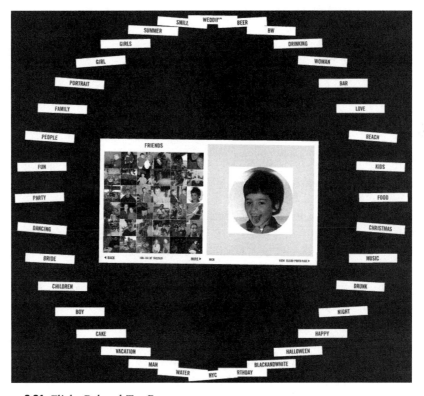

Figure 3.31 Flickr Related Tag Browser.
Source: http://www.airtightinteractive.com/projects/related_tag_browser

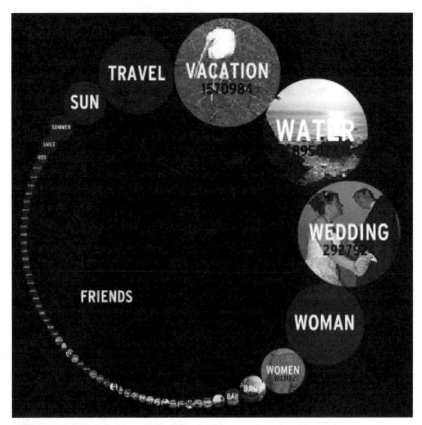

Figure 3.32 Tagnautica.
Source: http://www.quasimondo.com/tagnautica.php

problem can be seen in Figure 3.29: Quite a number of tags in the cloud refer to geographic locations (e.g., *australia, berlin, california, london, newyork*, also present as *newyorkcity* and *nyc*). In order to be able to use these tags for deriving the geographic locations of photos, one would need to ensure that all of these tags indeed have the same semantics (i.e., that the photo has been shot at the particular location mentioned in the tag). This is further complicated by the fact that the tags refer to very different levels of a geographic hierarchy: Some refer to countries, others to states, others to cities. Finally, the obvious ambiguity in writing the name of a place would need to be resolved. As a consequence, it would seem difficult to create mash-ups involving tags, since they connect services based on programs, and tags processing appears difficult to automate.

Nevertheless, there are already various attempts to use tags in and for mash-ups, and since there are several that try to do this for map mash-ups, we will stick with our previous example. The services in the category

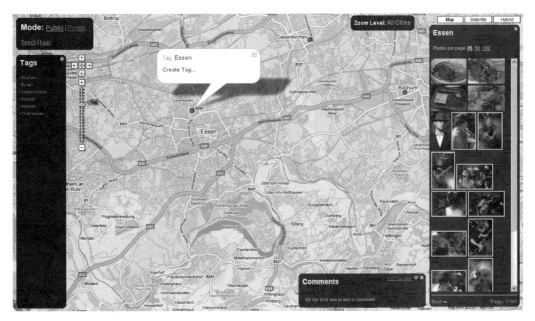

Figure 3.33 The city of Essen in Fotoland.
Source: http://fotoland.us

include Trippermap (see flickrmap.com), Mappr! (see mappr.com), and Virtual Places (see apps.nikhilk.net/VirtualPlaces). The *Fotoland* service (see fotoland.us) mashes up photos from Flickr with Google Maps. To determine the location of a photo, this service utilizes a database of tag names which are linked to geographic coordinates. For example, in Figure 3.33, the map is centered on the German city of Essen. The tag "Essen" has been placed relatively close to the city center. On the right side of the figure one can now see photos that are tagged with "Essen." When checking the tags the pictures shown have associated with them, it turns out that a lot of them have tags like "Europe, Germany, Essen"; in other words, the tags were really intended to be interpreted as tags specifying the location of the photo. However, the food items in the top of the list, while also sharing the three tags mentioned above, have "Munich" and "food" as additional tags. This indicates that the city in which the photos were taken is actually Munich, and "Essen" was just used as a tag because it is the German translation of the word *food*.

This example shows that extracting the geographic location by assuming that tags are used as place names can yield false positives. In general, there will be false negatives as well: When a tag is spelling a place differently (e.g., as an abbreviation), the photos will not show up. It is important to say that although this is true, it nevertheless makes sense to try this approach: Even

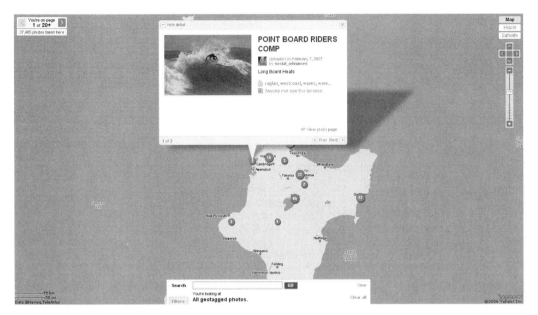

Figure 3.34 Flickr map.
Source: http://www.flickr.com/map
Reproduced with permission of Yahoo! Inc. © 2007 by Yahoo! Inc. YAHOO! and the YAHOO!
logo are trademarks of Yahoo! Inc.

for a city with an ambiguous city name such as Essen, numerous pictures are correctly shown!

Flickr itself offers a map as a service. It does not try to interpret tags as such, however. It gives users a map interface to Yahoo! Maps, which allows placing photos on a map by dragging them onto the desired location. Figure 3.34 shows such a map. Bubbles on the map indicate where there are photos already with the size of the bubble indicating the number of images.

For users who have tagged their photos with geographic coordinates, an import is possible. There are three tags needed to do this (see www.flickr.com/account/geo/import):

1. `geotagged`,
2. `geo:lat=` followed by a valid latitude value in decimal format, and
3. `geo:long=` or `geo:lon=` followed by a valid longitude value in decimal format.

This is a convention frequently used for *geotagged* photos (i.e., resources tagged with geographic information). Flickr uses this information to automatically put the photos on the map and save this information as additional information, separated from the tags. This is a step towards making tags *structured*; for this to work tags obviously cannot be chosen freely anymore. Flickr calls these tags *machine tags*, as they can be securely interpreted by an

Figure 3.35 Mash-up based on tags: "Spell with Flickr."
Source: http://metaatem.net/words/

algorithm if always used as intended. This is why machine or structured tags are, in our view, an important step in the direction of the Semantic Web.

As a final example for a use of tags in a mash-up, we mention *Spell with Flickr* (see metaatem.net/words/). This application spells out words one can enter into a text field with images from Flickr. Figure 3.35 shows the word "mash-up" spelled out using images from the Flickr database. The application downloads for each letter of a given word a random photo from Flickr that is tagged with that particular letter. However, since single letters will hardly be used as tags, the actual trick is to refer to a Flickr group named "One Letter" (see www.flickr.com/groups/oneletter), which allows photos to be added only when they show a letter. Photos that do not fulfill this requirement are deleted from the group on a regular basis. The script of Spell with Flickr therefore also checks that the photo has been added to this group, thus ensuring that the words are readable. This can be seen as another way of ensuring that tags have well-defined semantics: The combination of tag letter and group membership leads to high-quality metadata, i.e., data about the data. This is one way of adding semantics to syntactic structure by employing the wisdom of people, an issue we return to in Chapter 6.

3.3.2 Social bookmarking

Social software introduces a new dimension to searching and other applications on the Web, for example by allowing users to add personal search logic to machine-based algorithms. A search result that is "good" from an individual's perspective is not necessarily the Web site ranked highest or linked to most often, as traditional search algorithms may make you believe. Rather, it is the site other users have considered useful or relevant to the topic at hand before. This section elaborates on the features of *social bookmarking services* and introduces two specific such services, del.icio.us and Yahoo!'s MyWeb 2.0. As shown next, social bookmarking can have an interesting impact on search.

A large number of social bookmarking services have evolved over the past few years. Both *del.icio.us* and Yahoo!'s *MyWeb 2.0* are such Web services where users can save the bookmarks they consider interesting and classify their content by means of user-created tags. Traditional search algorithms, which do not employ user-generated metadata to rank their search, can be said to base their search results on the anonymous mass of Internet users and content providers. In contrast to this, basing a search on explicitly created metadata and relations within the communities of social bookmarking services, one can build searches that are guided by a person's social contacts' judgment.

Technically, the most significant differences in the variety of social bookmarking services relate to the distinct handling of tags on the one hand, and to the different community and bookmark visibility concepts on the other. Generally, RSS feeds are available for the different sites. The import of existing bookmarks is possible, while browser support varies from one service to the next, and *bookmarklets*, respectively, toolbars, are offered in order to simplify adding a link.

Launched in 2003, del.icio.us is said to have been the first considerable Web service integrating the combination of social bookmarking and tagging. Yahoo! succeeded with a social bookmarking service in 2005, before acquiring del.icio. us later the same year. Yet both services have continued to run separately since. In order to develop a deeper understanding of the Web services and their relevance as Web 2.0 applications, del.icio.us and Yahoo!'s MyWeb 2.0 will be individually introduced and the most significant functionality identified next.

del.icio.us

Web service del.icio.us (the name is actually the URL, see del.icio.us), developed by Joshua Schachter, came online in late 2003; see O'Connor (2007) or Orchard (2006) for detailed programming introductions. According to Schachter, the motivation for the development of del.icio.us originated from his personal need for help in managing large amounts of collected bookmarks. The "about" section of the del.icio.us site captures its very philosophy in the catchy slogan "del.icio.us is a collection of favorites – yours and everyone else's." The service is generally open to anyone, allowing users to browse an entire range of saved bookmarks. However, the use of the more powerful managing tools for bookmarks requires a user to register; yet registration is kept at a minimal level of personal data. The user base has grown steadily ever since the service's initialization and was estimated around 300,000 when acquired by Yahoo!.

The functionality offered by del.icio.us is exclusively about bookmarks. Reduced to its underlying concepts, none of them is revolutionary, yet the

description	folksonomies edit / delete
notes	fun to read, yet grasps the concept behind social bookmarking services
tags, number of sharing users, date	to del.icio.us web2.0 folksonomy ... saved by 11 other people ... on april 10

Figure 3.36 Metadata on a del.icio.us bookmark.

combination was a novelty when first developed. Del.icio.us' social book-marking strategy can be broken down into two generic elements: *bookmarks* (i.e., Web addresses representing Web sites users consider worthwhile), and *metadata* (i.e., data on the bookmark data).

This metadata is what makes del.icio.us a powerful Web service. Overall, it can be classified into user-created metadata and systemic metadata, with an emphasis on the former. At the lowest level, the metadata related to a bookmark merely comprises the three attributes *description*, *notes*, and *tags*. Together with the systemic metadata, which, for example, consists of the number of other users sharing a specific bookmark and the date a user saved it to his personal bookmarks, the user-created metadata is displayed as the representation of a bookmark, as shown in Figure 3.36.

While both the metadata description and the metadata notes are informative and searchable data, there is a much broader concept behind the metadata in form of tags. First, when adding or saving a bookmark, tags are easy to handle as they are space separated, and both word prediction and choice-by-click functionality is supported for previously allocated tags. Note that this can be characterized as being viewable and suggested tagging support. Second, tags are the most important tool for managing personal bookmarks. For this purpose – in addition to a number of tag display options – each tag can be arranged in one of several *bundles*, enabling users to add personal logic to the composition of tags. Finally, tags form the crucial element for browsing and searching bookmarks, elaborated upon in the following subsection. For example, the support of structured tags such as media or file types (e.g., `system:media:[video|audio|document|image]`) lays the foundation for complex search potential. We refrain from going into detail and postpone the further discussion of structured tags to Chapter 6 on the Semantic Web.

The key functionality of del.icio.us can be best explored by means of the links integrated in del.icio.us. The front page, which can be seen in Figure 3.37, presents the hotlist – a list of pages currently added a lot. The "recent page" offers a collection of a list of most recently shared bookmarks, aligned by time elapsed since being shared, as well as the top seven most popular tags, featuring four bookmarks for each. Page "popular" has a similar approach, displaying the day's most popular items in accordance with the number of recent shares. Whereas the two previous sites are generally accessible, the "your bookmarks" link leads to those bookmarks saved by a registered user, and to corresponding

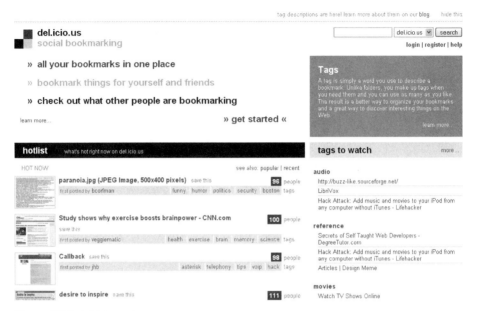

Figure 3.37 del.icio.us home page.

search and tag-focused management functionalities. Logically preceding the managing of bookmarks, the "post" page enables a user to save a bookmark.

In addition, del.icio.us provides another interesting concept for exploring bookmarks shared by other people. It is implemented within the links "inbox" and "links for you," taking into consideration the user name as systemic metadata on top of the concept of tagging, and thereby extending the power of search. The inbox, for example, contains the results of an individual user's subscription, empowering her or him to subscribe to bookmarks by tag and optionally user name. This is particularly useful in order to track all sites related to a certain topic (i.e., tag combination) shared by a particular user who appears to be an expert on that specific field. *Links for you* displays all those bookmarks that other users have designated to an individual user by means of assigning a tag `for:USERNAME`.

The concept of a user name-related search is additionally reflected in the structure of the human readable del.icio.us URLs, allowing direct access to another user's bookmarks by means of the site address `http://del.icio.us/<user name>/<tag name>`. Also, instead of a concrete user name, "recent," "popular," or "tag" can be used, resulting in the most recent, most popular, or all bookmarks holding specific tags. Similarly, other user's inboxes can be accessed, empowering to explore who is watching whom and to identify individuals who are interesting in terms of similar interests, the quality of their data and the connectedness of their community.

Yahoo! MyWeb

A Web service vastly equivalent to del.icio.us has been developed by Yahoo! under the name *MyWeb* (see myweb.yahoo.com) and was launched in April 2005. It has been integrated into the personal communication portal Yahoo! 360° under the motto "Search, with a little help from your friends." MyWeb enables "users to search the knowledge and expertise of their friends and community." Building and accessing the community requires non-Yahoo! users to sign up and create a Yahoo! ID, which implies the provision of personal information. Due to this crossover with users of other Yahoo! services, the number of MyWeb users is difficult to quantify. However, one year after its launch, the number of referenced sites already exceeded 1 million, supported by more than 180,000 tags.

In June 2005, David Ku and Eckart Walther from Yahoo! Search identified the key concepts behind the MyWeb social search service, outlining the following five main ideas (see ysearchblog.com/archives/000130.html):

- The trusted Web: MyWeb enables a user to build a community by inviting friends or importing existing contacts from other Yahoo! Web services.
- Personalized search: Yahoo's MyRank search technology is incorporated, basing search results on the shared knowledge of the personal community.
- Control over what is shared and with whom: Three different levels of visibility can be assigned to stored bookmarks.
- Structured tagging: In additional to tagging in general, structured tags such as "geo:[location]" – which we already know from Flickr are supported – allow complex search results (e.g., including maps to locations to a Web page).
- Open APIs: MyWeb's use of open APIs lays the foundation for the development of new applications based on the Web service.

The body of the MyWeb home page incorporates the key concept behind the service. It is separated into the areas "My Saved Pages," "My Contacts' Pages," and "Everyone's Pages," showing three bookmarks for each category and representing the three degrees of separation for sharing data. Consequently, the visibility of bookmarks can be restricted to personal usage only, access granted to certain groups of contacts or stored pages can be made available unrestrictedly. This concept of access levels, enabling to construct interest and target groups and to share links purposefully with friends and familiar people, dominates the entire logic of the Web service and makes it stand out from other social bookmarking services. The specific

title
number of sharing users
note
tags
access level
cached copy

Koranteng's Toli: Frisson de Folksonomie
Shared by: Me - Details - Edit
Note: **fun to read, yet grasps the idea behind social bookmarking services**
Tags: del.icio.us, folksonomy, web2.0
Access: Everyone
http://koranteng.blogspot.com/2.../04/frisson-de-folksonomie.html - My cached copy

Figure 3.38 Metadata on a Yahoo! MyWeb 2.0 bookmark.

access level forms part of the metadata to a bookmark, originally defined
when stored to MyWeb and edited whenever necessary.

Apart from the access level, common user defined metadata are *url*, *title*,
note, and *tags*. *Suggestion* is supported for tags by means of an interactive
drop-down menu. Noticeably, tags are comma-separated, allowing com-
pound words such as "MyWeb" to form tags, rather than necessitating a
convention for the handling of those (see Figure 3.38).

Another distinct feature in the context of storing a Web page is the possibility to choose saving a cached copy rather than having to face nonper-
sistent content or the loss of a page due to removal. This concept of caching
proves to be particularly powerful when keeping a history or backup of
changing sites (e.g., synchronizing a personal blog on a daily basis).

Beyond the main page, the MyWeb functionality is provided via the three
tabs "Pages," "Tags," and "Contacts," where both Pages and Tags can be viewed
at the different levels of either personal, contacts' or everyone's bookmarks,
respectively tags. Pages (i.e., the collection of bookmarks) can be filtered by
one or several tags, whereby search results can be gradually narrowed down.
In order to provide this filter function, tags – assigned personally, community-wide, or globally – are listed together with their number of occurrences.
The Tags site offers the collection of tags – again at the three different levels
– supporting a tag cloud as well as sorting by name, date, and popularity.
However, this site is limited to an informative character rather than enabling
the organization of tags. For example, tags cannot be predefined into bundles of tags, which would significantly ease the accomplishment of reoccur-
ring searches.

Finally, the Contacts site combines the functionality to invite and manage
contacts. While formerly adding a user as a contact required knowing them
earlier and involved a complex routine of mutual agreements, the MyWeb
community concept was modified to be less restrictive. A user can add
another user he deems interesting at any time for browsing publicly shared
bookmarks or to his contacts' contact lists. For the purpose of sharing sites,
a contact can optionally be categorized into "family" or "friends," which
in turn can be relabeled individually. A "contacts in reverse" link informs
about any other user who has added a particular user as a contact. Once

added and, if applicable, grouped, the main feature in the context of contacts is browsing their pages, tags, and contacts. Ultimately, there also is an indirect denotation to the community, impacting a user's search results in the course of Yahoo!'s MyRank personal search technology.

Generally, bookmarks can be found by tag, title, note as well as by page content. Yet searching is not restricted to MyWeb, but alternatively the entire Web can be searched. Integrating the general Yahoo! search into the Web service, a single click plus entering the site's metadata is sufficient for saving any search result as a bookmark to MyWeb. This clearly is a convenience as opposed to isolated social bookmarking services.

3.3.3 Folksonomies

All three services we have discussed (i.e., Flickr, del.icio.us, and Yahoo! MyWeb) are based on the concept of *folksonomic* tagging, with del.icio.us being one of the most commonly referenced example for folksonomies. The term "folksonomy" was originally coined by Thomas Vander Wal, blending together the words "folks" and "taxonomy" and thereby expressing the impact of people (folks) on classification (the Greek word *taxis* stands for *classification*), respectively its management (the Greek word *nomia* means *management*). We refer the reader to his Web site's *Off the Top* category for his original as well as more recent statements on this term and topic; see www.vanderwal.net/random/index.php. A classification is generally understood as the result of classifying within a predefined, hierarchical system, fundamentally disagreeing with the nonhierarchic and nonexclusive approach of a folksonomy, which is why the use of the term in this context is discussed controversially. The neologism is also defined as "user-generated classification, emerging through bottom-up consensus" (see agwright.com/blog/archives/000900.html) and is prominent for its "socially created, typically flat name-spaces" (see many.corante.com/archives/2004/08/25/folksonomy.php).

Breaking down these definitions, folksonomies first of all are about *classification*, therefore they are about metadata. Generally, three classes of metadata can be differentiated: first, professionally created metadata, typically a catalog compiled by a group of professionals; second, author-created metadata which refers to people describing self-created documents; and third, user-created metadata assigned by any user of a document and typically shared throughout a community. A folksonomy avails itself of the third, admitting an *unrestricted vocabulary* for tagging objects.

Moreover, folksonomies are attributed *a bottom-up consensus* and *socially created* due to their "democratic approach, [. . .] [avoiding] many of the ethical and political concerns of top-down, centrally imposed systems" (see davidsturtz.com/drexel/622/communal-categorization-the-folksonomy. html). They essentially characterize a consensus which is obtained due to the observation that, despite the use of an uncontrolled vocabulary, a system of largely agreed upon terms evolves from collaborative tagging, which even coexists next to personal and minority categories.

Finally, a *flat name-space* is another defining characteristic for a folksonomy, causing it to develop into a nonhierarchical and nonexclusive collection of tags. This concept exploits the general perception that hierarchies are both subjective in their structure and expensive in terms of the time necessary to build and maintain. An article on Linux for PCs, for example, would be classified as *PC* within a *Linux* folder by one individual, while the perception of others is that it is about *Linux* within a *PC* context. Consequently, the idea is to strip labels from their inter-relational logic and solely assign them at a unique and equal level.

We note that folksonomies, although having been characterized as bottom-up, socially created, and nonhierarchical, also face several limitations. Generally, these can be grouped around the three linguistic constructs of *homonyms*, *polysemes*, and *synonyms*, as discussed next.

Similarly to a word that may have different meanings, a tag may, too. Homonymous tags (i.e., syntactically equal tags with distinct meanings) directly affect search results, as they do not filter correctly but combine all results relevant to the superset of different connotations. For example tag *apple* produces sites relating to Apple Computer, Apple Records, or simply the fruit itself. Or take the example from earlier: "Essen" as both the name of a city in Germany as well as the German word for eating or a meal. Similarly, acronyms (e.g., "SOAP" for Simple Object Access Protocol) are subject to the risk of mixing together completely different ideas in the same tag (soap in this example). These ambiguities can largely be tackled by including additional, univocal tags when searching; polysemes, however, – describing terms with different, but closely related meanings – present a greater hurdle. Synonyms, on the other hand, refer to different terms with identical meaning and therefore being usable interchangeably, tamper search results by artificially narrowing them. Continuing the apple example, browsing for *apple* in the context of computers will deprive users from any page others have, for whatever reason, tagged with *mac* or *macintosh*. The *apple* example further points to related problems arising from singular versus plural forms of substantives. Issues linked to case sensitivity or the handling of terms consisting of multiple words complement the picture of challenges faced by a folksonomy as opposed to a controlled vocabulary.

Folksonomies represent an important development in the direction of creating a common understanding, agreement, and maybe even trust within communities on the Web. They essentially are formed in a bottom-up fashion, as it is hardly known from the very beginning what exactly a folksonomy will consist of. As we discuss in Chapter 6, this is in remarkable contrast to *ontologies*, which have become popular in the context of the Semantic Web and which typically undergo a stringent design process prior to their publication and usage. However, the two concepts may also be pivotal in the attempt to bring the Semantic Web and Web 2.0 developments closer together.

3.4 Summary

What we have seen in this chapter are the three main technical mechanisms that characterize Web 2.0: RIAs, mash-ups, and tagging. In some way, all three increase the options and possibilities Web users have in delivering and accessing information.

RIAs directly impact what a Web site can do. New uses of Web pages are possible since the interfaces allow more *functionality* to be efficiently provided. This enables applications to be migrated to the Web. Yet, also, Web pages that still serve their original purpose can benefit from RIA concepts and now deliver their content more economically. The consequence of an increased need for "Web software development" is something we look at in Chapter 4.

Mash-ups allow for applications that make better use of the information accessible on the Web. APIs explicitly allow the reuse of functionality and data with an emphasis often on *data*, and provide access mechanisms that enable (syntactic) data integration. Several forms of integration have been seen in this chapter: Simple textual inclusion is enabled by Web feeds, while the interleaving of complex data structures is supported by WPCs. The general hope that information sources will become better integrated is fast turning into reality for mapping, and is disseminating and spreading into other fields.

Finally, tagging is by no means Web specific, but on the Web can create folksonomies if implemented appropriately. Folksonomies then benefit from network effects: They grow evolutionary and are shaped by the *social* interaction of users adding content and linking this content to keywords. This supports *associative* data exploration based on those keywords that are commonly used together. Whether and how folksonomies can evolve into agreed-upon, common vocabularies remains to be seen. This discussion continues in Chapter 6.

Based on what each of the three mechanisms discussed in the chapter emphasizes, it is near at hand to align them to the three dimensions of functionality, data, and socialization we already introduced at the end of Chapter 1 as follows:

RIA $\rightarrow$ increased functionality
Mash-ups $\rightarrow$ better data usage
Tagging $\rightarrow$ more social interaction

While this association is generally valid, we have seen in the course of this chapter that there is more to these concepts. As RIAs transform off-line to online applications, data moves with the application and goes online, too. This leads to more data becoming available online, with increased possibilities for better uses of that data. In the course of mash-up creation, interaction has to be increased. Developers bind their services together for long-term and lasting relationships. In order for this to work, there needs to be communication. Lastly, while tagging is an important way to allow content to be structured, ordered, and evaluated by users, it again produces more data. Tags, tag evolution, and usage data can be valuable input for new services.

Sample Frameworks for Web Application Development

This chapter sheds some light on the question of "how to." We have seen in Chapter 2 what Ajax programming looks like when there is no support through programming libraries or the like. In this chapter, programming frameworks will be presented that are intended to help Web developers to efficiently bring new sites and new functionalities to life. Before we do so, we briefly discuss design and development principles that underlie the development of Web applications in Section 4.1. While these are mostly standard and generally applicable, developing software for the Web comes with some specialties we cover here.

The number of frameworks that support the development of Rich Internet Applications has exploded over the last year. Among the available implementation languages for RIAs, Ajax has by far had the most popularity, only counting the number of frameworks that have sprung up to claim they are "Ajax frameworks." The tools in this group can be classified into client-side and server-side frameworks, where the former are usually just JavaScript files that can be downloaded by the user and to which the Web application makes references. The range in this category starts with simple wrappers of the XMLHttpRequest (XHR) and goes up to full-fledged, object-oriented JavaScript libraries attending many programming needs. Server-side frameworks give Ajax support to various programming languages such as Java, DotNet, C++, PHP, and Ruby. A wide range of products has been cataloged on www.ajaxpatterns.org during 2006. Indeed, as of December 2006, the site lists more than 150 frameworks. In this chapter, we just look at one sample framework for each of the client-side and the server-side groups.

We use the Kabuki Ajax Toolkit as an example for client-side frameworks in Section 4.2; Kabuki offers an XHR wrapper, support for events, network communication, SOAP, cookies, and visual interfaces with drag and drop functionality. As an example for server-side frameworks, we show in Section 4.3 how Web development is conducted with Ruby on Rails. The interest in this framework has skyrocketed since it allows rapid prototyping and takes away a lot of the pains of developing for the Web.

One reason for the popularity of Ajax is its seamless integration with the current generation of Internet browsers. There is no need to install additional software since all that is needed is offered by standard installations on virtually all operating systems. However, there are browsers that do not support JavaScript, such as the text-only browser Lynx (lynx.isc.org). Other users have JavaScript turned off or their firewalls are blocking it. Statistics indicate that about 94 percent of users can run JavaScript (see www.w3schools.com/browsers/browser_stats.asp). As a drawback, Ajax does not support playing rich media contents such as audio or video. Applications that want to use these can nevertheless be built using Ajax, but need to resort to other technologies to handle media contents.

The popularity of Ajax sometimes seems to conceal that there are alternatives to Ajax that have in fact been around for quite a while already. Adobe Flash has been available for several years, but under the name Macromedia Flash for most of the time, and offers excellent support for rich media and animation; Java Web Start offers the execution of Java applications in the browser. These and other alternatives, however, share one drawback in that they require extensions to be installed in the browser to support their execution. This may not only limit their respective user groups, as not all extensions are available for all operating systems, but it also interferes heavily with the structure of the Web (e.g., by disallowing hyperlinks and granular addressability). We nevertheless look at one example from this category as well, namely OpenLaszlo, in Section 4.4. This suite has been released under an Open-Source license. The project is interesting as it is now heading towards supporting multiple deployment platforms. It has started with Flash, and is now also supporting Ajax and working on more target implementations as well.

4.1 Development methodologies

In this section, we briefly discuss how application development for Web 2.0 fits into the overall picture of software development.

Traditional software development methodologies

A common distinction in design tasks (e.g., database design, information system design, process design) is between a *model*, such as the Entity-Relationship model, the *Unified Modeling Language* UML, or state charts, and a *methodology* for its application. Regarding the latter, there is typically a distinction between *top-down* design (i.e., starting from a general level and specializing as far as necessary) and *bottom-up* design (i.e., starting from components and generalizing them as far as necessary). Methodologies typically employ one or – in the case of UML, several models – to structure the results of the various steps that are carried out. To a certain extent, methodologies favor certain models over others. The Unified Process, for example, heavily relies on UML (see www.uml.org), which incorporates several diagrams such as for use cases, components, classes, or activities.

The oldest approach to software development methodologies is said to be the *Waterfall* method (Royce, 1970). It employs a top-down approach, starting with the *requirements analysis*. This step identifies the wishes and requirements of the customer which, as simple as it may sound, is of greatest importance as it codifies what actions need to be carried out in the subsequent steps. With the requirements available, the software under development and a precise description of what it is supposed to do can be specified. When a system interacts with other systems, it is especially important that interface definitions are precisely specified and remain stable, so that the codevelopment of system components and their successful interconnection are enabled. Dealing with how a specification is transformed into a running system, a software *architecture* defines what the coarse structure of the software will look like. This may include defining layers or distribution scenarios. The *implementation* takes the architecture and transforms it into running code, and for that it has to fill in the details not covered by the architecture. After the code has been written, it has to be *tested*. Starting with the testing of smaller parts, such as individual classes possibly performed by the respective programmer, testing goes all the way up to testing the entire system working in a realistic test environment. In this process the last step of the development can be seen in the *deployment* of the system, after which further processes ensure that the system is maintained.

It has to be noted that Royce never proposed a purely linear walk through these steps, but was already aware that there will be loops in the process, which are needed in order to be able to return to earlier steps once errors, contradictions, or omissions in later ones are encountered. This, ultimately, leads to an iterative take on the software development process, where steps similar to what we just described are repeatedly gone through. A popular iterative approach is the *Unified Process* (Jacobson et al., 1999), which in addition blurs the sequentiality of the steps of the process by proposing them to be executed in parallel. Milestones then take over the role from the distinct steps for capturing the state of the development process.

Agile software development

The software development methodology and its variations we have described have been criticized for the overhead that they bring to a project. It is inherent to all of them that documentation has to be created that contains the outputs of the different steps (e.g., the specifications written or the diagrams created) which, at the same time, are input to subsequent steps. Moreover, they have been criticized for their assumptions of externals as well. For a software project, it is often not the case that the entire program can be prespecified by the customer, as his or her demands adapt with the ripening of the product.

Consequently, software development methodologies have been created that try to circumvent the problems of the former ones. Generally speaking, these try to be more lightweight on what has to be present at the beginning and during development. *Extreme Programming* (XP) is one such methodology, which centers around the values of simplicity, communication, feedback, and courage as shown with the relevant principles in Figure 4.1. We do not want to go into the details of every value or principle here, but highlight a few of them only. The value of simplicity aims at the simplest possible solution for a problem at hand. Feedback refers to feedback among all participating persons, including the customer. Developers should be courageous in their action and communicate often and intensively with all others involved in the team. The principles tie these rather abstract values to actionable practices. For example, XP's take on communication leads to three principles, namely *on-site customer* demanding that the communication between programmer and customer is to be very intense, with the customer somehow being part of the development team, *pair programming* requiring two programmers engaging in team work on one computer, providing instant review of every line of code to each other, and finally *coding standards* that everyone adheres to. To learn more about how XP can be implemented in practice, refer to Jeffries et al. (2001).

There are other methods closely related to XP, which can all be subsumed under the term of *agile software development*. This name was sparked by a group of prominent figures from the community who has published the

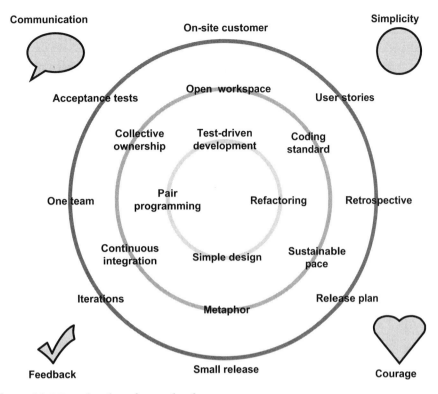

Figure 4.1 XP and agile software development concerns.
Source: http://uk.builder.com/i/b/illo/diagrams/agile-chart.gif

Manifesto for Agile Software Development (see www.agilemanifesto.org/), whose new core values are:

- *Individuals and interactions* over processes and tools
- *Working software* over comprehensive documentation
- *Customer collaboration* over contract negotiation
- *Responding to change* over following a plan.

One can see that the items on the right of this list can be repeatedly found in the traditional development methodologies we discussed. The manifesto, however, does not completely discard these, since it says "while there is value in the items on the right, we value the items on the left more."

Web development today

It has been shown how the general methodologies for software development can be applied to the special case of Web application development in Kappel et al. (2006). RIAs are just a special case of Web applications, so that methodologies and their models such as use case diagrams, class and interaction diagrams, and such can be applied here as well. We indicate in this section that there is a tendency among the developers of Web 2.0 applications to follow the agile approach more.

In his blog entry, "What is Web 2.0?" (see www.oreillynet.com/pub/a/oreilly/tim/news/2005/09/30/what-is-web-20.html), Tim O'Reilly has started to lay out patterns that are common to Web 2.0 projects. This work has been continued in Musser and O'Reilly (2007), which names eight core patterns that can be found in Web 2.0 projects, some of which are related to our discussion here: "Perpetual Beta" and "Lightweight Models and Cost-Effective Scalability." For the most part, these patterns are reformulations and concretizations of agile values for the context of Web development.

The first pattern, with some of the best practices Musser and O'Reilly (2007) name for it including "Release early and often," "engage users as codevelopers and real-time testers," and "instrument your product" clearly mirrors the third agile value of "customer collaboration." In the case of most Web 2.0 applications, there is no customer at the start of the project, which is why the implementation of this value has its specifics. The practices work together to generate a customer base that is using the product, which of course has to be released for that base. Customers subsequently give feedback about the service allowing the developers to improve the product. The feedback can come as comments from the users, but is not limited to that, as the usage of the service can directly be monitored on the server in real time. If usage information is used to generate a "data warehouse of user actions" this can then be exploited in further development. A typical example here is Flickr, of which its lead developer Cal Handerson reportedly has said that a new version is released every half an hour (see www.plasticbag.org/archives/2005/06/cal_henderson_on_how_we_built_flickr/).   Sticking with this example, the uptake of structured tagging, which we mentioned in Chapter 3, is an example of how Flickr has changed the product after observing a change in usage.

As said, the implementation of this first pattern actually drives the development of new features, but at the same time prevents something one could call overdevelopment: features no one needs (or has asked for) – these prevent a fast time to market and thus increase the risk of failure for the entire project. Notice that there may be a sharp contradiction between "don't overdevelop" and the application of a traditional development methodology. These try to fix the requirements at the start of a project and may lack the ability to adapt to changes or may waste efforts when detecting changed requirements too late. It is also important to note that the prevention of overdevelopment should never kill creativity, since without it none of the Web 2.0 companies would have been created in the first place!

The second pattern ("Lightweight Models and Cost-Effective Scalability") closely resembles the agile value of "responding to change." Some of the best practices associated with this pattern are "scale with demand," "scale your pricing and revenue models," and "syndicate business models." All of these practices directly address change: change in demand for the own service, change in possibilities to monetize a service (which we cover more in Chapter 5), and change in service assembly through content syndication and WPCs (which we have covered in Chapter 3). This final practice is a good representative of "lightweight models": outsource to services wherever practical and thus rely on proven business models to leverage your own business idea. Chapter 5, in particular, presents a number of examples of services which could not have been developed without applying this pattern.

What we recognize with respect to software development methodologies is that in the context of Web 2.0 projects, traditional methodologies and models are often considered to be burdened with an unnecessary overhead, and that agile methods appear better suited and are definitely applied more often. We discover a similar discrepancy in Chapter 6 when we discuss the Semantic Web and its formal frameworks and compare them to Web 2.0 concepts such as tagging.

4.2 Client-side Ajax frameworks

There is a multitude of frameworks available that fall under the category of client-side Ajax frameworks; just take a look at Mahemoff (2006) or the corresponding Web page at www.ajaxpatterns.org, which list more than thirty of them. They cover quite a range of functions and differ in size, focus, or license. There are specialized frameworks that handle specific needs, such as handling network communication including XMLHttpRequest, visual effects, integration with Flash technology, or XML. Most of the bigger projects cover several of these areas, allowing a programmer to rely on them for a lot of his or her needs when developing Ajax applications. The most popular frameworks include *Dojo* (see dojotoolkit.org), where developers have started to work on a version that will also support off-line operation, and *Script.aculo. us* (see script.aculo.us), a project with exceptional graphical effects capabilities for an Ajax framework. The latter is based on the client-side framework *Prototype* (see prototype.conio.net) that ships with Ruby on Rails, the server-side Ajax framework for Ruby, which is covered in Section 4.3.

We discuss yet another client-side framework here, namely the *Kabuki Ajax Toolkit*. We do this because it is an integral part of an initiative to promote Ajax by creating an integrated development environment for it. It also offers a simple way to implement *Zimlets*, a neat way of developing special types of mash-ups, where the content of one application is fetched or accessed when references to it are discovered and highlighted in another application.

4.2.1 Kabuki Ajax toolkit

The Kabuki Ajax Toolkit (*AjaxTK* for short) is an object-oriented JavaScript library for generating standard dialog elements. It also includes methods for event handling and for communication. For presentation, it uses the functions of DHTML; to interact with remote services it uses Ajax technology.

AjaxTK has been developed for the Zimbra Collaboration Suite (ZCS, see www.zimbra.com), which is a Web-based collaboration and groupware tool whose primary eye catcher is the rich-featured user interface. Due to the extensive usage of Ajax and DHTML, Zimbra's Web applications behave much like any rich-client application found on desktop systems. Users will find all common functions such as context-menus, copy and paste, interactive dialog boxes, and many more. Before we look at AjaxTK, we will take a quick look at Zimbra's software and the Open Ajax Initiative, the former being the product that AjaxTK was developed for, the latter being a group of companies that have joined to enhance the development of Ajax.

Zimbra

The idea of Zimbra has been to create a messaging and collaboration system "from scratch" (Zimbra, 2006a). It is therefore consistent that Zimbra uses only open Web standards such as SOAP, XML, and RSS instead of proprietary access formats. Also, it is thus very much in the spirit of the applications we have discussed in Chapter 3. Since Zimbra is targeted at an enterprise level, it supports a range of desktop applications including Outlook, Thunderbird, Apple Mail, and others. As the standard way of access, it provides an Ajax-based Rich Internet Application. Figure 4.2 shows the various options to connect to the ZCS and surveys the architecture it is built upon. As alternatives to accessing the suite via a browser, it is possible to connect via the MAPI, a framework specifically made for message exchange, and via the typical mailing protocols such as IMAP, POP, and SMTP.

When accessing the ZCS via the Ajax interface, quite a bit of application code has to be sent to the client, a good portion of which is sent from the AjaxTK. It covers the basic functions related to presentational issues, network communication, XML processing, and event handling. AjaxTK is released under the Apache License and is available at www.zimbra.com/community/kabuki_ajax_toolkit_download.html. This is because AjaxTK is intended to play a major role in the work of the Open Ajax Initiative.

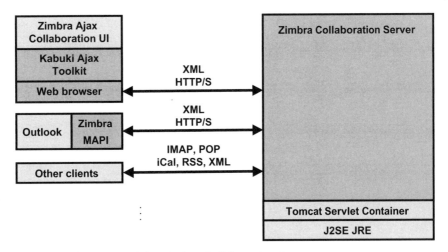

Figure 4.2 Architecture of the Zimbra Collaboration Server.

Open Ajax Initiative

The Open Ajax Initiative was founded by a host of companies with the intention of providing a common toolkit for developing rich client applications using Ajax, while remaining independent of browser, client and server operating system and programming languages used on the server. Zimbra is a founding member of the this initiative, alongside of IBM, the Eclipse Foundation, Mozilla Corporation, the Apache Foundation, Google, Yahoo!, Red Hat, Bea, and others.

Zimbra has provided AjaxTK to the initiative to make the development of Ajax empowered applications easier by offering a set of tools to create widgets, to handle events, and to initiate communication. At the same time, the Open Ajax Initiative supports other Ajax runtime libraries, such as the aforementioned Dojo or Rico (see openrico.org), in order to bring some of them to a critical mass and ensure that they are well integrated with Eclipse and Mozilla technologies. All the currently existing frameworks are combined into the Ajax Toolkit Framework (ATF, see www.eclipse.org/atf/), which is an Eclipse project aiming at integrating all the toolkits into the Eclipse development platform. Within this initiative Eclipse is providing the preferred development environment, while Mozilla is contributing a debugging framework to debug Ajax enabled applications.

AjaxTK components

AjaxTK (Zimbra, 2006) is an object-oriented, JavaScript runtime library with a standard set of controls to create user interface components, also called widgets, a framework to handle events, and a set of tools to initiate communications. It provides a comprehensive set of tools to develop rich client applications using extensively DHTML techniques and core Ajax functionalities to communicate with remote services. Although AjaxTK eases the development of creating client-server applications using Ajax, there is, at least for the time being, still not quite the sophisticated support one is used to from other programming languages, which allow for visual creation of user interfaces. It can be expected that this situation will change with the progress of the Open Ajax Initiative. Because of its features, AjaxTK can be classified as a multipurpose JavaScript framework (see ajaxpatterns.org). Although the details differ, other such frameworks offer similar capabilities.

The key components of the AjaxTK are user interface development, network communications (synchronous and asynchronous), SOAP programming, XML document creation and manipulation, event handling, and management of the user interface. Applications implement their own logic on top of the toolkit as shown in Figure 4.3.

The *event model* is based on the publish-and-subscribe model, where subscribers register certain events with event publishers. Whenever an event fires, the publisher notifies the listener that are subscribed to the event type by providing an event object that encapsulates the actual event data. This enables the creation of Model-View-Controller (MVC) style applications, as it takes care of the event notification needed to connect components in an MVC style application. MVC is an architectural pattern for software design based on a distinction between a data *model*, presentation or *view*, and program control or *controller* (see also the discussion of Ruby on Rails that follows, or Thomas et al., 2006). The model is responsible for managing the data, state and business logic, whereas it is the job of the view to provide the user interface. The controller in between translates the interaction with the user interface into transactions on the model. This separation leads to two benefits. The code gets less complicated and the architecture more flexible and extensible, because the

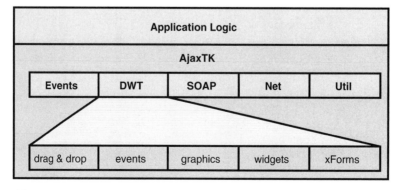

Figure 4.3 AjaxTK components.

areas of activity are split into the three components. In terms of Web development, this also means that a Web designer can focus on designing HTML templates and the Web developer on programming the application.

The *DHTML Widget Toolkit* (DWT) provides and supports many common components. It is similar in spirit to traditional user interface toolkits such as Java AWT/Swing or SWT. The DWT hides most of the DOM handling from a user, thus allowing the development of browser independent applications without having to worry about browser mismatches or memory leaks. While the DWT already provides a rich set of prebuilt widgets, developers can create their own widgets, using as many features of the DWT as they like, by inheriting from existing DWT classes. Another way of using the DWT functionality is by importing a static class from DWT, which comes with methods that allow for extensive DOM manipulation and other functions. The components offered by DWT range from simple user interface elements, such as label, button, and text to more complex elements and windows such as list, tree, dialog, menu, calendar, color picker, HTML editor. The DWT also takes care of the drag-and-drop functionality. Its event model extends the general event model and provides user interface specific events such as events from keys, the mouse, or parts of the UI. The XForms subcomponent allows the creation of forms for HTML that in contrast to standard HTML forms separate what a form does from how it looks. XForms is a W3C recommendation available at w3.org/TR/xforms.

To exchange data with servers, the AjaxTK provides two levels of *network communication*. In any case the direct implementation – whether using the XMLHTTP object in Internet Explorer or the XMLHttpRequest in Firefox or Safari – is hidden from the developer. The first level is a low-level communications layer, allowing direct execution of HTTP requests. These requests can either be synchronous or asynchronous or may use the POST method for example to upload a file to the server. The second layer enables the usage of document-style SOAP protocols. This layer provides core functionality to create and manipulate SOAP documents, to handle SOAP exceptions as well as to handle SOAP faults.

Last, but not least, the toolkit provides a number of utilities that help working with dates, strings, cookies, and that allow the scheduling of actions. These utilities allow manipulation, processing and reformatting of all of these items.

When developing applications using the AjaxTK, developers should no longer think in terms of HTML elements to design Web applications, but rather in designing user interfaces using standardized controls. Ideally, these applications should run and behave alike on different platforms, since the toolkit is providing an abstraction layer between the logical design of the user interface and the "physical HTML" that is being produced by the toolkit. In order to be able to achieve this, the toolkit is aware of existing browser differences. AjaxTK supports the Internet Explorer, Firefox, and Safari browsers. Thus, for example, it takes care of the different implementations of the XMLHttpRequest (see Chapter 3).

4.2.2 Development of a Zimlet using AjaxTK

Zimlets

Zimlets (Zimbra, 2006b) are the standardized way of extending the functionality of the ZCS and they are what AjaxTK was designed to primarily support. In essence, Zimlets are widgets that access APIs and implement mash-ups. This can avoid context switches that would be necessary if the content were not available directly from within the application in question. Moreover, Zimlets are also used to add new custom applications to Zimbra. Finally, Zimlets provide a mechanism to link any messaging content directly to any service on the intranet or the Internet. There are two different kinds of Zimlets.

Zimlets as *panel items* appear in the application overview panel. A user can interact with such Zimlets by dragging content such as e-mails or contacts onto them. Additionally, a Zimlet can be programmed to react to double-clicks and produce items in context menus. An example of such a Zimlet is shown in Figure 4.4. In this example, a contact is being dragged onto the SalesForce Zimlet. SalesForce is a Web-based customer relationship management application (see Chapter 5).

Some of the possibilities of panel item Zimlets are "drag an e-mail to an SMS icon to edit/forward to your coworker's phone; drag an e-mail, contact, or appointment to an IM session with a buddy; ... drag a contact to Yahoo! or Google Maps to see where they are located" (Zimbra, 2006b).

Next to their name, panel items need to specify which objects they want to interact with and how. Possible objects include e-mails, conversations, appointments, or contacts. It is possible to define the action for the panel item in the event of such an object being dragged onto it. Moreover, it can be specified what the actions of the panel item are in case of a single and double click.

Zimlets as *content objects* are triggered whenever a certain keyword is discovered. While the mouse is hovering over such a keyword, either a context menu is created to offer actions that can be taken or detailed information regarding the keyword is displayed. Figure 4.5 shows an example where the preview of a URL over which the mouse has been moved is displayed as a tooltip. This is similar to the smart-tag technology of recent Microsoft Office products, the difference being that Zimlets are not restricted to a usage with Office applications. Indeed, ZCS or Zimlets will run with any

Figure 4.4 Dragging a Contact onto the SalesForce Zimlet.
(Zimbra, 2006b)

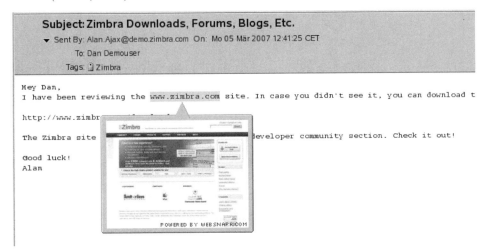

Figure 4.5 A content-sensitive Zimlet.
Source: http://demo.zimbra.com/zimbra/mail

major browser on most operating systems. Examples of what can be done with content object Zimlets include

- mouse-over a date or time to see the corresponding calendar content
- mouse-over a contact to see a telephone number
- mouse-over a physical address to see a map or driving directions and estimated arrival times (Zimbra, 2006b).

Content objects are objects based on parts of bodies of content such as e-mails, notes, or contacts. Two things need to be specified for these objects: how they are recognized and what will happen after they have been clicked. The former is specified using regular expressions, as we see in the following text. If a regular expression is not sufficient, more complex recognition patterns can be programmed by overwriting the Zimlet class that matches the content.

ZCS comes with several built-in Zimlets, which including integration with Yahoo!/Google Maps, Alexa, Amazon.com, Bugzilla, SMS, Wikipedia, ZCS calendar, ZCS address book, and Skype. Beyond this, users can start building their own Zimlets.

The central element of a Zimlet is an XML file where all its configuration is stored. Most Zimlets can be defined declaratively in XML, specifying basic user interface features and behavior and associated URLs. The user interface is using AjaxTK from the specification of the XML file without any further customization. Because of this, simple Zimlets do not need a single line of code.

Zimlets can also contain custom application logic. In this case the front-end logic is implemented using AjaxTK and JavaScript. The declarative XML file as well as any other resource like JavaScript files, images, or style sheets are deployed on the server to be made available to clients. In order to deploy Zimlets, all content is bundled into a zip file. Some of the most typical files to be found in such a bundle are listed next:

- `name.xml`: This file contains the main Zimlet definition, as we just described. It specifies the behavior of the Zimlet and can be the only file, should simple Zimlets not need any further programming.
- `name.js`: This file is used to extend the Ajax client with custom JavaScript code.
- `name.jsp`: If a Zimlet requires custom server implementation, such as retrieving data or any other processing, a Java Server Page (JSP) file is needed. The JSP is being called via a generic proxy structure provided by the ZCS.

Creating a Zimlet using AjaxTK

To show some of the capabilities of AjaxTK, we look next at what it takes to create a Zimlet. Specifically, we build a content object whose goal is to provide on-demand access to customer information. If, for instance, a customer number is detected in the message body of an e-mail, additional data relating to this customer should be made available instantly. By clicking on the customer number, a small info box is to appear, showing contact data as well as past invoices and open items of this current customer. Figure 4.6

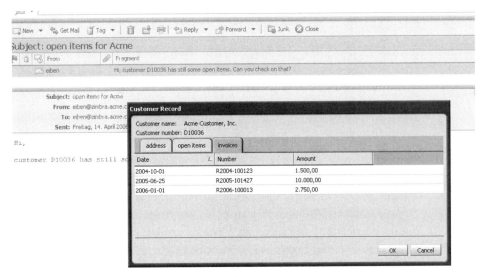

Figure 4.6 Zimlet for a customer record.

shows the user interface of this Zimlet opened for customer "D10036," with an open tab showing the previous invoices sent to this customer.

The user interface consists of a dialog box which has a general information area where the name of the customer and his or her number are shown. A tabbed navigation displays various customer-related details such as address, open items, and past invoices.

To implement this Zimlet, at least two components are needed: a Zimlet definition file and a custom JavaScript file containing the presentation logic. First, a suitable name has to be chosen; we have chosen "com_acme_accounting," complying with the general naming convention. `com_acme_accounting.xml` then has to contain the registration of the custom JavaScript file as well as the definition of a regular expression which identifies keywords within the content. Here, our keywords are customer numbers, and these start with a "D" followed by five digits. Finally, a handler has to be declared that will take care of all further actions (e.g., displaying the actual customer information) whenever a matching expression is found in the content. This is done by specifying a `handlerObject`, which in this case references a class that is implemented in the `accounting.js`. The XML file should look like the one shown in Listing 4.1.

Listing 4.1: Zimlet code example.

```
<zimlet name="com_acme_accounting" version="1.0"
    description="Accounting integration to Zimbra">
  <include>accounting.js</include>
```

```
<handlerObject>Com_Acme_Accounting</handlerObject>
<contentObject>
 <matchOn>
  <regex attrs="ig">D([0-9]{5,5})</regex>
 </matchOn>
 <toolTip>Showing customer record ${src.$1}</toolTip>
</contentObject>
</zimlet>
```

The second step involves the actual implementation of class Com_Acme_ Accounting, which will be contained in the accounting.js file. In order to inherit the more general features and functions, this class is derived from base class ZmZimletBase. Thus, the registration of events like clicking on a content object is ensured via inheritance. To react to click events, a method named clicked needs to be implemented. This method is then called whenever a click on a content object is recognized. In our example, the method is responsible for creating the dialog box and the other elements of the user interface.

As already mentioned, when creating a user interface using AjaxTK, almost no HTML code needs to be written. Instead, just widgets need to be instantiated, which in turn can create their own HTML code transparently. In our example, three different widgets are needed: a dialog box that will act as a container for all other controls, a control which will hold the general customer data, and the tabbed navigation. In order for the tabbed navigation to display three tabs, three corresponding controls need to be created. Last, but not least, all those controls need to be filled with actual data that is supposed to be displayed. This is the only part of this Zimlet where HTML code would need to be written, for example, when a table is to be used to display the data in a proper form.

To create the main user interface controls (general customer data, tabbed navigation, and corresponding pages), the appropriate widget classes of the DWT need to be instantiated. Listing 4.2 only shows the code relevant to the application logic. Note that there is more code needed preceding and following this code that creates the dialog-box window containing all elements.

Listing 4.2: Creating a table.

```
// the general customer data is "stored" in a composite control
customerPanel = new DwtComposite(view);
this._addCustomerData(customerPanel);

// the tabview contains the customer details
tabView = new DwtTabView(view , null, DwtControl.ABSOLUTE_STYLE);

// we need three pages in the tabview, one for each detail
pageA = new DwtTabViewPage(view);
pageB = new DwtTabViewPage(view);
pageC = new DwtTabViewPage(view);
```

```
// add the actual content to the tabviewpages
this._addAddress(pageA);
this._addOpenItems(pageB);
this._addInvoices(pageC);

// finally add the tabviewpages to the tabview
tabView.addTab("address", pageA);
tabView.addTab("open items", pageB);
tabView.addTab("invoices", pageC);
```

In addition to calling the DWT methods, we have to build several functions, namely _addCustomerData, _addAddress, _addOpenItems, and _addInvoices. We do not want to go into details here and only show what the last function will look like. The list view class (DwtListView), can be considered an abstract class, as the look of the list items needs to be implemented in a subclass inheriting from the list view. This is done within class SimpleList which is the value of variable invoiceList in Listing 4.3. We skip the details of this class as well.

To use a list view, first the headers of the list need to be declared, which is done by constructing an array of DwtListHeaderItem, which in turn is passed to the list view. After instantiating the list, the actual content items can be added, and finally the rendering of the list can be triggered. This is what is shown in Listing 4.3 for the list of invoices.

Listing 4.3: Context-sensitive Zimlet: customer record.

```
Com_Acme_Accounting.prototype._addInvoices = function(parent) {
  var headerList = new Array();
  var i = 0;
  headerList[i++] = new DwtListHeaderItem("Date--c", "Date", null,
50, "Date", true, true);
  headerList[i++] = new DwtListHeaderItem("Number--c", "Number",
null, 50, "Number", true, true);
  headerList[i++] = new DwtListHeaderItem("Amount--c", "Amount",
null, 50, "Amount", true, true);

  var invoiceList = new SimpleList(parent, headerList);
  invoiceList.addItem(new Array("2004-10-01", "R2004-100123",
"1.500,00"));
  invoiceList.addItem(new Array("2005-06-25", "R2005-101427",
"10.000,00"));
  invoiceList.addItem(new Array("2006-01-01", "R2006-100013",
"2.750,00"));

  invoiceList.setUI();
}
```

A completed Zimlet is deployed onto a running server with the Zimlet Management Tool. This tool controls the entire lifecycle of a Zimlet from deployment and activation, control of access rights, to deactivation.

We have seen in this section how a special form of mash-up, namely content objects, which create a convenient way for accessing data from one Web application from within another, can be created. AjaxTK offers many pre-built controls to develop rich client interfaces. If a developer is familiar with creating user interfaces in common programming languages without using a visual designer, creating user interfaces using the AjaxTK is no problem at all. We believe that it is with the further development of such libraries that the possibilities of Ajax will increase, as it becomes easier to use by a broader audience. We expect to see an ever more spreading use of Ajax.

4.3 Server-side frameworks

The number of frameworks that fall into the category of server-side frameworks is even larger than the number of client-side frameworks. This does not really come as a surprise, as it just resembles the fact that so many server-side languages are used for Web development nowadays and where developers now want easier access to and handling of functions related to page generation and, of course, Ajax. For this category, Mahemoff (2006) and ajaxpatterns.org list more than fifty frameworks, for languages such as C++, ColdFusion, .Net, Java, Lisp, Perl, PHP, Python, and Ruby. The only framework that exists for Ruby, namely *Ruby on Rails* (see rubyonrails.org), is, certainly, the leader of the pack. While it is a general Web development framework, it has supported Ajax from the start (in 2005, very early into the time where Ajax got a huge momentum) by including the client-side framework Prototype (see prototype.conio.net) and other smaller JavaScript libraries. We do not cover the Ajax capabilities of Ruby on Rails in what follows, as we want to focus on its server-side features.

This section covers Ruby on Rails to show the basics of how Web applications can be generated with an advanced framework, which takes away much of the programming efforts that would be needed without the availability of such a framework.

4.3.1 Ruby on Rails

Based on the Ruby programming language – see Carlson and Richardson (2006) or www.ruby-lang.org – the framework Ruby on Rails, or *Rails* for short, allows the fast development of database-backed Web sites, see Black (2006) or Tate and Hibbs (2006). The basic idea of this framework is to ease the process of programming by using the model view controller (MVC) software design pattern mentioned earlier and two principles: *do not repeat yourself* (DRY) and *convention over configuration* (Thomas et al., 2006). The framework is written in Ruby, an object-oriented script language.

The DRY principle demands that neither data nor functionality should be implemented more than once in a system. An obvious consequence of this basic principle of programming is that code complexity is reduced, as there is always just one place where some configuration needs to be changed in order for a change to be fully implemented. This hopefully leads to lower costs of maintenance.

The second principle, *convention over configuration,* not only applies to configuration files, where it is common to have useful default values and where configuration is only necessary if special requests need to be taken care of. When creating new objects, the Rails framework takes care of the relationships between objects or between objects and databases via conventions for object names, location, or files.

MVC and Rails components

As mentioned, Ruby on Rails implements the model-view-controller (MVC) design pattern explained earlier. Thus, Rails has three main subframeworks, each of which corresponds to a part of the MVC.

Figure 4.7 shows how the components of Rails work together. The client sends an HTTP request to the Web server. There, a router figures out which action has occurred and which method of the controller should therefore be executed. It also parses all information sent by the client. The action processes the request by invoking other actions or by retrieving or manipulating data of the model. Finally, when the action has gathered all necessary information for

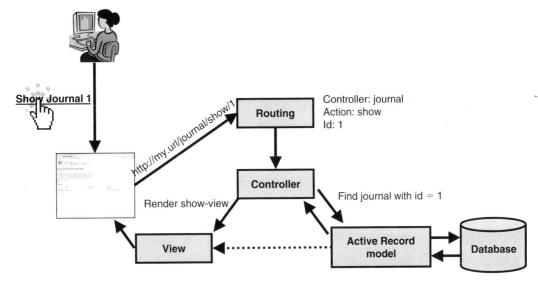

Figure 4.7 Ruby on Rails overview.

the view, the view is rendered to the user. Actions do not necessarily replace the current view, but by using Ajax they may replace only parts of it, or just add data.

Based on a database scheme, Rails can generate controllers and views appropriate for the model that the database resembles, which is called *scaffolding*. The three then instantly work together to allow performing basic operations on the models. At this point, an application is already executable. For illustration purposes, let's assume in this section that we want to build an application that allows users to share travel experiences, which we will call "GTravel." We want users to be able to create journals for trips they are doing or have done, so that they can subsequently add entries (e.g., containing notes on the events of every day of a travel). Journals and travelers should then be searchable via the GTravel home page. For a sneak preview of what we created at the end of this section, have a look at Figure 4.10. To start writing an application with Rails, the directory structure needs to be generated. This is simply done by the command `rails travel`. Rails then starts creating a set of subdirectories in the directory named `travel`, which will later contain the different parts of the application. Rails comes with its own Web server for testing purposes, WEB-Rick, which if started now already shows a welcome page. The next step is to set up a database connection for Ruby to use, after which scaffolding of an application can begin.

As quickly as one is able to build the first parts of an application, one is simultaneously building the beginnings of a test suite for the same application. By convention, test skeletons are present as unit tests for models and functional tests for controllers. It is still the task of the programmer to add test information, but he is put right on track for this task by Rails' scripts.

4.3.2 Creating a Web application with Rails

Active Record

Subframework *Active Record* realizes the connection between model and database. A model in Rails is a domain object. It contains all data and business logic relevant for an entity of the domain which it represents.

An Active Record class corresponds exactly to one database table, and an instance of this class to one row in that table. As all attributes of database table and object class need to be the same, Rails can generate the necessary attributes as well as methods that get and set values on its own. So, the only place where the structure of a model is defined is within the database. Redefining those again in the specification of the model would be a violation of the DRY principle. The generation happens at runtime, so it is even

Figure 4.8 Journal-Entry relationship (UML notation).

possible to add additional fields to the table dynamically while the application is running, and it will adapt instantly.

The connection between model and database is established automatically by the name of the database table and the Active Record class. This is a good example for the principle *convention over configuration*. The name of the database table needs to be the plural form of the name of the class. Consequently, even irregular plurals are supported, such as entity – entities. Figure 4.8 shows the relationship we want to model: A journal can have several entries. The same information is given in the SQL statements of Listing 4.4, which needs to be executed on the database server in order to create the tables that will store the model data. For the journal, we are creating a table where entries are identified by an integer key, have a title of up to 100 characters, a textual description, and a date, signifying the beginning of the trip. The table for entries is similar, but, additionally, also references the journal's table, which ensures that every entry belongs to exactly one journal. If class and table need to be named differently and thereby do not adhere to the default convention, one needs a little configuration.

Listing 4.4: SQL statements for the models.

```
create table journals (
  id int          not null auto_increment,
  title varchar(100) not null,
  description text  not null,
  trip_date date    not null,
  primary key(id)
);

create table entries (
  id int          not null auto_increment,
  journal_id int    not null,
  title varchar(100) not null,
  description text  not null,
  content text      not null,
  trip_date date    not null,
  constraint fk_entries_journal foreign key
        (journal_id) references journals(id),
  primary key(id)
);
```

Now, for example, a scaffold for a travel journal can be created by executing `ruby script/generate scaffold Journal Journal`. Again, Rails creates a

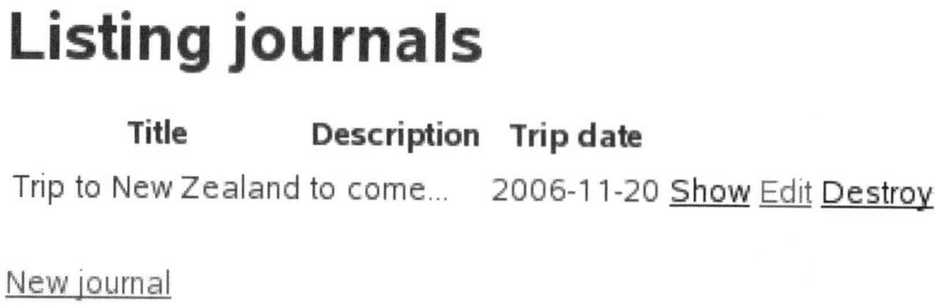

Listing journals

Title	Description	Trip date			
Trip to New Zealand to come...		2006-11-20	Show	Edit	Destroy

New journal

Figure 4.9 Maintenance application for journals after scaffolding.

set of directories and files. The first "journal" parameter is the name of the model we have just created, the second is that of the controller. This makes a small maintenance application for the journal model available, which offers the standard methods for manipulating the model (see Figure 4.9: new, show, edit, and destroy). These methods are often summarized by the acronym CRUD which stands for create, read, update, and delete. Note that we have this preliminary application running without having looked at, let alone edited, Ruby code yet. So far, the Ruby on Rails framework has done all the work in this respect. This will change now, as we add features and change the standard behavior.

Listing 4.5 shows the contents of the two model classes we have created in our example so far: journal and entry. This is Ruby code using Ruby on Rails methods. Each class starts with the definition of the class in the first line and are both based on the Active Record base class.

The association between models cannot always be created from the database. The problem is that not all databases provide a way to distinguish between one-to-one and one-to-many relationships on the basis of foreign keys. However, Rails offers a nice workaround to minimize additional implementation. Every class that has an association with another class needs to include a so-called *association macro*. The models are shown in Listing 4.5; we assume that a model for entries has also been generated. The association macro of the journal class is the line `has_many :entries`, the entry class has the corresponding line `belongs_to :journal`. The macro extends the model class at runtime with all methods that are necessary to work with the association at the model level.

Active Record also includes methods for validation of data records. In our case, `validates_presence_of` is used on the title attributes of entries and the journal. It ensures that the titles are present and nonempty. There is also a `validate` method present in the entry model, which ensures that its trip date is later than that of the corresponding journal. For this, it is checked, whether the `trip_date` of the entry is lower than that of the journal. If this is the case, an error message is displayed.

Listing 4.5: Ruby code statements for the Active Record.

```
Ruby code of the "Journal"-model:

app/models/entry.rb
class Journal < ActiveRecord::Base
 validates_presence_of :title
 has_many :entries
end
```

```
Ruby code of the "Entry"-model:

app/models/entry.rb
class Entry < ActiveRecord::Base
 validates_presence_of :title
  protected
  def validate
   if trip_date < journal.trip_date
    errors.add(:trip_date, "must be equal or later
            than the journal's trip date")
  end
 end
 belongs_to :journal
end
```

Action View

Action View is bundled with the Action Controller in sub-framework *Action Pack*. The view is a presentation of the data. It is sent by the controller as a response to an action typically in form of an HTML or XML file.

A view is generated by HTML templates. As those templates include Ruby code, they also are referred to as RHTML templates. Not too much Ruby code should be in a view to keep with the clear MVC separation between controller and view. For this purpose, a helper module can be used, where methods for use in the HTML template are defined. Action View is already shipped with various helpers for formatting, creation of form elements and HTML tags (see Listing 4.6, which has the method names highlighted). The code for "New Journal" first contains a heading in HTML, after which some lines of Ruby code generate the rest of the view. The first block, starting with `start_form_tag` and ending with `end_form_tag`, creates an input form for a journal using the partial view `form` (see below). `submit_tag` creates the HTML code for the submit button, which is labelled "Create."

One controller is typically responsible for several views, as each action needs one view. To stick to the DRY principle, Rails offers different ways to reuse parts of the code. The first possibility is to use *partial views*. These are ordinary templates, but they do not get their data from a controller, but from a template that calls them. The idea is that one can reuse parts of views wherever they are needed. Listing 4.6 has a partial view for the generation of the code for an HTML form. As can be seen, XHTML code and Ruby commands are mixed to generate not only the form, but also its contents. For example, the HTML code that generates the form element for the journal title contains `<%= text_field 'journal', 'title' %>`, which is the Rails command that generates a text field containing the stored of the corresponding attribute. Note that this partial view is used in both, they create and the edit action.

Listing 4.6: Automatically generated RHTML files of the Action View.

```
app/views/journal/new.rhtml - RHTML for the "New Journal"-view
<h1>New journal</h1>

<%= start_form_tag :action => 'create' %>
 <%= render :partial => 'form' %>
 <%= submit_tag "Create" %>

<%= end_form_tag %>

<%= link_to 'Back', :action => 'list' %>

app/views/journal/edit.rhtml - RHTML for the "Editing Journal"-view
<h1>Editing journal</h1>

<%= start_form_tag :action => 'update', :id => @journal %>
 <%= render :partial => 'form' %>
 <%= submit_tag 'Edit' %>
<%= end_form_tag %>

<%= link_to 'Show', :action => 'show', :id => @journal %> |
<%= link_to 'Back', :action => 'list' %>

app/views/journal/_form.rhtml - RHTML for the partial view "form" used by the
   previous views
<%= error_messages_for 'journal' %>

<!--[form:journal]-->
<p><label for="journal_name">Title</label><br/>
<%= text_field 'journal', 'title' %></p>

<p><label for="journal_description">Description</label><br/>
<%= text_area 'journal', 'description' %></p>

<p><label for="journal_trip_date">Trip date</label><br/>
<%= date_select 'journal', 'trip_date' %></p>
<!--[eoform:journal]-->
```

Components provide another way of reusing code; however, we have not been using them in this example. They do not offer the possibility to reuse presentational aspects, but only functionality. Typically a view just has access to actions of the controller it is associated with. Components allow reusing the functionality of every other controller as well.

Action Controller

As mentioned, the controller is what mediates between view and model. It needs to implement the actions that are sent from a client via an HTTP request. Rails makes use of the fact that Ruby is a *reflective* programming language and thus can extract the responsible controller and action name from the HTTP request. Other data that is sent by the request (e.g., all the information the user has typed into a form) is provided to the controller as a hash table. Its keys correspond to the names of the form fields of the view. Then, a view can directly use the controller's instance variables to access the data made available by the controller.

As a response, the controller delivers the views described earlier in the section. Before these can be sent to the client, they need to be processed by the *Embedded Ruby Processor* which generates pure HTML from the RHTML files. By default, the controller delivers the view whose name corresponds to the name of the action (another example for *convention over configuration*). Listing 4.7 shows the code for the journal controller (which was created through the scaffold); the methods made available are `create`, `show`, `update`, and `destroy` (i.e., the CRUD methods are all covered).

In an extended version of our example, Travelers are models representing users, and we require a login before a creation or edit of journals is possible. As typical Web applications are stateful, but HTTP is a stateless protocol, Rails offers sessions realized through cookies. A session can be seen as a temporary storage for all data, which needs to be present for a sequence of HTTP transactions, but is not meant for permanent storage in the underlying database. So, in our example, a session will be used to track users who are logged in. To this end, the session variable needs to be accessed, which can be seen in the "Sign On" section of `traveler_controller.rb` in Listing 4.7.

Another feature of the Action Controller is filters. A filter is a method that is called automatically before or after an action is executed. We use it to restrict editing to users who are actually logged in: The filter can be seen in Listing 4.7 in the first line of the `TravelerController`. Therefore, in our example, the session is tested for whether or not it contains the information of a user who is logged in; if not, access is denied.

Listing 4.7: Ruby code statements for Active Controller.

`app/controllers/journal_controller.rb` – Ruby code of the "Journal"-controller's automatically created CRUD actions

```ruby
def create
  @journal = Journal.new(params[:journal])
  if @journal.save
    flash[:notice] = 'Journal was successfully created.'
    redirect_to :action => 'list'
  else
    render :action => 'new'
  end
end

def show
  @journal = Journal.find(params[:id])
end

def update
  @journal = Journal.find(params[:id])
  if @journal.update_attributes(params[:journal])
    flash[:notice] = 'Journal was successfully updated.'
    redirect_to :action => 'show', :id => @journal
  else
    render :action => 'edit'
  end
end

def destroy
  Journal.find(params[:id]).destroy
  redirect_to :action => 'list'
end
```

app/controllers/traveler_controller.rb – Ruby code of the "Before Filter" guaranteeing an authentication for "Edit" and "Destroy", and the "Sign on"-action allowing a traveler to login

```ruby
class TravelerController < ApplicationController
  before_filter :authenticate, :only => [:edit, :destroy]

  def sign_on
    traveler = Traveler.find(:first,
        :conditions => ["username = BINARY ?
                AND password = BINARY ?",
                params[:traveler][:username],
                params[:traveler][:password]] )
    if traveler
      session[:traveler_id] = traveler.id
      redirect_to :action => 'show', :id => traveler
    else
      flash[:notice] = 'Invalid user/password'
      render :action => 'login'
    end
  end

  protected
    def authenticate
```

```
   unless session[:traveler_id] == Integer(@params[:id])
     redirect_to :action => 'login'
   end
 end
```

The result of our programming exercise can be seen in Figure 4.10. Based on the scaffold, which is at the core, the application now has the ability to edit travel journals and their entries. The scaffold is now surrounded by the image and the entries that belong to a trip. We have omitted an implementation of the full code for the traveler classes, and we have also not shown updates to the views that we have made after the scaffolding.

Designed for agility

While the sample application we have just seen is small, it still illustrates the main characteristics, possibilities, and the agile nature of Rails. It is fair to state that Ruby on Rails is designed for programming Web applications that are subject to continuous change. The basic idea of the underlying MVC design pattern is to be flexible. The two principles *convention over configuration* and *DRY* make it easier to alter parts of an application, especially when it comes to communication with a database. Moreover, the entire development environment, starting with the integrated Web server WEB-Rick, which allows a testing of changes in development mode without redeploying, the possibilities of the even more powerful testing tools for which the basis is created on the fly, and the scaffolding practice, suggests implementing functionality step by step.

It is the demand for eased Web development that creates frameworks such as Ruby on Rails. Moreover, the competition between such frameworks clearly enhances the productivity of the entire field. We can therefore

Figure 4.10 The GTravel application.

encourage monitoring pages such as ajaxpatterns.org that inform about trends in Web development as they happen.

4.4 Frameworks for other RIA technologies

The previous section has shown an example of a framework for various programming languages to ease the process of Web application development. Most such frameworks are specifically and only designed to make the world of the Web and Ajax more easily accessible to these languages.

A complementary task for Web development frameworks is to span a bridge between these same programming languages and other RIA technologies, such as Flash. The next logical step is to have frameworks that translate from one programming language to multiple RIA technologies at a click. With *OpenLaszlo,* we have chosen such a product as the topic for this section. It started out supporting RIAs based on Flash but, now, also allows the creation of Ajax-based RIAs. This gives us the opportunity to highlight how these technologies differ and where the possibilities of each of them lie.

4.4.1 RIA development with OpenLaszlo

OpenLaszlo (see www.openlaszlo.org) is an Open-Source RIA development platform. Laszlo applications are coded in a combination of XML and JavaScript and compiled into SWF (Small Web Format) to be displayed by the Adobe Flash Player (see www.adobe.com/de/products/flash/flashpro/). The latter is a widespread browser plug-in available for most browsers and operating systems as well as for handhelds and mobile phones. Flash is able to display animated vector graphics and, in newer versions, supports audio and video integration and XML data-binding features. Laszlo applications can be used together with the OpenLaszlo Server to enable support for streaming media as well as for advanced data interchange using XML with SOAP Web services or J2EE remote procedure calls. This has been the situation with OpenLaszlo at the end of 2006.

Laszlo Systems has started to build OpenLaszlo with the goal of creating a framework for the development of RIAs, which follow the rule of "code once, deploy everywhere." With one single code base, a developer should be able to create an application that runs on every system in every browser. For future releases, even deployment as a desktop application has been envisioned. However, for several years Flash has been the only output language of OpenLaszlo, which is why it has commonly been seen as an approach competing with Ajax. In October 2004, the Laszlo Presentation Server (LPS), as it was called at that time, was placed under the IBM common public license

(CPL) as the OpenLaszlo project. The CPL allows free commercial use of the LPS, but demands that every improvement of the code has to be returned to the global code base. The first output format that now complements Flash is Ajax, which has been added to OpenLaszlo in the beginning of 2007, being the first major extension of the open-sourced system. We show how OpenLaszlo works with Ajax to make clear that it now is more a platform that helps to create Ajax applications than just an Ajax contender. Laszlo Systems is cooperating with Sun on the "Orbit" project, where the two companies are implementing Java Platform, Micro Edition (see www.openlaszlo.org/orbit), as a new target, which when completed will extend the reach of OpenLaszlo even further.

The development process

An OpenLaszlo application consists of one or more files written in the LZX programming language, the *OpenLaszlo XML Definition Language* (Laszlo Systems, 2005). LZX is an XML-based description language that also supports the integration of JavaScript-style code. The handling of LZX is to some extent similar to the creation of DHTML or Ajax pages. In addition, LZX allows basic use of object-oriented programming, mainly to allow code refactoring.

Using the special set of XML tags provided by LZX, developers can fill their application with standard GUI components like windows, buttons, text boxes, and so on. Besides the GUI components, LZX tags can be chosen out of various categories for layout, animations, drag-and-drop support, XML data binding, or debugging (Laszlo Systems, 2005a).

The LZX code of Listing 4.8 shows how the language can be used to create a small Laszlo application. The script will create an area of unformatted text and a simple button, vertically aligned inside a window. In this listing, no JavaScript is used, and because of this the window will not react to any user actions.

Listing 4.8: Window with OpenLaszlo.

```
<canvas>
  <window name="main" title="This is a window!"
      resizable="true">
    <simplelayout axis="y" spacing="8" />
    <text>This s just text</text>
    <button>This is a button</button>
  </window>
</canvas>
```

To get the code compiled, the LZX files have to be put into any directory below the folder for Web applications of the OpenLaszlo Server. When accessing that folder or, actually, the location where the folder is found on the Web server through a browser, the compiler transforms the source code to an SWF file and displays it using the browser's Flash plug-in. The result will be a window as shown in Figure 4.11.

To demonstrate the scripting functionalities of LZX, let's assume that the code from Listing 4.8 is extended to replace the title of the window through a click on the button:

```
<button onclick="main.setAttribute('title', 'New Title')">
   This is a button
</button>
```

After pushing the button, the window title will change to "New Title" as shown in Figure 4.12.

To make the development process easier and more comfortable, there is a development environment for OpenLaszlo called *IDE4Laszlo*, which is a plug-in for the Eclipse platform. Additionally, developers can use the Laszlo Debugger to print out messages into a debugging window that appears in

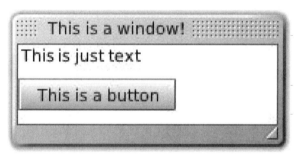

Figure 4.11 OpenLaszlo window.

Figure 4.12 Modified OpenLaszlo window.

the application on demand. The debugger also allows entering JavaScript commands to change the application state in real time.

Deploying an application

OpenLaszlo provides two ways of deployment that mainly differ in the way the OpenLaszlo Server is used. The deployment options can also be seen in Figure 4.13, which already includes the Ajax runtime that is new to OpenLaszlo in Version 4. The two methods are:

- *SOLO Client* (Figure 4.13, left-hand side): Applications that do not make use of streaming media or WPC features do not need the OpenLaszlo Server. They can therefore be deployed on a standard Web server like Apache or Microsoft's IIS. This way of deployment is called *SOLO* (for *Standalone OpenLaszlo Output*). After an SWF file has been compiled from the source code, it can be played or downloaded and subsequently be displayed by Flash Players even without a connection to the Internet.

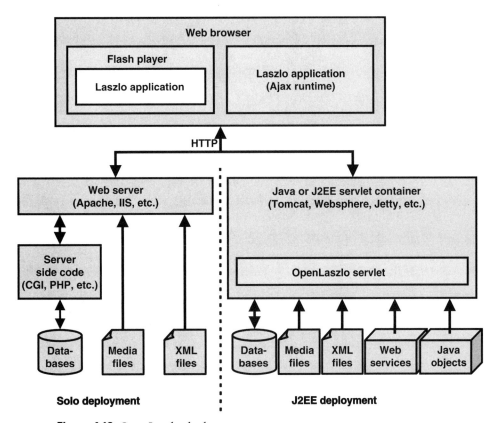

Figure 4.13 OpenLaszlo deployment.

- *Proxied Client* (Figure 4.13, right-hand side): Developers can choose whether resources have to be statically compiled into the SWF, like images or fonts, or dynamically loaded from the Internet, which is common, for example, for audio files. For those resources, the application has to be deployed on the OpenLaszlo Server. The source code is compiled and cached at request time. As a consequence, the loading time of proxied applications is longer than that of SOLO-deployed applications. Apart from loading media at runtime, proxied deployment is necessary to enable support for SOAP Web services or XML-RPC calls.

Architecture of the OpenLaszlo Server

The services of the OpenLaszlo Server are accessed via a Java servlet. Therefore, the server needs to run at least in a standard Java servlet container such as Apache Tomcat. The server architecture comprises three major components:

- The OpenLaszlo *Compiler*: This converts LZX and JavaScript source code into Actionscript 2 syntax, which can be displayed by Flash Players in Version 6 or later. Nonstreaming media types, currently images, fonts, MP3, simple Flash graphics or animations without scripting are compressed and bundled into one target SWF file. The compiler itself is coded in Java and can be accessed through the OpenLaszlo servlet.
- The *Data Manager*: This is used for data interchange. It is accessed through the servlet and is able to handle requests to various data sources such as XML-based Web services or databases. It also supports XMLHttpRequest. If the OpenLaszlo Server runs in a J2EE environment, the usage of XML or Java Remote Procedure Calls is also possible. The Data Manager collects incoming responses and converts the data into a compressed binary format before returning them to the client. For that, the client only has to handle one single format for displaying data, so unified list and table components can be used at the client side.
- The *Persistent Connection Manager*: Through this, an OpenLaszlo application can establish a session-wide connection to the server, either as simple HTTP or as secure HTTPS connection. This connection can be used for authentication as known in standard Web applications, yet it mainly provides streaming media support, which can be used for real-time messaging and notification as well as for video or audio streaming.

4.4.2 Flash versus Ajax

Laszlo Systems' choice to start building their RIA framework around the Flash plug-in was based on mainly three reasons: First, the Flash Player is currently the only cross-browser runtime environment that allows the integration of a graphic user interface (GUI) together with bundled or streaming media in one canvas, without the need of other third-party software. Recognizing also the XML data exchange capabilities, Flash includes all features to implement powerful RIAs. Second, the Flash Player is widely spread among computers all over the world. Statistics point out that around 97 percent of all PCs have a version of the Flash Player installed, with typically more than 45 percent using the latest one (see www.adobe.com/products/player_census/flashplayer/; note that these statistics have been compiled on behalf of Adobe). Third, the implementations of Flash Players across different browsers and operating systems are relatively equal, which is a huge advantage considering the cross-browser incompatibilities we have seen earlier with Ajax (see Chapter 3).

Projects demanding support for streaming media have long relied on Flash capabilities. Especially sites such as cinema movies, music groups, design agencies, or, more recently, streaming video sites such as YouTube have long relied on Flash. OpenLaszlo is partly used for the same reason. The project Pandora (see Figure 4.14) offers a music service, which selects music that is similar in musical style to songs or artists specified by the user. It employs OpenLaszlo for its user interface, the streaming of music to a client, and it makes sure that most users do not have to install any additional software.

But despite its advantages, companies especially are often reluctant to buy products relying on Flash technology. This has mainly security reasons. One point of criticism is the so-called *Local Shared Object (LSO)*, a Flash pendant to the HTML cookie. While a user has full control over cookies, which means accepting, denying, and deleting them as well as completely switching them off is at a user's discretion, LSOs are stored without asking for permission,

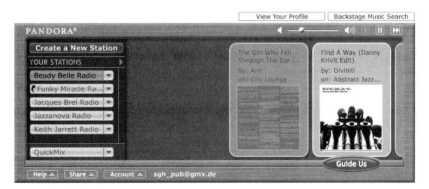

Figure 4.14 The Pandora Music Discovery application.
Source: http://pandora.com/

do not expire, and cannot be deleted easily. A tool for complete deletion of all LSOs can be found on the Macromedia site (see macromedia.com/support/documentation/en/flashplayer/help/settings_manager07.html).

Another point leads us back to the Ajax design principles, and that is inextricably linked to the use of Flash: It changes the browser model of pages and links, and for example always breaks the functioning of the back button. Flash applications reside inside the browser, but in a way lead a separate life from the usual Web content the moment they are started.

Up to the end of 2006, the dependency of OpenLaszlo on Flash as its only deployment language was huge. Although the specifications of the SWF file format used by OpenLaszlo are officially published by Macromedia/Adobe, the file format could easily be changed for future Flash releases, thereby preventing OpenLaszlo applications from running on the latest players. It remains to be seen whether this situation will persist, with Adobe's move to develop Flex (see www.adobe.com/de/products/flex/), a platform similar in spirit to OpenLaszlo and also based on Flash technology.

OpenLaszlo 4 and Ajax

Beginning with Version 4, OpenLaszlo will fully support Ajax. At the time of this writing, the stable release of Version 4 is yet to appear, and there are some features missing in the Ajax version that are included in the Flash version of OpenLaszlo applications. These are mostly graphics-related, such as setting opacity, rotation, or visual transformations, and one can expect these to be cleared up before the final release. Parts of the Ajax support of OpenLaszlo are provided by the Dojo Toolkit, a client-side Ajax framework. Available demo applications that run in the two different runtimes are at first sight indistinguishable in looks and behavior. One of these, the LZPix interface to Flickr images, is shown in Figure 4.15, for which the source code is available from labs.openlaszlo.org.

4.5 Summary

In this chapter, we have discussed various technical aspects of the development of Rich Internet Applications as well as tools available for their development. The first topics were approaches to software development and what we see as anecdotal evidence for Web development concentrating very much on being agile.

After that, we have presented three different frameworks supporting different aspects of RIA development in some detail. First we have covered the client-side framework *AjaxTK* and have looked at its capabilities for creating Zimlets. Next, we have looked at *Ruby on Rails* as a server-side framework

Figure 4.15 The LZPix demo application.
Source: http://labs.openlaszlo.org/

for creating Web applications on the basis of the Ruby language. We have mentioned that Rails makes use of a client-side Ajax Framework to provide advanced functionalities out of the box. Last, we have looked at *OpenLaszlo* with its powerful usage of Flash. It also employs a client-side framework to offer Ajax functionality. The last aspect we have discussed about this framework gives an important indication of what can be expected in future developments of Web frameworks.

The first result is that client-side and server-side frameworks do not compete. Rather, they complement each other, the former easing the implementation of Ajax by taking away the details, the latter by easing the Web development for various programming languages. The actual competition that we see and which is going to continue is between the bundles of frameworks. The prime aspect of their success is going to be their ability to support Web development processes from project start through the various phases to maintenance of the resulting application. The second result we see is the competition between approaches to delivering rich user interfaces, the basis for RIAs through the browser. We have mentioned the "battle" between

Ajax and Flash and the pros and cons of both. It is through the decision for one of these technologies that the frameworks compete. And it is the decision of OpenLaszlo to support both that makes its position so interesting and worth looking at.

Overall, we expect the competition among frameworks to continue in the mid-term future. The competition will probably even increase, as desktop and online applications converge. Adobe's Apollo project is one example of a framework that brings the ideas of RIAs to the desktop (see labs.adobe.com/technologies/apollo).

Our presentation was not intended to be complete. It can obviously not cover the up-to-the-minute news that is occurring in this area on an almost daily basis. For continuous coverage, we recommend blogs on the topic, for example Ryan Stewart's blog titled *The Universal Desktop*, which can be found at blogs.zdnet.com/Stewart/.

Impacts of the Next Generation of the Web

In this chapter, we take a look at various impacts that the next Web generation is likely to have or is having already, and we do so by following again the three dimensions of data, functionality, and socialization we have introduced as our fundamental "navigational space" for Web 2.0 at the end of Chapter 1. While that chapter has shown the evolution of the Web and its development over the years, and while the previous chapters have looked more into technological aspects behind all that, this chapter looks at the situation from the perspective of the individual user, from the perspective of a community of users, and from a business-oriented point of view. In particular, we discuss what impact the Web is likely to have on single users with respect to interaction of publication of data or on existing or evolving communities of users. We do so by discussing the business opportunities arising from being the owner of a large data collection, from providing software as a service, or from providing or using social software. To this end, we start with a brief review of the most essential business models that have been developed in the context of the Web or that have been transferred to the Web from physical reality. Then, as we go along, we point to these business models here and there and indicate how they pop up again in the new context of Web 2.0. We also see how the technical possibilities of the present-day Web allow combinations of business models that were unthinkable several years ago.

Not every aspect of our discussion in this chapter is business-oriented, however, and even if it is, it does not reach as far as, say, return-on-investment calculations or other financial aspects a company may be interested in. The chapter presents a number of ideas that have emerged in the context of the Web 2.0 phenomenon, mostly by way of mentioning a number of sample companies whose businesses are based on an ingenious and sophisticated combination of aspects from all three of our dimensions. These examples may even inspire the reader as to where possibilities for his or her own adoption of Web 2.0 concepts should be looked for.

5.1 Business models for Internet and Web

In order to be able to evaluate potential (business) impacts that Web 2.0 might have, we first close a gap we have so far left open in this book and briefly talk about the most relevant business models for the Internet and the Web. We then, later in this chapter, explain how these models may or will evolve in the various dimensions that Web 2.0 is characterized by, and how they may even reappear in contexts we would not have expected them to yet.

Recall that we discussed in Chapter 1 the major components of an e-commerce system and the various forms of e-commerce today: B2B, B2C, C2C. Yet, the only way of making money we have mentioned, besides selling something over the Web, has been advertising. We now take a broader look at the monetization side of the Web and clarify what other business models are in use. In essence, a *business model* is a method or way of doing business for a company or an enterprise by which that company can sustain itself and in particular generate revenue. A business model is typically comprised of several components, including, but not limited to

- a *value proposition* (i.e., a statement of how the products or services offered by the company or enterprise in question can create a value or be of value for a customer)
- a *revenue model* (i.e., a description of which cash flows into the company will actually bring along a profit)
- a specification of the *target customer* or the *market segment* to which the products or services are to be offered for the purpose of creating value and revenue
- *distribution channels* through which the company plans to reach its customers.

We here follow Michael Rappa, a professor from North Carolina State University, in his distinction of the following business models that are in use on the Web:

- Commission-based Brokerage and Merchants
- Advertising

- Information Intermediaries
- The Community Model
- Subscriptions

Rappa's categorization, which can be found at digitalenterprise.org/models/ models.html, contains three other models, which will be mentioned as we go along. We briefly describe each of the five categories we consider essential next. For a more technical view of electronic business, refer to Papazoglou and Ribbers (2006).

5.1.1 Commission-based brokerage and merchants

A *broker* is an intermediary who brings buyers and sellers together and facilitates transactions between them based on a commission. One of the best known Web examples is Amazon.com, which started out as an electronic bookstore and nowadays sells products in more than thirty different categories and lets other sellers use their platform (see Bellomo and Elad, 2006). As we see below, Amazon.com goes even further by offering a variety of software and hardware *services*. A broker typically charges a commission only for each successfully completed transaction, with another prominent example being eBay.

A variant of models based on commissions is the *affiliate* model, also made popular by companies such as Amazon.com, which offers opportunities to buy goods or services in places where people may be surfing. The model offers incentives in the form of a percentage of revenue to partners who are affiliated. Affiliates place click-throughs on their sites that directly lead to the merchant. Commission is based on a pay-for-performance model (i.e., only when sales are generated will the affiliate get paid).

As shown in Figure 5.1, a brokerage platform often involves more than just a meeting place with a catalog and shopping facilities. Search functionality, negotiation support for dealing with offers, and fulfillment capacities needed after a deal has been closed might be supported as well. Various combinations of functions supported exist, where the choice of features may also depend on the target group or the main focus of the platform; for example, selling used cars is different from selling airline tickets.

Brokerage can take various other forms. Amazon.com is actually a combination of a virtual *store*, where customers can browse a catalog and fill a market basket, and a virtual *marketplace* or mall, where third-party online sellers can be hosted and get charged for setup, listing, and the sales transactions that are completed on their behalf. Further examples of the latter category include Alibaba and mySimon, the latter of which can also be classified as *search agent* since it provides personalized shopping or information

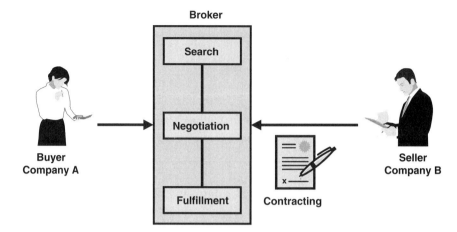

Figure 5.1 Business transactions involving a broker.

services via intelligent agent or "shopbots," or DealTime. Another form of brokerage is the buy/sell *fulfillment*, which accepts customer orders to buy or sell a product or service; an example being CarsDirect. Places like Travelocity and Orbitz specialize in travel and go beyond pure fulfillment by also offering assessment and negotiation. A wide area within brokerage is *auctioning* in its various forms (e.g., English auction, Dutch auction, second-prize auction, or sealed-bid auction). Examples besides eBay include uBid as well as Liquidation. A *transaction broker* provides a third-party payment mechanism for both buyers and sellers in order to settle the financial aspects of a transaction in a trustable way; examples include PayPal and Escrow. For several other subcategories of the brokerage business model, refer to Afuah and Tucci (2003), or to Laudon and Trevor (2006) for additional discussions of this particular model.

Closely related to the brokerage model is the *merchant model*, where, again according Michael Rappa, wholesalers and retailers of goods and services are brought together (as opposed to businesses and potential end customers). Sales may be made based on list prices or through auctions of the aforementioned types. Merchants can be entirely virtual, or they can be a mail-order business with a Web-based catalog. The subcategory of a *bit vendor* deals strictly with digital products such as electronic music. The *click and mortar* category derives its name from the fact that it is comprised of companies combining a traditional store-based ("brick") business with an electronic store ("click") and are hence called click-and-mortar instead of brick-and-mortar. Examples include Wal-Mart or Barnes and Noble. Another subcategory of the merchant model is the *manufacturer* (i.e., a company creating a product or a service) which sells directly over the Web to buyers without any intermediaries. A well-known example is Dell.

5.1.2 Advertising

Advertising is the most prominent and lucrative business model on the Web today; spending on search-related ads alone has risen considerably over the past five years. We have mentioned in Chapter 1 already that Web advertising has become a major business model since the arrival of Google AdSense and Google AdWords. We briefly follow their roots here and discuss what impact they are having today.

Advertising by itself is an old technique for getting consumers or potential customers interested in products or services. Advertising happens in the classical media (i.e., newspapers, radio, television, in cinemas, in sport arenas) as well as in many other contexts. Two features have always been characteristic of traditional "broadcast" advertising:

1. The advertiser can never be sure to hit the right audience. For example, the reader of a newspaper may currently not be in the market for a new car, so he or she will simply ignore ads of whatever size for new cars for which the car manufacturer has paid a lot of money.
2. The advertiser has to pay independently of whether there is the slightest chance of generating revenue from his ad.

In other words, broadcast ads may totally fail to hit their target, and then represent a waste of money. On the Web, this type of advertising has been and still is repeated in the form of *banner ads*, which are typically images that are placed within a Web page and that link to some provider of goods or a service. Banners are often random ads within a Web page and in this case hardly different from traditional broadcast ads.

Paid clicks

What has been recognized by people like Bill Gross, founder of GoTo.com (renamed Overture in the fall of 2001, which in turn was acquired by its largest customer Yahoo! in 2003), and others is that the Web can essentially turn these two issues around by 180 degrees: The Web allows ads to be placed that target consumers very specifically ("narrowcasting"), and advertisers can be charged only if their ad attracts traffic. Indeed, if people can be shown precisely what they are interested in, advertising may create revenue much more often. The key to this again is search: The observation initially made by Bill Gross was that if people *search* for a particular item, it may not be a bad idea to place an ad for items in the same category next to the search results. Thus, for example, if someone would enter the search terms "camera+digital" into the search box of a search engine, the assumption that this person is interested in information about digital cameras and may even be interested in *buying* one is not entirely wrong. So placing an ad for a digital camera right next to the search results appears to be considerably more appropriate than anywhere else, which is the essence of what is called *search marketing*.

Now it is obviously not enough to just let advertisers choose the keywords and terms they are interested in, since that would create many clashes among them. So the GoTo idea was to let advertisers pay for their high or early listing in search results and make them pay one cent per click if a user clicked through to them, at least initially. Thus, advertisers could decide for themselves how much they were willing to spend so that their ad would appear at the top of results in response to a specific search. The notion of *paid clicks* or *pay per click* (PPC) was born, also known as *cost per click* (CPC). There are also other ways of charging an advertiser, as described, for example, in Mordkovich and Mordkovich (2005).

Google AdWords

In 2002, Google introduced the current version of its AdWords service (and got into legal issues with Yahoo! since they also used the PPC model), following another version that had already been launched two years earlier. In Google AdWords, an advertiser cannot pay for being listed early in a search result, but can buy "advertising words." A provider of some goods or service formulates an ad, which is restricted to a few lines of text, and chooses one or more keywords that are relevant to the ad. If a user searches for one of these keywords, the ad may be placed next to the search results, so that the advertisement is directed to people who are already interested in the products in question. Users can then click on the ad in order to be redirected to the advertising store and, ideally, make a purchase from there. Details of how to use AdWords and how to run, say, a marketing campaign with it can be found, for example, in Davis (2006), Goodman (2005), and Miller (2007).

Again, the advertiser only has to pay Google when a searcher clicks from a result page through to the advertiser's site. However, the amount to be paid is determined in an auction in which everyone interested in particular search terms or ad words can participate. This auction is run as a 24/7 marketplace where terms and phrases that people may search for are constantly bought and sold. Google originally applied a "cost per thousand impressions" or CPM model, in which advertisers got charged based on the number of times a page with their ad on it appeared in front of a searcher.

Since Google's strategy of listing search results is based, among other parameters, on the PageRank of sites, it is not surprising that ranking has also been introduced into advertising at Google. Indeed, Google has integrated the popularity of an ad or its "click-through rate" into its overall ranking. Thus, an advertiser whose ad never gets clicked may lose in terms of ranking independently of how much he has agreed to pay for a click. Conversely, popular ads that get frequent clicks may have delivered a lower bid, but might get a better position due to their popularity. Thus, ads are ranked based on the two parameters of (a) the bid of an advertiser and (b) the frequency of how often the ads get clicked. As Battelle (2005) explains, this is absolutely feasible from an economical perspective. When the advertiser with the lower bid is clicked more often than the one with the higher bid, the former generates more revenue for Google, since Google is paid for every click.

Other issues

Ads that an advertiser has to pay for when clicked nowadays appear as "sponsored links" (Google) or "sponsored results" (Yahoo! and Ask) or with similar designations atop or near search results. The PPC model may give rise to *click fraud*, for example when the competitor of an advertiser constantly clicks on his ad in order to make him pay to the search engine. A possible workaround here is the *click per action* (CPA) model employed, for example, by Snap.com, in which an advertiser only pays if both his ad has been clicked and some transaction that is of value to the advertiser has subsequently been completed. Companies like Google and others also apply other measures to fight click fraud, such as filtering of suspicious clicks, "forensic" analysis of advertisers' Web server log files, or observation and corroboration of click traffic by third parties. Mordkovich and Mordkovich (2005) deal with this topic in further detail.

Google has taken the ad business a step further by introducing *AdSense* in 2003 by supporting the long tail of advertising as discussed in Chapter 1, Section 1.1.4, in yet another way. AdSense gives Web site publishers access to Google's network of advertisers so that they can place ads from the Google pool on their own sites. After sign-up, AdSense scans a new customer's site and distributes contextually relevant ads on that site or places them next to the results of searches on that site. The Web site publisher then gets a percentage if someone clicks on such an ad and hence – through Google – to the advertiser. Google AdSense has allowed even small Web pages to create revenue streams without the need for big administrative forces. AdSense also comprises a *Referrals* program which, essentially, is an affiliate model. Referrals connect site visitors to products on other sites and are made via a button that is placed on a page at a participating site.

We do not need to delve into the financial successes a company like Google has had since it has entered the advertising business. The important point is that *Web* advertising has been able to turn an entire business around and to create a market, the dimensions of which nobody could initially antic-ipate. Web advertising is another perfect example of a long tail phenomenon. Businesses of all sizes, not just big ones with considerable marketing budgets, have received unprecedented access to markets of all sizes, in particular to niche markets. As other Web business models, advertising is to a large extent also based on *micropayments* (i.e., very small amounts of money that are paid for a transaction or a service). It is then the huge number of such pay-ments that ultimately results in a considerable amount of money.

However, advertising on the Web is no longer limited to search appli-cations. Indeed, new advertising channels are opening up as consum-ers produce more and more data themselves. And, customized advertising is penetrating an increasing number of uses of the Web, as we see later in this chapter. Since consumers are starting to even *create* the advertisements other consumers will look at, it may soon be the case that the providers and consumers will become indistinguishable, a phenomenon for which econ-omists and others have created the combined term *prosumer* already. An interesting archive of online ads can be found at adverlicio.us.

5.1.3 Information intermediaries

The next category of business models is the *information intermediary* or "infomediary." In essence, this is an evolution of the information broker model we mentioned in Chapter 1. Recall that an *information broker* col-lects market data, data on market development, information on the compe-tition both domestically and internationally, typical figures of how much is spent on advertising and what common distribution channels are, and real or estimated consumer demand. As more and more people got connected to the Web, and as e-commerce became considerable business, data about consumers, their habits, and their click streams became more and more val-uable for businesses. While raw data obtained from, say, the log of a Web server may not be very interesting yet, it becomes relevant when it is prop-erly analyzed by data mining techniques, since it can then be used for rec-ommendations, page optimization, target marketing, and other activities.

A prominent example in this area is Nielsen//NetRatings, a company measuring a variety of aspects in Internet audience and an excellent source for analyses of online advertising effects (see www.nielsen-netratings.com). Another example is DoubleClick, which collects and distributes information on advertising and brings together agencies, marketers, and content pub-lishers for the purpose of digital marketing. For an example of what such information intermediaries can come up with, including aspects such as the total number of visits or the number of visits classified by source, Figure 5.2

Reports: www.kix.in

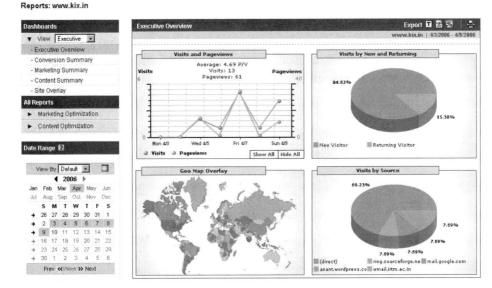

Figure 5.2 Google Analytics overview.
Source: http://anant.files.wordpress.com/2006/04/analytics.jpg

shows an overview of a page created by Google Analytics (see www.google.
com/analytics). Among the many tools falling into this category, we mention AWStats (see www.awstats.net) as well as Webalizer (see www.mrunix.
net/webalizer).

The latter three can actually be used by anybody, including businesses
and private people who are interested in analyzing the traffic on their sites.
Another target of data collection, besides traffic as such, is producers and their
products, for which suitably prepared information will be of value to consumers when considering a purchase. While the recommendations a user can
get at Amazon.com and other places are an example in this category, better
ones are *Consumer Reports* (see www.consumerreports.org) or *Trip Advisor*.

5.1.4 The community and the subscription models

The *community model* came into existence through movements such as
Open-Source software development, where programmers share and develop
program code freely and in particular without license fees, and open content sharing on networks such as Wikipedia. Open-Source software in itself
is free, yet some revenue may be generated from product support or other
services that are related to the software. Other forms of community models
exist in Web radio and Web television, since these are often set up as nonprofit sites that are supported by donations (e.g., SHOUTcast and others).

Thus, the community model consists of a community of developers, users, or both providing its members with some free product or service and building upon user loyalty, since contributors typically invest quite a bit of their time and skills. Revenue can be generated from combining the community model with other models such as advertising or subscriptions to a premium service. It is such a combination that turns the community into a true business model in the sense defined earlier. As we see in our discussion of socialization that follows, the Internet and the Web have become *the* place for community business models, since communities are typically formed around a particular topic or purpose and hence represent an excellent target audience. It is therefore no surprise that the community model is a very valuable one and under constant development and expansion. It is actually seen as the major model for the future of the Web, which, in the medium- to long-run, may even outperform advertising.

The last model we look into here is the *subscription model*. In this model, users are charged for a subscription to some service (e.g., the exclusive right to use a domain name, storage space rental with an Internet service provider (ISP) for the personal or enterprise Web site, DSL access to the Web provided by the local telecommunications company, or television programs provided by a channel that uses the Internet). The ways of charging customers vary; charging can occur periodically (e.g., on a monthly or annual basis; it could be one-time) or it could be based on a pay-as-you-go model; the latter is a "metered" subscription, also known as the *utility* model. We see in the text that follows that the subscription model is particularly relevant to services on the Web.

5.1.5 Summary

Afuah and Tucci (2003) give a concise summary of Web business models, their taxonomy, and their typology. They organize business models along the four dimensions of *revenue model* (e.g., commission, advertising, subscription, and such), *commerce strategy* (e.g., B2C), *pricing model* (auction, fixed), and *profit side*. They also compare Rappa's classification to several others that have been proposed in the relevant research literature.

While these models are not new in general, the major difference to classical ways of doing business that has come along on the Internet and the Web is the aforementioned *micropayments* (i.e., the fact that payments can now be arbitrarily small, often in the range of just several cents). Yet providing a service at this level can still be profitable now, since these micropayments may come, as mentioned, in large numbers.

Our goal in the following sections is to indicate how (if at all) these different business models are affected by the Web 2.0 developments. To this end, we look at the three major dimensions in turn and discuss them in light of what we've just discussed. As we see, numerous combinations of the models discussed in this section presently exist on the Web, and it is not difficult to see that more are invented on an almost daily basis.

5.2 Data ownership

As we said in Chapter 1, data and data streams are one of the core features of the Web today. Indeed, data is not only written to the Web by users who are into blogging, write wikis, or produce reviews and recommendations. Data is automatically generated in many applications (e.g., in transaction-based e-commerce based on one of the models described in this chapter, in digital telephony, or in Web server logs, to mention just a few), and data is collected on purpose by applications such as search engines or satellites, sometimes even government agencies. As a result, and enabled by cheap storage technology, huge data collections are nowadays a frequent reality, and large data centers are being set up by Internet providers all the time.

In these areas of human-generated as well as machine-generated data, we can see different patterns that govern data accumulation. While human-generated data should ultimately remain under the control of the human or the community who is creating this data, this is not always the case. For example, a product review written for Amazon.com is explicitly not the writer's property anymore, once it has been delivered to their site. A blog may be "owned" by the blogger who has set it up, and this person is in charge of the things that happen to or within the blog. Although, if the blog is hosted, control over the blog may actually be exercised by someone else. If a comment to a blog entry is unacceptable or inappropriate, the blog owner can erase it. If an individual blog entry gets too long, the owner can edit it and cut it down to its essence. If a larger community is behind a particular data collection, rules might explicitly or implicitly be in place that control the writing. In Chapter 1, we mentioned the Wikipedia rules and Charlene Li's Blogger Code of Ethics, which are an example here.

Human-generated data may be intentionally collected and then machine processed; for example, the data that goes into the index of a search engine is typically created by others, but then copied into the data collection of a service provider. For example, search engines like Google or Yahoo! crawl the Web, copy pages they find, and analyze them in various ways, as we discussed in Chapter 1.

With machine-generated data, ownership of the data often arises "by itself," since considerable amounts of data are simply collected and stored on the servers of a company or a provider. A typical example is transaction data arising from business execution in e-commerce (i.e., data that relates buyers, payments, orders, shipments, and suppliers in a way that must be accountable and trusted). Often, machine-generated data contains redundancy, and in general the amount of data generated is so vast that techniques such as data integration, data warehousing, and data mining have to be employed for transforming raw data into information or for generating new information from it. Other machine-generated data, in particular the logs that a Web server keeps and that can be analyzed by tools such as Webalizer mentioned in the previous section, is analyzed for traffic statistics or click stream optimization.

Collecting data and owning a data collection are not novel issues that only arose in the context of the Web. Indeed, telephone books and directories were introduced in the late nineteenth century and have always been a value for the phone company who composed them and kept them up-to-date. The point is that having a data collection such as the phone book in *electronic* form allows for integration into other applications. It also allows for making it the basis for new services, such as an inverse phone directory (i.e., connecting phone numbers to names and addresses instead of the other way around), tracing old-to-new number transitions, or creating directories of unlisted phone numbers (see www.phonesearchcentral.com for an example), applications that integrate other sources into the area of phone numbers.

The telephone book is a good example for what we can often observe on the Web as well: It is distributed for free, but there are still ways of making money through the phone book, for example by selling ads for inclusion in the Yellow Pages. The same principle applies to a service such as Google: The search engine with its huge index can be used for free, yet, as we have discussed, advertising is the principal revenue creator.

The Web has enabled the establishment of *unique* data collections or ones that are hard to re-create. For example, Navteq is a service that offers digital map coverage currently in fifty-eight countries on six continents in the world. Their maps are the basis of car or PDA navigation systems and are constantly updated by people who actually inspect roads and collect data for up to 200 different attributes. So, here, the data collection is the essential ingredient for the map service, a feature for which Tim O'Reilly has coined the statement "data is the next 'Intel inside,'" as similar observations apply to auction databases, search indexes, or media collections.

Musser and O'Reilly (2007) list a number of ways in which a data collection can be used for creating or adding strategic value, including:

■ *Creation* strategies are used, in particular for creating and owning data that is difficult to re-create, as in the case of Navteq.

- *Control* strategies include custom file formats or specific ways of accessing the data (e.g., through registries).
- *Framework* strategies refer to data that form the underlying framework or base for a variety of other services (e.g., location data, time data including events and calendars, catalog data, product indexes, or digital identities).
- *Access* strategies provide access to data that was previously difficult to find or to get to. An example here is Zillow, which provides estimates for real estate values for homes in the United States based on calculation tools formerly available to brokers only. Chicago Crimes (see www.chicagocrimes.org) provides access to a database of crimes that have been reported in the city of Chicago, and access can be by crime type, street, date, police district, zip code, or other characteristics.
- *Infrastructure* strategies are about providing an infrastructure for storing and accessing data that may be owned by others. An example is Photobucket, which provides free video and photo sharing and allows users to link images and videos to online social networks, auction sites, blogs, and message boards. Another example is Limelight Networks, which provides platforms for content delivery such as on-demand video streaming or Internet games.

Clearly, once a data collection is being used for creating strategic value, there is often more than one way to also monetize it.

Data ownership, while being the basis for numerous services and service compositions, also has a number of usage issues relating to copyright, security and safety, privacy protection, or the right to delete someone's personal data. For example, an ISP might sell user data to an advertising company for a marketing campaign. While this is certainly considered unethical, it may be legal due to the "terms and conditions" a user might have agreed to during sign-up.

As Loshin (2002) writes,

> ... data ownership refers to both the possession of and responsibility for information. Ownership implies power as well as control. The control of information includes not just the ability to access, create, modify, package, derive benefit from, sell or remove data, but also the right to assign these access privileges to others.

As a consequence, data ownership implies a variety of responsibilities, including but not limited to the following:

- Access and security management: In a system that contains sensitive data, whether it is confidential information, human resource data, corporate intelligence, and such, it is necessary to define a security and authorization policy and to provide for its enforcement.

■ Data quality: This includes determining and setting user data quality expectations, instituting gauges and measurements of the levels of data quality, and providing reports on the conformance to data quality. This also includes defining data quality policies for all data that flows into the system and any data cleansing, standardization, or other preparation for user applications.

■ Management of business rules: All data processing operations have business rules. Whether these rules are embedded in application code, abstracted into a rules format, or are just documented separately from their implementation, the data owner is also responsible for managing business rules.

While some of these issues might be pure infrastructure problems, a good basis for beneficial results is given when "users own their data and the provider owns the aggregate" (Musser and O'Reilly, 2007).

5.3 Software as a Service (SaaS)

An interesting calculation on the amount of IT spending needed when someone starts a new company or is asked to reduce that spending in an existing company, which is shown in Figure 5.3, has been published by Igniter Ltd. (see www.igniter.co.nz). The resulting monthly figure of roughly 63 dollars (New Zealand) translates into about 33 Euros or about 43 dollars (United States). The setup does not have any major omissions and even includes some sophisticated items (e.g., CRM or project management software)!

The point of this little calculation is that there are serious opportunities for a company to reduce its IT spending by making appropriate use of current Web technology and the services that are offered there. While we have seen in hardware prices over the past forty years already that IT is becoming a cheaper and cheaper technology, the same may soon apply to software as well and actually does apply to Open-Source software already. One of the keys to this development is the *Software as a Service* (SaaS) paradigm, which we have mentioned already several times in previous chapters and which we now discuss in more detail. SaaS is seen by Musser and O'Reilly (2007) as *the* enabler of what they call the *Enterprise 2.0.*

What we have seen so far is the conceptual framework of Web services (see Chapters 1 and 2), where service providers prepare a specification of the services they are able to provide and publish this in a generally accessible

The $100 IT Application setup

1.	Website - use Joomla / Mambo / Drupal / osCommerce and host at Siteground.com. Modify/customise an existing or free template	US$4.95/month
2.	Domain name and website stats - Google Apps and Google Analytics	Free
3.	Email system - Gmail with Google Apps	Free
4.	Office automation - use Star Office , Open Office or Google Docs and Spreadsheets / Google Calendar	Free
5.	PDF writer - use Google Documents and Spreadsheets instead	Free
6.	Project Management - use Basecamp Basic	US$24/month
7.	CRM / Contact management - use SugarCRM hosted on Siteground.com	US$4.95/month
8.	Telephony - use Skype Out or JaJah	US$10/month
9.	Accounting - Xero (to be released)	Unknown*
10.	[Operating System - use Ubuntu]	[Free]
	Total	**NZ$ 62.77 / month**

* Xero is currently in private beta testing but is expected to be available in Q1 2007. Given that it is targeting SME's using a Software as a Service model it is likely that the monthly cost is not more than $50 for the most basic version.

Figure 5.3 The Igniter $100 IT Application Setup.
Source: http://www.igniter.co.nz/index.php?option=com_content@task=view&id=101&Itemid=207

registry. Service clients, on the other hand, can query this registry for services they are looking for and, if something appropriate is found, contact the respective provider for contracting and service execution. What we have also seen is that this conceptual model, although implemented in various platforms such as ebXML or RosettaNet, has gotten a sibling that does without the registry and that we have termed *Web procedure calls* (WPCs). WPCs are the vehicles used when programs connect to a public API such as that of Google Maps we discussed in Chapter 3.

SaaS is a reality today in two major forms: for developers in the form of mash-ups or WPCs, for end users (companies as well as individuals) in the form of feature-rich services (RIAs) or widget collections which either are for free (as shown in Figure 5.3) or can be purchased or rented. In this section we continue our SaaS discussion, both from a provider and from a consumer perspective. The provider is essentially interested in offering a service that clients can use on-demand and for which he can charge a fixed or pay-as-you-go fee. The consumer, on the other hand, may be interested in specifying parameters in advance which the service should meet as well as in the customization of a service, or the consumer may simply be interested in putting a service together himself (i.e., without any specific prescription from a provider).

5.3.1 A look back: the ASP model

We mentioned in Chapter 3 that Rich Internet Applications provide a kind of functionality and interactivity today that has previously been reserved for desktop applications. RIAs can, hence, be considered as a materialization of the network computer that had been predicted by companies such as Sun Microsystems and Oracle in the mid-1990s already. The motivation for such announcements at the time was derived from the concept of *Application Service Provisioning* (ASP), which was based on the idea of providing software functionality over the Internet. In the ASP model, a provider would not sell software as a package that a customer needs to install on its own server. Instead, the software or the application is hosted on a machine owned by the provider, and it is used via an Internet connection whenever needed.

In the mid-1990s, the ASP model was seen as a way to make software cheaper, since the cost of software by then had typically risen to be a multiple of the cost of hardware. Moreover, especially small to medium businesses without their own system administration department often found software installation and maintenance too difficult. Thus, instead of buying an expensive software and then have it sitting idle when it was not used, the ASP idea is to provide an on-demand service. The need for installation and maintenance is eliminated, and the service provider can now upgrade the software or install bug fixes without a complicated distribution process that needs to reach each and every customer.

The applications provided can range from simple access to a specific program, such as a currency converter or some billing software via virtual conference and meeting platforms to complex application packages such as a business process modeling (BPM) tool. Typically, a single provider would host a number of different applications, as illustrated in Figure 5.4. When applications are provided remotely, the technical tool employed is, for example, remote method invocation (RMI), the Java equivalent at the level of single services and APIs.

A considerable responsibility rests with the provider in the ASP model, since the provider needs to make *service guarantees* regarding availability, security, backups, technical support, and maintenance, issues that had previously rested with the client. When the ASP model was introduced in the 1990s, the hope was that ultimately the *entire* software on a computer could be hosted somewhere on the Internet, including the operating system, which was the idea behind the aforementioned net computer.

While a number of applications exist in which the ASP model has been successfully utilized, and while clients for ASP services especially in the United States include businesses, government agencies, nonprofit organizations, and

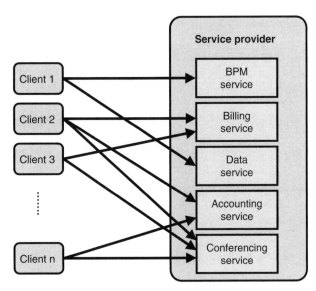

Figure 5.4 The ASP model.

others, the model has never reached the level of success that was originally anticipated and predicted. The major reason for this has been technical in nature, in particular the fact that Internet connections in the late 1990s were far from being as reliable and fast as they are today.

The technical problem of limited bandwidth and stability have mostly been overcome today, although there will always be a demand for improvement and higher rates here. However, it is not only the technical side of cables and connections that let the ASP model enter a new stage of evolution. Thanks to the technical mechanisms we have described in Chapter 3, in particular thanks to RIAs, where a particular kick is derived from the fact the RIAs can be enriched by mash-ups (e.g., Google Desktop, which is not a Web application), the concept is becoming a reality, and we look into its various facets next.

5.3.2 The provider-oriented view

When a software service is provided over the Web, such as in the case of the Google Maps API, the provider is essentially fixing the ways in which the service can be used. The API for the service typically consists of a number of procedures that can be called or invoked, yet the services are fixed and have to be used as is. We distinguish application services and infrastructure services in this subsection.

Application services

The business model of application services, where some software functionality is provided that a customer uses as an application, is typically the subscription model. The service might be free, but more common is a subscription or a pay-as-you-go fee. Thus, using the service is what clients have to pay for, yet there is essentially no need for an initial investment in hardware or software (see again the calculation shown in Figure 5.3), except for the cases where the application provided is integrated into other applications at the client's side.

As an example, let us consider the *Google Apps* service (see www.google.com/a), which has been launched in a Premier Edition in February 2007. Google Apps is a suite of tools that include Gmail, the Google mail application, Google Talk for chatting and sending instant messages, Google Calendar, a tool for scheduling events and meetings and for sharing these with others, Page Creator for designing Web pages, Start Page for creating a personalized browser start page, and Google Docs & Spreadsheet, a Web-based text processing and spreadsheet program that allows several people to work on documents or spreadsheet calculations together. All components as well as the required data storage run on Google servers. The intended price is fifty U.S. dollars per user account per year for the Premier Edition, while basic services with, for example, reduced storage space for the mailbox remain free of charge.

Services like Google Apps exist in a variety that is enriched almost daily, and examples range from individual service calls to entire complex applications. To give an impression of what is available and why the calculation shown earlier in Figure 5.3 is indeed appropriate, we just summarize a few categories in which software is available as a service at present in Table 5.1. As a sample, Figure 5.5 shows the calendar application by 30 Boxes. These applications range from individual office functions, such as an organizer or a calendar, to planning, collaboration, accounting, and CRM tools; even databases can be set up as a service over the Web these days. A practical consequence of this increasing availability of software on the Web is that many start-up companies, at least in the beginning, do not rent office space anymore, but work in virtual teams.

While there is a clearly visible trend to make applications that formerly were exclusively running on a desktop computer now available as a service on the Web, with the ultimate Web operating system on the horizon, with projects underway from players such as YouOS, Goowy, DesktopTwo, Xin, eyeOS, there are two other trends that try to combine desktop and Webtop software, or that develop something intermediary. One is the idea of having desktop applications tapping into the Web, which is the case, for example,

Table 5.1 SaaS applications.

Application	Company	URL
Organizer and Calendar	Kiko	www.kiko.com
	37signals Backpack	www.backpackit.com
	30Boxes	www.30boxes.com
Planning	PlanHQ	www.planhq.com
Word Processing and Spreadsheets	EditGrid	www.editgrid.com
	ThinkFree	www.thinkfree.com
	Google Docs & Spreadsheets	docs.google.com
	Ajax 13 ajaxWrite, ajaxXLS	ww.ajaxwrite.com
	Num Sum	ww.numsum.com
	Zoho	www.zoho.com
	Peepel	www.peepel.com
	ShareOffice	www.sharemethods.com/products/shareoffice.html
Distributed Database Applications	Smallthought Systems Dabble DB	www.dabbledb.com
Invoicing and Time Tracking	FreshBooks	www.freshbooks.com
Project Management, Collaboration, Shared Workspaces, Conferencing	37signals Basecamp	www.basecamphq.com
	CentralDesktop	www.centraldesktop.com
	WebEx	www.webex.com
	GoToMeeting	www.gotomeeting.com
	activeCollab	www.activecollab.com
	TeamWork Live	www.teamworklive.com
	LiveOnTheNet	www.liveonthenet.com
	Zimbra Collaboration Suite	www.zimbra.com
Group Chat	37signals Campfire	www.campfirenow.com
Accounting and Payroll	Xero	www.xero.com
	Intacct	www.intacct.com
	KeepMore	www.keepmore.com
Customer Relationship Management	Etelos CRMforGoogle	www.crmforgoogle.com
	salesforce.com	www.salesforce.com
	RightNow	www.rightnow.com

for SongBird (see www.songbirdnest.com). The other is that future browser versions are expected to comprise support for off-line applications. In other words, a user will be enabled to use his or her Web applications such as Google Calendar in the browser even when he or she is off-line; a corresponding announcement has been made in early 2007 for Firefox 3.

SongBird is an interesting combination of a desktop music player with a Web browser and a digital jukebox. It is not a service, however, but a mash-up, and

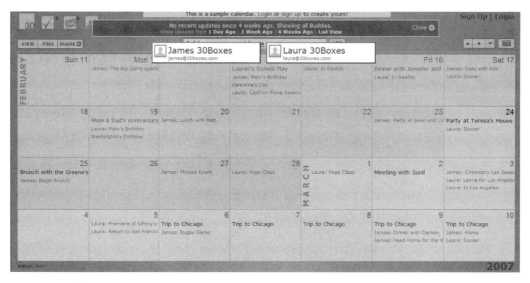

Figure 5.5 30Boxes calendar application.

nicely illustrates the concept of having desktop applications reach out onto the Web. We may expect more such online/off-line integrations in the future.

Infrastructure services

While the services we have described in this section so far represent *applications* with certain functionality, there is another category of *infrastructure services* that are being offered over the Web. Services in this category take the ISP concepts of providing storage or computing power or both a step further, but also add other types of functionality.

As a prominent example in this category, we mention the Amazon Web Services (see aws.amazon.com). Amazon.com currently offers ten different Web services, which are genuine infrastructure services in the sense that they enable product development and are not intended for individual users. During product development or for a start-up company, issues to be dealt with include server hosting, contract negotiation, bandwidth management, purchase decisions, moving facilities, scaling and managing physical growth, heterogeneous hardware, as well as coordinating large teams. The Amazon Web Services target these issues; they came into existence as a by-product of the enormous computing infrastructure that is meanwhile owned by this Internet marketplace. We take a closer look at just two of them.

Amazon S3 (*Simple Storage Service*), which we have already mentioned in Chapter 2 in the context of Web Services, provides storage over the Internet that is priced at fifteen cents per gigabyte per month of storage used and twenty cents per gigabyte of data transferred, without base fees or setup costs. According to Amazon.com, S3

> ... provides a simple Web services interface that can be used to store and retrieve any amount of data, at any time, from anywhere on the Web. It gives any developer access to the same highly scalable, reliable, fast, inexpensive data storage infrastructure that Amazon uses to run its own global network of Web sites. The service aims to maximize benefits of scale and to pass those benefits on to developers.

Amazon S3 offers the typical features associated with a storage service (i.e., the capability to write, read, and delete objects containing from one byte to five gigabytes of data each) where each object is stored and retrieved via a unique, developer-assigned key. S3 includes authentication mechanisms to prevent unauthorized access. Objects can be made private or public, and rights can be granted to specific users. It uses standards-based REST and SOAP interfaces designed to work with any Internet-development toolkit. Finally, protocol or functional layers can easily be added to S3; its default download protocol is HTTP, and a BitTorrent protocol interface is provided to lower costs for high-scale distribution. Amazon S3 is not the only storage service on the Web; another one is Omnidrive.

Amazon EC2 (*Elastic Compute Cloud*) is a computing service that allows customers to assign varying computing power to their tasks and that charges ten cents per computer hour used. It provides a "virtual computing environment, allowing you to use Web service interfaces to requisition machines for use, load them with your custom application environment, manage your network's access permissions, and run your image using as many or few systems as you desire." The on-demand service is scalable, so that a user can use, for example, a single machine for an entire month (thirty days of twenty-four hours) for a total of seventy-two dollars or, if necessary, 720 servers for one hour for the same amount. Thus, EC2 is a commercial form of grid computing.

A platform that helps programmers and system developers to keep up with Web-based APIs, newly available mash-ups, and anything relevant to the Web as a computing platform is the ProgrammableWeb. The site was created by John Musser. Figure 5.6 shows the API Dashboard with a featured API, newest APIs, a tag cloud, and other ingredients.

From the perspective of business models, SaaS is from the provider perspective based on the subscription model, since service providers charge service customers for usage. SaaS may as well be based on a combination of the subscription and the community models, where contributions to a, say, developer community may be honored by lower subscription fees.

Figure 5.6 ProgrammableWeb API overview (as of March 21, 2007).
Source: http://programmableweb.com/apis

The SaaS model may not just be considered entirely advantageous. For example, a *service lock-in* may arise due to the fact that some business organizes all its processes around a certain service provider, thereby becoming heavily dependent on this provider. This can even refer to such trivial issues as e-mail addresses following the syntax of a particular ISP; if the company switches to another ISP, all these addresses are likely to change. On a larger scale, a service provider may exploit lock-ins in various ways, such as to start charging for an initially free service after some time. In addition, there may be contractual hazards that need to be considered. Other potential problems are that the service provider may be down at unpredictable times or may even go out of business. The questions that need to be looked into here are not new, yet may easily be overlooked in this particular context.

5.3.3 The consumer-oriented view and service customization

There is a second way of looking at the SaaS approach, namely from the consumer perspective. Under this perspective, a consumer or service client may have an understanding of the service he or she is looking for and may even be able to set up a specification that includes the desired functionality, the price he or she is willing to pay, the required service availability, a frequency of service execution, and other parameters. The client would then search for a provider who is able to meet this specification. Notice that this is the original idea behind Web services that we introduced in Chapter 1 (see Figure 1.17), and which may ultimately be done automatically. Another motivation is the consumer's desire to be independent of any subscriptions and commit to self-service offerings only which can be dropped any time.

While available in its full generality only in limited settings so far, there are approximations of the concept of service-spec publication in the form of *service marketplaces*. In a marketplace, a service requester can specify the parameters a service has to meet; if a provider is able to meet the specification, the service can be provided and the requester pays for it.

As an example for such a service marketplace, we look at the *Amazon Mechanical Turk*, which is another one of the ten Web services currently offered by Amazon.com. Amazon Mechanical Turk is not a marketplace for automated services, but provides an API through which programmers or *requesters* can submit tasks that are to be completed by *humans*; they can also approve completed tasks, and incorporate the answers into their own software application. From the programmer's perspective, putting up a service request is done via WPCs to the Turk API. However, it is important to keep in mind that the service requested is actually provided by humans who look for a "HIT" (Human Intelligence Task), execute it, and get paid for it. Figure 5.7 shows the Amazon Mechanical Turk home page.

A typical task or HIT description states an expiration date for the HIT, a time allotted, and a reward for each completed HIT, where the latter is typically in the range of several cents only. A task published by a requester could be the following: For a GIS image tagging application, a *worker* (i.e., a human willing to take this assignment) is given fifty images and has to go through each, clicking on road edges in the images as he goes along. Each completed HIT is rewarded with eight cents. The point is that tasks offered as HITs are often hardly doable by a computer, and this is where human workers come in. However, the results achieved by a human, such as the image completed with tags for road edges in our example, can be incorporated back into a computer-based application such as a mapping service.

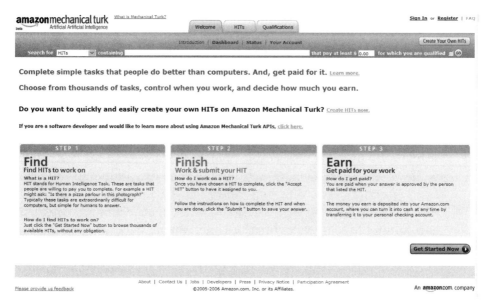

Figure 5.7 Amazon Mechanical Turk home page.
Source: http://www.mturk.com/mturk/welcome

A task with an extremely sad background appeared on Amazon Mechanical Turk in February 2007 shortly after Jim Gray, one of the most famous computer scientists and database researchers, had not returned from a Sunday sailing trip. It read:

> You will be presented with 5 images. The task is to indicate any satellite images which contain any foreign objects in the water that may resemble Jim's sailboat or parts of a boat. Jim's sailboat will show up as a regular object with sharp edges, white or nearly white, about 10 pixels long and 4 pixels wide in the image. If in doubt, be conservative and mark the image. Marked images will be sent to a team of specialists who will determine if they contain information on the whereabouts of Jim Gray.

An amusing example that has employed the Mechanical Turk has been the seemingly simple task of drawing a sheep. Ten thousand drawings were collected in this way and are now displayed at TheSheepMarket.

The business model in this consumer-oriented category again is that using the service drives home a commission, to be paid to the provider of the platform. The Mechanical Turk platform makes sure that direct commissions flow from the service requester to the human provider.

An increasing number of companies offer platforms for creating individual applications through mash-up services or widget integration, and it is

Table 5.2 Service integration into applications.

Application	Company	URL
Mash-Up Services	Teqlo	www.teqlo.com
Widgets Integration	Coghead	www.coghead.com
Application Creation	Yahoo!Widgets	widgets.yahoo.com
	ZCubes	www.zcubes.com
	Zimki	portal.zimki.com
Shop-Building Services	GoodStorm	www.goodstorm.com
	Zlio	www.zlio.com
	Zazzle	www.zazzle.com
	Amazon aStore	astore.amazon.com

becoming easy even for end users to set up an electronic shop today. Table 5.2 surveys several available sites that enable such service integrations and that are customer-oriented in the sense that, essentially, no programming skills are required to use any of these more comprehensive offerings. Many are based on widgets (i.e., small reusable components that enable an easy integration of content from multiple services and that were mentioned in Chapter 3). For shops that almost anybody can now create easily, the term *MeCommerce* has already been created as a synonym for "my own shop." What we see here is yet another manifestation of the long tail phenomenon; it is now easy to set up a business in an arbitrarily tiny niche without a lot of effort.

One of the next steps in consumer perspective on services obtainable from the Web will be customization (i.e., the idea of adapting a given service precisely to the needs of a particular customer). A development in this direction is app2you ("the apps you make are up to you"), which emerged from the database research group of the CSE Department of the University of California in San Diego. The intention is that app2you enables Internet users to build database-driven hosted Web applications without any coding and without specific database knowledge. Thus, the promise is that there will not be programming involved, but only a customization of given programs or services.

A general expectation is that service marketplaces will soon spread on the Web, and specialized brokers will provide services such as payment, mediation, identity management, provisioning, or authentication. The latter two issues refer to the fact that a user or customer may need to be logged in with many servers at the same time when using a mash-up of services from different providers. To alleviate this problem, the concept of *single-sign-on* (SSO) has been developed and is currently standardized within the *openID* project, a decentralized framework for digital user identities. Another aspect of service marketplaces is that consumers will be able to design their own portfolio depending on goals and prospects, but deep technical knowledge will no longer be needed. On the other hand, application integration may still be an issue, and it is here where semantic technologies, as discussed in Chapter 6, may enter the picture.

Yet another direction of future development is brought along by technical progress: At present, more and more applications become available on mobile devices such as cell phones and PDAs. As a consequence, the SaaS model is also starting to become available on mobile platforms. To this end, a recent survey on the Read/Write Web blog shows fifty-five tools that are readily available for taking search and a number of other services to a mobile environment, to be found at www.readwriteweb.com/archives/the_55_piece_mobile_search_tool_kit.php.

5.4 Socialization and cocreation of content

We now turn to the third major stream of the current Web development, which we termed "socialization" in Chapter 1. As we have discussed in various places already, socialization covers the aspect of user-generated content as it occurs in blogs or wikis, in tagging as well as in social bookmarking. In the context of our discussion, socialization does not, however, refer to the process of learning social skills. In this section, we encounter additional aspects of socialization, in particular ones that relate to software. In a nutshell, "social" software is software that gets better as more people use it; see also Musser and O'Reilly (2007). To be precise, it is often not the software itself that benefits from intensive usage, but the application that the software is providing. As we are interested in looking at impacts in this chapter, we explore how socialization and the cocreation of content on the Web go together with the business models we presented in the beginning of this chapter.

5.4.1 Social search

The well-known dilemma with Web search technologies is that, on the one hand their crawlers and indexers are still not smart enough to provide an automatic decision-making process to assess and evaluate the information a Web site contains. On the other hand, every individual is capable of deciding which information is useful for a particular purpose, yet does not have the time to browse the millions of hits a search engine typically supplies in return to a query. In Chapter 6, where we discuss the Semantic Web, we present several proposals for search engines that address this problem. Here, we look just at the aspect of socialization in relation to search.

For determining a user's intention when a query is posed to a search engine, there is a simple and obvious element that can help: past behavior. This just requires that the user register with the search engine so that his or her reactions to previous search results presented by the engine can be tracked and saved for future use. Evaluating user reactions with respect to previous searches can be utilized to anticipate the user's true interests for future queries. For instance, a long history of searches through the sites of car manufacturers indicates a high interest in this subject. If the user then starts a search, say, for "Jaguar," it is very likely that he or she intends to retrieve information on the car of this brand and not on the animal. Conversely, an animal welfare activist issuing the same query would probably be more interested in the animal and the environments it may be living in.

Based on the idea of incorporating history into search, search engine providers have already started offering services for a *personalized search*. A personalized search aims at improving search results by taking the empirical information about the user's search behavior into account and amounts to an analysis of user queries to identify additional information about the user, such as his or her preferred fields of interest or location. Optionally, a user's bookmarks can be employed as well. Then, all available information beyond the query proper is additionally applied to the computation of relevance for the distinct entries in a result list.

There are two main approaches to personalization of a search engine: One is employing cookies, the other one is based on explicit registration. The latter approach specially shows good potential for improving search results, since favorite sites are weighted higher for a recognized user than for an anonymous individual using a standard search.

However, there are ways of going even further, namely by spreading the insights about individual search behavior within a community and additionally allowing and encouraging users to label or tag the information they have used. The techniques we discussed in Chapter 3 in connection with Flickr and del.icio.us may be applied to search as well. As we have seen, tags can represent keywords, personal ratings, or other forms of comments or metadata. A search becomes *social* when such metadata, be it from an individual or a community, is taken into account during the process of answering a search query. The various evolutionary steps in search just described are summarized in Figure 5.8.

Recall from Chapter 3 how tagging and social bookmarking can lead to collaboratively created, open-ended labeling systems called *folksonomies;* there is no reason why folksonomies should not be applied to search.

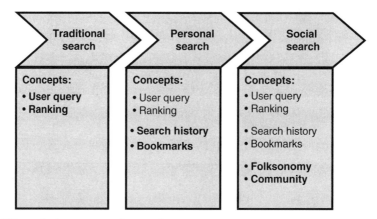

Figure 5.8 Evolutionary steps in search.

Indeed, the concept of tagging can be adopted for pictures, movies, Web sites, articles, and so on. Moreover, when tagging is conducted in the context of a community, experts for a specific domain can share their knowledge and make it available to others. Finally, there seems to be a tendency that the larger the community, the more the tags used will converge towards a common point of view or understanding.

Clearly, search based on a folksonomy will face exactly the same problems as other exploitations of folksonomies. In particular, there may be semantic issues brought along, for example, by homonyms and synonyms. This is where techniques under development in the context of the Semantic Web may come in. These are discussed in Chapter 6.

Rollyo as a social search platform

We next discuss Rollyo, whose name is an abbreviation for "roll your own search engine." Rollyo incorporates both personalized and social elements into search. The personalization can be done by creating individual *search rolls,* a construct comprising up to twenty-five Web sites which are subsequently used for search exclusively. Rollyo builds on the Yahoo! API and thus uses the Yahoo! search engine, but restricts the search to the predefined sites. However, to promote the idea of social search, search rolls can additionally be tagged, shared, and searched among all users, which is the crucial point of Rollyo. The restriction of search to a particular domain or a specific set of Web sites is neither new nor complex, but the sharing of expertise and knowledge makes it a valuable search platform. A concept for promoting this advantage is the "Exploring a Searchroll" feature. Based on collected statistics, it can be seen which search rolls are most frequently used and which

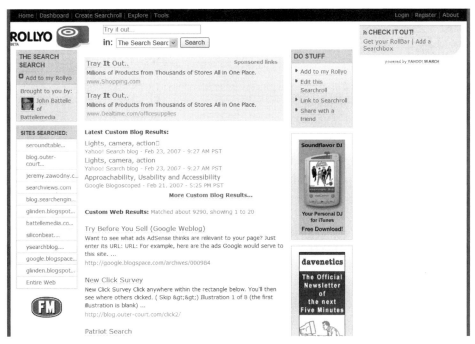

Figure 5.9 Rollyo Search Roll "The Search Search" by John Battelle (February 2007).

have been recently added. Thus, a user's attention can be drawn to this collection of Web sites, and he or she might discover a new search roll that may be helpful for his or her own search intentions.

As an example, Figure 5.9 shows a search roll named "The Search Search" created by John Battelle (see www.rollyo.com/search.html?q=Try+it+out … &sid=213&x=15&y=10). The left-hand side shows the sites it will go through when a search is actually started. Other than that, the page shows blog entries, sponsored links, and a few banners. In addition, there is a prestigious group of "High Rollers" involving widely accepted experts from science, press, and business. These professionals announce their personal search rolls and spread their search experience to anyone who might be interested and who thinks could benefit from it. To amplify the community effect and to foster user discoveries, search rolls can be tagged, and the resulting folksonomy can improve search results even further. For example, searching a search roll for "Harlem OR Manhattan OR Queens" will also discover search rolls for "New York," assuming the tagging has been done properly.

To illustrate the usage of the Yahoo! API as the technical foundation of Rollyo, consider an example of a user creating a search roll called "social search" and aiming at specialized academic institutions such as the

University of Muenster in Germany and the University of Poznan in Poland. Rollyo would build a query as a WPC call as follows:

```
http://api.search.yahoo.com/WebSearchService/V1/
webSearch?
appid="rollyo"
&query="Forms of Search in Web 2.0"
&site=www.wi.uni-muenster.de, www.kti.ae.poznan.pl
```

In line 1, the base URL of the Yahoo! Web search API is provided. In line 2, the Web search method is invoked. Lines 3 to 5 provide the relevant WPC parameters: line 3 supplies the application ID, in this example "rollyo," line 4 contains the search query, and line 5 restricts the search to the desired sites.

Since manual search as this one just shown can be tedious, Rollyo is automatically doing most of the work, once an appropriate search roll has been chosen. The user only needs to specify the query and the search roll that he or she wants to engage.

In order to resolve ambiguities in the meaning of search terms, new ways of consistency checking must be developed. Rollyo already uses automatic completion for the tagging process to help unify the vocabulary used. However, more profound and sustainable mechanisms need to be introduced in order to supervise and standardize the semantic contributions of the masses. As a solution to this problem, the Semantic Web is offering the possibility of creating ontologies (see Chapter 6). Finally, it has to be pointed out that Rollyo can be perceived as a solely personalized platform for search in the first place, since the user can exclusively make use of his or her own search rolls. Social idea is actually exploited only when a user takes other search rolls into account.

Other social search engines

Rollyo is not the only company working on social search. For another approach in this direction, refer to *Yahoo!Search MyWeb2* (see myweb2.search. yahoo.com), which embraces most of the available concepts for social search such as bookmarks, search history, tagging, and the cultivation of a community. Another example is *Eurekster*, a Christchurch, New Zealand-based company that has combined search and wikis into what they call "swickis." Among other things, swickis let people within specific communities or niches (like a sports publication site) rank results for that particular community. Thus, a swicki is essentially a community-powered search engine, tailored to produce only the targeted search results that this community wants. To this end, it comprises a variety of algorithmic technologies. Yet another example is *PreFound*, where users can see what other users have gathered on the Web and shared with the PreFound community. Summize is a product search engine that returns products in various categories, shows their price, and lists comments on the product that people have previously delivered.

5.4.2 Social aspects of software

Socialization in the form of user contributions to Web content *and* of sharing these contributions among communities has not only arrived at search engines and their core business; it is also, nowadays, seen as a phenomenon that has far-reaching consequences even for other types of software, and it has in fact been around for quite some time already. As briefly mentioned earlier in this chapter, social software is software that gets better the more people use it. While most of the time the software itself (i.e., the program system) does not change based on the number of its users or the frequency with which it is used, it is the *application* that the software is enabling that is actually getting better. Several examples support this claim:

■ The Amazon recommendation service ("Customers who bought this item also bought") can be more precise when more people have bought on Amazon, since it can then do more evaluations and analyses. By a similar token, reviews at Amazon that end in the question "Was this review helpful to you?" and that show how many people found it helpful become more reliable and meaningful when more people answer this question. While the former is the result of an automated software application, whose results improve with a larger database, the latter depends on human input to the Amazon Web site.

■ The eBay seller evaluation and the profile that is created for every seller are more significant when more people have entered their experience with a particular seller. Again, the basis is the input provided by buyers; eBay then evaluates this input and turns it into a profile that even comes with a summary of the evaluation results.

■ The Google PageRank, which essentially mimics a citation system discussed in Chapter 1, improves for a given page the more back links that page has to pages that have a high PageRank themselves. Here it is the creation and linking of Web pages as well as the authoritativeness of linking pages that impact the PageRank of a page, but again it is the users who ultimately decide which links to put in a page.

■ Google AdSense has been explained as a way to generate revenue for a Web site that includes references to Google ads and the AdWords behind them. Here, again, the more people participate, the more advertising can be placed next to respective content.

■ Wikipedia is, as we have seen, an encyclopedia crucially depending on user input, be it for new entries or for editing as well as commenting on existing ones. Here it is, again, the application (i.e., the encyclopedia itself) that is getting better with every new listing or with most user input sent to it.

- By a similar token, even a blog that focuses on a particular topic gets better as more and more experts on the topic write to the blog. As an example, we have described Bob Lutz's blog in Chapter 1 as a novel approach to customer interaction for a large car manufacturer. It takes its information from GM officials who *know* what is going on in the company. Again, the application benefits from contributions, not the blogging software itself.

- As a final example, even Skype, the VoIP communication platform we discussed in Chapter 2, deserves mentioning here. The more people have a Skype account, the more people a user can reach via Skype, as long as we consider just the option of free communication from computer to computer. Conversely, the application is hardly useful as long as only a few people have signed up. Notice that this is a classical network effect that has also applied, for example, to the telephone network in the nineteenth century: Each new addition of an end node increases the number of connections that can be established by the number of end points already in the network.

Most of the examples just described take advantage of socialization aspects by evaluating and subsequently exploiting user input (i.e., evaluations, recommendations, citations, and sometimes just increased usage) in response to contacts, search results, or transactions they have been experiencing. As demonstrated by Flickr, however, there is another impact that socialization can have, namely that of improving some given software on a constant or *perpetual* basis. Traditionally, software has never been free of bugs, security holes, or errors, and it has been common for a software company to fix them and distribute new releases or versions of the software from time to time. The new paradigm is to do this at a much higher pace. As mentioned in Chapter 3, software on the Web may nowadays be in a permanent beta state of release and never finished. Thus, for outsiders, maintenance occurs on a permanent basis. As mentioned in Chapter 1, such a state of *perpetual beta* may apply to a service that can only be accessed through an API, in which case a user is not bothered by constant release changes, at least as long as the behavior of the API is only extended, but not fundamentally modified. Alternatively, it may apply to the actual software underlying a site; in this case, short delays in service may occur during moments of software update.

Flickr is an example of a perpetual beta site, which is where the software actually gets better with increasing numbers of users, since the more often it is used, the more bugs or missing features are detected, and the faster the company can react and release a new version of the software. Users may even be invited to become codevelopers.

Social software or, more precisely, social aspects of software, are not only more and more relevant in personal Web applications or in B2C e-commerce, it is expected that social software will also have a major impact on how people connect with their colleagues and coworkers, partners, and customers, and hence on how they work or how companies do business with each other and with their customers. Companies not only expect improved knowledge management among their workforce, but also increased productivity and better customer relationship management. As a consequence, large IT companies building software have meanwhile discovered this area as a market that can even be reached via a traditional distribution channel; examples of recent products in this category of social software include IBM's Lotus Connections, Oracle's WebCenter Suite, or Intel's SuiteTwo.

5.4.3 Impacts of online social networks

As we stated in Chapter 1, online social networks bring a dimension to the Web that goes beyond simple links between pages; they add links between people and between communities. In such a network, direct links will typically point to our closest friends and colleagues, indirect links lead to the friends of a friend ("FOAF"), and so on. We have also said that a *social network* on the Web is typically the result of employing some software that is intended to focus on building an online community for a specific purpose. Social networks connect people with common interests and may be as simple as a blog, or as complex as MySpace, which we have already discussed. We have also mentioned a number of social network sites that emphasize professional use (e.g., LinkedIn or openBC) or that can be used for sharing any kind of media, nowadays preferably videos (e.g., YouTube). As mentioned, a social network can act as a means of connecting employees of distinct expertise across departments and company branches and help them build profiles in an often much easier way, and it can do so in a much cheaper and more flexible way than traditional knowledge management systems. Once a profile has been set up and published within the network, others can search for people with particular knowledge and connect to them. Finally, platforms such as LinkedIn, openBC or Ryze enable such networks to go online.

The primary impacts that the current Web developments are having in this area are that connecting people and communities constantly becomes easier, and it is not difficult anymore to maintain a professional or personal network of buddies worldwide. Yet another impact is that a social network may open up novel sources of revenue. Indeed, some of the business models we have discussed can easily be applied to a social network, most notably advertising. For example, MySpace has a "Classifieds" section that comprises ads in categories such as jobs, services, housing and rentals, cars for sale, and several others, and that can be localized to a number of cities in the United States and beyond. Similarly, YouTube presents "Ads by Google" obtained via the Google AdSense program. As noted by Sloan and Kaihla (2006), advertising is big business even in blogs today. Moreover, since the number of newly created blogs is still growing exponentially, blogs that are proven to attract high traffic rates have started to ask for more and more money for the placement of ads.

What companies have recognized and what is a direct continuation of the concept of focused advertising invented by search engine providers is that social networks, especially those on the Web, may be able to do much more for a brand or for a product to become popular than traditional marketing approaches. For example, German car manufacturer BMW has recently produced a number of three-minute videos on a new engine that was downloaded from the BMW Web site, watched online, or put on other sites several million times within a short period of time. If people like the video, they may bookmark it and share that through del.icio.us, or they may replicate it on their own site or on a site such as YouTube and tag it, thereby essentially recommending it to other users or to their friends. The business phenomenon behind this is called *viral marketing*, since announcements, messages, and ultimately ads get spread like a virus without the company behind it having to do much about it or having to invest a lot of money for the creation or purchase of a channel. Besides BMW, other examples of companies having started to exploit and utilize social networking effects directly and having actually started to reorganize their marketing budgets correspondingly include Coca-Cola and Adidas. There is also an indirect way, which we talk about in the context of Second Life.

Since ultimately the business goal even on the Web is to create revenue, a new term in this context is "social shopping," which is the idea of making electronic shopping a social experience through an intensive sharing of recommendations or product reviews. Chitika ShopCloud$ and eMiniMalls (see www.chitika.com for both), Chitika ShopLinc (see www.shoplinc.com), Loomia, PowerReviews, or Kaboodle are developments in this direction. PowerReviews, for example, provides its service for free, yet their business model is based on monetizing the content of a review through advertising and a PPC mechanism from their shopping portal.

5.4.4 User-generated content in advertising

While social networks and blogging, as well as content-sharing sites, have long been identified as good places for targeted advertisements, and while this has meanwhile become big business due to its enormous reach and success, there is a second side to a business model such as advertising in this context. While ads have so far mostly been presented *next* to user-generated content, another evolutionary step would be its *integration* into such content, an approach that has been taken by the online gaming industry (e.g., Massive Inc. and others) already. Yet another step would be to base advertising directly on user-generated contributions; in other words, users become the *creators* of ads.

A recent example of the integration approach is given by companies such as Podcaster Ads, Visible World, or Audioads (see www.audioads.de), which integrate advertising into podcasts or videocasts (an activity also called *podvertising*). Using such a platform, a user creating a podcast can make money by having ads injected at the beginning or the end of the podcast; every time the podcast is downloaded, the creator gets paid. The United States alone saw more than three million dollars spent on podcast ads in 2005, and it is expected that this market will grow considerably over the next couple of years, as advertisers are looking for new channels. This development is another example of the long tail we have mentioned several times.

An example of the second evolutionary step of advertising mentioned was observed during Super Bowl XLI in 2007, the biggest annual event in U.S. football. For this event, advertising costs had risen to more than two and one-half million U.S. dollars for a thirty-second commercial spot on television. Since an ad during Super Bowl gets highest visibility nationwide, companies are willing to spend large amounts of money here, yet some have started looking into production alternatives. In particular, they have experimented with *user-generated ads*. For example, Chevrolet asked college students from all over the United States to submit ideas for ads presenting the company's latest lineup of cars; snack producer Doritos ran the "Crash the Super Bowl" contest in 2006, in which consumers could submit their own thirty-second spots to the company's Web site, where Internet users could then vote. The submissions to Doritos led to a shortlist of five, out of which the winner was then shown on national television during the Super Bowl game; for further details, see promotions.yahoo.com/doritos. Even the National Football League itself, which runs the Super Bowl, sponsored a "Best NFL Super Bowl Commercial Ever" contest (see www.nfl.com/superad) in which fans could create their own spots and have some of them broadcasted during the game.

The important aspects of activities such as the ones just described is that in the context of the Web today, media companies and advertisers are moving away from the traditional approach, in which ads were prefabricated with a specific audience in mind, but independent of it, towards an approach in which users and hence consumers have a more active role and start developing their own media. This trend will see more exploitation within online social networks in the near future. Moreover, if spending on advertising is shifted from traditional media to the Internet, this trend will soon have an impact on the traditional media as well. Many newspapers, noticing such effects already, have added an online edition to their traditional print edition, and started relying on user input by providing a blog for discussions. Other media will certainly follow.

5.4.5 Second Life

The final example of a Web 2.0 application whose importance appears to be emerging quickly is Second Life. Ever wished for a second life? Well, this can now be made a reality, but it has to occur *during* your first life, not thereafter. Second Life is essentially an online role-playing site created by San Francisco-based Linden Lab. It provides a three-dimensional virtual world that is built and owned by its "residents." In order to become a resident, users need to register in one of several categories and choose an *avatar* (i.e., their named virtual representation, whose appearance can be changed if the avatar does no longer please the user it represents). Second Life can be considered as a 3D variant of the Internet: Instead of just having a home page, users can create a house or even an island in Second Life; instead of just having an e-mail address or a user name, there is now the personalized avatar whose movements and actions are controlled from the keyboard of the user's computer.

Since its start in 2003, Second Life grew explosively to more than four million registered users at the end of February 2007. Once inside, users can discover and explore this virtual world and the entertainment and opportunities it offers. Users can build a house or a business, and can buy, sell, and trade with other residents. The *Marketplace* currently supports monthly transactions valued at millions of U.S. dollars, where the actual currency is the *Linden dollar*, which can be converted to and from U.S. dollars at an online exchange. The exchange rate varies, but was pretty stable in early 2007 at around 270 Linden dollars for one U.S. dollar (see www.secondlife. com/whatis/economy-market.php). Orientation within the virtual world is achieved through maps, menus, or contact with other avatars that are met.

An introduction to Second Life can be found in Rymaszewski et al. (2007). The NewScientist Technology Blog wrote on Second Life in February 2006:

> Ever wished you could give up the day job and play video games for a living instead? You're not the only one. Some people are doing it too – abandoning the real rat race to pursue a virtual fortune instead, within the online game Second Life. Second Life "citizens" can create in-game objects – including clothes, vehicles and buildings – and sell them on to other players. Very talented crafters can make serious money too, hawking their wares for virtual credits that can be converted into real-world cash.

The point for us is that not just private users are flocking to Second Life for various reasons. An increasing number of companies are also discovering Second Life as another advertising, marketing, presentation, contact, and business platform. In mid-2006, Adidas Reebok opened a store in Second Life, and Toyota has started using the platform for marketing its Scion xB model (see Figure 5.10) primarily to a young audience. Other companies that are already using Second Life for product presentation, marketing, or customer relationship activities include BMW, Nissan, Mazda, General Motors, Dell, Sun Microsystems, IBM, Circuit City, or German Bild.T-Online, which offers a virtual newspaper called *The AvaStar;* this list is growing almost daily. DaimlerChrysler runs a virtual showroom in Second Life as well as a test circuit onto which their cars can be taken for a virtual test drive. Circuit City opened a store on IBM's premises in December 2006; both companies are investigating how this virtual world and the 3D Internet can be integrated into future, multichannel marketing concepts and whether it appears promising as another sales channel. To this end, the store exhibits virtual mock-ups of products that Circuit City is also offering in its real-world stores. Clearly, products can be ordered directly from this store, which thus essentially replaces the online catalog. The company expects to be able to improve its customer relations, for example through three-dimensional and interactive instruction manuals of products such as digital cameras.

IBM has used Second Life already for a number of other activities, including an alumni meeting in October 2006, a virtual Wimbledon tennis match later the same year, or meetings of consultants with customers on one of their virtual islands. The company has used this platform for announcing new business ideas and generally considers 3D Internet applications as an appropriate platform for future Web stores as well as global commerce.

Companies like Sears are experimenting with *virtual commerce*: When a new product is presented on a platform such as Second Life, the company can test its market acceptability through observing, for example, what people say about the product on blogs. If the product is mainly criticized, there

Figure 5.10 Toyota Scion xB product presentation at Second Life.
Source: http://secondworld.files.wordpress.com/2006/09/toyota_sion_02.jpg

may be little point in taking it to the real-world market. Otherwise, it can go into production. An approach like this is also called *consumer-owned marketing,* since the value of a product or its potential success is determined in advance through consumer feedback loops on a large scale. Moreover, potential customers can check how the company's product would fit into their homes, for example, by changing colors of furniture.

Second Life is not the only player on this field. Another one is the Entropia Universe (see www.project-entropia.com or www.entropiauniverse.com), with more than 500,000 registered users, which was founded by actor and director Jon Jacobs and which is run by Swedish software company MindArk. Entropia is similar to Second Life in many respects; real dollars have to be exchanged against *Project Entropia Dollars* (PEDs) for being able to make payments; PEDs can also be changed back, for which the provider charges a fee. Other recent developments in this category include China-based HiPiHi and Sony's PlayStation 3 Home project that can only be accessed using a PS3.

Second Life and its competitors open entirely new fields for B2C as well as for B2B and other forms of e-commerce, and the business models we have discussed in the beginning of this chapter are beginning to be carried over into these virtual worlds that heavily exploit user contributions as well as interactions and the various forms of socializations we have discussed.

5.5 Summary

In this chapter, we have touched upon a variety of issues that are currently in motion thanks to the vast possibilities of the Web today and to the core dimensions along which it keeps evolving. The main theme has been the various business models for the Web, in particular advertising, subscriptions, and pay-as-you-go and their interaction with paradigms such as Software as a Service, data ownership, and the many facets of socialization. In previous years, the business models we have discussed have been transferred or applied to the Web only one after the other. What can be observed in the context of the Web as we see it today is that various *combinations* of business models become common. For example, blogs can combine the community and the brokerage models, since they allow interested communities to exchange their views *and* enable transactions through which goods or services are exchanged. The SaaS paradigm combines community and subscription models, while social software can be seen as a confluence of transactions, advertising, and the community models.

Through various mechanisms and developments we have described, social networks are turning into social *value* networks at a large scale, and our traditional economies are becoming *economies of relationships* as well as economies of attention (see the article by Alex Iskold at alexiskold. wordpress.com/2007/03/02/the-attention-economy-an-overview). While this has been observed by many commentators, the media, and bloggers for quite some time now, the scientific study of the interaction of the social as well as the engineering dimension of the Web has only just begun (Berners-Lee et al., 2006)

While it appears that the importance of traditional media is decreasing and on the other hand the number of blogs around the world doubles every six months (see Figure 1.19), the Web has become a place where users are more and more in control of content, and businesses are looking for new ways of tapping into this situation and of taking advantage of it. An obvious trade-off that has to be investigated is control over content, including privacy and copyright issues, versus the many opportunities arising through participation and cocreation of content. Finally, it is clear that unintended uses will happen, such as the discovery made by the *New Scientist* magazine "that Pentagon's National Security Agency, which specializes in eavesdropping and code-breaking, is funding research into the mass harvesting of the information that people post about themselves on social networks" (see www.newscientisttech.com/article.ns?id=mg19025556.200). Other misuses through spamming or phishing will also occur, and participating users will have to protect themselves against it.

We are aware that a discussion like the one led here may outdate relatively soon, which is why we mention keeping up-to-date with online sources such as Richard MacManus' blog entitled *Read/Write Web*, a tech Web log maintained at www.readwriteweb.com, which is part of the blogger network web20workgroup.com/. We are also aware of the fact that many other blogs discuss the topic of Web 2.0 as well, but any attempt to be comprehensive here would be very difficult.

The Semantic Web and Web 2.0

In their introductory paper to Pellegrini and Blumauer's (2006) book discussing the development of the networked information society and the role semantic technologies can and will play in it, authors Tochtermann and Maurer sketch two scenarios. In these, they highlight the difference between one scenario, the Web as we know it today, and another, the "Semantic" Web of the (near) future. They roughly go like this:

In Scenario 1, a woman, Ms. Maler, is searching for a homeopathic doctor in her home town, the Austrian city of Graz. She enters "doctor," "homeopathic," and "Graz" into the search field of her favorite search engine, and receives a long list of links. Ms. Maler next works through that list to figure out which are doctors that do have the desired expertise, that do offer visiting hours that would fit into her schedule, and that are reachable using public transportation. To figure out the third, she needs to consult a city map and look up the addresses. Finally, she takes a quick look at evaluations the remaining doctors may have received and, after twenty minutes, ends up with three who might be appropriate.

In Scenario 2, set in the not-too-distant future, the project manager of a transnational enterprise is working on a ground-breaking space tourism project, together with two other large and a number of smaller companies, as well as a network of independent specialists and consultants. They collaborate through a service-oriented, Web-based platform that allows them to plan, schedule, calculate, monitor, and administer the project electronically.

An unexpected court decision has just changed the basic conditions of the project completely. However, in that real-time economy his project partners, the investors, and also his boss expect fast and precise reactions instantly; obviously, this requires quite a bit more than Ms. Maler's search for a doctor. Indeed, the enterprise has to decide how to cope with the court rule, and that decision has to be made in a virtual collaboration carried out on the Web via multiple time zones and technical disciplines.

The question in Scenario 1 is: *Could* this be done easier, faster, and better? Wouldn't it be nice to have this search task executed a bit more intelligently, based on the search terms Ms. Maler has provided? For example, we can imagine that a localization of the search results concentrates on doctors in Graz and mashes up names with addresses and location pointers on a map. In particular, the manual "post-processing" of the initial search results should be taken over by a machine that comes up with suggestions and even itineraries of how to get to them.

The question in Scenario 2 goes quite a step further; it is: *Must* that not go easier, faster, and better than today? For example, communication devices at each participating party should initiate a Web-based meeting immediately after an event (such as the court decision) changing the project's conditions has occurred, calling in a representative from each side automatically, and taking time zones and personal calendars into consideration. Moreover, agents should start evaluating the options to carry on the project prior to the meeting and have them available for review at its start. Activities like these would require the respective machines to take action autonomously, and to collect information from various other machines on their own.

The *Semantic Web* that we introduce in this chapter was born out of the recognition that the answer to both questions must be "yes" and that there are emerging and maturing technologies available that even indicate *how* this could be accomplished.

The Semantic Web represents another important Web development, besides Web 2.0, that has emerged roughly since 2001, when Tim Berners-Lee and others wrote their famous paper "The Semantic Web – A new form of Web content that is meaningful to computers will unleash a revolution of new possibilities" in the *Scientific American* (Berners-Lee et al., 2001). It essentially describes the idea of adding more meaning to what can be found on the Web today and to do so in such a way that this information becomes not only machine-*readable* (as it is already today), but also machine-*understandable*; today it is only understandable to humans. We first elaborate on this idea a bit, which requires linguistic (as well as other) concepts to be applied to the Web so that the "meaning" or semantics of data found there can be made explicit and manageable. These concepts have led to the development of a stack of languages and protocols that have in part already arrived and are increasingly in use. Two of these languages, RDF/RDFS (the Resource Description Framework and its Schema language) and OWL (the Web Ontology Language), are described in more detail, as they form the underlying foundation for the important concept of *ontologies* which, in essence, provides common reference terminologies, languages, and inference mechanisms for specific application domains.

We then contrast and compare the features available through Web 2.0 technology, in particular, social bookmarking, tagging, and folksonomies, with Semantic Web developments such as taxonomies and ontologies. We will argue that here is where the two currently have the best chance of growing together into something that Wahlster and Dengel (2006) as well as others already call "Web 3.0." Thus, in light of what we have discussed in the previous chapters, we can term the Semantic Web the "logical future" of the Web. While Web 2.0 represents its "physical presence," it of course remains to be seen whether Web 2.0 technology can indeed become the "implementation vehicle" for the Semantic Web. The interesting challenge arising is to get the most benefit out of both.

For a picture of what we are aiming at, preview Figure 6.20, where the lower portion summarizes the concepts we have seen in previous chapters, the upper portion surveys what we deal with in this chapter, and the middle section indicates points where the two could meet.

6.1 Basics

In this section, we introduce the basic concepts of the Semantic Web. We start out from a look at possible augmentations and enhancements to traditional search engines, then present the core idea of the Semantic Web, and finally introduce its structure as it is foreseen today. The structure in particular positions various languages relevant to the Semantic Web, which we discuss in more detail in the next section.

6.1.1 Search revisited

Let's come back to an issue we have discussed already in a little bit of detail in Chapter 1 and that was also on Ms. Maler's agenda above: searching the Internet. As we have described, search engines typically crawl the Web and build an index that, together with some ranking mechanism, is then used to answer user queries and in particular to order the respective search results in "most appropriate" form. However, as everybody will certainly have experienced, search results are often still far from optimal or at least appropriate or relevant to what the user wanted or had in mind. There are various work-arounds to this situation, both commercially available and under development, that justify a little detour into current search technology.

The first is to experiment with new ranking and ordering approaches such as customized ranking suited to particular user requirements (Tsoi et al., 2006), or to enhance search otherwise. Clearly, this would have to be done on the side of the search engine, since its algorithms and other mechanisms cannot be controlled from outside. For example, Nextlinks (wortschatz.uni-leipzig.de/nextlinks/nextlinks.html) has been an attempt to set up a search engine that, whenever the user clicked on the link provided in a search result, showed up to ten links of "similar" Web pages. Another example would be IBM's WebFountain project (www.research.ibm.com/journal/sj/431/gruhl.html), which uses (de-) tagging of HTML and PDF documents as well as data mining techniques to derive semantically meaningful content through linguistic analyses on full texts, as described by Tretau and Lelescu (2004). Related is the idea of employing a visualization tool that may or may not have been developed by the search engine provider; an example of an independent one is *Touchgraph* which displays the connections between Web pages as stored in the Google database in the form of a network. Another example, Snap, provides a split screen for search results with a list of URLs in the left half and a preview of the currently active position in that list in the right. An even more sophisticated service, actually a mash-up, is under development by Google itself under the name SearchMash. For yet another example, Powerset is experimenting with natural language processing in the context of search.

The second type of approach in current search technology is to request and exploit user interaction or feedback. This is, for example, done in approaches that use sliders (like mindset.research.yahoo.com). A slider typically allows setting a value by moving an indicator along a horizontal axis. It is operated by the user once an initial search result is available in order to refine it. Another example here is Getty Images, which combines keyword-based search with semantic refinement requested from the user. The ChaCha search engine combines automated search with *people-powered* search. ChaCha starts with a standard search box as seen in Figure 6.1 (left). When a query is typed in, there is an option of doing just a search or of searching with a guide. In the latter case, the system tries to connect you, through a chat interface, with a (human) Search Guide that will help refine the search results. Figure 6.1 (right) shows the initial result of "what is the area of Germany" typed into the search box and indicates in the left-hand side bar that it is trying to connect to a guide. Other recent enhancements to search include Hakia, which also accepts questions or complete sentences

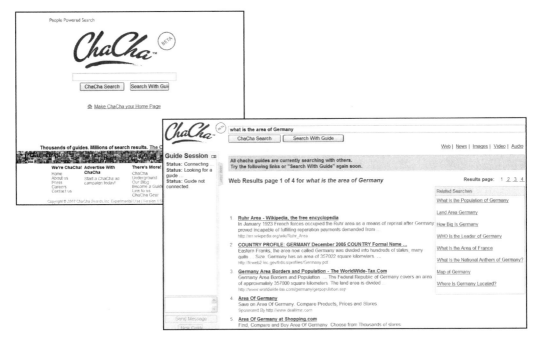

Figure 6.1 ChaCha search interface and query result.

in addition to simple search keywords, and attempts to get to the meaning of a question with the help of a proprietary *SemanticRank* algorithm. Yet another attempt to provide personalized search results is Collarity.

Ask X tries to accommodate the user's intention by coming back not just with topical links, but with a three-part result screen as shown in Figure 6.2. This screen contains in its left field a *search control panel* with *Zoom Related Search* and *Search Suggestions* that are updated as the user refines the search. The middle field contains the current set of search results with a *Binoculars* function to preview individual results. On the right-hand side, a preview of other types of search results is provided, including video, news, images, blogs, shopping, encyclopedia, and more. Another example in this category is Wikipedia founder Jimmy Wales' Wikiasari project (see search.wikia. com/wiki/Wikiasari), a search engine where a community of trusted users is asked to evaluate the quality of search results.

Finally, something could be done at the site of the information provider, and this is where the Semantic Web comes in. Indeed, it would be easier for search engines to distinguish "relevant" content from irrelevant content, or to replace full-text search by content-driven search, if the content itself was semantically annotated and not just plain text, an approach that IBM's Web Fountain tries to apply by itself. For example, consider a search

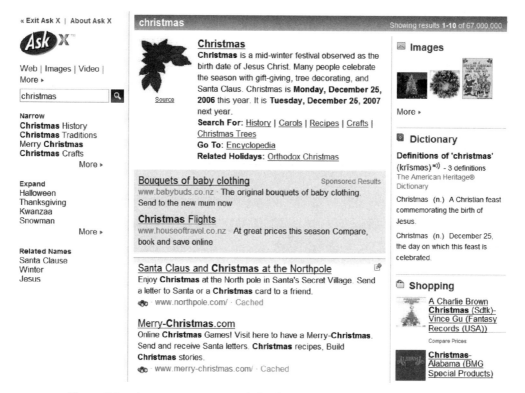

Figure 6.2 Ask X response to search for "Christmas."

for book titles. This can easily be done within the database of a Web-based book store, since that store would allow distinguishing "title" from "author" or from "keywords." In this case, the user query will most likely be translated into a query against a database that has a book table. This table, in turn, will have attributes such as "title" or "author" and hence return the desired information in an instant. This can be seen as a precursor to the idea of providing annotated information that can be crawled by search engines, correspondingly indexed, and then given as an answer to a query within the appropriate, user-intended context, for the simple reason that the database behind this Web site most likely has a "schema." The schema contains semantic information such as attributes, their types, and their integrity constraints. So it appears near at hand to transfer the idea of a "schema" to the Web.

Currently, most general-purpose search engines do not allow entering something like "book title = ..." into their search fields, since no metadata or schema information is available for the search engine through which it could identify a piece of text found on an HTML page as a book title. There are exceptions to this. For example, Google allows a user to enter a string such as "Semantic Web filetype:pdf" into its search box and will then return only the Adobe type objects that relate to the Semantic Web. We have seen in previous chapters what could be used as a general solution here: XML as well as tagging. Indeed, if publishers would provide their book information uniformly encoded in XML format (by using the same collection of tags, prescribed in a DTD or an XML Schema, across publishers), a solution to the problem would come in sight, as the crawler of a search engine could now exploit these tags for generating index entries. Similar comments apply to tagging, since user-generated tags attached to items or pages on the Web can also enhance search considerably. We mention that the *Knowledge Sifter* project at George Mason University in Virginia is among the few approaches in this direction; details are in Kerschberg et al. (2004).

As Battelle (2005) puts it, the Semantic Web could be an important step on the way to a "perfect search" (i.e., a search that indeed *understands* what the user has in mind and no longer guesses or makes assumptions about it). For a search to be considered perfect, it would have, for example, to become ubiquitous (i.e., searches everywhere on the Web and not just within its visible part). It would also have to take personal preferences and intentions into account via an analysis of stored clickstreams, or it would have to be able to grasp an understanding of what a document or file found on the Web means. It is here where the Semantic Web enters the picture. We mention that a speculative scenario for search in the presence of the Semantic Web in 2009 has been outlined in Ford (2002), a famous article by Paul Ford.

6.1.2 Data and information integration

The penetration of our world with computers and the ubiquitousness of the Web have led to giant aggregations of data, as we have discussed in previous chapters of this book. This can be observed both at a small and at a large scale. It can be seen in large enterprises that collect transaction data in a data warehouse or their satellite data for making it publicly available, as well as for private people who organize their digital media collection electronically. One of the major challenges the area of data collection and management has seen over the past twenty years has been *data integration* (i.e., the integration of data on a common subject or similar subjects, yet from several distinct sources into one consistent collection). Consider, for example, a company that buys another company and now wants to integrate two existing human-resource databases. Both databases might contain different data, such as home addresses only in one case and home and business addresses in the other. One might store an employee's age and the other only his or her birthday; one may record annual salaries, the other monthly payments; this list could go on. Even if there is the same type of information in both databases, it could be named and formatted differently (e.g., names broken down into first-name, last-name pairs in one case and last, middle, first name in another), each with its distinct type (such as strings of fixed or varying length). Numerous challenges arise here, including the question of which attributes to take over to the integrated data set, how to determine that attributes in the two database have different names but identical meaning, how to deal with missing or incomplete values, and, last but not least, how to derive company-relevant *information* from all this data. Notice that the basic problem just sketched is about *data* integration. Once this data is given a meaning or an interpretation, it may become *information*, with the data integration problem turned into an information integration problem. Health care systems or geographical information systems are typical examples.

Types of integration

The database area especially has developed a considerable number of techniques and approaches to deal with data integration problems. The approaches fall into two basic categories: virtual integration and materialized integration.

In a *virtual* integration system, the integration is done virtually only (i.e., the integration result is not stored). For a given application or query that needs to access several data sources, the task at hand is decomposed into subtasks that can be run on the relevant sources individually; the results are then combined into a uniform answer. Thus, integration essentially occurs *on demand* (i.e., when data from several sources is requested) and without the need to bother with integration issues as long as there is no application looking for it.

In a *materialized* integration system, on the other hand, integration of data from multiple sources occurs *in advance* (i.e., without a particular query or application demanding it). Thus, relevant sources are addressed, data is extracted from there, eventually filtered and consolidated, and finally placed into an integrated database. If a query occurs, this is run against the integration result; similarly, application referring to the integration result can do so without delay.

Materialized systems include search engines with their index, but also data warehouses as used in online analytical processing (OLAP) applications. Virtual systems include meta search engines such as Mamma, multidatabase systems as well as systems building on so called *mediated* integration. A virtual integration, in principle, also takes place in e-commerce scenarios where, for example, a customer transaction refers to user data from the database of a shop, to the database of a credit card company the customer wants to use for making a payment, and to data relevant to a proper delivery of purchased goods. All three sources must contain consistent data. Otherwise, the transaction will hardly complete successfully, and to achieve this there may be a mediator at the e-commerce provider's site.

We mention that both virtual and materialized systems can occur in combination with another integration dimension, which distinguishes *loosely* from *tightly* coupled federations of systems. For example, a data warehouse as a materialized system could be a loose federation of data sources, some of which are internal and others external to a given application or a company.

Among the challenges to all data integration tasks is the fact that enterprise databases are typically autonomous; they are used for particular applications and cannot change their structure without potentially harming these applications. Moreover, the heterogeneity among the integration objects may be and often is huge. Indeed, even similar databases often mismatch in many ways, both from a syntactic and from a semantic point of view. As a consequence, the integration techniques actually applied today often have to rely on human intervention. An expert has to determine which attributes from a database represent equal or just similar information, or how data from one representation can be converted into another. The Semantic Web is intended to help here as well, as we see, for example, through the provision of suitably built ontologies. Help from the Semantic Web in this area is confirmed by several success stories including Elsevier's EMTREE or the On-To-Knowledge projects at Swiss Life and EnerSearch, as reported, for example, in Antoniou and Harmelen (2004).

6.1.3 The Semantic Web idea

As first published in Berners-Lee et al. (2001),

> . . . the Semantic Web is a vision: the idea of having data on the Web defined and linked in a way that it can be used by machines not just for display purposes, but for automation, integration, and reuse of data across various applications. [. . .] The Semantic Web is an extension of the current Web in which information is given well-defined meaning, better enabling computers and people to work in cooperation.

Thus, Berners-Lee et al. (2001) and, meanwhile, many others see the Semantic Web as a (natural as well as necessary) evolution of the current Web that overcomes its mostly syntactic data handling limitations. In the context of the Web, "semantic" means machine-*processable*, where the semantics determine what a machine can do with the data beyond simply reading it.

In a nutshell, the core ideas of the Semantic Web are the following, all aimed at providing information models and languages that explicitly embed metadata and semantic contexts in such a way that an automated *processing* becomes possible:

1. Information agents produce semantically annotated Web pages that are enhanced with explicit semantic information. To do so, they use standardized syntax for representing information as well as annotations.
2. The information available on the Web is hence provided in a way so that humans can understand and machines can read and process it, so that both a user-friendly presentation of information as well as automated processing, aggregation, or evaluation is enabled.
3. Search on the Web and, in particular, within semantically enhanced Web pages will be accomplished by software agents. Humans will be enabled to query search engines in natural language and will receive meaningful answers in return.
4. Both information providers and search agents make use of common terminologies and knowledge structures that are manifested in what is known as *ontologies*.

As a result, it should become possible to gather and combine information from various sources better on the Semantic Web. Software agents should be enabled to integrate information automatically, so that, ultimately, the end-user is comprehensively supported in his or her use of the Web. We mention that the word "ontology" originates from the Greek philosopher Aristotle, who was looking for a classification of all entities that can be talked about into "categories," and it contains the Greek terms "onta" (being) and "logos" (science), see Sowa (2000).

As already stated in Chapter 1, an *agent* in this context is a program or a service that can act, on a limited scale, autonomously. An agent is also supposed to be able to make decisions, for example, on whether some information found on the Web is relevant to the integration task or search it is currently involved with or executing. This, in turn, will make it possible not just for humans, but also for information systems to access Web-based information and make use of it within the processes they are part of.

Metadata

The core of enhancing information available on the Web with meaning or semantics lies in the use of unique identifiers for all kinds of resources available on the Web (including Web pages, images, audio files) and of tags and metadata for describing or annotating the data. Since the Web keeps expanding rapidly and new resources are added to it on a continuous basis, it is important to add this metadata and the annotations in a way that avoids extensive restructurings of resources in the face of this growth. To meet a

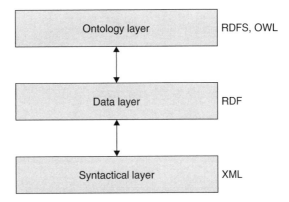

Figure 6.3 Semantic description at various levels of abstraction.

challenge like this, it has become common in computer science applications to introduce several layers of abstraction. In the context of the Semantic Web, three such layers are under discussion, where each level comes with a specific language framework and forms the basis of the next higher level. These layers, which are not entirely without controversy (Legg, 2007), are shown in Figure 6.3. They are roughly based on the perception that common vocabularies (ontologies) need languages (such as RDFS or OWL) in which they can be specified. In addition, a data model (such as RDF) is needed for describing relevant metadata; finally, an underlying syntactical framework (such as XML) is needed for tagging raw data.

As can be seen and is no longer surprising, the lowest, syntactical layer typically refers to XML as the language of choice. It is in wide use today for data exchange and integration purposes and well-suited as a basis for defining higher-level languages at the data layer. XML is used at the data layer for the creation of a namespace and as a framework that allows the representation of data instances (i.e., individual – meta – data items and their properties); as is discussed and illustrated shortly. This is where RDF comes in. At the highest ontology layer, the elements of the data layer are finally described in a semantic fashion. At this level, an abstraction is employed from concrete values towards descriptive items and their relationships; this leads to RDFS and OWL.

We mention that the choice of these layers (as well as the techniques associated with them) draws on experience from a variety of fields, such as knowledge representation, knowledge engineering, machine learning, automated deduction, expert systems, statistical data analysis, or case based reasoning, which are not the subject of this book. For more information on this field, typically attributed to the broader area of *artificial intelligence*, refer, for example, to Nilsson (1998), Russell and Norvig (2003), or Brachman and Levesque (2004).

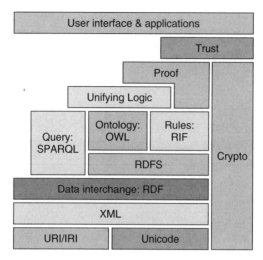

Figure 6.4 Semantic Web technology stack.
Source: www.w3.org/DesignIssues/diagrams/sweb-stack/2006a.png

6.1.4 The structure of the Semantic Web

The layer structure foreseen for the Semantic Web is actually a bit more involved than presented above. To this end, Figure 6.4 shows an entire stack of concepts, languages, and standards attributed to the Semantic Web. XML is seen as the basis. Although XML is appropriate as a foundation, this framework by itself is not enough. As has been done in areas such as e-commerce (think of RosettaNet or ebXML) and others (for example, in the biological or medical domains), an agreed-upon linguistic framework is needed. This framework fixes a namespace, a DTD, or an XML Schema for a specific domain, and possibly a number of issues beyond that. Since it would probably not make sense to come up with a number of distinct XML-based languages for the multiplicity of application domains that exist nowadays, a more promising approach is to devise "meta-frameworks" that can be employed independently of a particular application.

Since XML has become a predominant standard for labeling and tagging information in an application-specific way, it is no surprise that XML and its concepts form the underlying foundation, together with the general use of Unicode for making everything language-independent and the use of URIs as well as IRIs for unique, global identification. IRIs (Internationalized Resource Identifiers) are an extension of URIs (Uniform Resource Identifiers) that allow the use of Unicode symbols. These base technologies together allow elementary structuring, correct representation, as well as correct referencing of data (or more generally: resources) for Web applications. Building on top of the XML foundation are the following layers:

- At the next layer up, the Semantic Web actually starts with RDF, the *Resource Description Framework*, a simple XML-based data model. In this model, any type of content can be uniformly described through subject-predicate-object triples denoting the object in question, one of its attributes, and a value for that attribute. This allows representing basic concepts and their (typically hierarchical) relationships and can be embedded in an HTML page or another data format. We discuss RDF and ontologies in more detail following; in this stack it has been assigned the role of a data interchange format.

- RDFS (RDF Schema) is a vocabulary for describing the attribute, properties, and classes of resources that are captured in RDF format; RDFS comes with an object-oriented semantics that allows the specification of generalization hierarchies between properties and classes.

- The choice of object identifiers and attribute names can be seen as the foundation of the most central component of the Semantic Web: ontologies, which are common metadata vocabularies that can be formulated using RDF. Ontologies can be used to describe a certain section of the real world with all its context information, to represent a terminology, or to unify data from distinct semantic environments. If used by a community, an ontology is an item that evolves over time, that gets updated and in particular extended, and for this it needs rules that have to be observed. OWL, the *Web Ontology Language*, has been chosen as the language here and as a higher-level vocabulary for describing properties and classes. OWL goes beyond RDFS in allowing a specification of relationships between classes (e.g., disjointness or equality), cardinality, or a richer typing of attributes (in a way XML Schema has added this to DTDs). In addition, OWL comes with a set of logical axioms that can be used for expressing and generalizing dependencies between concepts.

- Next, SPARQL (Protocol And RDF Query Language) is a query language for accessing collections of RDF data currently under development at the W3C (see w3.org/TR/rdf-sparql-query). RIF stands for the *Rules Interchange Format* also under development by a W3C working group (see w3.org/2005/rules).

- For specifying the meaning of the components and terms included in an ontology, a logical language is often used, as it is for defining the formal semantics of an ontology in general. A logical language (or logic for short), in turn, comes with a proof theory or a model theory in order to be able to make statements about consistency, completeness, or correctness (Ben-Ari, 2006). Care needs to be taken so that the language chosen is not "too powerful" in the sense that certain questions relating to the language can no longer be algorithmically decided. On the other hand, a logical language allows inferences in order to derive information implicitly contained in the data as well as the ontology, or for classifying new data properly. A logical language can also provide formal semantics for a query language for ontologies.

■ If all of these items are indeed used for automated integration of information, for eliminating inconsistencies or incompleteness, and for consolidating distributed information from the Web, and if accompanied with proper security, verification, and encryption mechanisms, the result will be a Web that goes far beyond the capabilities of what we are used to today. Trust can be seen as a top goal for the development of the Semantic Web, where users can trust the information that is accessible via the Web or the information processes are that executed on the Web.

■ Finally, a user interface and applications layer appears at the top of the stack.

In order to be able to understand the meaning of information content, the participants in a communication process need to have a common background and use a common vocabulary. While humans can do this intuitively, by associating basic or foundational knowledge with context information provided, for example, by encyclopedias, textbooks, or indexes, this is entirely different when computers have to communicate. For being able to combine and integrate information in an application- and context-specific way, for example, to deliver better search results or to enable meaningful data integration from distinct sources, a formal representation of the relevant terms and their relationships is needed that can be read and interpreted by a machine. In other words, both syntax and semantics must be made explicit, and must be equipped with an appropriate and efficient inference mechanism. This is a prerequisite for *automated reasoning*, an area of artificial intelligence where deductions and logical consequence are done by programs. As we expect is clear by now, the interest of the Semantic Web is to extend this approach to the Web and the information it contains, and the vehicle that looks most promising for this purpose at the moment are ontologies.

In light of Figure 6.4, it is fair to say that the Semantic Web as seen by Berners-Lee and the W3C can be considered to be a major standardization effort, whose goal is to make the information on the Web representable in a suitably chosen syntax so that computers can process it. Ultimately, and as stated earlier, semantic technologies should enable humans to query the

Web in natural language and to receive meaningful answers. So, we are moving from a "Web of links" towards a "Web of meaning" according to Fensel et al. (2005). However, while these ideas are both valuable and needed for future development of the Web, it remains to be seen how fast and comprehensively the emerging standards will be adopted. While we discuss RDF and OWL in more detail next and indicate how to exploit them in a particular application domain, we emphasize that ontology development is a nontrivial process best left to professionals. This fact will eventually lead us towards a possible confluence of the Semantic Web and Web 2.0 at the end of this chapter.

6.2 Languages of the Semantic Web

In this section, we take a closer look at the languages we mentioned as being at the core of Semantic Web development. We start with RDF, then look at the schema language extension of RDF, and finally describe OWL as a prerequisite for developing ontologies. These languages are in use in a number of ontology projects these days. For example, the Gene Ontology maintains an ontology on model organisms and proteins for biological research and provides it in both RDF and OWL formats (see www.geneontology.org). RDF is also used for the Wine Ontology (available from www.schemaweb. info/schema/SchemaDetails.aspx?id=62) as well as a number of other ontologies dealing with such diverse topics as airports, conferences, purchase orders, to name just a few. Refer to www.schemaweb.info for further information. A number of examples of ontologies written in OWL can be found at protege.cim3.net, the Web site of Stanford University's Open Source ontology editor, Protégé.

Most of the examples we show here deal with multimedia data (such as images, music, or video files); we do so in light of the fact that we describe the development (and usage) of an ontology for multimedia data as a larger case study in the following text.

6.2.1 The Resource Description Framework (RDF)

RDF, the Resource Description Framework, is a W3C development for a simple XML-based data model that can easily be represented graphically (see w3.org/RDF). RDF is based on three core concepts: resources, properties, and statements. A *resource* is the subject or the object of an RDF description; it can be a concrete information object (e.g., a music file) or an abstract concept (e.g., a company) and is always uniquely identifiable (by a URI). A *property* (partially) describes a resource; its value is either a literal

Figure 6.5 General form of an RDF statement.

or a reference to another resource (i.e., its URI). A *statement* combines the property of a resource with a value and is broken down, as mentioned earlier, into a subject, a predicate, and an object, where both subject and object may be URIs and the predicate is the property linking the object to the subject. This is straightforwardly expressed graphically as shown in Figure 6.5.

Thus, RDF allows expressing general concepts based on a simple and uniform syntax. It should be obvious that larger graphs can be built in this way, by using the target resource of one predicate as the source of another. Even more expressive power is gained by adding subset relationships, through which subjects can be made subsets (or specializations) of other subjects. Different from what is commonly done in object-orientation, where properties are attached to classes and hence are inherited by subclasses, RDF allows a user to form specializations of properties independent of class specializations. The result of specializing is a *semantic net*; an example exhibiting animals (with some properties and their respective values) and their specializations into birds and persons (with further specializations and properties) is shown in Figure 6.6. RDF descriptions can be stored in databases, and can be queried by languages such as the aforementioned RDF query language SPARQL or SeRQL (Sesame RDF Query Language); see Haase et al. (2004) for a survey.

For being able to search, link, and access resources and their properties at a larger scale and in particular on the Web, RDF uses *URI references* (which, according to Figure 6.4, is an underlying concept). RDF also comprises constructs for *multivalued* properties. Such properties can implicitly be represented by multiple value triples; the alternative way is to use a *container*. A container is itself a resource and can associate multiple properties with a resource within a single statement. Containers can take the form of an unordered bag, an ordered sequence, or list of alternatives. As an example (borrowed from www.w3schools.com/rdf/rdf_containers.asp), the following short RDF document describes a CD entry for the Beatles found in a fake record shop; the CD was made by several artists, namely John, Paul, George, and Ringo:

```
<?xml version="1.0"?>
<rdf:RDF
xmlns:rdf="http://www.w3.org/1999/02/22-rdf-syntax-ns#"
xmlns:cd="http://www.recshop.fake/cd#">
```

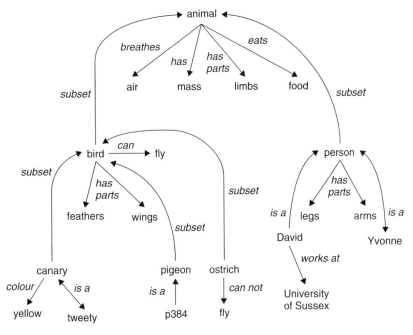

Figure 6.6 A semantic net describing certain animals.
Source: http://www.cogs.susx.ac.uk/users/davidy/atcs/semnet.gif

```
<rdf:Description
  rdf:about="http://www.recshop.fake/cd/Beatles">
  <cd:artist>
      <rdf:Bag>
          <rdf:li>John</rdf:li>
          <rdf:li>Paul</rdf:li>
          <rdf:li>George</rdf:li>
          <rdf:li>Ringo</rdf:li>
      </rdf:Bag>
  </cd:artist>
</rdf:Description>
</rdf:RDF>
```

The Beatles example also shows a number of other RDF features, which should be vastly self-explanatory once the concept of an XML-based language (as explained in Chapters 1 and 2) has been understood. In particular, RDF has its own namespace, and for identification purposes, each RDF tag starts with the "rdf:" prefix. The rdf:Description tag starts a statement, which in this example has a subject mentioned as value of the rdf:about attribute; the remainder is the object in this statement. We mention that the example could be represented in graphical form, by linking an *artist* to a *bag* containing the four names.

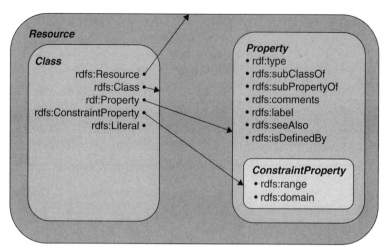

Figure 6.7 RDFS resources and classes by containment.
Source: http://www.w3.org/TR/2000/CR-rdf-schema-20000327/#s2.1.2

RDF also supports the use of typed literals and uses the data types known from XML Schema for their declaration. This carries over to the schema language of RDF.

6.2.2 RDF Schema (RDFS)

In order to allow for more type information to be expressible, RDF has been equipped with a schema specification language called *RDF Schema* (RDFS). RDFS comes with its own namespace (to be found at w3.org/TR/2000/CR-rdf-schema-20000327). The major extension of RDF in RDFS is the notion of a *class* in addition to resources and properties, as shown in Figure 6.7. A class is depicted there by a rounded rectangle; a resource is depicted by a dot. Edges are drawn from a resource to the class it defines. A subclass is shown by having a rounded rectangle (the subclass) completely enclosed by another (the superclass). If a resource sits inside a class, then there exists either an explicit or an implicit rdf:type property of that resource whose value is the resource defining the containing class. As a straightforward exercise, the reader should try to represent the animal example from Figure 6.6 above in RDFS.

The RDF Schema type system is similar to the type system of an object-oriented programming language such as Java or that of an object-relational database system following the SQL:2003 language standard. However, RDF is different in that, instead of defining a class in terms of the properties its instances may have, an RDF schema will define properties in terms of the classes to which they apply. For example, while an object-oriented system would define a class *Book* to have an attribute *Author* of type *Literal* or *String*, RDFS would define a property *Author* of domain *Book* and with range *Literal*. In other words, an author would "map" a book to a literal or a string. More generally, RDFS is property-centric, while object-oriented systems are typically class-centric. The former is generally considered more appropriate in the context of the Web, since individual properties can now be associated with several classes.

While classes are used to group related RDF instances, it is also possible to specify the type of a resource by associating it with several classes. As indicated by the animal example, classes can also be arranged into a hierarchy of subclasses and superclasses, which reflects the common notions of specialization and generalization and implies property inheritance. Multiple inheritance is allowed in RDFS, and ambiguity stemming from inheriting attributes with the same name from multiple sources is avoided by the fact that properties can be addressed in RDFS independently of the class membership.

Figure 6.8 shows the RDFS class hierarchy. Notice that the information in this figure is just a different representation of what we have previously seen in Figure 6.7. In Figure 6.8 subclass relationships between classes are indicated by an `rdfs:subClassOf` edge from the subclass to the superclass. Similarly, if a resource is an instance of a class, then there is an `rdf:type` edge from the resource to that class. Notice also that, as is common in class hierarchies, the subclass relationship between classes is transitive. In the figure, a distinction is made between subclasses (i.e., edges labelled with an "s") and types (i.e., edges labelled with a "t") meaning, for example, that an `rdfs:label` is of type `rdf:property`, while `rdf:property` is a subclass of `rdfs:resource`.

Among the various, predefined RDFS classes shown in Figure 6.8, several are of particular importance. `rdfs:Resource` is the superclass of all class and property definitions of a schema, and each resource or property implicitly is an instance of this class. `rdfs:Class` is a subclass of `rdfs:Resource` and at the same time the superclass of all class definitions in RDFS. Thus, each class definition implicitly is an instance of class `rdfs:Class`. Finally, each property occurring in a schema is an instance of class `rdfs:Property`.

As mentioned, attributes are specified for describing resources in an RDF schema by defining properties, and the definition of a property is not bound to the existence of an associated class. Properties can also be arranged in a property hierarchy. For example, to define a subproperty `exterms:lastEdit` of property `exterms:date` we can write:

```
<rdfs:Property rdf:about="&exterms;lastEdit">
  <rdfs:subPropertyOf rdf:resource="&exterms;date"/>
</rdfs:Property>
```

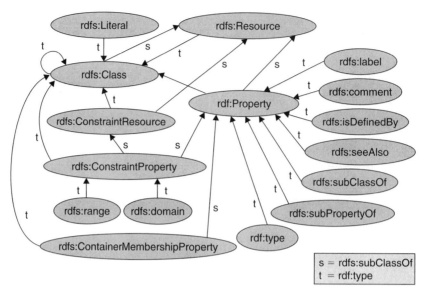

Figure 6.8 RDFS class hierarchy.
Source: http://www.w3.org/TR/2000/CR-rdf-schema-20000327/#s2.1.2

The example assumes the availability of an external namespace called exterms, in which tags and attributes are defined that may be used in RDF and RDFS definitions. On the other hand, the values that attributes can assume are specific to RDF. As is common in XML applications, a complete RDFS document would need to contain a URL of that namespace within its opening lines.

As we have said, the optional binding of properties to classes is done in RDFS by assigning a domain containing all classes in which these properties can be used. This supports a reuse of properties within various class contexts. The following example defines a property exterms:hasOwner, to be used as owner description for an instance of class exterms:file.

```
<rdfs:Property rdf:about="&exterms;hasOwner">
  <rdfs:domain rdf:resource="&exterms;file"/>
  <rdfs:range rdf:resource="&exterms;person"/>
</rdfs:Property>
```

Figure 6.9 shows the graph of an RDF schema with three classes exterms: file, exterms:imageFile, and exterms:person, where the second is a subclass of the first; for other examples, refer to Antoniou and Harmelen (2004). The schema also contains the declaration of property exterms:hasOwner with class exterms:file as domain and class exterms:person as range. The dotted line separates schema from instance, where ex:image1.jpg is shown as an instance

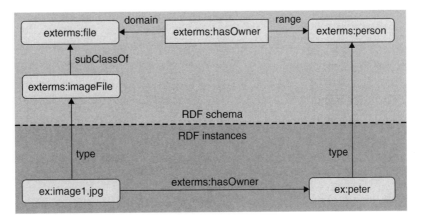

Figure 6.9 Sample RDF schema with instance.

of class exterms:imageFile. This instance has property exterms:hasOwner for which ex:peter, an instance of class exterms:person, is assigned as value.

We conclude our brief introduction to RDF and RDFS by taking a look at one of the prominent application examples of these languages, which has been specified by the *Dublin Core Metadata Initiative* (DCMI), "an organization dedicated to promoting the widespread adoption of interoperable metadata standards and developing specialized metadata vocabularies for describing resources that enable more intelligent information discovery systems" (see dublincore.org). Specifically, the *Element Set* that has been developed by DCMI and that is well-known nowadays in a number of Web applications is a set of fifteen distinct properties for use in the description of a resource. This set, which is briefly referred to as the "Dublin Core," has the following elements, a more detailed description of which can be found at dublincore.org/documents/dces. (This is also where the following definitions are taken from, in their December 2006 versions.)

1. *Contributor*, an entity responsible for making contributions to the resource
2. *Coverage*, the spatial or temporal topic of the resource, the spatial applicability of the resource, or the jurisdiction under which the resource is relevant
3. *Creator*, an entity primarily responsible for making the resource
4. *Date*, a point or period of time associated with an event in the lifecycle of the resource
5. *Description*, an account of the resource
6. *Format*, the file format, physical medium, or dimensions of the resource

7. *Identifier*, an unambiguous reference to the resource within a given context
8. *Language*, a language of the resource
9. *Publisher*, an entity responsible for making the resource available
10. *Relation*, a related resource
11. *Rights*, information about rights held in and over the resource
12. *Source*, the resource from which the described resource is derived
13. *Subject*, the topic of the resource
14. *Title*, a name given to the resource
15. *Type*, the nature or genre of the resource

These fifteen elements are part of a larger set of metadata vocabularies and technical specifications maintained by the initiative, which also includes resource classes as well as a type vocabulary. The terms in DCMI vocabularies are intended to be used in combination with terms from other, compatible vocabularies in the context of application profiles. They are also intended to be used on the basis of an underlying abstract model of the resources described by a metadata description. These and the descriptions themselves can be found at dublincore.org/documents/abstract-model. The following is a brief example of a Dublin Core document describing a family Web site in some the terms listed above:

```
<rdf:RDF
  xmlns:RDF="http://www.w3.org/1999/02/22-rdf-syntax-ns#"
  xmlns:DC="http://dublincore.org/2003/03/24/dces#">
  <RDF:Description
  about="http://www.family.org/smithfamily.html">
      <DC:Title>The Smith Family</DC:Title>
      <DC:Author>H.B. Smith</DC:Author>
      <DC:Date>2006-05-20</DC:Date>
      <DC:Language>en</DC:Language>
  </RDF:Description>
  <RDF:Description
  about="http://www.family.org/H_B_Smith.jpg">
      <DC:Title>Henry Smith on vacation</DC:Title>
      <DC:Creator>Sonja Smith</DC:Creator>
      <DC:Type>Image</DC:Type>
      <DC:Date>2005-07-16</DC:Date>
      <DC:Publisher>One Hour Photo Shop</DC:Publisher>
  </RDF:Description>
</rdf:RDF>
```

Along the lines of Figure 6.4, RDFS can be used to specify simple ontologies in the form of taxonomies for classes and properties, where domain and range specifications can be used for expressing restrictions as well as a mild form of integrity constraints; see Antoniou and Harmelen (2004). This exposition should have indicated that this is not too difficult, yet already requires considerably more effort than simply tagging a Web resource. This effort, which will be even higher in OWL, is justified from the point of view of reusability and being able to make inferences, and it can be seen as a first approximation of the goals of the Semantic Web, as stated earlier in this chapter. It should be clear by now that there exists a clear trade-off between an RDFS description of a collection of Web resources and a tag cloud for that collection. While the former can carry more semantics, will be independent of the individual user – ideally representing the consensus of an entire community – and will allow for some form of formal inference, its design and specification require a process of considerable complexity. The tag cloud, on the other hand, may mostly come into existence through an ad hoc and fast interaction among a random group of users, yet the result will still be of benefit for many of them.

From a semantic point of view, RDFS is not expressive enough for meeting several requirements of complex ontologies, in particular with respect to integrity and interpretation. For example, it is impossible to express the requirement that two classes should be disjoint, or to form new classes as a Boolean conjunction or disjunction of existing classes. Moreover, local restrictions of properties that may apply to specific classes where the property is valid or cardinality constraints stating a lower or upper bound for the occurrence of certain values are not expressible either. This is where OWL comes in, a language specifically designed to overcome such limitations.

6.2.3 Web Ontology Language (OWL)

The *Web Ontology Language* (OWL) is a language for specifying ontologies and was developed by the W3C Web Ontology Working Group. OWL functionality goes considerably beyond that of XML, RDF, and RDFS, since additional modeling primitives with a formal semantics are defined, and OWL comprises a set of logical axioms that can be used for specifying set operations, equivalence of concepts, or disjointness. OWL has been developed based on the observation that an automated processing of annotated data needs a more formal foundation and also constructs specifically targeted towards ontologies. It also combines concepts from frame-based knowledge representation (see Brachman and Levesque, 2004, or Sowa, 2000), predicate logic (see Ben-Ari, 2006, or Kifer et al., 1995), and Web standards.

OWL functionality is contained in three distinct sublanguages that have increasing expressive power and computational complexity: *OWL Lite* is the most basic language, containing constructs for defining class hierarchies and simple mechanisms for specifying restrictions such as cardinality constraints. The language is restricted enough so that efficient processing can

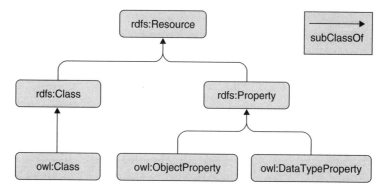

Figure 6.10 Central OWL classes and their subclass relationships to RDFS.

always be guaranteed. *OWL DL* is an extension of OWL Lite that is based on *Description Logics* (Baader et al., 2003) and that can guarantee efficient inferences only under certain circumstances, for example if a class is not a subclass and an instance of another class at the same time. Finally, *OWL Full* contains the complete language capabilities, but does not generally guarantee decidability, so that processing OWL Full documents does have its limitations. Description logics can provide a formal foundation for frame-based systems, object-oriented representations, semantic data models, and type systems in general; it is an area of knowledge representation aimed at expressing structured information and at reasoning about this information. Refer to Legg (2007) for an exposition of the various (versions of) ontology languages, their expressive power, and their complexity.

We introduce the main constructs of OWL next, where examples from the multimedia domain are again used; they can be found in more detail in Hüsemann (2005). A full description of the language can be found at w3.org/TR/owl-features; a good overview is also provided in Antoniou and Harmelen (2004). Essentially, OWL uses the constructs known from RDF and RDFS. In particular, OWL Full comprises all of RDF and RDFS, so that each valid RDFS document is also a valid OWL Full document; we mention that this does not hold for OWL DL and OWL Lite, which has consequences, for example, for the layering process outlined in Figure 6.3. Indeed, in order to make to language layering strict, a restriction has to be made to the highest layer to OWL Full.

It should no longer come as a surprise that an association of RDF, RDFS, and OWL constructs to their respective specifications is done via individual namespaces, which are indicated by corresponding prefixes. Figure 6.10 shows the central OWL classes and properties as well as their relationships to RDFS classes, explained further in Antoniou and Harmelen (2003).

OWL defines class `owl:Class` in which all OWL classes are contained. In addition, OWL distinguishes two classes of properties, `owl:ObjectProperty` and `owl:DataTypeProperty`. We will look at classes first and then at these property classes. An example of a class definition is given by the following statement defining a class named `imageFile`:

```
<owl:Class rdf:about="&exterms;imageFile">
  <rdfs:subClassOf rdf:resource="&exterms;file"/>
</owl:Class>
```

A class definition has two parts. The first contains the name declaration for the class and the second defines an optional set of restrictions for the class (such as the subclass specification in the example). Every class defined in OWL is a subclass of class `owl:Thing`, conversely, there is a class `owl:Nothing`, which is an empty class and contained in every other class. Table 6.1 shows the OWL constructs for defining classes together with local restrictions.

Similar to RDFS, properties in OWL are binary relations describing classes and their instances in more detail. However, different from RDFS there are two distinct types of properties. *Object properties* establish relationships between the instances of two classes, while *data type properties* establish relationships between class instances and literals. For both property types domain and range, restrictions can be specified via the RDFS properties `rdfs:domain` and `rdfs:range`, respectively. Moreover, OWL supports the definition of property hierarchies via `rdfs:subPropertyOf`.

As an example, the following piece of code declares an object property `exterms:hasOwner` which is valid in class `exterms:file` and restricted to range over `exterms:person`.

```
<owl:ObjectProperty rdf:about="&exterms;hasOwner">
        <rdfs:domain rdf:resource="&exterms;file"/>
        <rdfs:range rdf:resource="&exterms;person"/>
</owl:ObjectProperty>
```

The next example shows a data type property `exterms:hasLyrics` which is valid in class `exterms:musicFile` and which ranges over the XSD data type String. In general, OWL supports almost all XML Schema data types.

```
<owl:DataTypeProperty rdf:about="&exterms;hasLyrics">
        <rdfs:domain rdf:resource="&exterms;musicFile"/>
        <rdfs:range rdf:resource="&xsd;string"/>
</owl:DataTypeProperty>
```

OWL provides a number of predicates for describing properties in more detail. Table 6.2 surveys the most relevant of these.

As is common in object-orientation, OWL *classes* describe a set of similar instances that are characterized by the same set of properties. A particular

Table 6.1 OWL constructs for defining classes and local property restrictions.

Category	OWL Construct	Description
Value restrictions	`owl:allValuesFrom`	The local domain of a property is restricted to the associated domain.
	`owl:someValuesFrom`	The local domain of a property takes at least one value from the associated domain.
	`owl:hasValue`	The local value of a property is restricted to the given constant.
Cardinality restrictions	`owl:cardinality`	A property has a given minimal and maximal cardinality.
	`owl:minCardinality`	A property has a given minimal cardinality.
	`owl:maxCardinality`	A property has a given maximal cardinality.
Set constructors	`owl:intersectionOf`	A class definition is derived from the intersection of the given classes.
	`owl:unionOf`	A class definition is derived from the union of the given classes.
	`owl:complementOf`	A class definition is derived from the complement of the given class.
Axioms	`owl:equivalentClass`	Two classes are declared as semantically equivalent. Instances of one class are also instances of the equivalent class.
	`owl:disjointWith`	Two classes are declared as being disjoint. An instance of one class is never an instance of the other.

Table 6.2 OWL constructs for describing properties.

Category	OWL Construct	Description
Relationship to other properties	`owl:inverseOf`	A property <a> is an inverse of property <b> if for each triple <X, a, Y> the triple <Y, b, X> is also valid.
	`owl:equivalentProperty`	A property <a> is equivalent to a property <b> if for each triple <X, a, Y> the triple <X, b, Y> is also valid.
Local properties	`owl:TransitiveProperty`	A property <a> is transitive if <X, a, Y> and <Y, a, Z> imply <X, a, Z>.
	`owl:SymmetricProperty`	A property <a> is symmetrical if <X, a, Y> implies <Y, a, X>.
Global cardinality	`owl:FunctionalProperty`	A functional property has at most one value, i.e., <X, a, Y> and <X, a, Z> imply Y=Z.
	`owl:InverseFunctionalProperty`	An inverse functional property <a> is a property whose inverse $<a>^{-1}$ is functional, i.e., <X, a, Z> and <Y, a, Z> imply Y=Z.

Table 6.3 OWL constructs for describing instances.

Category	OWL Construct	Description
Identity of instances	owl:sameAs owl:differentFrom owl:AllDifferent	An instance is declared equivalent to another instance. An instance is declared different from another instance. The instances of the set specified are declared to be pair-wise disjoint.

OWL instance is the concrete description of an information object. The definition of an OWL instance is done by declaring a name for the object as well as the class to which it belongs. In the following example, OWL instance ex:title1.mp3 of class exterms:musicFile is defined:

```
<owl:Thing rdf:about="&ex;title1.mp3"/>
        <rdf:type rdf:resource="&exterms;musicFile"/>
</owl:Thing>
```

As the example shows, RDF constructs can still be used within the definition of OWL instances. By the same token, the specification of instance properties follows RDF. The following example associate with OWL instance ex:title1.mp3 the properties exterms:hasOwner and exterms:hasLyrics as were just defined:

```
<exterms:musicFile rdf:about="&ex;title1.mp3">
        <exterms:hasOwner rdf:resource="&ex;person1"/>
        <exterms:hasLyrics rdf:datatype="&xsd;string">
          This is a songtext</exterms:hasLyrics>
</exterms:musicFile>
```

OWL provides constructs for expressing logical connections between individual instances (e.g., for expressing equivalence or nonequivalence). Table 6.3 shows the available constructs for describing instances.

We next look at *inferences* that can be made in OWL. To this end, it is worth mentioning that OWL has had two precursors, the *DARPA Agent Markup Language* (DAML) and its DAML Ontology language specification (DAML-ONT), and the *Ontology Inference Layer* (OIL), a language based on the aforementioned Description Logics. DAML-ONT and OIL were combined into the ontology language DAML-OIL in 2001 (see www.daml. org/2000/12/daml+oil-index), which finally resulted in OWL as a W3C recommendation in 2004. As a consequence, the OWL specification contains not only a description of the individual language elements, but also the definition of a formal semantics. This allows for a precise evaluation of ontologies specified in OWL based on Description Logics. Inferences can, for instance, refer to the following:

- Derived classification: If an instance I is associated with class A and A is a subclass of B, then I is also associated with B.
- Derived equivalence: If class A is equivalent to class B and B is equivalent to class C, then A is also equivalent to C. This transitivity property is useful for unifying classification structures from distinct ontologies.

Further details on OWL can be found, as mentioned, in sources such as Antoniou and Harmelen (2004). We note, in light of what has been said at the end of the previous subsection, OWL adds more expressive power to semantic descriptions at the expense of additional complexity. Thus it should not come as a surprise that the process of developing an ontology has not been made easier through the arrival of OWL, but has been made more adequate. What we look at in the next section is how OWL actually relates to ontologies and how these can be designed.

6.3 Ontologies

We now consider the concept of an *ontology*, the central component of the Semantic Web, in more detail as well as its usage for modeling vocabularies and domain knowledge. We do so mostly by way of a case study that centers around personal multimedia data management. In particular, we use this case as a running example during the explanation of an approach to ontology *design* that essentially resembles database design. While other approaches might be feasible for ontology design as well, the point here is that ontology design is a complex task that should be (and typically will be) broken down into several clearly distinguished phases. Moreover, it is a task that requires attendance from a domain expert who is capable of (pre-) structuring the domain in question in a way a community will be able to agree to. The expert's view will typically determine the basic outline of the ontology under design and will thus, in a sense, prescribe to the rest of the world how the domain under consideration is to be viewed. Clearly, this is in sharp contrast to user-driven and mostly ad hoc tagging as we have discussed in previous chapters. However, as we discuss in the next section, there is an emerging link between the two ways of adding meaning or domain knowledge to a certain set of Web resources.

To conclude this section, we briefly discuss a system for multimedia data management that is based on the ontology designed as a case study and that has originally been developed under the supervision of the first author of this book. This system, called *OntoMedia*, is just one of many examples where ontologies are "at work" already these days. Many others exist, in particular in the life sciences, in health application, in law, or in pharmaceutical applications.

6.3.1 Introduction

A succinct definition of the notion of an ontology has been given by Gruber (1993): "*An ontology is a formal, explicit specification of a shared conceptualization.*" A conceptualization, in turn, refers to the modeling of concepts, items, their relationships, and their deduction rules. Thus, an ontology is a common model for the terminology of a specific domain of knowledge. It has an explicit representation in the form of a schema, commonly together with a set of rules that state that the concepts of this domain are related. An important point is that ontologies are generally considered to be the result of a common process of conceptualization in which many people are involved. On the other hand, several user communities may develop ontologies for the same knowledge domain, so that multiple ontologies may exist for a single domain. An interesting and vastly open challenge then is the *integration* of these ontologies in case some common ground is needed.

From a more technical perspective, an ontology is a collection of terms or concepts associated with real-world entities that are related by generalization and specialization relationships and that have properties. Formally, relationships are binary relations, for which additional properties (such as transitivity, reflexivity, or symmetry) may hold, which can then be exploited during inferences. For example, referring back to Figure 6.6, typical rules relating to animals as shown in this figure would be the following:

Canary *is-a* Bird,   Bird *is-a* Animal,   Animal *has* Limbs

As in other contexts, *is-a* relationships represent specialization or subset relationships, while *has* denotes a property. Conclusions already possible from these rules are

Bird *has* Limbs,   Canary *has* Limbs.

Moreover, if, say, Charly is the name of new instance of type "canary" not yet represented in the picture, we could immediately conclude that

Charly *is-a* Bird   or   Charly *has* Limbs.

Ontologies are thus related to *indexes* or registers (i.e., alphabetically ordered collections of keywords in a book), *thesauri* (i.e., controlled vocabularies of words that are related), *semantic nets*, and *topic maps*, an ISO standard for the representation and interchange of knowledge (see www. topicmaps.org or www.ontopia.net/topicmaps/materials/tao.html); see Legg (2007) for a more complete exposition. All of these tools allow some form of knowledge representation and storage and using that collected knowledge for navigation, derivation of new knowledge, and search. An ontology describes terms like a thesaurus, serves classification purposes like a taxonomy, allows for logical deduction like a semantic net, and can be used for navigation knowledge structures like indexes or topic maps. For clarification purposes, we mention that a *thesaurus* is a collection of words with similar, related, or strictly opposite meanings, sometimes restricted to a particular field, and not necessarily alphabetically ordered. A famous example is *Roget's Thesaurus*, published in 1852. A taxonomy is an arrangement of terms in a specialization hierarchy for a particular field that is typically fixed (i.e., does hardly, if at all, change over time). A famous example is Carl von Linné's botanical taxonomy from the eighteenth century.

The languages needed for specifying ontologies have been introduced earlier. In particular, OWL is the language of choice here. However, instead of discussing general thoughts on ontologies, what we do in this section is present something like a case study. We do not delve into all the details of the case, personal multimedia data management, but we indicate how an ontology for this application domain could look and how it can be designed. The design methodology presented in the next subsection is general enough to be applicable in other contexts as well, yet here it delivers the desired ontology for multimedia data. Thereafter, we briefly showcase a piece of "semantic technology," a (software) system for handling and utilizing this multimedia ontology in the context of personal information management.

6.3.2 Design of an ontology

The development of an ontology is a nontrivial engineering task almost comparable to other complex design processes such as software engineering or database design. While many different ontology editors or processing systems (e.g., Protégé from Stanford University, or OntoEdit from the University of Karlsruhe in Germany and KAON, *The Karlsruhe Ontology and Semantic Web Tool Suite*) are nowadays available for that purpose, the foundations of systematic ontology design and engineering are still in their infancy. In this section, we sketch an ontology design proposal originally made in Hüsemann and Vossen (2005) that is based on the four-phase model of traditional database design consisting of requirements analysis, conceptual design, logical design, and physical design. We indicate how this phase concept carries over to ontology design.

Table 6.4 Metadata attributes of sample media files.

music file	image file	movie file	file
music title	image title	movie title	file name
music album	image width	movie series title	file type
music artist	image height	director	
music band		film genre	
music genre		soundtrack	
music cover		movie cover	

Running example and design approach

The running example to be used is from the multimedia domain. It is assumed that private users want to manage their personal multimedia file collections, typically including music, images, movies, and ordinary files, using metadata extracted from the files in their collection as well as other sources. The general problem motivating the use of an ontology in this context is the huge number of files a user typically collects. And, especially for media files, there is hardly a way to associate any meaning with a file name (e.g., think of associating with an image named "IMG_4148.JPG" the fact that is shows the New Zealand natural rain forest). Typical metadata attributes used in this domain are shown in Table 6.4. In the sequel, it will be indicated how to develop a multimedia ontology for the description of this metadata as well as for relevant concepts from the application scenario.

The ontology design methodology employed here generally aims to achieve the following major goals according to Hüsemann (2005):

- It should provide structured guidelines and detailed methods for the ontology engineering process.
- It should provide a clear separation between the conceptual, logical, and physical schemas of an ontology.
- It should include quality management and control mechanisms providing evaluation guidelines throughout all design stages.

To this end, analogies between ontology instances and databases are exploited. Indeed, the extension of an ontology schema can technically be understood as a conventional database in which the concepts describe different classes and properties of instances. Thus, it makes sense to perceive ontology design as a specific form of database design and hence adapt the traditional database design process, see Batini et al. (1992) or Teorey et al. (2006), regarding the development of ontologies. However, we mention that the resulting methodology still has similarities with others, for example the one described in Noy

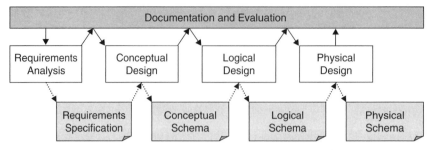

Figure 6.11 The phases of a database or ontology design process.

and McGuinnes (2001) (see also Antoniou and Harmelen, 2004). There are also differences between an ontology, which can easily be extended even after its design has finished, and a database schema, which typically remains vastly stable over the lifetime of the corresponding database.

Database design is traditionally performed in four sequential design steps: requirements analysis, conceptual design, logical design, and physical design, as shown in Figure 6.11. We use these phases here for ontology design as well. The output of each design phase delivers the input for the next, and each design phase ends with an evaluation activity in which specific validation and verification methods provide a quality assessment of the produced output. As indicated in Figure 6.11, documentation and evaluation should be done continuously along the process. We describe the four phases in more detail next.

Requirements analysis and specification

Requirements analysis of an ontology analyzes the relevant "information space" of an ontology. It consists of a *context analysis* via three different views in conjunction with a *value analysis* to scope all identified requirements in relation to a specific value for their use. These views refer to the organization at hand, relevant processes, and data:

- *Organization analysis:* The goal of organization analysis is the identification and analysis of relevant user groups, potential target hardware, and software systems for the ontology under design. Relevant organization elements of our running example include "multimedia creator," "multimedia user," or "multimedia device."
- *Process analysis:* The aim of process analysis is the identification and analysis of relevant application processes or activities in which the ontology will be used or which should be modeled with the ontology.

Relevant activities of our running example include "play audio CD," "burn music collection," or "search music album."

- *Data analysis:* Data analysis is the identification and analysis of relevant data sources that are described by the ontology or which are useful for determining relevant concepts in the application domain. In our example we identify, among others, the EXIF-specification relevant to describe images of digital cameras, or the ID3V2-specification relevant to describe metadata of MP3 audio files.

Requirements specification comprises a specification of all relevant concepts within the identified scope of an ontology obtained from requirements analysis. It integrates the output of an analysis of the various views. Requirements specification is decomposed into the sequential steps of

- specification of use-case diagrams (to figure out data, activities, and users)
- specification of competency questions to analyze the domain and the usage of its resources
- specification of an initial glossary of all concepts relevant to the ontology
- glossary refinement
- evaluation.

The specification of use cases should be straightforward and is described in Hüsemann and Vossen (2005); it follows standard UML techniques from software engineering or database design (Teorey et al., 2006). For each use case (e.g., music file creation, video file playing), competency questions are defined that comprise all concepts relevant to the context of a use case. These competency questions (e.g., "Which music title, artist, album, band, and genre, are related to a specific music file?" or "Which *cover* is related to a *music file, music album, movie,* or *movie series*?") relate use cases to information sources and can be used to evaluate the completeness of the resulting ontology at the end of the design process.

Given all relevant concepts for the specified competency questions, an initial glossary of all concepts in the scope of the ontology can be built, which is then refined by specifying for each entry a sample value, a context, and generalized concepts. A concept *value* is either a literal or an instance of another concept defined in the glossary. The *context* of a concept comprises concepts that may use a given concept as a valid description. All *general concepts* of a given concept relate to an abstract IS-A relation. The result of these steps for the example of multimedia data is shown in Table 6.5.

Table 6.5 Sample glossary at the end of requirements specification.

Concept name	Concept values	Concept context	Concept generalization
Collection	Collection	–	Concept
Cover	Cover	Movie file, Movie series, Music file, Music album	Image file
File	File	–	Concept
Image file	Image file	–	File
Movie file	Movie file	Movie series	File
Movie series	Movie series	–	Collection
Music album	Music album	–	Collection
Music file	Music file	Music album	File
Music title	Literal	Music file	Title
Title	Literal	–	Concept

Conceptual design

The goal of the *conceptual design* phase is the modeling of the ontology according to all specified requirements at a conceptual level. Similar to what happens in database design, the output of conceptual design is the *conceptual schema* of the ontology. The conceptual schema is specified by using a conceptual notation to represent the requirements in a suitable semiformal language. This language should include all elements necessary to model the requirements without restraining itself to potential logical processing restrictions.

The following steps can be distinguished within the phase model for the conceptual modeling of an ontology: Definition of naming conventions; modeling of concept hierarchies, of concept roles, and of class and property hierarchies; extension of the conceptual property schema; extension of the conceptual class schema, and evaluation.

The modeling of concept hierarchies means to apply the modeling abstractions *generalization* and *aggregation* to all specified concepts within the glossary of the requirements specification. In a *generalization hierarchy*, a subconcept is related to all superconcepts, while in an *aggregation hierarchy*, each component is related to all aggregates. Figure 6.12 shows parts of the generalization hierarchy for our sample multimedia scenario along with parts of its aggregation hierarchy in Figure 6.13. The aggregation hierarchy can exploit the generalization hierarchy to simplify the modeled graph. A specified aggregation for a superconcept of the generalization hierarchy is also valid for all its subconcepts.

The next step is to associate roles with concepts, where a role can be either a class or a property. The instances of an ontology database are concrete entities of associated *classes*. The instances of a class are described

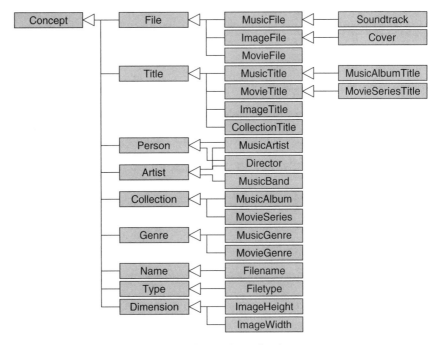

Figure 6.12 Generalization hierarchy for multimedia data.

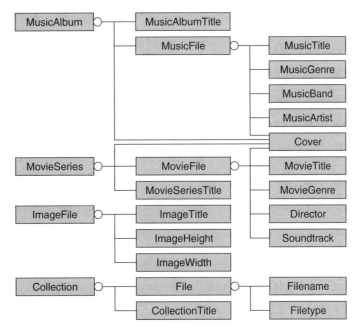

Figure 6.13 Aggregation hierarchy for multimedia data.

by *properties* that have a data *value*. All instances of a class share a common set of properties that describe the schema of the class. One way of achieving this is by marking all aggregate concepts as *classes* and all component concepts as *properties*. In a similar way, this can be done for the generalization hierarchy, and roles already assigned in the aggregation hierarchy carry over. Now, given the associated roles for each concept, classes can be separated from properties in the generalization concept hierarchy, which leads to separate generalization hierarchies for classes and properties. Recall from our discussion of ontologies languages earlier that properties are first-class elements in the conceptual schema of an ontology, which is different from conventional object-oriented conceptual models like UML. Finally, additional conceptual information for the property schema of the ontology under design can be added, such as range, domain, and global cardinality.

Finally, property constraints in the local context of a specific class can be defined. For this extension, class properties with local range and cardinality definitions are added to the class schema. The local range of a property in the context of a specific class is determined by looking at its global range definition given by the property schema. The local range of a property is a (nonstrict) restriction of its global range. Thus, to ensure schema consistency, the local range of a property must be a subset of its global range.

Figure 6.14 shows the extended class-schema of the example. The classes "Soundtrack" and "Cover" do not have local properties. All "title" properties in the schema are mandatory and existential to a specific class, thus they have the conceptual cardinality "(1,1)" meaning that there must be at least and at most one value. The property "file" has the global range "File" which is restricted to "MusicFile" (resp. "MovieFile") in the context of the class "MusicAlbum" (resp. "MovieSeries").

Logical design

The *logical design* step that follows next expresses the conceptual schema in terms of a logical schema based on a formal ontology language such as OWL. For this transformation, rules are needed to derive the base of the logical schema from the conceptual one. We indicate briefly how to use OWL for the construction of a logical ontology schema from its conceptual counterpart. To this end, a phase model for logical design is used consisting of:

1. definition of namespaces
2. transformation of the class hierarchy
3. transformation of the property hierarchy
4. transformation of global restrictions for properties
5. transformation of local restrictions for properties
6. evaluation.

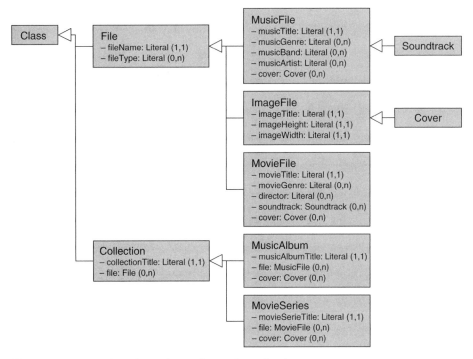

Figure 6.14 Extended class schema for multimedia data.

The definition of logical namespaces is common to ontology languages that provide global identification mechanisms for concepts in conjunction with other ontologies. The assumption here is that logical concept names are enclosed in angle brackets (e.g., <Cover>) to denote the logical namespace of the example ontology. In larger applications, it could become necessary to define more than one logical namespace to create appropriate logical partitions of an ontology.

The transformation process proper starts with the class hierarchy. For any conceptual class <A> of the conceptual schema an OWL class is specified as follows:

```
<owl:Class rdf:ID="<<A>>">
</owl:Class>
```

For any superclass <B> of a subclass <A> of the conceptual schema the definition is extended as follows:

```
<owl:Class rdf:about="<<A>>">
  <rdfs:subClassOf rdf:resource="<<B>>"/>
</owl:Class>
```

Next, the property hierarchy is transformed. For any property <a> of the conceptual schema with a range "Literal" an OWL data type property is specified as follows:

```
<owl:DatatypeProperty rdf:ID="<<a>>">
</owl:DatatypeProperty>
```

For any property <a> of the conceptual schema with a range consisting of a set of classes, an OWL object type property is specified as follows:

```
<owl:ObjectProperty rdf:ID="<<a>>">
</owl:ObjectProperty>
```

For any subproperty <a> of a superproperty <b> of the conceptual schema, the respective definition is extended as follows:

```
<owl:(Datatype|Object)Property rdf:about="<<a>>">
  <rdfs:subPropertyOf rdf:resource="<<b>>"/>
</owl(Datatype|Object)Property>
```

The transformation of global restrictions for properties includes the following two steps: First, a transformation of global range restrictions is carried out. For every OWL data type property <a> a logical OWL range is specified by choosing an appropriate XML Schema data type <dataType>:

```
<owl:DatatypeProperty rdf:about="<<a>>">
    <rdfs:range rdf:resource="&xsd;<<dataType>>"/>
</owl:DatatypeProperty>
```

For every OWL object property <a> a logical OWL range <Ri> is specified for every class i in the conceptual range as follows:

```
<owl:ObjectProperty rdf:about="<<a>>">
  <rdfs:range rdf:resource="<<R1>>"/>
  <rdfs:range rdf:resource="<<R2>>"/>
</owl:ObjectProperty>
```

For all properties with a conceptual range "All," no explicit OWL property restriction is necessary. Second, a transformation of global domain restrictions is done. For every property <a> with a domain <D> in the conceptual schema, a logical OWL domain is specified as follows:

```
<owl:(DataType|Object)Property rdf:about="<<a>>">
  <rdfs:domain rdf:resource="<<D>>"/>
</owl:(DataType|Object)Property>
```

The transformation of local restrictions for properties again proceeds in two steps: First, a transformation of local range restrictions is carried out. For every property <a> with local domain <D> in the context of a specific class $<A>$ of the conceptual schema, a logical OWL domain restriction is specified as follows:

```
<owl:Class rdf:about="<<A>>">
    <rdfs:subClassOf>
     <owl:Restriction>
        <owl:onProperty rdf:resource="<<a>>"/>
        <owl:allValuesFrom rdf:resource="<<D>>"/>
     </owl:Restriction>
    </rdfs:subClassOf>
</owl:Class>
```

Second, a transformation of local cardinality restrictions takes place. For every property $<a>$ with a local cardinality (min,max) in the context of a specific class $<A>$ of the conceptual schema, a logical OWL cardinality restriction is specified as follows:

```
<owl:Class rdf:about="<<A>>">
    <rdfs:subClassOf>
     <owl:Restriction>
        <owl:onProperty rdf:resource="<<a>>"/>
        <owl:minCardinality><<min>>
        </owl:minCardinality>
        <owl:maxCardinality><<max>>
        </owl:maxCardinality>
     </owl:Restriction>
    </rdfs:subClassOf>
</owl:Class>
```

This concludes our brief discussion of the transformation, which should have highlighted some of the issues to be resolved here. Further details can be found in Hüsemann (2005) as well as in Hüsemann and Vossen (2005).

Physical design

Last, but not least, the final *physical design* step of an ontology will adapt the logical schema to the specific needs of a target application system. It is quite common that application systems have specific requirements regarding the physical format of an ontology.

We mention that the methodology just described is not based on any specific tool support, which an industrial-strength methodology would certainly need. While we have indicated what principles can be applied to ontology design and what it requires to apply them, the main issue again is that, clearly, the help of one or more experts is mandatory. We should also mention that commercial tools for ontology development are beginning to arrive; an example is OntoStudio from German ontoprise GmbH.

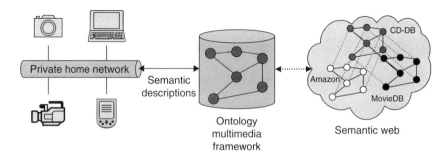

Figure 6.15 The OntoMedia personal entertainment framework.

6.3.3 OntoMedia: an ontology-based personal entertainment system

In this section, we take a brief look at a system for personal multimedia data management that supports an ontology as designed in the previous subsection. In this application domain, an ontology can come in pretty handy, and it may be expected that, in the near future, ontologies might even be supplied together with the relevant appliances.

Today, more and more information is stored in digital form, and information services like newspapers, radio, and television are becoming digitally available. The capacity of digital storage devices provides enormous space at affordable prices to save all this digital information into a giant personal multimedia archive (which may go as far as Gordon Bell's MyLifeBits project at Microsoft's Bay Area Research Center in San Francisco, see research.microsoft.com/barc/mediapresence/MyLifeBits.aspx). The creation and storage of digital content has never been easier, but with increasing volume, the management of multimedia archives turns out to be a nontrivial task with vital research problems. Indeed, ACM's SIGMM ranks "*to make capturing, storing, finding, and using digital media an everyday occurrence in our computing environment*" one of three major goals for multimedia research for the future.

However, as is well known, the more data is stored, the more difficult it is to manage it in an intelligent way. As it turns out, and has been researched in Hüsemann (2005), Semantic Web technology can fruitfully be used in this context, in a way indicated in Figure 6.15. Multimedia files within a private home network represent a resource collection a personal user wants to work with, and for many of the files therein, metadata is available on the Web (e.g., in the Internet Movie Database, the CD Database, or at Amazon as already shown in Chapter 2). A "middle tier" is needed to bring these worlds together and to help improve the usability of multimedia files through an augmentation with metadata; OntoMedia provides such a middle tier.

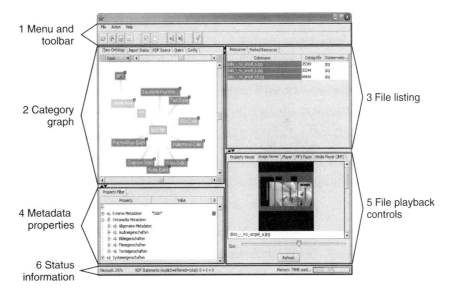

Figure 6.16 OntoMedia user interface.

OntoMedia is an Open Source software system based on a multimedia ontology that is intended for personal usage (see sourceforge.net/projects/ontomedia). It has been developed with two main goals in mind: Automatic extraction and semantic integration of multimedia metadata should be supported, and convenient organization and search of multimedia documents based on semantic metadata should be provided. The main user interface of OntoMedia is divided into six different parts, which are shown in Figure 6.16. The main part of the user interface between status and menu bars is divided into four different areas, where the left half shows schema information of the current ontology and the right half shows instance data about indexed documents in the database.

The left-hand side shows the category graph (area 2), and the metadata properties (area 4) of the OntoMedia database. The category graph is a visualization of the class hierarchy to categorize files with OntoMedia. The user can navigate, select, and modify the category graph in order to search or organize document collections. There are different colors of categories that denote different select modes, which we explain in detail later. In area 4 (below the category graph), users can define metadata based search criteria using the displayed metadata property tree. The user can navigate all metadata properties available in the database and define search criteria to filter the results of a search request.

On the right-hand side, the user interface shows a tabular listing of files (the file browser) in the database (area 3), and a playback panel with further file specific details (area 5). The file listing contains all files relevant to the current selection of categories and defined filter criteria. The File Viewer area contains different panels to display all metadata about a selected file, display a set of images, or playback audio/video files selected in the File Browser/Basket.

The menu and toolbar at the top of the user interface (area 1) provides access to the main functionality concerning data import/export, organization, and search commands available to the user. The user can export the database in RDF/XML format or import any RDF data to the current database. Thus it is possible to include any RDF-based information that is useful (e.g., to import external databases into OntoMedia). The status bar contains information about the current size of the database, and the memory resources used by OntoMedia.

The architecture of OntoMedia, as well as further details of how it works and how it has been designed, is described in Hüsemann and Vossen (2006) as well as in Hüsemann (2005). The User Interface Layer (UIL) of OntoMedia consists of several components to browse or query the underlying database and to display information about files in the database with related metadata. The UIL comprises a class browser, which displays a graphical representation of the category hierarchy, and is based on the Touchgraph framework; it also comprises a property browser, a file browser, and various viewers. The Property Browser shows the available metadata properties and their hierarchical relationships in a tree-like representation which is based on the OntoMedia Core Ontology. This ontology defines basic categories suitable as a generic starting point for building up personalized organization structures within the category browser. OntoMedia supports searching in the OntoMedia database by using the Category Browser and the Property Filter to define search criteria.

OntoMedia was built using platform-independent Java technology, which provides an easy test ride of the application without complicated installation procedures using the Java WebStart access point at www.ontomedia.de/webstart. It has been described here as a sample system in which the use of an ontology is fundamental, yet appropriately supported by tools that make the exploitation of the underlying ontology convenient for a user.

Once an ontology for a domain such a multimedia data has been designed and is accepted by a user community, it can fruitfully support the domain in a number of ways (e.g., search, organization, maintenance, and so on). However, this section should have shown that it takes a while to get to this point, since knowledge description and representation are nontrivial tasks that require considerable engineering effort. In the next section, we return to tagging, as previously discussed in Chapter 3, and see that what arises is a valuable supplement to ontologies.

6.4 From tagging to ontologies and back

What we have seen in the previous sections of this chapter is a typical scenario we encounter in many areas of computer science and elsewhere. A systematic approach to an exploration of the respective area requires quite a bit of "machinery" (i.e., technical tools, models, languages, and methodologies) and may also impose computational and organizational overhead (we mentioned a similar situation in Chapter 1 in connection with the development of languages based on XML). This is particularly true for ontologies, their design, and their exploitation, as we have tried to indicate in this chapter. An ontology is an excellent vehicle for creating and maintaining a common understanding of a domain, to represent a certain amount of knowledge about that domain, to organize its terms and vocabulary, and to augment and update it as it grows or as changes occur over time.

On the other hand, there is a different solution, at an instance as opposed to a schema level that is more efficient at first glance, requires less initial overhead, and therefore has wider acceptance. This particularly refers to *tagging* as we have presented and discussed it in Chapter 3. Tagging, in particular, *collaborative* tagging, also represents a form of establishing a common vocabulary, but one that is essentially unstructured and most often developed in an ad hoc fashion. Users attach tags to Web resources primarily based on their personal understanding and usage purpose for these resources, possibly for easing future reference, or for socializing them within a certain community (i.e., to share them with other users). As we have seen, this can easily result in a tag cloud that shows in an associate way which tags a community of users has been using and with what frequency. In particular, the maintenance of a tag cloud occurs via tools (available at sites like Flickr or del.icio.us) that evaluate the number of times a certain tag is used or referred to, so that tags contained in a cloud may grow or shrink according to user behavior.

As an example not given before, consider the tag cloud shown in Figure 6.17: share.loc (shared repository for learning object content). This is an e-Learning repository under development at the University of Muenster that offers a single point of access to learning objects developed and used throughout the university; see Dahl et al. (2006) for details. As an alternative to common user interfaces like search and directory views, share.loc exploits the concept of tagging in the context of e-Learning resources. Tags are primarily attached to the resources by students, but also but tutors and teachers or even content authors; see Dahl and Vossen (2007). For a different example, refer to change.org, a portal for nonprofit organizations and private people showing an up-to-date tag cloud on its home page. We note

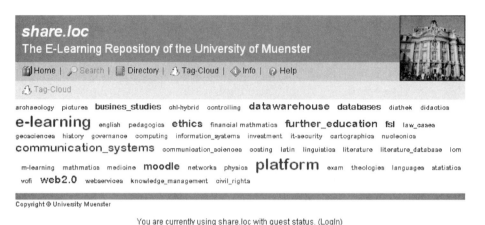

Figure 6.17 Tag cloud in share.loc.
Source: https://shareloc.uni-muenster.de/

that, as with other tag clouds, a problem may be seen in the fact that tags may enter the cloud in an uncontrolled way. In other words, in collaborative tagging, there may not be a "moderator" who controls that only tags that are in some way or another relevant to the resources in question are used. As we see, this could be a key to the usefulness of tags.

We can see that the collection of tags gathered in a tag cloud is initially far from an ontology, simply because there is no *a priori* way of limiting the tags included in the cloud to a particular set of terms or to a certain area. Moreover, there is no form of structuring involved which would, for example, use tags from certain classes that have either been predefined or are created on the fly. Users often do not tag objects with the goal of establishing a common understanding or common vocabulary in mind in the first place. And, since users involved in tagging a particular set of Web resources (in our example, learning objects) often do not even know each other, it cannot be expected that they quickly converge to something like the raw model of an ontology.

However, there are ways to overcome this apparent gap between well-structured ontologies with classes, attributes, and relationships on the one hand and unstructured tags and tag clouds on the other, and which, hence, contribute bringing the two areas closer together. In the remainder of this chapter, we discuss primarily two of the ways; we note that this is an emerging area with lots of research currently underway. One way is the emerging concept of *micro-formats*, the other *collaborative tagging*. Especially the latter gives rise to being combined with new forms of mash-ups, as we discuss using RealTravel as an example.

In either case, there is a simple idea behind the approach: A micro-format introduces a little bit of structuring (as opposed to the large structuring body of an ontology) and can basically be used in any HTML or XML context for adding some semantic information. Collaborative tagging utilizes the community approach to tagging with the effect that reaching an agreement about the tags being used is one of the goals. If combined with the concept of mash-ups we have discussed in Chapter 3, this can approximate a provision of semantic information also very well.

We discuss each briefly in this section and thereby try to make the point that Web 2.0 is beginning to make the Semantic Web a reality "from below." Indeed, we can consider both developments, Web 2.0 and the Semantic Web, as layers in the style of what we have seen in Figure 6.4, where the Semantic Web acts as an "upper" logical layer, providing the semantics, and Web 2.0 acts as a "lower" physical layer, providing the syntax and the technology.

6.4.1 Micro-formats

The first approach to filling the gap between ontologies and tag collections can be seen as an intermediary between the two ends of the spectrum we have just tried to outline. While an ontology might be too heavyweight for everyday and, in particular, ad hoc usage, and while a tag collection might be too unstructured for goal-oriented classification or integration of information, a compromise would be something lightweight, yet structured. Such a compromise has recently been proposed in the form of so-called *micro-formats* (Allsop, 2007). Micro-formats are simple data formats built upon existing standards such as HTML and XHTML. They provide tags or markup that can be used within an HTML or XHTML page and that build upon CSS classes with their identification capabilities and their limited form of inheritance, in order to provide easily identifiable semantic information. As a consequence, a page containing micro-format markup is, to some degree, machine-*understandable*, thereby addressing one of the goals of the Semantic Web. One has to be aware that this can only be a first step, as understandability in the sense of the Semantic Web requires the presence of a formal semantics, which is not the case here.

As a simple example, we consider *hCard*, a micro-format for representing people, companies, organizations, and places. hCard was developed by Tantek Celik and Brian Suda (the latter is also the author of an e-book on the subject, see www.oreilly.com/catalog/microformats) and resembles the internationally standardized vCard format. vCard has been devised for digital business cards and contact information that, for example, can be attached to an e-mail and then be easily added to the address book of the recipient of that e-mail. A typical vCard entry might look as follows:

```
BEGIN:VCARD
VERSION:3.0
N:Vossen;Gottfried
FN:Gottfried Vossen
ORG:University of Muenster
URL:http://dbms.uni-muenster.de
EMAIL;INTERNET:vossen@uni-muenster.de
END:VCARD
```

This simple vCard states a beginning and an end, a version number, followed by the name, full name, organization, URL, and e-mail address of a person (in this case the first author of this book). Micro-format hCard, which is based on vCard, uses XHTML and CSS classes, attributes, relationships, and reverse links to represent equivalent information, in our example as follows (here written as a div element):

```
<div class="vcard">
 <a class="url fn" href="http://dbms.uni-muenster.de/">
   Gottfried Vossen</a>
 <div class="org">University of Muenster</div>
 <div class="email" href="mailto:vossen@uni-muenster.de">
   email vossen</a>
</div>
```

Notice that this entry might be displayed as

```
Gottfried Vossen
University of Muenster
email vossen
```

where the first line would contain a link to dbms.uni-muenster.de and the last line a link to a local e-mail program and addressee vossen@uni-muenster.de. The important point is that the specific classes that can be used here (e.g., org or email) are not visible in the displayed information, but can be read by a program in order to figure out what the meaning (or semantics) of a particular part of the card is.

As can be seen from this simple example, the hCard micro-format can be used to mark up personal details appearing, say, on a Web site; once this admittedly rudimentary semantic information is in place, a program could be used to create a business card from that information and transfer it, say, to an address book or a mobile phone. A number of more sophisticated uses of hCard can be found at microformats.org/wiki/hcard-examples, and as shown there, it comprises straightforward ways of expressing addresses, phone number, nicknames, titles, roles, and a variety of other information.

Since hCard is based on common XHTML tags. It can be used wherever XHTML may appear, including Web pages, Atom, RSS, and blogs. In the case of blogs, a micro-format can even introduce some structure into an otherwise unstructured text. For example, if hCard markup is added to a blog entry containing, say, the name of a person, this person could be referred to explicitly. In addition, the blog author could even indicate his or her relationship to this person by using the `rel` attribute (e.g., in the form `rel="friend colleague met"`) indicating that this person is a friend, a colleague, and has been met before.

The site microformats.org provides a number of additional examples of micro-formats, all of which add some semantics to (X)HTML via specialized IDs, class names, or attribute values. Among them are the following:

- hCalendar is a calendaring and events format by the same authors as hCard and based on the iCalendar standard, with classes such as `vevent`, `URL`, `summary`, or `location`.
- hReview is a format, suitable for embedding reviews of products, services, businesses, events, and so on in (X)HTML, Atom, RSS, and arbitrary XML, with classes such as `summary`, `reviewer`, or `rating`.
- Rel-Tag is a micro-format for describing tags, keywords, or categories. By adding `rel="tag"` to an HTML hyperlink, the respective page will indicate that the destination of that link is an author-designated tag for the current page, and will display the tag as such.

Micro-formats are already well established in calendar and address book applications today, as they can help, for example, migrating data from calendar application to another. We mention that, similar to Web services, there is a distinction already between *elementary* and *composite* micro-formats. The ones mentioned here fall into the latter category, as they are composed of one or more elementary micro-format. Elementary ones, on the other hand, can be as simple as a single attribute (e.g., just consisting of `rel="tag"` for tagging or of `rel="license"` for attaching a license to a Web page).

Micro-formats are currently under development for a number of applications that refer to Web publishing and blogging; this goes together with a provision of tools (such as editors) that support the easy creation or consumption of content in a particular such format. As a good further introduction to the topic and an extended example of their usage, refer to Herrington (2006). Another application example can be seen at worldcup-kickoff.com, a site set up for the soccer World Cup in 2006 that used hCalendar to help users bookmark games in their own calendars. As mentioned, micro-formats are currently considered as a promising way to add structure to information on the Web, and they do so in a simpler way than ontologies can. There are also other developments going in the same direction, including *profiles* (Dubinko, 2005) (i.e., subsets of larger markup languages which still serve a similar purpose as the original language). The W3C itself has suggested the PICS (*Platform for Internet Content Selection*) specification (see w3.org/PICS) to have metadata associated with Internet content. Segala is promoting *content labels* as a potential PICS replacement; these are files containing metadata that describes Web site content and that enable search engines and browsers to indicate some form of trust in search results.

One objection to micro-formats, also discussed in Dubinko (2005), is that micro-formats may still encourage screen scraping in the style of Lixto, that we discussed in Chapter 3, instead of motivating the design of a service API, since the information still sits in HTML. On the other hand, this is what search engine crawlers are still going for, and this is unlikely to change in the foreseeable future. We also mention that alternatives to micro-formats exist in the form of combining tagging with RDF and to embed RDF in HTML. Examples include the dbpedia project (see dbpedia.org) that aims at providing database query capabilities for Wikipedia or the Semantic Wikipedia project (see wiki.ontoworld.org).

6.4.2 Collaborative tagging and folksonomies

Recall that in Chapter 3 we discussed tagging. In particular, we looked at Flickr, the Web-based community for organizing and sharing photos, and del.icio. us, the combination of social bookmarking and tagging, and how they both allow the development of folksonomies. Flickr allows users to associate keywords or tags with their photos, and since tags are free-form, they can be anything: a word, a number, or a phrase. Del.icio.us is about links. When a user stores a bookmark, he or she can thereafter access it from anywhere, since it is now stored on the Web. Moreover, the sites tells users which others users have saved the same link. Finally, folksonomies are the result of tagging and social bookmarking, as they represent collections of categories created by "folks" or users.

Folksonomies could be created in various ways. These include randomly, unsupervised, and uncontrolled; under the supervision of an individual (possibly the content creator) who checks the metadata about the subject in question from time to time and may even modify it; or by a community of users including content creator and content consumers. In the last case, we speak of *collaborative tagging* since the community is now creating metadata together.

Through sites like Flickr and del.icio.us, collaborative tagging has recently not only become very popular, but has also started to attract research attention (Golder and Huberman, 2006). The process by which many users add metadata in the form of tags and keywords to shared content does not aim at deriving a common terminology from the outset, yet may deliver just that if done in collaboration with common goals and interests.

While some people have termed the result of socialization processes on the Web "collective intelligence," Tom Gruber has suggested speaking of "collective knowledge" instead. Collective knowledge, as he defines it, refers to the capacity to provide useful information based on human contributions, which is genuinely social in the sense that it gets better as more people participate in it, contribute to it, and use it. He continues to note that many examples of collective knowledge are already out there, including FAQs (or Frequently Asked Questions), a functionality on many consumer Web sites today, and product reviews for all kinds of products. The interesting situation arises when user-contributed data such as tags or bookmarks are collected across multiple sites and applications, consolidated, and integrated. The result could then give rise to the creation of aggregate value, and an example of this is RealTravel (see below).

We mention that tags and tag clouds also bring back the long tail concept we have discussed in Chapter 1. Indeed, while ontologies and taxonomies may have a "cut-off" point below which no further specialization is accepted into it, since the community interest is too low, the same is not the case in the tag space. Any such space will always contain keywords and tags stemming from a user minority or even from single users. While rarely used tags may be considered spam by others, and while a tagging system in general will contain a certain amount of irrelevant entries, this may, on the other end, add to the usefulness of the tags as it continues to cater to the thin end of the long tail of system users.

We also mention several research issues related to folksonomies that have recently been identified. Quantitative and qualitative analysis of tags and user behavior are examples of research fields arising around Web services implementing folksonomies. Indeed, a number of evaluations have been carried out by Golder and Huberman (2006) on data extracted from del.icio.us. This data analysis, based on data shared within a three-day period and retrieved together with its complete history, provides a number of key insights. First, consider the regularities in user activity and the tagging frequency. There are weak relationships between the time a user has been signed up to the service and his or her respective activity, on the one hand, and, on the other, between the number of Web links an individual shares and the number of different tags allocated. They further identify seven key qualitative classes of tags, the most significant being the following:

- Subject tags ("what or who it is about"): These typically utilize nouns at different levels of abstraction.

- Genre or form descriptors ("what it is"): These, for example, identify a link as a `blog`, `article` or `book`.
- Task-organizing tags: These add personal logic; an example is self-reminders such as `toread` or `wishlist`.

Another result relates to the examination of relative proportions of tags for a specific URL over time, which proved to be significantly stable. With the proportion of each tag in this context being nearly fixed, Golder and Huberman (2006) consider this the empiric confirmation that increasing numbers of users have a stabilizing rather than a disturbing influence on the pattern of tags.

Despite their limitations, as we identified earlier, folksonomies combine a number of strengths, making them a widely powerful tool. As we have seen, tags and thus folksonomies are focused more on browsing than on finding; that is, they emphasize exploring interesting content unexpectedly and randomly, as opposed to a goal-oriented finding of relevant documents. Enabled by tagging in the context of folksonomies, this characteristic is generally referred to by the term *serendipity*.

From a user perspective, the use of a flat namespace also saves costs in terms of time, effort, and cognitive cost. Being quicker, easier, and involving less expertise, the complexity of tagging is significantly lower than that of classifying objects within limited, predefined, and hierarchical schemes.

Studies like the one just mentioned support our claim that folksonomies and ontologies are in the process of moving towards each other, and there are concrete projects underway. For example, as Gruber (2005) writes,

> . . . a group of people from the tagging community is beginning to work on a common ontology for tagging – the *TagOntology*. . . . The TagOntology is about identifying and formalizing a conceptualization of the activity of tagging, and building technology that commits to the ontology at the semantic level.

For an example of how the result of such an effort might look, refer to the site robustai.net/folksonomy/Tag-ontology.html. However, the development in this area is surprisingly slow; a reason might be that service providers still have little interest in cross-site tagging or cross-site ontologies.

Different from controlled vocabularies, a folksonomy, in a sense, directly reflects the vocabulary of users, thus mirroring their level of education, the language they use, and the accuracy with which they go about categorizing. Additionally, the immediate feedback experienced in the course of collaborative tagging – for example seeing an object personally associated with a certain tag within the cluster of items tagged identically – provides both inspiration and influence for future tagging, paving the way to the "bottom-up consensus" discussed earlier. Taking this a bit further, Peter Merholz formulates a folksonomy's potential to provide a basis for a self-developed, gradually emerged, *controlled* vocabulary "that truly speaks the users' language" (see adaptivepath.com/publications/essays/archives/000361.php).

Structured tagging

Let's look at an important step in the evolution of tags by recapitulating what we have discussed on the topic in Chapter 3. We saw how difficult it is to base mash-ups on tags, as these are designed for human usage and do not have an *a priori* defined vocabulary. This gives great flexibility and ease of writing and storing tags, but their meaning and the intention with which they were written is stored with them. Relying on tags is therefore risky, as we have seen with the map example. We also saw one way to make tags more reliable: humans organized the group "One Letter," which is now a reliable pool for photos of letters.

There are other approaches in this direction. The first one we cover is connected to *structured tags*. We have talked about how the vocabulary of users converges, and it can be observed that certain objects are regularly tagged in a certain fashion. One of the earliest examples must be the development that led to the "tags for two" feature in del.icio.us (blog.del.icio.us/blog/2005/07/ tags_for_two.html). The tag `for:<usename>` had been used to indicate that this tag had been saved with a specific user in mind, or was deemed interesting for him or her. It is obviously structured as the `for:` carries one part of the meaning, whereas the username carries the second. However, to the del.icio.us service, this tag was in no way different than all other tags. It was the programmers behind del.icio.us that eventually picked up on the use of this tag and incorporated its syntax and meaning (more correct would be: tags of this structure) into their system. They did so by providing a special page (del.icio.us/for) on which a user could view all the pages that had been saved for him by other users. The other users did this by just adding a tag of the aforementioned form. This decision to give these tags a defined meaning was controversially discussed among del.icio.us users, since this has tremendous consequences. Clearly, the new page eases their process of going through a new link saved for them by others. This is bought by reducing the flexibility since `for:<usename>` were not visible to everyone anymore. Moreover, users feared this inbox might be spammed by malicious users.

We note that any tag in which the user has encoded structure can be considered a structured tag (e.g., `food!fruit!apple`, or `name_JohnDoe`). For this, it is also not important whether the system in which the tags are used endorses these structured tags. As long as the user has reasonable incentives

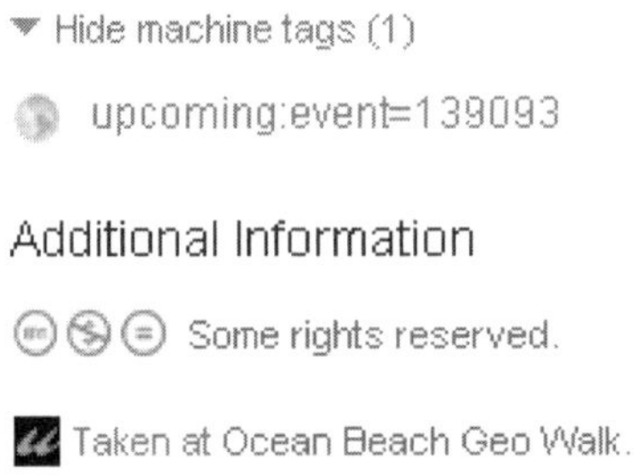

Figure 6.18 Example of a machine tag in Flickr.
Source: http://flickr.com

and can make use of them, he or she might just make them up. Other popular structured tags on del.icio.us include `filetype:*` or `system:*`.

As we have explained, structured tags have been used on Flickr as well. As mentioned, they are especially popular to tag photos with location information. In January 2007, Flickr started supporting what they call *machine tags* (www.flickr.com/groups/api/discuss/72157594497877875/). These are structured tags of a special form:

```
<namespace>:<predicate>=<value>
```

There are certain rules on what character strings namespace, predicate, and value can be, but these are only technicalities. Whenever a user enters a tag, which follows this syntax it is stored in specially, separately from the other tags, and it is also presented separately, that is it is shown under machine tags at the bottom of the list of tags (see Figure 6.18 for an example).

We have already mentioned one place where machine tags are used in Flickr, namely when importing a geo-tagged photo into the map system of Flickr. Another example can be seen in Figure 6.18: Here the namespace indicates that the tag belongs to the domain of the upcoming service (upcoming.org). This service allows creating events, giving information about these, and inviting people to them. `upcoming:event` thus indicates that this tag is referencing an event on upcoming.org. Which event is referenced is encoded into the value of this machine tag. Whenever Flickr encounters such tags on a photo, it will display a link to the upcoming event as can be seen at the bottom of Figure 6.18.

Note that the form of the structured tags we have seen here resembles that of the subject-predicate-object triples that are used with RDF, and which we discussed earlier in this chapter. Indeed, structured tags serve a similar purpose (but are much less powerful); this is the reason they have been called "Poor Man's RDF" (weblog.scifihifi.com/2005/08/05/meta-tags-the-poor-mans-rdf).

The potential for structured tags and machine tags seems great, to what extent they will flourish remains to be seen. A real boost of structured tags can be expected when they start to be created by machines (and not only used by machines). An example for the automatic creation of machine tags for Flickr is the research project Zonetag Photos from Yahoo! (zonetag. research.yahoo.com). This project allows camera phones to automatically attach tags with information on the location of the photo (derived from the mobile cell the phone was in when the photo was shot) to be uploaded to Flickr with the picture.

It is important that all systems that base their working on tags are aware that whether structured or not, the meaning of a tag could always be wrong. This is why any system using them should always "fail gracefully," in that it should always expect that something could go wrong. We expect many machine tags to remain unimportant on a global scale, but this is unimportant itself, since it is the architecture in which they are used that, at the core, allows for the emergence of uses that are now unforeseen. Structured tags still do not impose the semantics of tags onto the users, but they can ease the process of automatically creating and consuming structured information. They do this in a way that is in line with the approach that tagging unstructured tags has. As such, we see it as a natural extension of this concept that may ease the emergence of semantics in the field of tagging.

To conclude this section, we briefly mention that tagging is, of course, not the best approach in every field. We follow Tom Gruber once more in this example and consider the Web site *RealTravel*, which he cofounded. The site explains itself as follows: "RealTravel is the best place for real people to find and share travel advice and experiences." Browsing the information available at RealTravel is done by "surfing unstructured content along structured lines." *Unstructured content* is present since people essentially blog about trips they do (i.e., they write prose). The *structured lines* are present since these trips can be linked with the locations that a traveler blogs at (or about). All data aggregation in RealTravel is driven by destinations; for example, stories users have supplied are grouped together by destination. Moreover, the site infers geo-coordinates from destinations that are the basis of route maps. In addition, destinations are the link into targeted advertising and to external sources of content. Destinations form a natural hierarchy (e.g., from cities to states to countries) and contributors place their content into that hierarchy. From a technical point of view, the destination hierarchy is one of several dimensions in a data cube (similar to what is used in online analytical processing and data warehouses), with the others including dimensions such as *author*, *date*, or *quality rating*. Browsing

Figure 6.19 Germany on RealTravel.
Source: http://realtravel.com

then occurs along any of these dimensions. Figure 6.19 shows Germany and how it is situated in the destination dimension in RealTravel.

Users do not enter locations by giving tags, but by selecting the place they want to blog about from drop-down boxes. As simple as it may sound, this is what ensures that the *categories* of destinations can be trusted and are reliable. Note that a destination could still be wrong, so the system cannot prevent incorrect data, only incorrect categories through this. Incorrect data is prevented as it is expected that it is the user's interest to document his or her travel properly.

We finally mention that several other projects are on their way towards an integration of Semantic Web and Web 2.0 concepts, among them the Semantically-Interlinked Online Communities (SIOC, see sioc-project.org), or the *labels* (not to be confused with the content labels mentioned before) recently proposed by Berners-Lee (2007).

6.5 Summary

In this chapter, we have tried to direct the discussion towards the Semantic Web. In particular, it was our goal to explain the basics of this Web development, which has gained considerable attention and attracted several major research efforts in recent years. The Semantic Web can be seen as an agenda whose goal is to make the Web more accessible to computers, thereby enabling new applications for humans. The topics on this agenda essentially start from XML, the format allowing user-defined tags we discussed in Chapters 1 and 2 already and which has become popular in many other areas as well. Recent languages built on XML, in particular RDF, RDFS, and OWL, capture increasing levels of semantics. They gain their expressive power at the expense of increasingly complex design processes, in particular, when it comes to the design of an ontology based on one of these languages. They also gain it at the expense of increased complexity of concepts, deductions, and other computations.

The stack of concepts we introduced in Figure 6.4 can nicely be contrasted with a grass-roots development that vastly can do without much formalism, tagging. The interesting question at this point is whether the tagging (as well as other Web 2.0 concepts) and the Semantic Web will eventually grow together or at least move towards each other. The good news is that a number of people indeed believe that this will be the case, and there is good indication that this may be a correct assumption. As Wahlster and Dengel (2006) write,

> Only the combined muscle of Semantic Web technologies and broad user participation will ultimately lead to a Web 3.0, with completely new business opportunities in all segments of the ITC market. Without Web 2.0 technologies and without activating the power of community-based semantic tagging, the emerging Semantic Web cannot be scaled and broadened to the level that is needed for a complete transformation of the current syntactic Web. On the other hand, current Web 2.0 technologies cannot be used for automatic service composition and open domain query answering without adding machine-understandable content descriptions based on Semantic Web technologies. The ultimate worldwide knowledge infrastructure cannot be fully produced automatically but needs massive user participation based on open semantic platforms and standards.

As our exposition in this chapter should have made clear, our view of the situation is similar. With the various developments that we have discussed in this and previous chapters, we see a clear convergence of the Semantic Web and Web 2.0, which we have tried to capture in Figure 6.20. On the one hand, and we consider this the lower layer of foundations, there is Web 2.0 with its concepts such as RIAs, mash-ups, tagging, its collaborative development of content, and its community effects that have led to the use of the term "social Web" as a synonym for Web 2.0. On the other hand, there is the

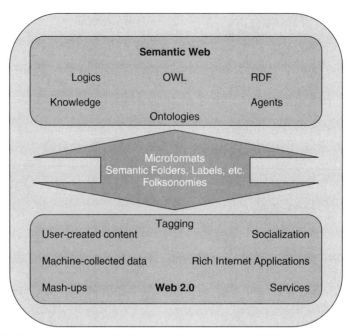

Figure 6.20 The convergence of Web 2.0 and the Semantic Web.

Semantic Web, the upper layer in our view, which brings along RDF, OWL, ontologies, and several other concepts.

We have tried to point out the pros and cons of both sides: While the Semantic Web has powerful and rigid structuring principles and allows for a specification of well-defined and reusable meaning for metadata, the price to pay for this is computational complexity as well as the fact that ordinary users will often have difficulties adopting its technologies. Web 2.0, on the other hand, is already used by the masses and technically allows for the developments of new and ingenious applications in short cycles and at a high frequency. However, it still lacks, for example, the expressive power of a well-engineered ontology.

As we have discussed in this chapter, a convergence of the two layers can indeed be achieved and is expected to involve concepts such as micro-formats, folksonomies, as well as a couple of others. The communities that are characteristic of Web 2.0 currently produce content in formats that do not have many capabilities (if any) for semantic evaluation. Thus, a goal can be to preserve the community approach and to provide it with tools such that a tagging process and the use of an ontology no longer exclude each other, but can converge.

References

Afuah, A., C.L. Tucci (2003): *Internet Business Models and Strategies*, 2nd edition. McGraw-Hill, New York.

Allaire, J. (2002): *Flash MX – A Next Generation Rich Client*. Macromedia Whitepaper.

Allsop, J. (2007): *Microformats: Empowering Your Markup for Web 2.0*. Friends of ED (Apress), Inc., Berkeley, CA.

Alonso, G., F. Casati, H. Kuno, V. Machiraju (2004): *Web Services. Concepts, Architectures and Applications*. Springer Verlag, Berlin.

Anderson, Ch. (2006): *The Long Tail. Why the Future of Business is Selling Less of More*. Hachette Book Group, Lebanon, IN. See also the following Web page of *Wired* magazine for a short article: www.wired.com/wired/archive/12.10/tail.html

Angel, K. (2002): *Inside Yahoo! Reinvention and the Road Ahead*. John Wiley & Sons, New York.

Antoniou, G., F. Harmelen (2003): Web Ontology Language; in S. Staab, R. Studer (eds.), *Handbook on Ontologies in Information Systems*. Springer-Verlag, Berlin.

Antoniou, G., F. Harmelen (2004): *A Semantic Web Primer*. The MIT Press, Boston, MA.

Asleson, R., N.T. Schutta (2006): *Foundations of Ajax*. Apress, Berkeley, CA.

Aspray, W., F. Mayadas, M.Y. Vardi (eds.) (2006): *Globalization and Offshoring of Software – A Report of the ACM Job Migration Task Force*. Association for Computing Machinery, New York.

Baader, F., D. Calvanese, D.L. McGuinness, D. Nardi, P. Patel-Schneider (eds.) (2003): *The Description Logic Handbook*. Cambridge University Press, Cambridge, UK.

Bates, C. (2006): *Web Programming – Building Internet Applications*, 3rd edition. John Wiley & Sons, Ltd, Chichester, UK.

Batini C., S. Ceri, S.B. Navathe (1992): *Conceptual Database Design – An Entity-Relationship-Approach*. Benjamin/Cummings, Redwood City, CA.

Battelle, J. (2005): *The Search – How Google and Its Rivals Rewrote the Rules of Business and Transformed Our Culture*. Portfolio (Penguin Group), New York.

Baumgartner, R., S. Eichholz, S. Flesca, G. Gottlob, M. Herzog (2003): Semantic Markup of News Items with Lixto; *Annotation for the Semantic Web*. IOSPress, Amsterdam.

Baumgartner, R., S. Flesca, G. Gottlob (2001): Supervised Wrapper Generation with Lixto; *Proc. 27th International Conference on Very Large Data Bases (VLDB)*. Rome, pp. 715–716.

Baumgartner, R., S. Flesca, G. Gottlob (2001a): Visual Web Information Extraction with Lixto; *Proc. 27th International Conference on Very Large Data Bases (VLDB)*. Rome, pp. 119–128.

Baumgartner, R., O. Fröhlich, G. Gottlob, P. Harz, M. Herzog, P. Lehmann (2005): Web Data Extraction for Business Intelligence: The Lixto Approach; *Proc. 11th German Biannual Conference on Databases for Business, Technology, and the Web(BTW)*. Karlsruhe, Germany, pp. 30–47.

Bausch, P., J. Bumgardner (2006): *Flickr Hacks – Tips & Tools for Sharing Photos Online*. O'Reilly Media, Sebastopol, California.

Bellomo, M., J. Elad (2006): *How to Sell Anything on Amazon . . . and Make a Fortune!* McGraw-Hill, Boston, MA.

Ben-Ari, M. (2006): *Mathematical Logic for Computer Science*. Springer-Verlag, Berlin.

Berners-Lee, T. (2000): *Weaving the Web: The Original Design and Ultimate Destiny of the World Wide Web*. HarperCollins Publishers, New York.

Berners-Lee, T. (2007): *Using labels to give semantics to tags*. Available from http://www.w3.org/DesignIssues/TagLabel.html

Berners-Lee, T., W. Hall, J. Hendler, N. Shadbolt, D.J. Weitzner (2006): Creating a Science of the Web. *Science,* Vol. 313, No. 5788, August, pp. 769–771.

Berners-Lee, T., J. Hendler, O. Lassila (2001): The Semantic Web – A new form of Web content that is meaningful to computers will unleash a revolution of new possibilities; *Scientific American*, Vol. 284, No. 5, May, pp. 35–43.

Black, D.A. (2006): *Ruby for Rails – Ruby Techniques for Rail Developers*. Manning Publications, Greenwich, CT.

Brachman, R.J., H.J. Levesque (2004): *Knowledge Representation and Reasoning*. Morgan Kaufmann Publishers, San Francisco, CA.

Brandes, U., Th. Erlebach (eds.) (2005): *Network Analysis – Methodological Foundations*. Springer-Verlag, Berlin, LNCS 3418.

Briggs, O., St. Champeon, E. Costello, M. Patterson (2004): *Cascading Style Sheets: Separating Content from Presentation*. Friends of ED (Apress), Inc., Berkeley, CA.

Brin, S., L. Page (1998): The Anatomy of a Large-Scale Hypertextual Web Search Engine. *Computer Networks* 30, pp. 107–117.

Bush, V. (1945): As We May Think, *The Atlantic Monthly*, Vol. 176, No. 7, July, pp. 101–108, see www.theatlantic.com/doc/194507/bush

Carlson, L., L. Richardson (2006): *Ruby Cookbook.* O'Reilly Media, Sebastopol, CA.

Cohen, A. (2002): *The Perfect Store: Inside eBay.* Little, Brown and Company, Boston, MA.

Crane, D., E. Pascarello, D. James (2006): *Ajax in Action.* Manning Publications Co., Greenwich, CT.

Dahl, D., G. Vossen (2007): Added Value for e-Learning Repositories through Social Tagging of Learning Objects. *Workshop Proceedings 12th BTW (Datenbanksysteme in Business, Technologie und Web)*, Aachen, Germany, pp. 270–279.

Dahl, D., G. Vossen, P. Westerkamp (2006): share.loc – A Multi-Tiered Interoperable E-Learning Metadata Repository. *Proc. 6th IEEE International Conference on Advanced Learning Technologies (ICALT)*, Kerkrade, The Netherlands, pp. 891–895.

Davis, H. (2006): *Google Advertising Tools: Cashing in with Adsense, Adwords, and the Google APIs.* O'Reilly Media, Sebastopol, CA.

Denning, P., J. Horning, D. Parnas, L. Weinstein (2005): Wikipedia Risks; *Communications of the ACM,* Vol. 48, No. 12, December, p. 152.

Dubinko, M. (2005): *Microformats and Web 2.0.* Available from http://www.xml.com/pub/a/2005/10/19/microformats-and-web-2.0.html

Fensel, D., J.A. Hendler, H. Lieberman, W. Wahlster (eds.) (2005): *Spinning the Semantic Web: Bringing the World Wide Web to Its Full Potential.* The MIT Press, Boston, MA.

Fielding, R. (2000): *Architectural Styles and the Design of Network-based Software Architectures.* Ph.D. Thesis, University of California, Irvine, Irvine, CA.

Ford, P. (2002): *August 2009: How Google beat Amazon and Ebay to the Semantic Web.* Available from http://www.ftrain.com/google_takes_all.html

Friedman, T.L. (2005): *The World is Flat – A Brief History of the Twenty-First Century.* Farrar, Straus and Giroux, New York.

Gehtland, J., B. Galbraith, D. Almaer (2006): *Pragmatic Ajax – A Web 2.0 Primer.* The Pragmatic Bookshelf, Raleigh, NC.

Gibson, R., S. Erle (2006): *Google Maps Hacks – Tips & Tools for Geographic Searching and Remixing.* O'Reilly Media, Sebastopol, CA.

Golder, S., B.A. Huberman (2006): Usage Patterns of Collaborative Tagging Systems. *Journal of Information Science*, Vol. 32, No. 2, pp. 198–208.

Goodman, A. (2005): *Winning Results with Google AdWords*. McGraw-Hill/Osborne, Emeryville, CA.

Gottlob, G., C. Koch, R. Baumgartner, M. Herzog, S. Flesca (2004): The Lixto Data Extraction Project – Back and Forth between Theory and Practice. *Proc. 23rd ACM SIGACT-SIGMOD-SIGART Symposium on Principles of Database Systems (PODS)*, ACM New York, pp. 1–12.

Grandinetti, L. (ed.) (2006): *Grid Computing: The New Frontier of High Performance Computing*, Vol. 14. Morgan Kaufmann Publishers, San Francisco, CA.

Gruber, T.R. (1993): A translation approach to portable ontologies. *Knowledge Acquisition*, Vol. 5, No. 2, pp. 199–220.

Gruber, T.R. (2005): *Folksonomy of Ontology: A Mash-up of Apples and Oranges*. First onLine conference on Metadata and Semantics Research (MTSR'05), see http://www.metadata-semantics.org/, available from http://tomgruber.org/writing/mtsr05-ontology-of-folksonomy.htm

Haase, P., J. Broekstra, A. Eberhart, R. Volz (2004): A comparison of RDF query languages. *Proc. 3rd International Semantic Web Conference*, Hiroshima, Japan, November, pp. 502–517.

Hammersley, B. (2006): *Hacking GMail*. John Wiley & Sons, New York.

Han, J., M. Kamber (2006): *Data Mining: Concepts and Techniques*, 2nd edition, Morgan Kaufmann Publishers, San Francisco, CA.

Harold, E.R. (2004): *XML 1.1 Bible*, 3rd edition. John Wiley & Sons, New York.

Harold, E.R., W.S. Means (2004): *XML in a Nutshell*, 3rd edition. O'Reilly Media, Sebastopol, CA.

Herrington, J.D. (2006): *Separate data and formatting with microformats*. IBM developerWorks article, available from http://www-128.ibm.com/developerworks/library/x-microformats/?ca=dgr-lnxw01Microformats

Hüsemann, B. (2005): Design and Realization of Ontologies for Multimedia Applications. *Dissertations on Databases and Information Systems*, Vol. 89, aka-Verlag, Berlin (in German).

Hüsemann, B., G. Vossen (2005): Ontology Engineering from a Database Perspective. *Proc. 10th Asian Computing Science Conference (ASIAN 2005): Data Management on the Web*, Kunming, China, Springer-Verlag, Berlin, LNCS 3818, pp. 49–63.

Hüsemann, B., G. Vossen (2006): OntoMedia – Semantic Multimedia Metadata Integration and Organization. *International Journal on Semantic Web & Information Systems* (IJSWIS). Vol. 2, No. 3 (Special Issue: Multimedia Semantics 2006), pp. 1–16.

Jacobson, I., G. Booch, J. Rumbaugh (1999): *The Unified Software Development Process*. Addison-Wesley, Reading, MA.

Jeffries, R., A. Anderson, C. Hendrickson (2001): *Extreme Programming Installed.* Addison-Wesley, Boston, MA.

Johnson, D. (2006): *RSS and Atom in Action – Web 2.0 Building Block.* Manning Publications Co., Greenwich, CT.

Kappel, G., B. Pröll, S. Reich, W. Retschitzegger (eds.) (2006): *Web Engineering – The Discipline of Systematic Development of Web Applications.* John Wiley & Sons, New York.

Keith, J. (2005): *DOM Scripting: Web Design with JavaScript and the Document Object Model.* Friends of ED (Apress), Inc., Berkeley, CA.

Kerschberg, L., M. Chowdhury, A. Damiano, H. Jeong, S. Mitchell, J. Si, S. Smith (2004): Knowledge Sifter: Agent-Based Ontology-Driven Search over Heterogeneous Databases using Semantic Web Services. *Proc. International Conference on Semantics for a Networked World, Semantics for Grid Databases*, Paris, pp. 276–293.

Kifer M., G. Lausen, J. Wu (1995): Logical foundations of object-oriented and frame-based languages. *Journal of the ACM* 42, pp. 741–843.

Langville, A.N., C.D. Meyer (2006): *Google's PageRank and Beyond – The Science of Search Engine Rankings.* Princeton University Press, Princeton, NJ.

Laszlo Systems (2005): *OpenLaszlo – An XML Framework for Rich Internet Applications.* Whitepaper, Laszlo Systems, available from www.openlaszlo.org/pdfs/LaszloNextGenWP.pdf

Laszlo Systems (2005a): *Working with the Laszlo Component Set.* Whitepaper, Laszlo Systems, available from www.openlaszlo.org/lps/docs/component-design/component-design-2.0.pdf

Laudon, K.C., C.G. Traver (2006): *E-Commerce: Business, Technology, Society,* 3rd edition. Prentice-Hall, Englewood-Cliffs, NJ.

Legg, C. (2007): Ontologies on the Semantic Web. *Annual Review of Information Science and Technology* 41, pp. 407–452.

Levene, M. (2006): *An Introduction to Search Engines and Web Navigation.* Addison-Wesley, Harlow, U.K.

Liu, B. (2007): *Web Data Mining – Exploring Hyperlinks, Contents, and Usage Data.* Springer, Berlin.

Loshin, D. (2002): *Knowledge Integrity: Data Ownership.* Available from http://www.datawarehouse.com/article/?articleid=3052

Magid, L., A. Collier (2007): *MySpace Unraveled – A Parent's Guide to Teen Social Networking.* Peachpit Press, Berkeley, CA.

Mahemoff, M. (2006): *Ajax Design Patterns.* O'Reilly Media, Sebastopol, CA.

Marlow, C., M. Naaman, D. Boyd, M. Davis (2006): HT06, tagging paper, taxonomy, Flickr, academic article, to read. *Proc. Hypertext*, pp. 31–40.

Melton, J., S. Buxton (2006): *Querying XML: XQuery, XPath, and SQL/XML in context*. Morgan Kaufmann Publishers, San Francisco, CA.

Meyer, E.A. (2006): *CSS: The Definitive Guide*. O'Reilly Media, Sebastopol, CA.

Miller, M. (2007): *Google.pedia – The Ultimate Google Resource*. Que Publishing, Indianapolis, IN.

Mordkovich, B., E. Mordkovich (2005): *Pay-Per-Click Search Engine Marketing Handbook: Low Cost Strategies to Attracting New Customers Using Google, Yahoo & Other Search Engines*. MordComm, Inc., New York.

Musciano, C., B. Kennedy (2006): *HTML & XHTML: The Definitive Guide*, 6th edition. O'Reilly Media, Sebastopol, CA.

Musser, J., T. O'Reilly (2007): *Web 2.0 Principles and Best Practices*. O'Reilly Media, Sebastopol, CA.

Nakhimovsky, A., T. Myers (2004): *Google, Amazon, and Beyond – Creating and Consuming Web Services*. Apress, Berkeley, CA.

Nilsson, N. (1998): *Artificial Intelligence – A New Synthesis*. Morgan Kaufmann Publishers, San Francisco, CA.

Norman, D.A. (1999): *The Invisible Computer: Why Good Products Can Fail, the Personal Computer Is So Complex, and Information Appliances Are the Solution*. The MIT Press, Boston, MA.

Noy, N.F., D.L. McGuinnes (2001): Ontology Development 101: A Guide to Creating Your First Ontology. *Stanford Knowledge Systems Laboratory Technical Report KSL-01-05* and *Stanford Medical Informatics Technical Report SMI-2001-0880*, March.

O'Connor, B. (2007): *del.icio.us Mashups*. Wrox Press, Hoboken, NJ.

Office of Communications (2006): *2006 Ofcom Report;* Ofcom, London, available from www.ofcom.org.uk/media/news/2006/08/nr_20060810

Olim, J., M. Olim, P. Kent (1999): *The CDnow Story: Rags to Riches on the Internet*. Top Floor Publishing.

Oram, A. (2001): *Peer-to-Peer: Harnessing the Benefits of a Disruptive Technology*. O'Reilly, Sebastopol, CA.

Orchard, L.M. (2006): *Hacking del.icio.us*. John Wiley & Sons, New York.

O'Reilly, T. (2005): *What Is Web 2.0 – Design Patterns and Business Models for the Next Generation of Software*. Available from www.oreilly.com/pub/a/oreilly/tim/news/2005/09/30/what-is-web-20.html

Paciello, M.G. (2000): *Web Accessibility for People with Disabilities*. CMP Books, Lawrence, KS.

Papazoglou, M.P., P.M.A. Ribbers (2006): *e-Business – Organizational and Technical Foundations*. John Wiley & Sons, Hoboken, NJ.

Payne, A. (2006): *Handbook of CRM: Achieving Excellence through Customer Management*. Butterworth-Heinemann Elsevier, Amsterdam.

Pellegrini, T., A. Blumauer (eds.) (2006): *Semantic Web – Wege zur vernetzten Wissensgesellschaft*. Springer-Verlag, Berlin.

Pogue, D., J.D. Biersdorfer (2006): *The Internet – The Missing Manual*. Pogue Press O'Reilly, Sebastopol, CA.

Pokorny, J. (2004): Web Searching and Information Retrieval. *IEEE Computing in Science & Engineering*, Vol. 6, No. 4, July/August, pp. 43–48.

Powers, D. (2007): *PHP Solutions: Dynamic Web Design Made Easy*. Friends of ED (Apress), Inc., Berkeley, CA.

Purvis, M., J. Sambells, C. Turner (2006): *Beginning Google Maps Applications with PHP and Ajax – From Novice to Professional*. Apress, Berkeley, CA.

Roberts, M.M. (2006): Lessons for the Future Internet – Learning from the Past. *Educause Review*, July/August, pp. 16–24.

Royce, W. (1970): Managing the Development of Large Software Systems. *Proceedings of the IEEE WESCON* 26, pp. 1–9.

Rundle, M. Ch. Conley (eds.) (2007): Ethical Implications of Emerging Technologies: A Survey. UNESCO, Paris.

Russell, St. J., P. Norvig (2003): *Artificial Intelligence: A Modern Approach*, 2nd edition. Prentice-Hall, Upper Saddle River, NJ.

Rymaszewski, M., W.J. Au, M. Wallace, C. Winters, C. Ondrejka, B. Batstone-Cunningham (2007): *Second Life: The Official Guide*. Wiley Publishing Inc., Indianapolis, IN.

Skype Limited (2006): *Skype – Guide for Network Administrators, Skype 3.0 Beta*. Available from www.skype.com/security/guide-for-network-admins-30beta.pdf

Sloan, P., P. Kaihla (2006): Blogging for Dollars. *Business 2.0 journal*, September, pp. 64–74.

Sowa, J.F. (2000): *Knowledge Representation: Logical, Philosophical, and Computational Foundations*. Brooks Cole Publishing Co., Pacific Grove, CA.

Tanenbaum, A.S. (2003): *Computer Networks*, 4th edition. Prentice-Hall, Upper Saddle River, NJ.

Tanenbaum, A.S, M. van Steen (2007): *Distributed Systems – Principles and Paradigms*, 2nd edition. Prentice-Hall, Upper Saddle River, NJ.

Tapscott, D., A.D. Williams (2006): Wikinomics: How Mass Collaboration Changes Everything Penguin Group, New York.

Tate, B., C. Hibbs (2006): *Ruby on Rails: Up and Running*. O'Reilly Media, Sebastopol, CA.

Teorey, T., S. Lightstone, T. Nadeau (2006): *Database Modeling and Design*, 4th edition. Morgan Kaufmann Publishers, San Francisco, CA.

Thomas, D., D. Hansson, L. Breedt, M. Clark, J. Duncan Davidson, J. Gehtland, A. Schwarz (2006): *Agile Web Development with Rails*, 2nd edition. Pragmatic Bookshelf, Raleigh, NC.

Tretau, S., A. Lelescu (2004): *IBM WebFountain and WebFountain Appliance Overview*. IBM Corp. Redbooks Paper, available from http://www.redbooks.ibm.com/redpapers/pdfs/redp3937.pdf

Tsoi, A.C., M. Hagenbuchner, F. Scarselli (2006): Computing Customized Page Ranks; *ACM Transactions on Internet Technology* 6, pp. 381–414.

Vise, D.A. (2005): *The Google Story – Inside the Hottest Business, Media and Technology Success of Our Time*. Macmillan, London.

Wahlster, W., A. Dengel (eds.) (2006): *Web 3.0: Convergence of Web 2.0 and the Semantic Web* (with contributions by Dietmar Dengler, Dominik Heckmann, Malte Kiesel, Alexander Pfalzgraf, Thomas Roth-Berghofer, Leo Sauermann, Eric Schwarzkopf, and Michael Sintek). Deutsche Telekom Laboratories, Technology Radar Feature Paper, Edition II/2006, June, pp. 1–23.

Wilkinson, D.A. (2007): *Flickr Mashups*. Wrox Press, Hoboken, NJ.

Witten, I.H., E. Frank (2006): *Data Mining – Practical Machine Learning Tools and Techniques*, 2nd edition. Morgan Kaufmann Publishers, San Francisco, CA.

Witten, I.H., M. Gori, T. Numerico (2007): *Web Dragons – Inside the Myths of Search Engine Technology*. Morgan Kaufmann Publishers, San Francisco, CA.

Yang, J. (2006): *The Rough Guide to Blogging – Navigate the Blogosphere*. Rough Guides Ltd., London.

Zhong, N., J. Liu, Y. Yao (2003): *Web Intelligence*. Springer, Berlin.

Zimbra (2006): *The Zimbra AJAX Toolkit (AjaxTK) – A Toolkit for Developing Rich, Browser-based Applications*. Whitepaper, Zimbra, Inc. Available from www.zimbra.com/community/documentation.html

Zimbra (2006a): *Zimbra Collaboration Suite Architectural Overview*. Whitepaper, Zimbra, Inc. Available from www.zimbra.com/community/documentation.html

Zimbra (2006b): *Zimlets™ – A Mechanism for Integrating Disparate Information Systems and Content with the Zimbra Collaboration Suite™*. Whitepaper, Zimbra, Inc. Version: 0.97. Available from www.zimbra.com/community/documentation.html

Index